The History of Anglo-Japanese Relations, 1600–2000

Volume II: The Political–Diplomatic Dimension, 1931–2000

THE HISTORY OF ANGLO-JAPANESE RELATIONS, 1600–2000

General editors: Chihiro Hosoya and Ian Nish

The five volumes which make up the series on The History of Anglo-Japanese Relations, 1600–2000 cover the relationship between these two island communities from the first contacts at the start of the seventeenth century through to the year 2000. While the studies cover the Anglo-Japanese relationship over the past four centuries, they tend to concentrate on features of the last 150 years. The volumes have been prepared independently over the last five years by Japanese and non-Japanese scholars who have met to debate and discuss their papers. These studies analyse the rise and fall of these relations in four dimensions: political and diplomatic; economic and business; military and naval; and social and cultural. The first two volumes are devoted to a chronological treatment of political–diplomatic exchanges.

Titles in the series:

The Political–Diplomatic Dimension, Volume 1, 1600–1930 (*edited by Ian Nish and Yoichi Kibata*)

The Political–Diplomatic Dimension, Volume 2, 1931–2000 (*edited by Ian Nish and Yoichi Kibata*)

The Military–Naval Dimension (*edited by Ian Gow and Yoichi Hirama*)

The Economic–Business Dimension (*edited by Janet Hunter and Shinya Sugiyama*)

The Social–Cultural Dimension (*edited by Gordon Daniels and Chushichi Tsuzuki*)

The History of Anglo-Japanese Relations, 1600–2000
Series Standing Order ISBN 0-333-79224-6
(*outside North America only*)

You can receive future titles in this series as they are published by placing a standing order. Please contact your bookseller or, in case of difficulty, write to us at the address below with your name and address, the title of the series and the ISBN quoted above.

Customer Services Department, Macmillan Distribution Ltd, Houndmills, Basingstoke, Hampshire RG21 6XS, England

The History of Anglo-Japanese Relations, 1600–2000

Volume II: The Political–Diplomatic Dimension, 1931–2000

Edited by

Ian Nish
Professor Emeritus of International History
London School of Economics and Political Science

and

Yoichi Kibata
Professor
University of Tokyo
Japan

With the assistance of Tadashi Kuramatsu

Foreword by Chihiro Hosoya and Ian Nish

First published in Great Britain 2000 by
MACMILLAN PRESS LTD
Houndmills, Basingstoke, Hampshire RG21 6XS and London
Companies and representatives throughout the world

A catalogue record for this book is available from the British Library.

ISBN 0–333–77098–6
Series ISBN 0–333–79224–6

 First published in the United States of America 2000 by
ST. MARTIN'S PRESS, LLC,
Scholarly and Reference Division,
175 Fifth Avenue, New York, N.Y. 10010

ISBN 0–312-23478-3

Library of Congress Cataloging-in-Publication Data
The history of Anglo-Japanese relations. The political diplomatic dimension /
edited by Ian Nish, Yoichi Kibata ; with assistance from Tadashi Kuramatsu.
p. cm. — (The history of Anglo-Japanese relations, 1600–2000)
Includes bibliographical references and index.
ISBN 0–312–23032–X (v. 1 : cloth)—ISBN 0–312-23478-3 (v. 2 : cloth)
1. Great Britain—Foreign relations—Japan. 2. Japan—Foreign relations—Great
Britain. I. Title: Political diplomatic dimension. II. Nish, Ian Hill. III. Kibata,
Yoichi, 1946– IV. Kuramatsu, Tadashi. V. Series.

DA47.9.J3 H57 2000
327.41052—dc21
99–055779

Selection, editorial matter and Preface © Ian Nish and Yoichi Kibata 2000
Chapter 1 © Yoichi Kibata 2000
Chapter 6 © Peter Lowe and Ian Nish 2000
Other chapters © Macmillan Press Ltd 2000

All rights reserved. No reproduction, copy or transmission of this publication may be made without written permission.

No paragraph of this publication may be reproduced, copied or transmitted save with written permission or in accordance with the provisions of the Copyright, Designs and Patents Act 1988, or under the terms of any licence permitting limited copying issued by the Copyright Licensing Agency, 90 Tottenham Court Road, London W1P 0LP.

Any person who does any unauthorised act in relation to this publication may be liable to criminal prosecution and civil claims for damages.

The authors have asserted their rights to be identified as the authors of this work in accordance with the Copyright, Designs and Patents Act 1988.

This book is printed on paper suitable for recycling and made from fully managed and sustained forest sources.

10 9 8 7 6 5 4 3 2 1
09 08 07 06 05 04 03 02 01 00

Printed and bound in Great Britain by
Antony Rowe Ltd, Chippenham, Wiltshire

Contents

Foreword		vii
Preface		ix
Abbreviations		xi
1	Anglo-Japanese Relations from the Manchurian Incident to Pearl Harbor: Missed Opportunities? *Kibata Yoichi (University of Tokyo)*	1
2	The Road to Anglo-Japanese Confrontation, 1931–41 *Antony Best (London School of Economics)*	26
3	Markets and Diplomacy: the Anglo-Japanese Rivalries over Cotton Goods Markets, 1930–36 *Ishii Osamu (Meiji Gakuin University)*	51
4	Economic Diplomacy in Anglo-Japanese Relations, 1931–41 *John Sharkey (School of Oriental and African Studies, University of London)*	78
5	Anglo-Japanese Relations, 1941–45 *Ikeda Kiyoshi (Aoyama Gakuin University)*	112
6	From Singapore to Tokyo Bay, 1941–45 *Peter Lowe (University of Manchester) and Ian Nish (Professor Emeritus of International History, University of London)*	135
7	British Prisoners of War of the Japanese, 1941–45 *Sybilla Jane Flower*	149
8	Uneasy Readjustment, 1945–58 *Peter Lowe (University of Manchester)*	174
9	Anglo-Japanese Relations in the 1950s: Cooperation, Friction and the Search for State Identity *Tanaka Takahiko (Hitotsubashi University)*	201

10 Anglo-Japanese Relations since the 1960s: Towards Mutual
   Understanding – Beyond Friction   235
   Kuroiwa Toru (Toyo Eiwa Women's University)

11 Distant Friends: Britain and Japan since 1958 – the Age of
   Globalization   263
   Christopher Braddick (Musashi University)

Index   313

Foreword

We write as chief coordinators of the Anglo-Japanese History Project, a Project for studying the history of the relationship of these two countries from 1600 to 2000. The Project originated in the statement of 31 August 1994 by Mr Tomiichi Murayama, on behalf of the coalition cabinet which he led. In this he announced the setting up of the Peace, Friendship and Exchange Initiative which would begin in 1995, the fiftieth anniversary of the end of the Asia-Pacific war. One part of the Initiative consisted of support for historical research, and particularly support for researchers in order 'to enable everyone to face squarely the facts of history'. The relationship between Japan and Britain was deemed to be one of the areas which came within the Initiative.

In order to implement this policy decision, the Japanese government announced that it would 'support the compilation of a series of volumes forming a comprehensive history of the UK–Japanese Relationship (Nichi-Ei kankeishi)'. The project was to be conducted by researchers from both Japan and the United Kingdom and to be funded over five years by a subvention administered by the Japan Society, London. Project offices were opened in London and Tokyo.

After preliminary discussions in London and Tokyo in 1995, it was agreed that the project would aim at conducting academic research and publishing volumes covering four central fields in Anglo-Japanese historical relations. Coordinators from the Japanese and British sides were appointed as follows:

The Political-Diplomatic Dimension (2 volumes)
(editors Yoichi Kibata and Ian Nish)
The Military-Naval Dimension (1 volume)
(editors Yoichi Hirama and Ian Gow)
The Economic-Business Dimension (1 volume)
(editors Shinya Sugiyama and Janet Hunter)
The Social-Cultural Dimension (1 volume)
(editors Chushichi Tsuzuki and Gordon Daniels)

These coordinators, in turn, selected experts in these fields and commissioned them to conduct research and write chapters for publication.

The first fruits of this research were discussed by both sides at Workshops held at the Civil Service College, Sunningdale, UK (July 1996), Shonan Village Centre, Hayama, Japan (September 1997) and Stephenson Hall, Sheffield University (August 1998). On these occasions draft chapters were presented by the contributors; and the discussion which ensued led to the revision of manuscripts.

It is too early for us to make sweeping generalizations about Anglo-Japanese relations over four centuries since the majority of papers from the four sections have not yet come in. But discussion at the Workshops has pointed out the positive aspects of the relationship between the two countries, which has been strong enough to survive setbacks and even disasters. Just as Britain's naval actions at Shimonoseki and Kagoshima in the 1860s were followed by the years of the Anglo-Japanese alliance (1902–23), so the dark years culminating in the Asia-Pacific war have been followed by the broadly favourable development of bilateral relations over the last 50 years, strengthened by wider common interests and deeper and more extensive exchanges in every field of activity. We recognize that there are problems outstanding between the two countries and hope that this series will make some contribution to their solution by clarifying some of the issues and will help to promote better understanding.

We as chief coordinators would like to thank the contributors who have devoted much time and effort to the Project. Thanks are due to the Japan Society (and the Tokyo office of the Project) for arranging its financial and administrative aspects. Finally, we are grateful for the co-operation of the officials of the Japanese Embassy, London, and the Japanese Ministry of Foreign Affairs. They have made it clear from the start that they would not take any part in the publication programme itself. What appears in these volumes is the work of independent scholars.

In conclusion, we should say that the joint project, which has been administered by a Steering Committee in London, presided over by Sir Sydney Giffard, and an Advisory Committee in Japan, has since its inauguration in 1995 been conducted most harmoniously.

Chihiro Hosoya and Ian Nish

Preface

This is one of two volumes devoted to the history of Anglo-Japanese relations covering the four centuries from 1600 to the present. This volume covers the more turbulent period of their relationship from 1931 to the present day. We have carved up the period chronologically in order to suit the special research interests of the contributors.

This volume consists of parallel essays by Japanese and British scholars. As in Volume I, they have exchanged drafts and discussed their papers, but they have written independently. The findings of their research are set out side by side. The editors have made no attempt to eliminate points of disagreement.

The British side is grateful to the Japanese contributors for undertaking the double burden of preparing their papers in English and for arranging for the translation of the British papers into Japanese. It is deeply grateful to the Japanese translators and to the Japanese coordinator for these efforts. The Japanese language version of these papers will be published by Tokyo University Press.

By agreement between the two sides, the Japanese counterpart to the paper by Ms Sybilla Jane Flower on prisoners-of-war will appear in the Military-Naval volume in this series, edited by Yoichi Hirama and Ian Gow.

Much thanks should go to Tadashi Kuramatsu who has acted as the London office manager for the History Project. He has played a special part in arranging these Political-Diplomatic papers. The editors wish to acknowledge his assistance by including his name on the title-page.

The editors have appreciated the guidance of those in the Tokyo office, notably Professor Takahiko Tanaka, Ms Eriko Jibiki and Ms Yoshie Takamitsu.

We have benefited greatly from the advice of Mr Lewis Radbourne, OBE, joint chairman of the Japan Society, and the hard work of Mrs Anne Hemingway and the staff of the Japan Society, London. In bringing these volumes to final publication, the editors wish to thank Mr T.E. Farmiloe, Ms Eleanor Birne and Ms Ruth Willats of Macmillan for their professional expertise and their cordial co-operation.

The editors, as they approach the end of the road, wish to express their gratitude to their wives and families, who have shared with them both the mishaps and the exhilaration of the journey.

Ian Nish and Yoichi Kibata

JAPANESE NAMES: In accordance with the established convention in academic works, Japanese names are ordinarily presented with the family name preceding the given name.

In view of the long period covered by these two volumes, the spelling of place-names, etc. has been left to the discretion of the contributors.

We acknowledge the use of Crown Copyright material in the Public Record Office, Kew. Our contributors wish to thank a large number of librarians, archivists and others in Japan and the United Kingdom.

Abbreviations

BAAG	British Army Aid Group
BIA	Burmese Independence Army
BIS	Bank of International Settlements
BOT	Board of Trade (UK)
DBFP	*Documents on British Foreign Policy*
DBPO	*Documents on British Policy Overseas*
FBI	Federation of British Industries
FO	Foreign Office (UK)
FRUS	Foreign Relations of the United States
GATT	General Agreement on Tariffs and Trade
ICRC	International Committee of the Red Cross
IHQ	Imperial Headquarters
IIL	Indian Independence League
IJA	Imperial Japanese Army
IJN	Imperial Japanese Navy
IMTFE	International Military Tribunal for the Far East
INA	Indian National Army
INF	Intermediate Nuclear Force
JCP	Japan Communist Party
JET	Japan Exchange & Teaching Programme
JETRO	Japanese Export and Trade Organisation
JLCSA	Japanese Labour Camp Survivors Association
LC	Government Liaison Conference
LDP	Liberal-Democratic Party
MFN	Most Favoured Nation
MOFA	Ministry of Foreign Affairs (Japan)
POW	Prisoners-of-War
PRO	Public Record Office
SACSEA	Supreme Allied Commander, Southeast Asia
SCAP	Supreme Commander Allied Powers
SDF	Self-Defence Force
SEAC	Southeast Asian Command
SEATO	Southeast Asia Treaty Organization
VSR	voluntary self-restraint
VRAs	voluntary restraint agreements

1
Anglo-Japanese Relations from the Manchurian Incident to Pearl Harbor: Missed Opportunities?

Kibata Yoichi

The Significance of Anglo-Japanese Relations in the 1930s

Discussions about Anglo-Japanese relations from the beginning of the Manchurian Incident in September 1931 to the outbreak of the Asia-Pacific War[1] in December 1941 cannot be separated from an examination of the historical process leading to that war. Until the 1970s research on international aspects of this process was dominated by that on US–Japanese relations. This was inevitable in view of the central role played by the United States in the Asia-Pacific war, and the papers presented to the Lake Kawaguchi Conference on US–Japan relations in 1969 were a testimony to the volume of research in that field.[2] But in the 1970s, when the British official records covering the 1930s and the Second World War were released, fresh light started to be shed on Anglo-Japanese relations after the Manchurian Incident, and the important position occupied by Britain in the international context of Japan's expansion came to be stressed. For example, Professor Hosoya Chihiro argued that a crucial aspect of the Asia-Pacific war was Anglo-Japanese conflict.[3] The Anglo-Japanese Conference on the History of the Second World War, which was held in London in 1979, was an indicator of this emphasis,[4] and the importance accorded to Britain at the Lake Yamanaka Conference on the Pacific war in 1991 reflected this trend.[5]

The significance of Anglo-Japanese relations is closely linked to the historical assessment of the course of Japanese expansion in the 1930s. The period between the Manchurian Incident and the end of the

Asia-Pacific war in August 1945 is often called the 15-year war. By employing this designation, which was first used by Tsurumi Shunsuke in the 1950s, historians aim to show the continuity from the Manchurian Incident through the Sino-Japanese War, which started in July 1937, to the Asia-Pacific war. According to Professor Kisaka Jun'ichiro this term is appropriate for the following reasons:[6]

> these three wars, despite changes of leadership and turmoil, vacillation, and vicissitudes concerning war implementation policies, were carried out and expanded under the consistently aggressive designs of Japanese imperialism – Japan wanted to rise to become the world's largest empire, reigning over all of Asia. Second, just as the contradictions arising out of past wars give rise to new wars, these three wars were in a cause and effect relationship, indivisible from one another.

As a general outline of the process of Japanese expansion which led to the Asia-Pacific war, such an explanation holds good, but at the same time it should be noted that the use of the phrase '15-year war' and the accompanying emphasis on the continuity tend to obscure the fact that there existed various alternative courses during this period which might have averted the escalation of hostilities, or at least changed the pace of subsequent events.[7]

Anglo-Japanese relations in the 1930s provide materials for considering such alternatives, for Britain was still the largest imperial power, and changes in Anglo-Japanese relations could have far-reaching repercussions in international relations in Asia. With this assumption in mind, I want to analyse the nature of diplomatic contacts between Britain and Japan in the 1930s. Emphasis will be put on their bearing on Japanese policy towards China. In his paper at the Anglo-Japanese Conference of 1979, Professor Ian Nish rightly stressed that the principal problem in Britain's view of Japan in the half-century after 1894 was Japan's activity in China.[8] This was especially true after Japan's invasion of Manchuria. For its part, Japan's view of Britain was inseparably connected to Britain's position in China and its stance towards Sino-Japanese confrontation. Economic relations between the two countries also loomed large in this decade, which started in the midst of the world depression. This aspect of Anglo-Japanese relations is dealt with in other essays in this volume and will not be discussed in detail in this chapter.

The Manchurian incident and Britain's magnanimity

The Japanese military started the Manchurian Incident on 18 September 1931 just at a time when the attention of the major powers was averted from East Asia because of domestic problems caused by the world depression. In contemporary eyes Britain's departure from the gold standard on 21 September was a much more crucial international event than the deployment of the Japanese army in a remote northeastern region of China. Though it cannot be said that the Japanese military deliberately chose this moment to invade Manchuria, an air of optimism prevailed among those who were contemplating the expansion of Japanese influence by military means. For example, according to the reminiscences of Suzuki Teiichi, one of the hard-liners in the army, the military planners expected that, as long as Japanese activities were confined within Manchuria, the League of Nations would make no more than verbal protests without resorting to effective means to halt the Japanese advance.[9]

In fact, the reaction of the great powers to Japan's action was lukewarm during the first phase of the Manchurian Incident despite strong appeals by China to the League of Nations. Among the powers it was Britain that displayed the most sympathetic attitude towards Japan. It is true that there were voices calling for economic sanctions and an arms embargo against Japan, but nothing came of it.[10] Britain would let Japan have its own way in Manchuria, as long as Britain's interests in the main parts of China were little affected. Perhaps what Sir John Simon, the British Foreign Secretary, jotted on a scrap of paper candidly reflected the overall British stance towards events in Manchuria:[11]

> Policy – conciliatory to Japan.
> To China – Don't rely solely on others: play your own part. Don't seek to transfer to Art. 16 [the article in the Covenant of the League of Nations about sanctions].
> To Japan: We don't want to apply sanctions.

In addition to the fact that the British government was preoccupied with the economic problems caused by the world depression, two factors can be detected behind Britain's stance.[12]

First, British policy-makers did not believe that Japan's actions posed a serious threat to its imperial interests, and thought that the Manchurian Incident could be concluded as a local conflict. The

Shanghai Incident in 1932, which will be discussed below, shook this optimism to some extent, but did not completely destroy it.

The Japanese government tried to exploit this attitude on the British side. A policy memorandum entitled 'A Draft Policy for Dealing with the Situation from the Viewpoint of International Relations', which was endorsed by the Japanese cabinet in August 1932, stressed the importance of cooperation with Britain concerning China, and stipulated:

> Bearing in mind that the important points for Britain exist in China proper, especially Shanghai, Canton, and the areas of the Yangtze valley and south China, it may be considered that we could, by respecting Britain's concerns appropriately, advance the cause of cooperation and thus create a favourable climate for our position over the Manchurian question.[13]

In pointing out the significance of this document, Nish observes that it is noteworthy that the advisers to the Japanese government at the height of the Manchurian crisis should be writing so optimistically of the possibility of cooperation with Britain. Then he adds that, since official British opinion was on the whole solidly in favour of China, historians who have the benefit of seeing the British archives would have to conclude that the Japanese perception of possible cooperation was wide of the mark.[14] This interpretation may be correct. However, it cannot be denied that the British attitude towards Japan did have some elements which led Japanese policy-makers to believe in the possibility of creating an imperialistic division of spheres of interest in China between Britain and Japan.

Such a consideration brings us to the second factor behind the British stance: Britain's sympathy for Japan as a country which shared the common cause (in China) of resisting the rise of Chinese nationalism. Immediately after the outbreak of the Manchurian Incident, Sir Francis Lindley, the British ambassador in Japan, noted that Japan's position had largely rested on treaty rights and surmised that Japan's action in Manchuria against China, which had tried to infringe these rights, would have a favourable impact on British interests in China.[15] The Japanese side did not fail to exploit such sympathy. When Sawada Setsuzo, secretary of the Japanese delegation to the League of Nations, met Lord Reading, Simon's predecessor as British Foreign Secretary, he referred to Reading's earlier career as Viceroy in India, and justified Japanese activities in Manchuria in the following way:[16]

[With that experience you] should have enough knowledge about Asia. In that case it will not be difficult for you to imagine what the situation of China and Manchuria is like. The situation in Manchuria is completely different from that in European countries. There are hundreds of thousands of disgruntled soldiers. Bandits are doing as they please. Under such circumstances the despatch of the Japanese army to places outside the area under Japanese jurisdiction cannot be called a war. Even if it is called a war, it is nothing but a 'colonial war', and can never be compared to the wars among European countries.

This kind of reasoning certainly accorded well with the attitude of imperially minded British politicians. Their reaction could be summed up by Leopold Amery's remark at the time of Japan's withdrawal from the League of Nations that 'our whole policy in India, our whole policy in Egypt, stand condemned if we condemn Japan'.[17]

Britain's magnanimous attitude towards Japan, which was based on such factors, was challenged by Japan during the Shanghai Incident (January–May 1932). Since Shanghai was the city where British economic interests were heavily concentrated, Britain adopted a relatively firm stance to rein in Japanese activities. This had some effect on Japan's policy-makers. In his book Nish notes that 'fleet movements, mediation efforts and financial pressures all ... gave confidence to the "internationalist" forces of Japan, who wanted to call a halt. The compromise and curbing of military activity tipped the balance between the nationalists and the internationalists in favour of the latter.'[18] The internationalists mentioned here comprised several prominent politicians and diplomats (Shidehara Kijuro, Yoshizawa Kenkichi, Takahashi Korekiyo, and Sato Naotake) and the notables in court circles (Saionji Kinmochi, Makino Nobuaki and the Showa Emperor himself). In various ways they realized the importance of not alienating the great powers, especially Britain and the United States. At the beginning of October 1931 the Emperor confided his anxiety to the elder statesman Saionji: 'I am very worried about the League of Nations. What would happen if economic sanctions were imposed on us? Thinking about these and other possibilities and the delicate position in which Japan is placed, I cannot help feeling apprehensive about the future.'[19] It is true that the temporary hardening of Britain's attitude towards Japan aggravated the concern of those internationally minded elites and made them more assertive, but this did not alter the course of the Manchurian Incident.

After the Shanghai Incident international interest in East Asian affairs focused on the publication of the Lytton Report and its reception at the League of Nations. In the discussion of the report in the General Assembly in December 1932, Sir John Simon, the British Foreign Secretary's speech stood out for its sympathetic line on Japan, and his speech was praised by Matsuoka Yosuke, the Japanese representative to the League, who was later to lead the Japanese delegation that walked out of the League at the end of February 1933.[20] Shortly before the Japanese decision to leave the League was taken, the British attitude towards Japan hardened somewhat. Henry Stimson, US Secretary of State, attributed this shift in British attitude to its fear of a Chinese boycott of British goods which might be carried out in protest at Britain's lukewarm stand on Japan's activities in China.[21] In order to solve the dilemma of keeping a balance between maintaining British interests in China and having a friendly relationship with Japan, some British policy-makers started to take policy initiatives in East Asia after the Manchurian Incident concluded with the Tangku Truce in May 1933.

Britain's abortive initiatives

The period after the Tangku Truce was a lull as far as Japan's military activities in China were concerned. Japan's political ambitions in China, however, became very visible during this period. The Chinese policy pursued by Hirota Koki, who served as Foreign Minister from September 1933 to April 1936 and as the Prime Minister from March 1936 to January 1937 (during the first month of his premiership he concurrently held the post of Foreign Minister), is sometimes called 'Hirota wakyo gaiko' (the friendly diplomacy of Hirota). This diplomacy aimed at expanding Japan's political and economic influence in China without recourse to strong military measures which would only have the result of completely destroying Japan's peaceful relations with the European powers. The so-called Amau Statement of April 1934 was an expression of this policy orientation. In that unofficial statement Amau Eiji, head of the Information Department of the Japanese Foreign Ministry, stressed that Japan had a special mission in East Asia, and that in order to realize peace and order in this region Japan would act independently and oppose any foreign interference in China, whether it took the form of financial or technological aid.[22] This statement had far-reaching international repercussions, since it was regarded as a clear enunciation of Japan's 'Monroe Doctrine in East Asia'.

What is noteworthy about the British government's reaction to this statement was its initial optimism. Foreign Office officials thought that the main target of the statement was not Britain but other powers, especially the United States, which had agreed to give a loan to China in the previous year.[23] Such optimism was typical of a country which had a stake in the preservation of the status quo. It should be emphasized, however, that Japan's China policy had an element which seemed to justify such an interpretation of Amau's statement. A memorandum drafted by the army in the autumn of 1933 and submitted to the Five Ministers' Conference, which was composed of Prime Minister, Finance Minister, Foreign Minister, War Minister and Navy Minister, pointed to the discrepancies between Britain and America and stated that 'if we give temporary and tacit approval to the expansion of British interests in the Far East, especially in China proper, it will not be impossible to keep Britain from standing on our enemy's side when our country faces a crisis.'[24] However, this did not mean that Japanese policy-makers were prepared to cooperate with Britain on the latter's terms, as was shown in Japan's reaction to repeated British initiatives towards Anglo-Japanese rapprochement: Neville Chamberlain's attempt to conclude a non-aggression pact with Japan in 1934 and Sir Frederick Leith-Ross's offer of Anglo-Japanese cooperation in 1935–36.

In the summer and autumn of 1934 Chamberlain, the Chancellor of the Exchequer, took the initiative in planning to offer a non-aggression pact with Japan as a means of improving Anglo-Japanese relations.[25] This plan was first suggested by Chamberlain at a cabinet meeting in March 1934 in conjunction with the discussion of the priorities in British defence, and strong support for it was given by his right-hand man, Sir Warren Fisher, Permanent Under-Secretary at the Treasury. In spite of the negative attitude of the Foreign Office, which feared that such a move would provoke adverse reactions in the United States, China and the Soviet Union,[26] they pushed ahead, anticipating that it would ease the tension between the two countries in terms of economic and naval competition.

This move gained momentum after Hirota Koki suggested his readiness to consider the possibility of concluding a non-aggression pact with Britain and the United States at his first meeting with the new British ambassador in Tokyo, Sir Robert Clive, at the beginning of July 1934.[27] It should be noted that in this meeting Hirota touched upon the problem of a non-aggression pact in the context of the forthcoming naval conference. Such a pact would show that Japan had no aggressive designs in constructing warships in excess of the existing limit, and his emphasis was placed not on the idea of a pact itself, but on the revision of the naval limits set. However, Chamberlain interpreted Hirota's suggestion to his own liking and started to make a concrete plan for a pact and only then would sound out Japan's reaction.

To Chamberlain's disappointment, the responses of Hirota and Shigemitsu Mamoru, Deputy-Minister for Foreign Affairs, were very negative. Referring to the British approach in his conversation with Harada Kumao, secretary to Saionji, Hirota said that an Anglo-Japanese rapprochement in general was desirable,[28] but despite his own remark in July, he was not thinking seriously of concluding a non-aggression pact. What Hirota and Shigemitsu had in mind was not a specific pact but a broader and more general improvement in bilateral relations on condition that such a rapprochement would 'not restrain Japan's position in East Asia'. According to Shigemitsu, it was not feasible to discuss a non-aggression pact or the way of guaranteeing the interests of the powers in China in relation to the naval negotiation. 'To propose such a thing does not do us any good for improving our negotiating terms in the naval discussion, and is likely to result in an uncomfortable situation in which Japan's hands will be tied in various ways.'[29] Those key foreign policy-makers were not ready to enter into an agreement which might impinge on Japan's freedom in international relations in Asia.[30]

In assessing the likelihood of Chamberlain's initiative succeeding, Professor Hosoya Chihiro wrote that, if the planned agreement had been in the form originally perceived by Chamberlain with the emphasis on reducing economic friction with Japan, and had not contained the provision about the future of China, which was added as a result of discussions with the Foreign Office, the Japanese government might have reacted more positively.[31] But it was inevitable that China would creep into the picture of any Anglo-Japanese rapprochement during this period. The view that the prospect of Japan's future in China was the crux of the matter in Anglo-Japanese relations has recently been stressed by Professor Sakai Tetsuya. According to Sakai, one possible course by which Japan could redress the balance of international order in Asia after its withdrawal from the League of Nations was to make effective use of Britain's appeasement policy towards Japan. However, the Japanese Foreign Ministry was at that time pursuing a 'pro-China' policy, demanding the removal of foreign vested interests from China, on condition that the existence of 'Manchukuo' be kept intact. Such a policy towards China inevitably conflicted with Japan's cooperation with Britain, which had the largest vested interests in China.[32]

Although it is arguable whether we can call the policy of the Japanese Foreign Ministry in those days 'pro-China', it does seem clear that China was the key obstacle to an attempt at Anglo-Japanese rapprochement in 1934.

The same factors can be detected behind the failure of the mission of the Federation of British Industries (FBI) led by Lord Barnby, which visited Japan and 'Manchukuo' in September and October 1934 with the aim of promoting British trade in 'Manchukuo'. During their stay in Japan and Manchuria the Japanese tried to present the mission as an indication of British willingness to recognize 'Manchukuo', but conceded nothing in concrete terms.

There has recently been an interesting attempt to reinterpret the significance of the FBI mission. According to Professor Inoue Toshikazu the mission could have offered Japan the opportunity to construct a new regional order with economic cooperation between Japan, Britain and 'Manchukuo', which China could be invited to join. He ascribes the reason for the failure of the mission not to Japan's military ambition in China, but rather to Britain's inability to provide 'Manchukuo' with the long-term investment necessary for its economic development.[33] This thesis, which discusses the problem in terms of financial capacity, is valuable in highlighting a factor which has not hitherto been discussed in depth, but seems to go too far in revising the currently accepted picture.

With regard to the FBI mission mention should be made of an important aspect of Anglo-Japanese relations: court diplomacy. In conveying information about the visit of this mission, Matsudaira Tsuneo, the Japanese ambassador to London, suggested that the royal family played a role in despatching it. According to Matsudaira, George V watched the development of the idea of the mission with great interest, and the Prince of Wales was so interested that he recommended members first.[34] Such an interest was echoed in Japan: when the mission visited the Emperor in Tokyo in October, the Emperor wanted to offer encouragement about the desirability of Anglo-Japanese economic cooperation and sought Makino Nobuaki's advice on this.[35] Although these moves on the part of the two royal families did not produce any substantial results, court diplomacy was an important undercurrent in Anglo-Japanese relations which should not be neglected.

In 1935 another attempt to bring about closer Anglo-Japanese cooperation in East Asia was made by the British side. The occasion was offered by China's economic difficulties occasioned by the rise in the price of silver. Neville Chamberlain and Sir Warren Fisher, who were the central figures behind the British overture in the previous year, arranged to send a mission led by Sir Frederick Leith-Ross, a currency expert, to China in the autumn of 1935 in order to help currency reform there. What was important from our viewpoint was that the mission carried with it a proposal to Japan about an Anglo-Japanese joint credit to 'Manchukuo', which could then be handed to China as compensation for the loss of 'Manchukuo'.[36] This was a clever idea to link Britain, Japan and China, but Leith-Ross was disappointed by the cool response he received in Tokyo during a brief sojourn there before he went to China in September.

The key personalities on the Japanese side, as on the British side, were the same as in 1934: Hirota and Shigemitsu. In conversation with Leith-Ross, Hirota said that, as far as the position of 'Manchukuo' was concerned, the Chinese government was already adopting a position which amounted to *de facto* recognition of that country, and he did not show any active interest in Leith-Ross's proposal. Shigemitsu, for his part, stressed that currency reform could not be undertaken in a country like China where there was no political stability; hence it would be premature to think in terms of joint financial aid.[37] In anticipating that currency reform would not succeed in China, Shigemitsu expressed the prevailing view among Japanese policy-makers.

Inoue Toshikazu has challenged such a negative picture. Inoue maintained that, even before Leith-Ross visited Japan, the Japanese Foreign Ministry was willing to grant a loan to China if the political basis of the 'pro-Japanese' leaders of China would not thereby be undermined. Furthermore, he stressed the domestic financial factor as the background to the cool reception which Leith-Ross encountered in Tokyo: Japan simply did not have enough resources to respond favourably to Leith-Ross's proposal.[38] Such an argument, which emphasizes economic and financial constraints on diplomacy, is certainly worth exploring,[39] but, as in the case of his analysis of Japan's response to the FBI mission, Inoue seems to have overstated his case.

Contrary to Japanese expectations, currency reform in China was successful, although the British desire to peg the new currency exclusively to sterling was not realized. The success of currency reform met with two kinds of response in Japan. On the one hand, there were those who wanted to destroy the new currency which threatened to bring about the economic unification of China. The capitalists in the Japanese textile industry were a typical example.[40] The Japanese military, which was at that time busy creating an exclusive sphere of interest in north China, were also critical of Leith-Ross's activities in China, and the intrigues of the Japanese army in north China increased after the success of currency reform. But there were also those who recognized the fact that China now had a fairly stable currency and who were ready to cooperate with Britain in supporting the new currency. Yoshida Shigeru, whose activities will be shortly discussed below, was one of them. Discerning this latter trend, from early 1936 some British diplomats began to hold the view that the power of the Japanese military was being curbed and the military was becoming more moderate.[41] However, the 26 February Incident pointed to the decline of civilian influence in Japan, and the possibility of Anglo-Japanese cooperation under the new condition of economically unified China further diminished. When Leith-Ross visited Tokyo again in June 1936, he found the same negative attitude as in September 1935. The Japanese government was determined to show that it would not allow Britain to interfere with the spread of Japanese influence in East Asia, where 'Japan alone could act as a stabilizing power'.[42] Leith-Ross had the impression that the Japanese government was unable or unwilling to modify the China policy of the military authorities,[43] and returned to Britain empty-handed as far as his (and Chamberlain's) initial desire to bring about Anglo-Japanese rapprochement was concerned.

As to the historical significance of the Leith-Ross mission in the whole course of the 15-year war, Professor Masuda Hiroshi, who is an authority on Ishibashi Tanzan, a perceptive economic journalist, argued that, given the British inclination for cooperation with Japan and the desire for a similar policy shown by several key Japanese policy-makers, such as Takahashi Korekiyo, the Finance Minister, Anglo-Japanese collaboration in a loan to China and in supporting activities for currency reform there would have changed the subsequent course of the relationship between Japan, Britain and China.[44] However, as Professor Masuda himself points out, such sentiments in favour of joint economic support for China were rare in Japan at the time. Among the newspapers and influential journals, it was only *Toyo Keizai Shinpo* under the editorship of Ishibashi, that openly supported such a policy.[45]

Yoshida's overtures and the Sato diplomacy

Unlike in 1934 and 1935 the next attempt at Anglo-Japanese rapprochement was initiated by the Japanese. Yoshida Shigeru, who was appointed Japanese ambassador to the Court of St James in June 1936, approached the British Foreign Office soon after he took up his position with a memorandum stipulating ten areas for Anglo-Japanese cooperation. Of these five covered the problem of China and the other five were related to trade, naval disarmament and the League of Nations.[46] Yoshida was a professional diplomat sympathetic to British culture and his father-in-law was Makino Nobuaki, the leading figure in the so-called '*shin'ei ha*' (pro-British group) among the Japanese political elites.[47] He went to London with the ambition of smoothing over the difficulties between Britain and Japan in China, and his memorandum was put forward as the starting point of this undertaking.

However, the memorandum covered too many points to serve as the basis for diplomatic negotiations between the two countries and was not thought out well enough.[48] In particular, the central proposal concerning China, in which Yoshida asked for discussions with the Chinese government on the question of assisting in checking the spread of communism by means of arms, ammunition and even military advisers from Japan, was nothing but reactionary and was correctly interpreted by the officials of the British Foreign Office as tantamount to subjecting China to Japanese rule. It should be noted here that before this memorandum was delivered to the Foreign Office, Yoshida discussed its content with Neville Chamberlain.[49] Chamberlain, whose indifference to Chinese nationalism had been revealed in his attempts at Anglo-Japanese rapprochement in 1934 and 1935, might have overlooked this crucial drawback in the Yoshida memorandum.

Yoshida's overture did not bear fruit both because of the anachronistic character of his proposals and because of Britain's mistrust of him, as it was believed he was acting without the full backing of the Japanese government.

While the British government was contemplating how to respond to Yoshida's proposals, the Anti-Comintern Pact between Germany and Japan was signed in November 1936. Together with the 'Plan for Imperial Defence', which was revised in June of that year and for the first time included Britain in the list of Japan's potential enemies, the conclusion of the Anti-Comintern Pact seemed to indicate that the opportunity for Anglo-Japanese cooperation had almost disappeared. In fact, this was not the case. Britain, it was felt, was still a country with which diplomatic accommodation should be sought. In June 1937 Togo Shigenori of the Japanese Foreign Ministry looked back at the previous year and referred to the agreement between the Foreign

Ministry, the Ministry of War and the Navy Ministry about the plan to approach Germany and Britain simultaneously.[50] However, a personal initiative like that of Yoshida was not enough to open a new chapter in Anglo-Japanese relations. The search for Anglo-Japanese rapprochement needed to be combined with a new orientation in Japan's policy in China.

In this respect it was important that, soon after Yoshida's first attempt failed to achieve its overall purpose at the beginning of 1937, a new Foreign Minister with the determination to improve both Sino-Japanese and Anglo-Japanese relations came on the scene. The diplomacy pursued by Sato Naotake, Foreign Minister in the cabinet headed by Hayashi Senjuro, has been highly evaluated by some historians as the one which had the greatest prospect of changing the course of events leading to the Asia-Pacific war, especially as it corresponded with a new and conciliatory attitude towards China on the part of the Japanese military.[51] Facing the increasing tendency towards domestic unity in China after the Sian Incident of December 1936, the Japanese army and navy started to modify their China policies. The basic policy document, 'Policies to be Executed towards China', adopted by the Foreign Ministry, the Finance Ministry, the Army Ministry and the Navy Ministry in April 1937 reflected this new policy orientation. Whereas the earlier version of this policy document adopted in August 1936 stressed the creation of a Japanese sphere of influence in north China, this version stated clearly that 'no political attempt should be made which aims at the creation of a separate sphere in north China or which is likely to disturb the domestic politics in China'.[52] Another policy document entitled 'Policies for Guiding North China', which was adopted at the same time, gave importance to economic developments in north China and to cooperation in this field with Britain and the United States.[53]

When the Hirota cabinet resigned at the end of January 1937, some British observers thought that moderate elements among the Japanese capitalists had at last begun to rein in the military,[54] and the advent of the Hayashi cabinet with Sato as Foreign Minister at the beginning of February was welcomed by the British side. Sato was regarded as a man who 'knows European diplomacy and the European mind as few Japanese do',[55] and his nomination was greeted as symbolizing the growing preponderance of 'moderate' elements in the Japanese ruling elite. It could perhaps be argued that, if Sato's penchant for a fundamental reorientation of Japanese foreign policy had been combined with active diplomacy in London, Anglo-Japanese relations might yet have taken a different course. The atmosphere of this period can be detected from the observation of a shrewd China watcher, Ozaki Hotsumi. Ozaki, who always regarded the Anglo-Japanese conflict as the most decisive element in the competition among the powers in China and had earlier stressed the difficulty of achieving Anglo-Japanese cooperation, began to perceive the possibility of such cooperation in the spring of 1937.[56] However, the Hayashi cabinet was very short-lived, and at the beginning of June the Konoe cabinet took power, with Hirota Koki being appointed Foreign Minister.

It was after the fall of the Hayashi cabinet that Yoshida Shigeru renewed his efforts to bring about an Anglo-Japanese concert, but again his attempt could not produce any concrete results. At the end of June, Prince Takamatsu, a younger brother of the Emperor, referred in his diary to a Foreign Ministry telegram to Yoshida sent on 19 June which proposed Anglo-Japanese cooperation in China, resolution of trade problems and closer contact concerning financial matters as the basis of negotiations. Discussing this despatch Prince Takamatsu noted: 'even when it is professed that Japan has no territorial ambitions in China, in reality no one can say so with enough confidence. This ambiguity lies at the basis of everything now, and, given such a state of things, it is impossible to bring Britain and Japan closer.'[57] This observation went to the heart of the problem. In other words, had the Japanese government made the change in its China policy much more explicit in both words and actions, Yoshida's renewed effort might have achieved something, but in fact the reorientation of Japan's China policy turned out to be imperfect and its territorial ambitions were to be unleashed by military means in July 1937.

Before going on to describe Anglo-Japanese relations after the outbreak of the Sino-Japanese war, I should mention here one aspect of this period to which insufficient attention has been paid. It is the importance attached to 'economic appeasement' by the British. In British policy towards Japan 'economic appeasement' centred on the proposal to abolish the import quota system in the British Empire, which had been laid down in 1934 to counter competition from Japanese goods, especially cotton products.[58] Frank Ashton-Gwatkin, an economic expert at the Foreign Office, for one expected that such a policy would lead to an improvement in the political relationship between the two countries.[59] Just like 'economic appeasement' towards Germany, the aim of the policy was to encourage those Japanese in economic circles who were thought to occupy a crucial position among the 'moderate' elements. It should be noted that Shigemitsu, who was by this time Japanese ambassador to Moscow, suggested that the key to Anglo-Japanese friendship, which he felt was growing at that time, lay in the economic and commercial fields, and that neither political nor Chinese problems should be allowed to come to the forefront.[60]

It is difficult to determine how much emphasis can be put on the prospect of such 'economic appeasement'. Perhaps Professor Ann Trotter was right in remarking:

> The change in outlook towards international affairs which had marked Japanese foreign policy since the Manchurian Incident, included the downgrading of the pursuit of economic interests as a national goal. There was, however, a tendency among British ministers and civil servants in the 1930s to assume that other nations sought peaceful economic cooperation as keenly as did the British.[61]

We should also bear in mind that during the period of the Yoshida initiative and the Sato diplomacy voices for closer Anglo-Japanese ties based on economic cooperation were heard in Japan. The most notable case was the advocacy of Anglo-Japanese friendship by Ishibashi Tanzan. Ishibashi, who had earlier forcibly criticized Japan's withdrawal from the League of Nations and at the time of the Leith-Ross mission advocated a joint loan to China with Britain and America, argued in the autumn of 1936 for a 'world-wide open door policy' (*sekai kaiho shugi*). What he proposed was the establishment of harmonious and equal relations of China, Japan, Britain and America with the open door principle in operation.[62] What is important here is that, as Ishibashi's argument showed, any economic arrangement between Britain and Japan could not be separated from the problem of China. In this sense 'economic appeasement' in itself was not sufficient to bring about closer Anglo-Japanese relations, but it was none the less a significant factor which should be probed further.

The road to the abyss

According to the account he gave immediately after the end of the Asia-Pacific war, in the early summer of 1937 the Showa Emperor summoned the Minister of War, Sugiyama Hajime, and the chief of the general staff, Prince Kan'in, to discuss a possible compromise with Chiang Kai-shek. The Emperor thought that, while events in Manchuria, a remote rural region, might not have any profound international repercussions, events in Peking or Tientsin would invite increased intervention from Britain and America and would be likely to lead to serious conflict with them.[63] Although at present we cannot establish the authenticity of this evidence, certainly the outbreak of the Sino-Japanese War in July 1937 and the expansion of Japanese military power in China widened the gap between Japan and Britain. This does not mean, however, that attempts to bring Japan and Britain closer were abandoned on both sides. But the general picture given by existing works on Anglo-Japanese relations after the summer of 1937 is that of Britain steadily leaning towards China in spite of the advocacy of a more friendly posture towards Japan by men such as Sir Robert Craigie, who became British ambassador to Tokyo in September 1937.[64]

One period which is deemed to be significant from the perspective of this author is spring and summer of 1938. In the aftermath of the failure of the negotiations with China through Oskar Trautmann, the German ambassador to China, and the reckless statement by Konoe Fumimaro in which he refused to deal with the Chinese Nationalist government, Japanese policy-makers again began to pay attention to Anglo-Japanese relations. At the end of February 1938 Deputy Ministers of the Foreign Ministry, the Army Ministry and the Navy Ministry met to discuss ways of improving relations with Britain as a step towards solving entanglement in China. Horinouchi Kensuke, Deputy Minister for Foreign Affairs, pointed to the difficulty of defeating the Chinese Nationalist government by military means and said: 'After all the only measure conceivable at present is to ameliorate our relations with Britain, on which China is most dependent, as much as we can, and thus put pressure on the Nationalist government with Britain as our ally.'[65]

The reshuffle of the Konoe cabinet in May 1938 was carried out along these lines. In a recent book on Japanese foreign policy during this period, Professor Matsuura Masataka called the policies pursued by Ikeda Shigeaki, a leading banker who became Finance Minister, the 'Ikeda line'. According to Matsuura, the 'Ikeda line' in Japanese foreign policy sought cooperation with Britain and America, while taking a hard-line stance towards China. The 'Ikeda line' aimed to 'enter into imperialistic cooperation with Britain by solving the difficulties about vested interests in China in concert with Britain, and thereby enticing Britain into a pro-Japanese position in order to create a condition for concluding peace with China on Japanese terms'.[66] This standpoint was based on the recognition of the weakness of the Japanese economy, but, as Professor Matsuura has rightly pointed out, it was extremely difficult to change the political/military course of action by the logic of economic thinking. He has also aptly stressed a crucial problem inherent in the 'Ikeda line': the optimistic and unrealistic tendency to think that it was possible to make peace with China by cooperating with Britain and America, especially with Britain. This line of thought was after all an aggressive one and took little account of Chinese nationalism, which was driving the Chinese people to war against Japan.

Professor Matsuura also maintained that the policy priority of Ugaki Kazushige, who was appointed Foreign Minister in May 1938 and conducted talks with Craigie in the summer of that year, was different from that of his colleague, Ikeda. While the latter attached the utmost importance to a deal with Britain, Ugaki wanted to limit the scope of mediation by Britain in Japan's relations with China, and in the course of his negotiation with Craigie he came to abandon the prospect of Anglo-Japanese cooperation in China.[67]

Though Ugaki was a professional soldier and had served successively as Minister of War and Governor-General of Korea in the 1920s and 1930s, his appointment as Foreign Minister was greeted very warmly by such a shrewd observer of Japanese diplomacy as Kiyosawa Kiyoshi, a liberal journalist, who remarked that with the coming onto the scene of Ugaki, an amateur in diplomacy, Japan had in fact regained its diplomacy after a long interval.[68] Kiyosawa also praised Ugaki's decision to begin his diplomacy with negotiations with Britain, stressing the importance of its international repercussions and arguing that there would be nothing that could not be solved by diplomacy between Britain and Japan. In spite of high expectations like this, the Ugaki–Craigie talks, which started at the end of July, collapsed as the result of Ugaki's resignation before much had been achievable. To say nothing of a general understanding between the two countries, no agreement was reached over the problem of trade discrimination in occupied China raised by the British side. It should be remembered here that there were many in Japan who did not share Kiyosawa's opinion and that Ugaki encountered strong opposition to his talks with Craigie, not only in military circles but also among young Japanese diplomats. Anti-British sentiment in Japan, which will be discussed later, also worked to the detriment of negotiations with Britain.

The intention of using Britain for the purpose of subduing China surfaced again in 1939 at the time of the crisis over the Tientsin Concession. The top brass of the Japanese army thought of using this crisis as a bargaining chip for making Britain recognize and support Japan's new order in East Asia.[69] On the British side Craigie expected that a British compromise in the negotiation over the Tientsin problem would strengthen the hands of the Japanese moderates.[70] This attitude led to the Agreement of 24 July between Craigie and Arita Hachiro, the new Foreign Minister, in which it was stated that the British government fully recognized the existing situation in China. This was a diplomatic success for the Japanese side, and in various parts of the world, especially in China and the United States, the Agreement was regarded as a sign of Britain's tendency towards appeasement. However, the subsequent negotiation about the handing-over of the silver, which the Japanese side regarded as crucial for strengthening Japanese position in China, ended in stalemate, and it was clearly shown that there was definitely a limit to what the British would concede even during a very difficult period in Europe. It should be added here that Foreign Minister Arita was conceiving an idea about the construction of an economic bloc in East Asia, which was largely different from the line of economic cooperation with Britain advocated by Ikeda in the previous year.[71] The scope for improved Anglo-Japanese understanding was very narrow in 1939.

A factor which should be mentioned in connection with the negotiation over the Tientsin concession was the trend of Japanese public opinion. The expression of anti-British sentiment was not rare in the early 1930s, but it became more rampant after the outbreak of the Sino-Japanese War. To take one example, Muto Teiichi, a right-wing journalist, published a book entitled *Eikoku o Utsu* (Attacking Britain) in December 1937, in which he argued that the war against China was 'a war between Japan and the Soviet Union in a different form, but at the same time and for more profound reasons a war between Japan and Britain', and urged that 'all the world should be mobilized in a fight against Britain'.[72] Fifty thousand copies of his book were sold in its first printing and in the next month 20,000 copies were printed as the second impression.

Such a discourse was accompanied by widespread anti-British mass demonstrations in many places. In his article about this important but hitherto rather neglected topic, Professor Nagai Kazu demonstrated that these movements gained momentum after the summer of 1937, and after a lull between March and May 1938 reached their peak at the time of the Tientsin Crisis between May and August 1939.[73] Even during the period of lull anti-British sentiment continued to spread, and unlike the first stage, when the promoters were almost exclusively right-wing elements, the second stage in 1939 was joined by others, many of whom were instigated to do so by the government with the aim of putting pressure on Britain.

On the British side there were also popular agitations against Japan, though they were smaller in scale than the anti-British movements in Japan and were led by left-wing people. For example, the Left Book Club, a popular front organization, conducted a mass campaign against Japan and called for aid to China; and dock workers in Southampton refused to unload Japanese cargoes.[74] Though it is difficult to gauge the political effect of these movements, such a situation certainly made it more difficult for those who aspired to Anglo-Japanese rapprochement to speak out.

It is true that in Japan the failure of the pro-Axis group to strengthen the Anti-Comintern Pact in 1938 and 1939 showed the persistence of the forces favouring cooperation with the Anglo-Saxon powers, but there was little chance of success for Anglo-Japanese understanding.

This situation did not change after the outbreak of the war in Europe in September 1939. In his excellent study Dr Antony Best makes an interesting point that May/June 1940 was a period in which Britain and Japan came closer to agreement than at any time since the summer of 1937,[75] but here it should be emphasized that the period after the outbreak and expansion of the Sino-Japanese war was very different from the preceding period in terms of the feasibility of talking about historical alternatives.

In the early summer of 1940 the Japanese leaders became more committed to a 'southern advance'. A policy document sanctioned at a liaison conference between the cabinet and the Supreme Command (*Daihon'ei*), 'Principal Lines of Action for Dealing with the International Situation under the Changing World Situation', contained a section on military confrontation with Britain: 'Should it go to war in the South Seas regions, Japan would endeavour to confine her employment of force solely against the British; but, in such circumstances, there would be some likelihood that war with the United States might not be avoided. In order to provide for that contingency, therefore, every possible precaution would be taken.'[76] The Konoe Cabinet, which adopted this policy, concluded the Tripartite Pact with Germany and Italy in September 1940.

Although there were still oscillations in Anglo-Japanese relations from that time on, the possibility of a rapprochement between the two countries became almost non-existent. In order to build up the 'Great East Asia Co-prosperity Sphere', it was inevitable for Japan to collide with Britain. When Matsuoka Yosuke, the Foreign Minister in the Konoe cabinet and the architect of the Tripartite Pact, drafted his plan for negotiations with the Soviet Union as well as with the alliance partners at the beginning of 1941, he indicated that only Australia and New Zealand would be excluded from the purview of the new international order in the Asia Pacific.[77] As Dr Peter Lowe pointed out, in 1941 Britain at last ceased to be centrally engaged in the confrontation with Japan, and the United States assumed this role.[78] During the protracted negotiations between Japan and the United States to avert a war, Britain did not and could not play any substantial role. So much so that it was ironical that a British territory (the Malay peninsula) was attacked by Japan one hour before Japan's pre-emptive raid on Pearl Harbor.

The beginning of the Asia-Pacific War was interpreted in various quarters in Japan as the start of the total collapse of the British Empire in Asia and the Pacific. This may be illustrated by the fact that, on hearing the news of the outbreak of the war, Tsunoda Jun, a historian, added a word *suibo* (decline and fall) to the title of his book on the British Empire in the Pacific which was then in the process of publication.[79] The leading article of the journal *Kaizo* asserted that the British Empire was now destined to collapse and the day of its break-up was quite close at hand.[80] Discourse like this became widespread in Japan, and, as was pointed out at the beginning of this chapter, the Anglo-Japanese war became a key aspect of the Asia-Pacific war.

Chances and limits of rapprochement

Despite all their efforts Japan and Britain could neither come to terms with regard to the treatment of China nor avert a military confrontation. But, as this chapter has shown, alternative courses existed, and the period from 1933 to 1937 appears to be the most interesting period when considering the prospect of an Anglo-Japanese rapprochement in the history of the 15-year war. At the same time, in saying so, I cannot help but ask the following question: had an Anglo-Japanese agreement been reached some time during that period, would it have lasted long? It is impossible to give a definite answer to such a hypothetical question. However, one thing is clear. Those who advocated Anglo-Japanese cooperation tended to ignore or underestimate the force of Chinese nationalism. For example, Neville Chamberlain and Sir Warren Fisher on the British side and Yoshida Shigeru on the Japanese side did not have sufficient understanding of it. Any plan for the imperialistic coexistence of Japan and Britain in China would have inevitably come into conflict with rising Chinese nationalism. It may be true that in 1935 Chiang Kai-shek was inclined to come to terms with Japan, and, if the Leith-Ross proposal had materialized, Anglo-Japanese cooperation might have materialized and China's acquiescence to it might have been secured. If Yoshida's proposal in 1936 had been more modest and he had had stronger backing from the Japanese government in his negotiations with Britain, some sort of Anglo-Japanese rapprochement might have come into being. But it is doubtful that such a state could have been sustained for long, given the intensifying strength of popular Chinese nationalism, which the Chinese Communist Party was effectively mobilizing.

Nevertheless to point out this problem does not diminish the importance of the quest for alternative courses in Anglo-Japanese relations in the 1930s. However precarious an agreement between the two countries might have been, it could have changed the power constellation in East Asia in a short-term context, and then it might have had a critical effect on the long-term development of the international situation in Asia in the 1930s.

Notes

1. The use of this expression for what has long been called the Pacific war is now fairly widespread in Japanese historical works, since it can denote both Japan's war against China and its war against the United States and Britain.
2. Hosoya Chihiro et al. (eds), *Nichi–Bei kankei shi: Kaisen ni itaru 10-nen,1931–41 nen* (US–Japanese Relations up to the Outbreak of the War, 1931–41), 4 vols (Tokyo Daigaku Shuppankai, 1971–72).
3. Hosoya Chihiro, 'Taiheiyo senso wa Nichi-Ei senso dewa nakattaka' (Was the Pacific War not an Anglo-Japanese War?), *Gaikoshiryokan shiryo*, 10 (1979).
4. Ian Nish (ed.), *Anglo-Japanese Alienation 1919–1952* (Cambridge, 1982); Hosoya Chihiro (ed.), *Nichi–Ei kankei shi 1917–1949* (History of Anglo-Japanese Relations 1917–1949) (Tokyo Daigaku Shuppankai, 1982).
5. Hosoya Chihiro et al. (eds), *Taiheiyo senso* (The Pacific War) (Tokyo Daigaku Shuppankai, 1993).
6. Kisaka Jun'ichiro, 'Recent Japanese Research on the Second World War', in The National Committee of Japanese Historians (ed.), *Historical Studies in Japan* (VII) 1983–1987 (Yamakawa Shuppansha, 1990), p. 246.
7. Ironically the author of a recent book, which tries to find as many alternatives as possible in Sino-Japanese relations between 1931 and 1938, used the term 'Fifteen-year War' in its title. Osugi Kazuo, *Nitchu jugonen senso shi* (A History of the Sino-Japanese Fifteen-year War), (Chuo Koron Sha, 1996).
8. Ian Nish, 'Japan in Britain's View of the International System, 1919–37', in Nish (ed.), *Anglo-Japanese Alienation*, p. 27.
9. Kido Nikki Kenkyukai/Nihon Kindai Shiryo Kenkyukai (eds), *Suzuki Teiichi shi danwa sokkiroku* (Records of Reminiscences of Mr. Suzuki Teiichi) (Tokyo, 1971), pp. 20–1, 297.

10. The two most important works dealing with British policy towards Japan during the Manchurian Incident are Christopher Thorne, *The Limits of Foreign Policy: The West, the League and the Far Eastern Crisis of 1931–1933* (London, 1972), and Ian Nish, *Japan's Struggle with Internationalism: Japan, China and the League of Nations 1931–1933* (London/New York, 1993).
11. Thorne, *The Limits of Foreign Policy*, p. 189.
12. See Kibata Yoichi, 'Nihon fashizumu keisei ki no kokusai kankyo' (International Background of the Rise of Japanese Fascism), in Eguchi Keiichi et al. (eds), *Taikei Nihon gendai shi* (Modern History of Japan), Vol. 1 (Nihon Keizai Hyoron Sha, 1978), pp. 96–8.
13. The translation is that by Ian Nish in Nish, 'Anglo-Japanese Alienation Revisited', in Saki Dockrill (ed.), *From Pearl Harbor to Hiroshima: The Second World War in Asia and the Pacific, 1941–5* (London, 1994), p. 15.
14. *Ibid.*
15. Lindley to Simon, 20 September 1931, *Documents on British Foreign Policy* [*DBFP*], Second Series, Vol. VIII, 509.
16. Sawada to Shidehara, 17 October 1932, *Nihon gaiko bunsho* (Documents on Japanese Foreign Policy), Series on the Manchurian Incident, Part 1, Vol. 3.
17. Thorne, *The Limits of Foreign Policy*, p. 343.
18. Nish, *Japan's Struggle with Internationalism*, p. 120.
19. Harada Kumao, *Saionji-ko to seikyoku* (Prince Saionji and the Political Scene), Vol. 2 (Iwanami Shoten, 1950), p. 115.
20. Usui Katsumi, *Manshukoku to kokusai renmei* (Manchukuo and the League of Nations) (Yoshikawa Kobunkan, 1995), p. 144.
21. *Ibid.*, p. 166.
22. 'Amau Eiji joho bucho no hikoshiki seimei' (Unofficial Statement by Amau Eiji), in Shimada Toshihiko et al. (eds), *Gendaishi shiryo*, Vol. 8, Nitchu Senso (1) (Documents on Modern History, Vol. 8, Sino-Japanese War, (1)) (Misuzu Shobo, 1964), pp. 25–6.
23. Minutes by Harcourt-Smith, Allen and Randall, in FO371/18096 [Public Record Office, Kew].
24. 'Kokusaku riyusho' (The Reasons of our National Policy), in Japanese Foreign Ministry papers, A.1.0.0.6-3.
25. See Ann Trotter, *Britain and East Asia 1933–1937* (London, 1975), Ch. 6; Stephen Lyon Endicott, *Diplomacy and Enterprise: British China Policy 1933–1937* (Manchester, 1975), Ch. 3.
26. The conflict of views between the Treasury and the Foreign Office is dealt with in Gill Bennett, 'British Policy in the Far East 1933–1936: Treasury and Foreign Office', *Modern Asian Studies*, 26–3 (1992). A very favourable reassessment of Chamberlain's foreign policy can be found in Peter Bell, *Chamberlain, Germany and Japan, 1933–4* (Basingstoke/London, 1996).
27. Clive to Simon, 3 July 1934, *DBFP*, Second Series, Vol. XX, 149.
28. Harada Kumao, *Saionji-ko to seikyoku*, Vol. 4 (Iwanami Shoten, 1951), p. 100.
29. Hirota to Matsudaira, 29 October 1934, in Japanese Foreign Ministry papers, B.10.4.0.2-5-1.; Matsumura to Morishima and Yamagata, n.d., in Japanese Foreign Ministry papers, A.1.1.0.10, Vol.3.
30. Kibata Yoichi, 'Nitchu senso zenshi ni okeru kokusai kankyo: Igirisu no tai-Nichi seisaku, 1934-nen' (Anglo-Japanese Relations in 1934), *Kyoyo-Gakka kiyo* (University of Tokyo) No. 9 (1977). For Shigemitsu's attitude, see

Antony Best, 'Shigemitsu Mamoru, 1887–1957', in Ian Nish (ed.), *Britain and Japan: Biographical Portraits*, Vol. II (Folkestone, Kent, 1997).
31. Hosoya Chihiro, '1934 nen no Nichi-Ei fukashin kyotei mondai' (An Attempt at a Rapprochement in Anglo-Japanese Relations in the Mid-Thirties: the Question of the Anglo-Japanese Non-Aggression Pact), *Kokusai seiji* (International Relations), No. 58 (1977), 85.
32. Sakai Tetsuya, *Taisho demokurasi taisei no hokai* (The Collapse of Taisho Democracy) (Tokyo Daigaku Shuppankai, 1992), p. 62.
33. Inoue Toshikazu, *Kiki no naka no kyocho gaiko* (Co-operative Diplomacy at the Time of Crisis) (Yamakawa Shuppansha, 1994), pp. 232–7.
34. Hosoya Chihiro, 'Britain and the US in Japan's View, 1919–37', in Nish (ed.), *Anglo-Japanese Alienation*, p. 19.
35. *Makino Nobuaki nikki* (The Diary of Makino Nobuaki) (Chuo Koron Sha, 1990), pp. 592–3.
36. For the Leith-Ross Mission, see Trotter, *Britain and East Asia 1933–1937*, Chs 8 and 9; Endicott, *Diplomacy and Enterprise*, Chs 4–6; Kibata Yoichi, 'Leith-Ross shisetsu dan to Ei-Chu kankei' (The Leith-Ross Mission and Anglo-Chinese Relations), in Nozawa Yutaka (ed.), *Chugoku no heisei kaikaku to kokusai kankei* (Currency Reform in China (1935) and China's Relations with Japan, Britain and America) (Tokyo Daigaku Shuppankai, 1985).
37. Hatano Sumio, 'Leith-Ross no kyokuto homon to Nihon' (Leith-Ross Mission's Visit to Far East and Japan's Response), *Kokusai seiji*, No. 58 (1977), 90–1.
38. Inoue, *Kiki no naka no kyocho gaiko*, pp. 242–4.
39. See Mitani Taichiro, 'Kokusai kinyu shihon to Ajia no senso: shumatsuki ni okeru tai-Chu yonkoku shakkandan' (International Financiers and the War in Asia: The Four Power Banking Consortium to China in its Final Stage), *Kindai nihon kenkyu*, No. 2 (Yamakawa Shuppansha, 1980).
40. Matsuura Masataka, *Nitchu senso ki ni okeru keizai to seiji. Konoe Fumimaro to Ikeda Shigeaki* (Economic-Political Dynamics during the Sino-Japanese War, 1937–1945. Konoe Fumimaro and Ikeda Shigeaki) (Tokyo Daigaku Shuppankai, 1995), p. 68.
41. Clive to the Foreign Office, 20 February 1936; Minute by Orde, 21 February 1936, in FO371/ 20242.
42. 'Riisu-Rosu kankei konpon hoshin' (Guideline of Responses to Leith-Ross), *Nihon gaiko nenpyo narabi ni shuyo bunsho* (Chronology of Japanese Diplomacy and Major Documents), Vol. 2 (Hara Shobo, 1966), p. 334.
43. Trotter, *Britain and East Asia 1933–1937*, p. 182.
44. Masuda Hiroshi, 'Nitchu-senso ka Ishibashi Tanzan no Nichi-Ei teikei ron, 1933 nen-40 nen' (Ishibashi Tanzan's Advocacy for Anglo-Japanese Cooperation during the Sino-Japanese Conflicts, 1933–40), *Ajia Kenkyu*, 34–3 (1988), 37.
45. *Ibid.*, 10.
46. See Trotter, *Britain and East Asia 1933–1937*, Ch. 11; S. Olu Agbi, 'The Foreign Office and Yoshida's Bid for Rapprochement with Britain in 1936–1937: A Critical Reconsideration of the Anglo-Japanese Conversation', *Historical Journal*, 21–1 (1978); Kibata Yoichi, 'Nitchu senso zenya ni okeru Igirisu no tai-Nichi seisaku' (British Policy towards Japan on the Eve of the Sino-Japanese War), *Ronshu* (Tokyo University of Foreign Studies), No. 29 (1979).

47. The most recent assessment of Yoshida's activities during this period is Ian Nish, 'Yoshida Shigeru and Mme Yoshida at the London Embassy', in Nish (ed.), *Britain and Japan: Biographical Portraits*, Vol. II.
48. Hosoya Chihiro, 'Gaikokan Yoshida Shigeru no yume to zasetsu: Nichi-Ei teikei e no mosaku' (Yoshida Shigeru's Attempt at Anglo-Japanese Cooperation: A Shattered Dream), in Hosoya, *Nihon gaiko no zahyo* (Historical Contexts of Japanese Diplomacy) (Chuokoron-sha, 1979), p. 39.
49. Neville Chamberlain diary, 25 October 1936, in Neville Chamberlain papers (Birmingham University), NC2/23a.
50. Inoue Mitsusada et al. (eds), *Nihon rekishi taikei*, Vol. 17, *Kakushin to senso no jidai* (Japanese History, Vol. 17, The Age of Reform and War) (Yamakawa Shuppansha, 1997), p. 113 n. 9.
51. See Usui Katsumi, 'Sato gaiko to Nitchu kankei' (Sato Diplomacy and Sino-Japanese Relations), in Iriye Akira/Aruga Tadashi (eds), *Senkanki no Nihon gaiko* (Japanese Diplomacy in the Interwar Years) (Tokyo Daigaku Shuppankai, 1984).
52. *Ibid.*, pp. 250–1.
53. *Nihon gaiko nenpyo narabi ni shuyo bunsho*, p. 362.
54. For example, *Manchester Guardian*, 23 January 1937; *The Economist*, 30 January 1937, p. 231.
55. *Spectator*, 12 March 1937, p. 462.
56. *Ozaki Hotsumi chosakushu* (Collected Writings of Ozaki Hotsumi) (Keiso Shobo, 1977), pp. 24–5, 178.
57. Agawa Hiroyuki (ed.), *Takamatsu no miya nikki* (Diaries of Prince Takamatsu) (Chuo Koron Sha, 1995), p. 456.
58. Ishii Osamu, *Cotton-Textile Diplomacy. Japan, Great Britain, and the United States, 1930–1936* (New York, 1981).
59. Memo. by Ashton-Gwatkin, March 1937, in FO371/21215. Ashton-Gwatkin's long-term relations with Japan is analysed by Nish. Ian Nish, '"In One Day Have I Lived Many Lives": Frank Ashton-Gwatkin, Novelist and Diplomat, 1889–1976', in Nish (ed.), *Britain and Japan: Biographical Portraits* (Folkestone, Kent: Japan Library, 1994).
60. Shigemitsu Mamoru, 'Oshu no seikyoku: Hosoku dai ni' (Political Situation in Europe. Supplement No. 2), 10 May 1937, in Japanese Foreign Ministry papers, A.2.0.0.X-1.
61. Trotter, *Britain and East Asia 1933–1937*, p. 153.
62. Masuda, 'Ishibashi Tanzan no Nichi-Ei, teikei ron', 14.
63. *Showa tenno dokuhakuroku* (Record of Talks by the Showa Emperor) (Bungei Shunju Sha, 1991), p. 35.
64. See Bradford A. Lee, *Britain and the Sino-Japanese War, 1937–1939: A Study in the Dilemmas of British Decline* (Stanford, 1973); Aron Shai, *Origins of the War in the East: Britain, China and Japan 1937–39* (London, 1976); Peter Lowe, *Great Britain and the Origins of the Pacific War: A Study of British Policy in East Asia 1937–1941* (Oxford, 1977); Sato Kyozo, *Japan and Britain at the Crossroads, 1939–1941* (Senshu University Press, 1986); Antony Best, *Britain, Japan and Pearl Harbor: Avoiding War in East Asia 1936–41* (London/New York, 1995).
65. Hosoya Chihiro, 'Nihon no Ei-Bei-kan to senkanki no higashi Ajia' (Japan's View of Britain and America and East Asia during the Interwar Years), in

Hosoya (ed.), *Nichi-Ei Kankei Shi 1917–1949*, pp. 24–5. This part is not included in the English version of the record of the 1979 Anglo-Japanese Conference.
66. Matsuura, *Nitchu senso ki ni okeru keizai to seiji*, p. 93.
67. *Ibid.*, pp. 162ff.
68. Kiyosawa Kiyoshi, 'Ugaki gaiko ron' (On Ugaki's Diplomacy), *Kaizo* (September 1938).
69. Nagai Kazu, 'Nitchu senso to Nichi-Ei tairitsu' (The Sino-Japanese War and Anglo-Japanese Confrontation), in Furuya Tetsuo, (ed.), *Nitchu senso shi kenkyu* (Studies on the Sino-Japanese War) (Yoshikawa Kobunkan, 1984), pp. 294–5.
70. Craigie's view was strongly refuted by Sir George Sansom, Commercial Counsellor in the British Embassy in Tokyo, and by the Far Eastern Department of the Foreign Office. Best, *Britain, Japan and Pearl Harbor*, pp. 79, 83–4.
71. Inoue Yuichi, 'Arita no "koiki keizaiken" koso to tai-Ei kosho' (Arita's Proposal regarding an Economic Bloc for Japanese Expansion and his Conversations with Ambassador Craigie in July 1939), *Kokusai seiji*, No. 56 (1976); Matsuura, *Nitchu senso ki ni okeru keizai to seiji*, p. 198.
72. Muto Teiichi, *Eikoku o utsu* (Attacking Britain) (Shinchosha, 1937), pp. 3, 19.
73. Nagai Kazu, '1939-nen no hai-Ei undo' (Anti-British Movements in 1939), *Kindai nihon kenkyu*, No. 5 (Yamakawa Shuppansha, 1983).
74. Kibata Yoichi, 'Sekai no kiro to 15-nen senso' (A Turning Point in the World History and the Fifteen-year War) in *Koza Nihon rekishi* (Lectures on Japanese History), Vol. 10 (Tokyo Daigaku Shuppannkai, 1985), p. 26.
75. Best, *Britain, Japan and Pearl Harbor*, p. 109.
76. The translation follows that by Sato Kyozo. Sato, *Japan and Britain at the Crossroads*, pp. 73–4.
77. Mori Shigeki, 'Matsuoka gaiko ni okeru tai-Bei oyobi tai-Ei saku' (Policies towards America and Britain in Matsuoka's Diplomacy), *Nihonshi kenkyu*, 421 (1997), 45.
78. Peter Lowe, 'Britain and the Opening of the War in Asia, 1937–41', in Nish (ed.), *Anglo-Japanese Alienation*, p. 113.
79. Tsunoda Jun, *Taiheiyo ni okeru Eiteikoku no suibo: kokusai seiji teki gaikan* (The Decline and Fall of the British Empire in the Pacific: A Survey in International Politics) (Tokyo, 1942).
80. 'Eiteikoku no kaitai to Nihon no shorai' (The Break-up of the British Empire and Japan's Future), *Kaizo*, (February 1942).

2
The Road to Anglo-Japanese Confrontation, 1931–41

Antony Best

Despite the termination of the Anglo-Japanese alliance in 1923, relations between Britain and Japan remained stable, if not as close as they had once been until the end of the 1920s. However, from the start of the Manchurian Crisis in September 1931 the friendship between the two countries began to disintegrate, and they entered into a prolonged period of mutual antipathy which eventually culminated in the Japanese assault on Britain's Eastern Empire on 8 December 1941. There were intermittent attempts during this troubled decade to address and overcome these feelings of hostility and to find a new common ground, and this subject has become central to the historiography of Anglo-Japanese relations in this period. Much of the literature has dealt in particular with the attempts at reconciliation between 1933 and 1937, and some Japanese scholars have gone so far as to contend that Britain tried during these years to appease Japan, but that the latter refused to accept its overtures. There is, however, a danger in focusing on how close Britain and Japan came to a rapprochement; that is, that one can forget just how serious were the political, strategical, economic and ideological factors that drove them apart. The object of this chapter is to study these divisions and account for the inability of the two states to overcome them.

It seems almost superfluous to state that at the heart of the dispute between Britain and Japan was the issue of Japanese expansion in East Asia and its impact on the British stake in China. It was this issue above all others that shaped the growth of tensions and it proved consistently to be the greatest obstacle to any settlement. However, it is also important to realize that any study of the rise of Anglo-Japanese alienation during this period cannot afford to look at this relationship in isolation. Both Britain and Japan were at this time making policy decisions against the background of a world in crisis, since the Great Depression that ravaged the world economy from 1929 onwards had unleashed destructive forces far and wide. These included not just the rise of the revisionist states such as Germany, Italy and Japan, but also the breakdown of the world economic order, the isolationism of the United States and the growing industrial strength of the ultimate pariah state, the Soviet Union. The Anglo-Japanese dispute was in itself a significant contribution to the breakdown of the postwar order, but it in turn was influenced by the growing tensions in Europe, the trade problems caused by the shift towards bloc economies, the disputes over armaments and the profound philosophical divide that opened up between the status quo powers and the 'revisionists'. It is vital to understand, then, that the dispute that arose between Britain and Japan was not just based on power-political rivalry over China, but was also shaped by wider economic competition and an increasing divergence of views about the development of international politics.

The legacy of Manchukuo

The rupture of the friendship between the two states began with the Manchurian crisis that broke out in 1931 and the subsequent fighting at Shanghai in January 1932. From the start, these incidents raised important political and ideological issues since this was the first major use of force by a great power since the end of the First World War and were thus the first real challenges to be faced by the new arbiter of the international order, the League of Nations.

The position of the civilian authorities in Japan was that the use of aggression by the Japanese military was a natural reaction to the constant provocations of the Chinese, such as the infringement of Japan's treaty rights and the introduction of boycotts of Japanese goods. Japanese actions were thus depicted as justifiable attempts to uphold the sanctity of treaties and to bring order to areas that were deemed essential to its economic survival. It was also noted that a precedent for the defence of treaty rights had been set in 1927 when Britain had sent a 10,000-strong expeditionary force to safeguard the International Settlement at Shanghai from the advancing forces of the Kuomintang. In addition, Japan stressed that its actions in Manchuria would guard against any expansion of Soviet influence in the region.[1]

There were some in Britain who sympathized with Japan's actions. Among the ranks of the Conservative Party and in the right-wing press it was argued that it was only natural, in the light of China's persistent political instability, that Japan should seek to expand in continental Asia, and that in so doing it was only mirroring the example of British imperialism. In addition, there was an acceptance of the idea that Japan's presence in Manchuria would act as a buffer to the Soviet Union, which many on the political right still saw as the greatest threat to Britain's interests in East Asia. Leading Conservative backbenchers such as Leopold Amery and Winston Churchill typified this right-wing consensus. The latter observed to the Oxford University Conservative Association in February 1934 that he could not think that 'Japanese foreign policy threatens our Empire', and noted for good measure that he thought Manchukuo 'a good thing'.[2]

However, to those in Britain who believed in the League of Nations and the concept of collective security Japan's actions in China from 1931 to 1933 were interpreted as a direct challenge to the tenets of the postwar world. The liberal view of the Manchurian issue was ably summed up by *The New Statesman and Nation*, which observed in October 1932, just after the publication of the Lytton Report, that although Japanese complaints about Chinese behaviour prior to the Mukden Incident were justified:

> What cannot be justified, either legally or morally, is the high-handed methods they have adopted for securing their rights – and not merely for securing their rights, but for expanding them to cover a wholesale annexation of territory and a defiance of treaty obligations far more flagrant than anything of which China could be accused. Japan in Manchuria a year ago had some title to the sympathy of the world. Japan in Manchuria to-day is an outrage and a danger to the world.[3]

The strength of feeling among those opposed to Japan did not rest only on the judgement that the Japanese government had broken international law; it was also strongly influenced by the manner of Japanese warfare and in particular the brutal dive-bombing of Chapei, the Chinese quarter of Shanghai, in February 1932.[4] Such actions were held to warrant not just condemnation but a firmer response such as sanctions or an arms embargo.

In this volatile atmosphere the British government, with its armed forces depleted after the disarmament of the 1920s, and deeply concerned about the effects of the Depression at home, attempted to follow a moderate line and construct a policy that would uphold the authority of the League but not alienate Japan. These aims were, however, incompatible, and once the League Assembly voted to accept the Lytton Report in February 1933 the need to be seen to act led to the decision to introduce an arms embargo against both Japan and China, a move which, despite its even-handedness, appeared to demonstrate the National Government's sympathy with anti-Japanese sentiment in Britain.[5]

At the same time another issue was raising tensions between Britain and Japan. In 1932 there were increasingly loud cries from the Lancashire cotton lobby for action to be taken against the flood of Japanese cotton goods that were entering India and the colonies. These demands were made in the full knowledge that Japan's unpopularity over Manchuria would lead to support for retaliation.[6] This indeed proved to be the case, and in the wake of the arms embargo the Indian government announced in April 1933 the abrogation of the 1911 Treaty of Commerce and Navigation with Japan, while in May the British government abrogated the Anglo-Japanese commercial treaty for its West African colonies.[7]

The critical response in Britain to Japan's military adventures and its export drive came as an unpleasant shock to Tokyo. Moreover to many Japanese it appeared to demonstrate the inherent hypocrisy of Western democracies which criticized Japan for seeking an empire while simultaneously exploiting their own formal and informal empires in order to construct closed economic blocs. To some there was one simple explanation for such behaviour, namely racism, which was already manifest in the West's refusal to grant naval equality to Japan and in the immigration policies of the United States and Australia. Goaded by the West's condemnations and faced with the dislocation of the world economy, the internationalists within Japan were increasingly eclipsed and the Japanese government became prey to the ultra-nationalists' demands for further expansion.[8]

The result was that from 1933 the objective of the Japanese government became the formation of its own autarkic bloc in East Asia. This led to a bold new policy which implicitly rejected the status quo established at the Washington Conference of 1921–22: Japan now began to assert that it was responsible for the security of East Asia. It demanded that China should enter into a cooperative, rather than confrontational, relationship with Japan, and insisted that it had the right to oppose any Western actions that were likely to threaten the peace of East Asia. This policy, which was tantamount to a 'Monroe Doctrine for East Asia', was encapsulated in a succession of memoranda and pronouncements by Japanese officials, most notably the infamous statement in April 1934 by the spokesman of the Japanese Foreign Ministry (Gaimusho), Amau Eiji. In addition, behind the scenes the Deputy Minister for Foreign Affairs, Shigemitsu Mamoru, began to propose a series of concessions in regard to Japanese rights in China, such as the withdrawal of military garrisons from China and abolition of the Maritime Customs Service, which were designed to foster Sino-Japanese friendship and undercut the position of the West.[9]

In justifying its views to the outside world, Japan's propagandists made much of the fact that the policies of the West had left Japan with no choice but to seek expansion on the Asian mainland and that it was thus unfair to criticize its policies in China. In an article published in the British journal *The Fortnightly* in November 1935 the former Japanese ambassador to Britain, Matsui Keishiro, observed of recent times that:

> Great Britain and her Dominions, while refusing Japanese immigration, took at the time of the Manchurian incident an attitude as if they were bent upon interfering with Japan's advance along the only path left to her. And finally they are closing their markets to Japanese trade. Are we to live or perish, flourish or wither away? We cannot but contemplate with grave concern the enormous obstacles that beset the path of our nation.[10]

Matsui argued that Britain should therefore change its policy in East Asia and warned that 'All these questions must be answered to the satisfaction of the Japanese, dispelling all misgivings.'

The idea of achieving Japanese dominance over East Asia did not, however, mean that the Gaimusho wished to evict Britain completely, as there was a belief that a British financial and commercial presence in the region could be useful as long as Britain did not attempt to sow division between Japan and China. The problem was obviously how to get Britain to accept this diminished role for itself and recognize Japan's regional pre-eminence. The Gaimusho thought that such a shift in British thinking was possible. This view was based on the belief that many of the ministers in the British government retained a pragmatic approach to foreign policy and had little time for the League of Nations. In addition, it was assumed that as the British Conservatives were vociferously anti-Soviet, they would be sympathetic to a Japanese military presence in East Asia which would restrain Moscow's ambitions. Moreover, underlying the desire to appeal to this circle was the feeling that Britain retained an oligarchic system of government and that ministers could act without necessarily taking note of the anti-Japanese sentiments expressed by the political 'left'.[11]

The Gaimusho attempted in its diplomacy to appeal to a pro-Japanese faction in Britain centred on the figure of the Chancellor of the Exchequer, Neville Chamberlain. This group included prominent ministers such as Sir Samuel Hoare and Sir John Simon, supporters in Whitehall such as the Permanent Secretary to the Treasury, Sir Warren Fisher, and the Chief Industrial Adviser to the government, Sir Horace Wilson, and right-wing newspapers and journals, such as *The Morning Post*, the most conservative daily newspaper, *The English Review* and *The National Review*, and on occasions *The Times*. Of particular importance was H.A. Gwynne, the editor of *The Morning Post*, who was close to Chamberlain and acted as a conduit to the Japanese Embassy through his friendship with Arthur Edwardes, the London representative of the Manchukuo government.[12] This faction was on the whole sympathetic to Japan, in favour of the recognition of Manchukuo and keen to see future Anglo-Japanese economic collaboration in China.

The influence of this group within British politics and its contacts with the Gaimusho during the period 1934–37 have led a number of scholars, particularly in Japan, to speculate about missed opportunities during this period. Some have gone as far as to talk of British policy as one of 'appeasement', and have criticized the Gaimusho for failing to take advantage of the olive branch offered by Chamberlain.[13] Western historians have, however, tended to be uncertain about the use of the word 'appeasement' in the context of Japan.[14] While acknowledging that the desire for reconciliation was present, they have emphasized that many of the concessions mooted in Whitehall fell prey to departmental rivalries or were set aside due to concern about the reactions of other states. In addition, it has been contended that Britain had no intention of retreating in the face of the Japanese advance and that there was a strong desire to see the rehabilitation of the British economic stake in China.

In assessing this debate it is important on the British side to look at two points: first, to assess to what degree the Chamberlain group had any flexibility of movement within the British political system and, second, to study what exactly Chamberlain hoped to achieve.

In regard to the former, it is vital to take account of the domestic and European pressures on the British government that restricted its manoeuvrability *vis-à-vis* Japan. One frequently overlooked factor is that Japanese behaviour during the Manchurian crisis meant that significant elements within British politics, such as the Labour Party, the Samuelite Liberals and the pro-League elements within the Conservative Party, were already averse to any compromise with Japan that would have infringed China's sovereignty. Japan's actions in China between 1933 and 1937, the rise of militarism with its attendant escalation of political violence, and the development of links with Germany, symbolized by the signing of the Anti-Comintern Pact, only strengthened this sentiment.[15] On 27 November 1936, two days after the initialling of the Anti-Comintern Pact, Winston Churchill, who previously had defended Japan's ambitions in China, noted in an article for the *Evening Standard* that, if there were to be a war in Europe, 'We may be sure that Japan will immediately light a second conflagration in the Far East', and observed of Japan itself in words that summed up British unease:

> Here ... is a State where the military mind is supreme; ... where every voice of moderation is silenced by death; where the murder of political opponents has been for some years accepted practice; where even trusted commanders may be slaughtered by their supporters for suspected luke-warmness.[16]

Japan was thus for many a fanatical, militarist state which should be treated as a pariah.

Added to those elements who objected to the 'immorality' of Japanese foreign policy was the industrial lobby which faced increasing competition from Japanese exports. It may have been that this competition was not as serious as they imagined, and indeed some contemporary commentators made this criticism, but many industrialists nevertheless perceived themselves to be facing a crisis.[17] Concern was not limited to the textile sector; the letters to the Federation of British Industry complaining about Japanese competition came from many areas of business and covered a range of products as diverse as electric lamps, concrete, bicycles, hair-combs and rubber footwear.[18] The fear of commercial ruin led to fierce language, including references to the 'Yellow Peril'. On one occasion a speaker at an extraordinary meeting of the Manchester Chamber of Commerce went so far as to declare that, if the government did not act to curb Japanese exports, 'it may eventually mean the ultimate ruin of every civilized country inhabited by white people'.[19] Such was the level of hostility towards Japan that within Parliament there was a constant barrage of questions from MPs representing industrial constituencies that were implicitly critical not just of Japanese trade practices but of all things Japanese. For example, in April 1934 it was notable that many of the questions and statements critical of the Amau statement came from Conservative MPs in Lancashire and the Midlands.[20]

The importance of public opinion, whether critical of Japan for commercial or moral reasons, was not lost on Whitehall. In January 1937 Sir Alexander Cadogan, the Deputy Under-Secretary of State at the Foreign Office, noted to the First Sea Lord, Admiral Sir Ernle Chatfield, who had just proposed moves towards reconciliation, that:

> an agreement with Japan ... is going to be very difficult on account of our real differences of fundamental interests. But even if we at the Foreign Office could disregard or surmount this Japan has intentions in the East which conflict with 'public opinion' here, which is now more vocal than it was and influences Houses of Commons and Governments much more easily (cf. Manchukuo, Abyssinia). This would be a real difficulty in the East.[21]

In this atmosphere it seems clear that to avoid a political backlash on both the opposition and the government benches, any agreement which the government negotiated with Japan would have required substantial Japanese concessions.

The pro-Japanese group based around the Treasury did not, however, have only public opinion to contend with; they also had to convince the Foreign Office of the wisdom of a rapprochement. The problem here was that closer relations with Japan clearly had the potential to complicate British foreign policy elsewhere. There was, for example, the possibility that if Britain was too conciliatory towards Japan it would alienate American public opinion, and thus jeopardize future access to the munitions factories and money markets of the United States which had proved so vital in the Great War.[22] Another problem was the position of the Soviet Union as both an Asian and a European power. There was a real danger that, if Britain were reconciled with Japan, it would encourage the latter to step up its war of nerves with Russia, which might in turn lead Stalin to reduce the threat of a two-front war by moving closer to Germany or France, thus deepening rather than alleviating the European crisis.[23] A further concern was that any deal with Japan would merely alienate Chinese opinion and thus lead to a boycott of British goods, thereby negating the benefit of any Japanese concessions.[24]

Over and above these problems the Foreign Office also had another reason to be circumspect about any permanent agreement with Japan, and this was its access to intelligence information about Japan's diplomatic and military activities. From as early as 1919 British intelligence had been able to intercept the Gaimusho's telegrams and thus had a valuable window on Japanese decision-making. During the mid-1930s this source provided information that underlined the need to be very wary of Japan. For example, following the Amau statement in April 1934 the Gaimusho attempted to explain away its spokesman's words as an unauthorized outburst which did not reflect Japanese opinion. However, intercepted telegrams between Tokyo and the Japanese ambassador in Peking, Ariyoshi Akira, revealed that the Amau statement was indeed a true reflection of Japanese policy. In addition, the intercepts provided a window on Japanese relations with Europe, and from 1934 to 1936 the Foreign Office was able to watch the steady progress towards the signing of the Anti-Comintern Pact, which again revealed Japan's unreliability.[25]

This intelligence information, added to the possible repercussions of a rapprochement on Europe, led the Foreign Office to contend that Britain had to be cautious in its East Asian policy and maintain a careful balance between China and Japan. It was thus deeply sceptical about the Treasury's stance and sought to dilute Chamberlain's initiatives.

It can therefore be seen that there were major obstacles to any settlement since it had both to satisfy public opinion and avoid any unwelcome consequences in foreign policy. However, it is also important to see that, even had Chamberlain been able to neutralize the opposition within Britain, what he wanted to achieve in East Asia was not in any case compatible with Japanese interests. Chamberlain first put forward proposals for better relations in 1934, but, as these had centred on the naval limitation issue and ignored the main area of contention, China, they had come to nothing.[26] By 1935, however, the Treasury recognized that the China issue had to be addressed and began to construct a plan for joint exploitation of the Chinese market by Britain and Japan. This concept led in August 1935 to the despatch to East Asia of Sir Frederick Leith-Ross, the Chief Economic Adviser to the British government, to negotiate an agreement between Japan, China and Britain which would involve Britain and Japan in granting a joint loan to China in return for Chinese recognition of Manchukuo. Leith-Ross duly made this offer during his visit to Tokyo in September 1935 but met with an unsympathetic response.[27]

It is this episode which has caused the greatest controversy in the debate about British 'appeasement'. Some Japanese scholars have taken it for granted that the offer was intended primarily to conciliate Japan, and have heavily criticized the Japanese government for failing to capitalize on the situation. For example, Sakai Tetsuya has observed that the rejection of these proposals was due to the Gaimusho's steadfast adherence to 'the principle of rejecting third power interventions in the China problem' and that consequently Japan 'lost the last great opportunity to reconstruct the international order in the Far East', while Akita Shigeru has described the idea of recognizing Manchukuo as an 'incredible concession ... certainly deserving of the label "British appeasement of Japan"'.[28]

In order to understand why Japan rejected the Leith-Ross proposals it is important, however, to look more closely at them and their origin. In particular, it needs to be understood that a key element in Chamberlain's plan was that it would provide the foundations for an expansion of British commercial and financial interests in China.[29] This policy clearly ran counter to the plans for China that had been constructed within the Gaimusho, which were far from envisaging the establishment of any Anglo-Japanese condominium in China. In addition, it is apparent that, on the financial side, Britain aimed at helping to reform the Chinese currency with the explicit aim of linking it to sterling, a plan which ran contrary to Japan's ambition to set up a yen bloc in the region.[30] With these two important British desiderata in mind, one can see that, as Ian Nish has noted, 'the Manchukuo concessions were only part of the negotiating hand that Leith-Ross took with him', and that the recognition of Manchukuo was contingent on Japan itself making some unpalatable concessions.[31]

Chamberlain's ability to negotiate a settlement was also undermined by his reluctance to engage in economic appeasement of Japan in British imperial markets. Clearly if Britain was not willing to accept Japanese domination over China, then some redress had to be made elsewhere to meet Japan's argument that it must have room to expand. Logically this meant easing the restrictions on Japanese trade with the British Empire. Ironically this was an argument which was accepted by some of the British critics of Japanese militarism, who postulated that the roots of Japan's desire for expansion lay in the disparities in the international economy between the 'haves' and 'have-nots'.[32] This argument even had some appeal to the Foreign Office: in spring 1937 the Foreign Secretary, Anthony Eden, who was not renowned for making pro-Japanese statements, noted that it seemed to make little sense to dam back Japanese goods from entry into the Empire only for Japan to seek 'a preferential area in Manchukuo and North China'.[33] Chamberlain and his political allies were, however, loath to move in this direction. In August 1936, after reading a League of Nations memorandum calling for trade liberalization, Chamberlain baldly noted: 'We are not ready to yield to Japan more of our export trade to British Colonies.'[34] Furthermore in May 1937 when the Inter-Departmental Committee on Trade Policy indicated that Lancashire might have to make sacrifices in order to reduce the Japanese security threat, this line was rejected by the Cabinet Foreign Policy Committee because of its domestic implications.[35] Thus in one of the key areas which any rapprochement would have to address the British government was not prepared to move.

In addition, it must be remembered that opinion about Britain was divided in Japan and that this also helped to impede any improvement of Anglo-Japanese relations. There were some elements in the Gaimusho and the Court, such as Yoshida Shigeru and Makino Nobuaki, who were keen to work in co-operation with Britain. Indeed there is evidence to suggest that Yoshida as a 'special envoy' in the autumn of 1934 helped to plant the seed of the idea that became the Leith-Ross mission in the mind of Fisher, Edwardes and Gwynne; and certainly as ambassador to London from July 1936 he worked hard to build up mutual trust.[36] The problem was, however, that Yoshida was following his own agenda and that his efforts only helped to build up false hopes on the British side, until it was realized from the evidence of Japanese behaviour and the information provided by intelligence sources that he was speaking without authority. Meanwhile in Japan the Gaimusho was steadily losing ground to the Imperial Japanese Army (IJA), which was becoming the final arbiter within Japanese politics. In spring 1936 the IJA vetoed Hirota's attempt to make Yoshida his Foreign Minister and then refused to allow Shigemitsu to become the ambassador to China, which hardly augured well for a policy of conciliation with Britain.[37]

It is therefore important to recognize in any discussion of the mid-1930s that there were grave difficulties in the way of any Anglo-Japanese rapprochement. It is clear that British opinion was deeply divided over relations with Japan, which severely limited the pro-Japanese faction's room for manoeuvre, and that Chamberlain himself was concerned not just with pacifying Japan but also with expanding Britain's economic stake in China. This contrasted with opinion within Japan where those in power in the Gaimusho envisaged better relations within their own strict parameters and where their own manoeuvrability was being undermined by the activities of the IJA both in China and in Tokyo.

The effect of the Sino-Japanese war

The opening of the Sino-Japanese War in July 1937 ended any potential for talks between Britain and Japan. To the majority of the British public there was no question that Japan was responsible for the opening of hostilities in China, and the result was an outpouring of anti-Japanese sentiment at many levels. Much of the press, including most significantly *The Times*, took an anti-Japanese stance, and public meetings, including one at the Royal Albert Hall at which the Archbishop of Canterbury was present, denounced Japanese aggression. In particular, the Japanese aerial bombing of Shanghai, Nanking and Canton alienated opinion, as it drew a direct parallel with the German destruction of Guernica earlier that year.[38]

The sense of disgust with Japan's actions was not restricted to what might be termed the 'liberal left'; it also extended into the heart of the National Government. In August and September 1937 a number of ministers, including Lord Stanhope, Earl De La Warr and Lord Halifax, wrote to the Foreign Secretary, Anthony Eden, expressing their horror at Japan's actions. Halifax's outburst, in which he stated that the Japanese bombing 'seems to me to be the worst thing – for morality and civilization – that we have yet seen!', was the most significant, as he would soon replace Eden as Foreign Secretary and was normally identified by the Japanese as being sympathetic.[39] Even a figure such as Arthur Edwardes, who worked within the Japanese embassy as the agent for Manchukuo, could not understand why Japan did not act with a little more sensitivity. In late December 1937, after the fall of Nanking, Edwardes wrote to Amau Eiji who was now the Japanese minister in Berne, to bemoan Japan's failure to put forth reasonable peace terms and observed:

> As you know Japan has no more understanding friend in this country than myself, but I deplore the manner in which the continuance of hostilities is damaging Japan's reputation throughout the world. The large body of people in this country friendly to Japan is unable to understand what military object there can possibly be in continuing the struggle.[40]

If even Edwardes was tiring of Japan, the situation was indeed desperate.

The tide of anti-Japanese opinion that swept Britain was reciprocated within Japan, where the Japanese press produced articles asserting that the British were the chief backers of Chiang Kai-shek's regime. This perception was based in part on reports that munitions were reaching China through Hong Kong, but also on the belief that the opinions expressed in the British press, and particularly *The Times*, represented the view of the British government.[41]

The effect of the Sino-Japanese war was to turn Britain and Japan away from any consideration of how to come to terms with each other; instead each sought to use pressure to make the other more amenable. In Japan's case this led to a revival of interest in its relations with the Axis Powers in Europe in order to sharpen Britain's fear of a three-front war. Japan very quickly turned to Germany as its mediator of choice for peace with China, and in November 1937 invited Italy to accede to the Anti-Comintern Pact.[42] On the British side, the autumn of 1937 saw a concerted effort by Eden to construct a common Anglo-American front in East Asia to curtail Japanese aggression. Central to this attempt at co-operation was the idea of introducing economic sanctions against Japan. In October 1937 a report on the effect that economic sanctions by the British Empire singly and in combination with the United States might have on Japan was produced for the Committee of Imperial Defence. The conclusion reached was that sanctions could seriously damage Japan but only in the long term and only if taken in concert with Washington. Eden was keen to pursue such a strategy but, both at the Brussels Conference in November 1937 and in the aftermath of the Japanese attacks on the gunboats HMS *Ladybird* and USS *Panay* in December 1937, it was discovered that American enthusiasm for robust action soon evaporated.[43]

Faced with the likelihood of American inaction if Britain resorted to coercion against Japan, Whitehall was forced at the beginning of 1938 to reassess its policy towards the Sino-Japanese war. The case put forward by Eden and his successor, Lord Halifax, was that Britain should increase its level of assistance to China by agreeing to provide funds to support the Chinese currency and helping to construct a new road linking Yunnan with Burma. This policy was, however, resisted by the Treasury, which clung to the belief that the European situation was too serious for Britain to take the risk of alienating Japan. Instead the Treasury and the British Ambassador to Japan, Sir Robert Craigie, argued that Britain should be strictly neutral. Crucial to this argument was the belief that a Japanese victory was inevitable and that Britain therefore risked being ejected from China if it supported Chiang Kai-shek, while the observance of neutrality might still allow British firms to be involved in the reconstruction of China. In addition, Craigie went even further and, under the influence of the Military Attaché in Tokyo, Major-General F.S.G. Piggott, propagated the idea that a moderate group still existed in the Japanese government which was prepared to cooperate with Britain and that, through a more conciliatory and less confrontational policy, their influence might be strengthened.[44]

At first the Treasury was able to win the battle over the issue of neutrality, and in the summer of 1938 the Cabinet rejected the idea of a loan to China. However, the Foreign Office, and even the Treasury, were sceptical about Craigie's wilder claims and, although he was given permission to begin conversations with the new Japanese Foreign Minister, General Ugaki Kazushige, the agenda was largely restricted to the possibility of negotiating a *modus vivendi* for the Japanese-occupied areas of China which would allow British firms to renew trading.

Craigie's perception that the moderates were gaining ground in Tokyo was not without foundation. Ugaki, with the enthusiastic encouragement of Ambassador Yoshida in London, was indeed keen to improve relations with Britain or at least to remove the obvious sources of tensions in order to allow Japan to pursue victory against China.[45] As a result Ugaki was willing to engage in talks with Craigie, although these failed to make any headway and, in September 1938, collapsed under the weight of the Sudeten crisis in Europe and IJA pressure on Ugaki.[46] In addition, Ugaki decided to appoint Shigemitsu Mamoru as the new Japanese ambassador to London. Shigemitsu arrived in London in late October determined to improve relations and to get Britain to understand and recognize Japan's paramount position in East Asia.[47] Over the next three months he unleashed his own diplomatic offensive in London, meeting civil servants such as Sir Horace Wilson and Sir Frederick Leith-Ross, parliamentarians such as Sir John Wardlaw-Milne (chairman of the House of Commons China Committee), and ministers such as Neville Chamberlain, Lord Halifax and the Parliamentary Under-Secretary of State at the Foreign Office, R.A. Butler. On each occasion he attempted to interest his interlocutor in the idea of recognizing 'Japan's unique position in China'; he met, however, with universal resistance.[48]

The obvious question to ask about this initiative, which seems in hindsight to have flown in the face of the majority of British opinion, is, why did Shigemitsu even imagine that this policy would be acceptable? It would appear from his writings that his enthusiasm for these meetings was based on the fact that he still believed in the existence of a pro-Japanese faction in the Conservative Party and felt that the anti-Japanese sentiment expressed in Britain was the result of a small but vocal minority, including Churchill and Eden, which was sympathetic to the League, China, the United States, and even the Soviet Union.[49] The dismissal of those opposed to Japanese aggression as unrepresentative of the mass of informed opinion was a grave error, for it failed to recognize that even within Chamberlain's entourage sympathy for Japan was running dry and that Halifax himself was one of the main figures arguing for resistance to Japan. Certainly a pro-Japanese group did still exist on the 'far right' of the Conservative Party, but it was powerless to influence British policy and its voices in the British press such as *The National Review* were left to lash out at the 'anti-Japanese propaganda' in the British press and the Sinophile 'faddists' of Chatham House in a state of impotent rage.[50]

One can speculate that Shigemitsu's unwisely optimistic view of the political right as representative of 'true' British sentiment was due to the Japanese Embassy's reliance on Arthur Edwardes for its entrées into London society. Edwardes himself appears to have been firmly on the right in the context of British politics, was vociferously anti-League and consistently played down the depth of anti-Japanese feeling in Britain. For example, in January 1938 he contended to Amau that the majority of Englishmen hoped for the dissolution of the League, and he dismissed the idea that the fiery criticisms of Japan in *The Times* represented British opinion by noting that the newspaper was after all owned by the Astors who were American; a point which Shigemitsu later repeated almost verbatim in his memoirs.[51] There is an interesting parallel here with Piggott's influence on Craigie and it seems probable that Edwardes distorted the true nature of British opinion in much the same way as Piggott did Japanese opinion.

Shigemitsu's efforts were also undermined by events. The failure of the Craigie–Ugaki talks marked a turning point in Anglo-Japanese relations as it demonstrated the extent of the impasse between the two countries. Over the next few months relations, in the wake of Munich, became steadily worse as Japanese coercive measures against Britain and its East Asian interests increased in intensity. One aspect of this was the mounting pressure exerted on the authorities in charge of the International Settlement at Shanghai and the British Concession at Tientsin in north China to co-operate with local Japanese forces and not to give any assistance to the Kuomintang. In addition to this the Japanese military began directly to menace British interests. In October 1938 the IJA seized the area around Canton and closed the frontier between Hong Kong and China. This was followed in early 1939 by a Japanese advance into the South China Sea through the seizure of Hainan and the Paracel and Spratly Islands. Above and beyond this, in November 1938 the Prime Minister, Prince Konoe Fumimaro, announced the establishment of 'The New Order in East Asia'. This declaration was a direct challenge to the British position as it envisaged the grouping of Japan, China and Manchukuo into one political, economic and cultural bloc to the exclusion of any Western influence.[52]

Affected by the turn for the worse in Japan's attitude and by knowledge from intelligence sources about Japan's recent alliance talks with Germany and Italy, the Chamberlain government's policy became perceptibly harsher. In December 1938 it decided to reverse its previous decision over the loan to China, and there was once again talk in Whitehall about the possibility of economic sanctions. The background to this shift was a growing perception that Japan lacked the capability to strike back at Britain. The war in China had suggested to the British intelligence community the perilous state of the Japanese war economy and even more significantly the relative weakness of the IJA and the Japanese air arms. This suggested to some in Whitehall that the danger of Japanese retaliation against British sanctions was not as great as previously imagined.[53]

This prognosis, however, only held true if there was peace in Europe; it was clear that if there was any danger of war from Germany then Britain could not afford to take risks in East Asia. This was to be the case in the summer of 1939 when the unrelenting Japanese pressure on the British concession at Tientsin finally developed into a fully-fledged crisis. In June the IJA, in response to the British authority's lack of cooperation over policing the concession, blockaded the British zone and subjected all those passing in and out to humiliating body searches. This led to outrage in Britain, many letters of protest being sent to the press. However, due to the seriousness of the European situation, with Germany and Poland on the verge of war and Mussolini stirring up trouble in the Mediterranean, Britain could not afford to be led by public opinion into a conflict with Japan. Instead it had to seek a way out of the Tientsin crisis, and a solution was offered when Craigie proposed that talks should be held in Tokyo.

It is often assumed that these talks fit into a general pattern of British appeasement in the 1930s, particularly because they led to the Craigie–Arita formula of 24 July in which Britain appeared to promise to co-operate with Japan in China. This, however, is a false conclusion, for the formula was so vaguely worded as to be meaningless, and it was negotiated only as a way to reduce tensions and not with the intention of leading to any wider Anglo-Japanese rapprochement. It may have been that Craigie himself saw the talks in grandiose terms and hoped that they would spur on the Japanese 'moderates' to take hold of the reins of power, but that was certainly not the view held by Chamberlain or Halifax, who only wanted a painless solution to the immediate crisis. In the end, however, it was not negotiations that brought the Tientsin crisis to an end, but the signing of the Nazi–Soviet Pact on 23 August 1939, which compromised Japan's pro-German foreign policy and led swiftly to the resignation of the Hiranuma government. This dramatic change was rapidly followed by the opening of the European war on 3 September.[54]

The road to war

The conflict in Europe raised important questions about the future of Anglo-Japanese relations. The fundamental issue Britain had to face was whether it could afford to remain at loggerheads with Japan in East Asia now that it was fighting for its survival in Europe. It might appear from hindsight that Britain should at this point have decided that Japan's friendship was of greater importance than China and thus made a deal with Tokyo. However, a full-scale policy of appeasement carried with it a heavy price, for any such action would still have had a calamitous effect on relations with the United States. In addition, the Chiefs of Staff made a strong case for arguing that Britain should continue its support for China on the grounds that as long as Chinese resistance continued Japan could not turn its attention elsewhere.

The decision taken in the autumn of 1939 was therefore not to change British policy drastically but rather to attempt to ease tensions in a way that would not provoke American suspicions or undermine the Chinese war effort. With its mind set on prosecuting the China war to a successful conclusion, Japan too had an interest in starting talks, although its hope was that, as well as calming British susceptibilities, it might be possible through negotiation to push Britain into a more neutral position in the Sino-Japanese War as a quid pro quo for Japanese neutrality towards the European conflict. From September 1939 to June 1940 the two powers engaged in a number of tentative talks in both Tokyo and London. In Tokyo Craigie's activities centred around negotiating a settlement of the Tientsin issue, talks which eventually led to a mutually acceptable agreement in June. Meanwhile in London Shigemitsu concentrated on the revived interest in Anglo-Japanese trade issues.

The start of the European war raised two problems in the area of trade. The first was Japan's concern about a possible decline in imports of raw material from the British Empire now that the latter was engaged in war mobilization against Germany. On the British side the main issue was how to stop Germany from receiving vital raw materials from Southeast Asia and Latin America via Japan and the Trans-Siberian Railway. It soon became clear that these two issues could be linked, and in May and June 1940 talks were held in London. However, the talks revealed once again the incompatibility of the interests of the two powers. The British were only willing to set quotas of raw materials for Japan if the Japanese committed themselves not to re-export any goods to Germany: the Japanese, however, felt that the quotas were too low and that the ban on re-export was an infringement of its sovereignty. The talks were thus doomed to failure.[55]

Meanwhile a far greater opportunity for Japan to improve its economic and political position came in the summer of 1940 when Germany conquered France and Holland, and was poised to defeat Britain. This meant that Japan could now press Britain and Vichy France to suspend the passage of munitions into China, and take advantage of the power vacuum in Southeast Asia caused by the collapse of the colonial powers in Europe to ensure easy and open access to the region's raw materials. On 19 June the IJA demanded that Britain close the Burma Road or face the threat of war. This brought home to Whitehall the danger of facing Japan alone in East Asia, and on 17 July the Burma Road agreement was signed in Tokyo under which the Road was to be closed for a period of three months and Japan promised to seek a negotiated settlement with China.[56] There was hope in some quarters that the agreement would mark a turning point in Anglo-Japanese relations. In particular R.A. Butler, with strong encouragement from Shigemitsu, put pressure on the departments in Whitehall to look for a way to reach a more permanent settlement with Japan.

Any hope that the Burma Road agreement could provide the basis for something more permanent was, however, dashed with the formation in late July of the second Konoe cabinet and the appointment of Matsuoka Yosuke as Foreign Minister. Matsuoka was determined to build upon Japan's newfound ability to exercise pressure on Southeast Asia, and within two months of taking office he had declared that Japan intended to build a Greater East Asian Co-Prosperity Sphere, sent a delegation to the Dutch East Indies to ensure the supply of raw materials, forced Vichy France to agree to the stationing of Japanese troops in north Indo-China, and signed the Tripartite Pact with Germany and Italy. This succession of events, added to the wave of arrests of British subjects in Japan in late July, revealed to everyone in Whitehall, including Butler, that there was no point in trying to reach an agreement with Japan. The only policy that could now be followed was one of containing the Japanese in co-operation with the United States.[57]

In October 1940 the British War Cabinet established a Far Eastern Committee which began to introduce a policy of economic warfare against Japan. Over the next few months the first steps were taken towards constructing an effective blockade of Japan, although progress was delayed due to the tardiness of the United States and the British fear of moving too far ahead of Washington lest Japan be provoked to attack. By the spring of 1941, however, British pressure on the Americans, combined with the effect of a 'war scare' in Southeast Asia in February, had helped to galvanize the Roosevelt administration, and the Anglo-American economic noose around Japan began to pull ever tighter.[58] In addition, there was increasing military co-operation between the British, the Americans and the Dutch and, although there was still nothing in the nature of guaranteed assistance from Washington in the case of war, there was a real sense that the security situation had improved since the Burma Road crisis. This perception was augmented by the intelligence information that was reaching Whitehall about Japan's military capabilities, which continued to raise considerable doubts about the effectiveness of the Japanese war effort in China and helped to perpetuate the idea in Churchill's mind that Japan's leaders were innately cautious. In such circumstances the calls from various quarters, in particular from Craigie and Shigemitsu, to keep a negotiated settlement as a possible option were cast aside, and instead Britain began to use propaganda to persuade Japan that Germany was an untrustworthy ally and that war against the Anglo-Saxons would be futile due to their massive potential for war.[59]

A similarly uncompromising view was taken of Britain in Japan. It was widely believed in Japanese military circles that Britain was doomed to defeat in the European war and that the inadequate British forces in Malaya could be swept aside with ease, a view that was reinforced by the information about British weakness passed by Germany to Japan in the *Automedon* affair of December 1940.[60] The only obstacle to such a scenario was the likelihood that the United States would come to Britain's aid, and thus in the first half of 1941 Japan's attention in the diplomatic field was focused on Washington rather than London in the hope that the American threat could be neutralized. From July 1941, however, once it was clear that the United States had decided to use oil sanctions against Japan in order to force it to relinquish its conquests or face complete collapse, the Gaimusho tried to persuade Britain that it was necessary to make the Roosevelt administration more amenable. Craigie duly relayed Japan's concerns to the Foreign Office, but they failed to move the British government to act as there was a fear that pressure on Washington would be misconstrued as 'appeasement' of Japan, and because the apparent panic in Japan only confirmed the idea that Japan was desperate to avoid war.[61] Blind to the last to each other's aims and policies Britain and Japan stumbled towards war.

Conclusion

During the years between 1931 and 1941 there existed in both Britain and Japan elements who desired a return to the friendship of former years, but such sentiments never came to dominate policy. Anglo-Japanese friendship had begun to ebb away even before this decade as the national interests of Britain and Japan had started to diverge prior to the Washington Conference; this tendency had been reinforced by the differences of opinion at the Peking Tariff Conference of 1925, by the Northern Expedition crisis of 1926–28 and by the Manchurian crisis of 1931–33. After Japan's departure from the League in March 1933 there was a period in which influential factions on both sides talked of the need for rapprochement between the former allies, but nothing came of these overtures and instead the divide grew ever greater; it stood no chance of repair once the Sino-Japanese War had broken out in 1937.

The failure to break away from this road to confrontation was due to a myriad of factors. If one looks at the 1930s it is immediately apparent that Britain and Japan had opposing opinions over virtually every issue that springs to mind, the existence of Manchukuo, the future of China, the legitimacy of Imperial Preference, and the naval arms limitation process being only the most obvious. The clashes over these issues were fierce and mutually reinforcing and help to demonstrate that Anglo-Japanese alienation, while largely the result of antithetical national interests in the fields of security and commerce, was also to a degree the result of an ideological divide. Thus it is possible to say that at one level the road to war was simply part of the age-old *realpolitik* story of the conflict of interests between rising and declining powers, in this case exacerbated by the dire effects of the Depression, but that at another it was a reflection of the very different lessons that political élites drew from the origins and course of the Great War. Britain emerged from that war traumatized and desperate for some means to police the world without recourse to conflict; Japan, which had not suffered the slaughter of the Western Front, imbibed the heady brew emanating from Germany that dictated that autarky and authoritarianism were the only ways to survive in a world of eternal strife. Therefore once Japan put its desire for expansion into action it not only clashed with British material interests but also appeared as an unwelcome, perhaps even barbaric, throwback to the past.

The desire to avoid war, to assuage Japan and to demonstrate that it did not need to follow this aggressive path led to the exposition by both the right and the liberal-left in Britain of solutions to the East Asian question. The right proposed a division of the spoils in China, a plan that ignored Japan's desire for regional leadership and the strength of Chinese nationalism, and did nothing to address the economic issues which led Japan to espouse a need for its own bloc economy. The 'progressives', on the other hand, developed the 'have-not' thesis, but in the midst of the slump of the 1930s it was too late to act in this sphere; in any case it is doubtful whether any such action would have appealed to the militarists in Japan who desired empire not for markets but for national economic security. With no easy way out Britain was thus faced with a choice: it could appease Japan and accept the tenets of the New Order in East Asia, which was what Japan sought to persuade Britain to do, or it could follow a policy of resistance. After years of debate finally, in order to defend its own interests in East Asia and, ironically, because of the need not to prejudice its chances of victory in Europe, it chose the latter and the result was war.

Acknowledgement

I would like to thank Saho Matsumoto and Philip Best for their help, and record my gratitude to Iokibe Makoto, Akita Shigeru, Tanaka Takahiko and Aizawa Kiyoshi and their colleagues and students for comments on an earlier version of this chapter.

Notes

1. I. Nish, *Japan's Struggle with Internationalism: Japan, China and the League of Nations, 1931–3* (London, 1993) *passim*, and S. Wilson, 'Containing the Crisis: Japan's Diplomatic Offensive in the West, 1931–33', *Modern Asian Studies*, vol. 29, no. 2 (1995), pp. 337–72.

2. 'Record of Churchill talk to Oxford University Conservative Association' by R. Storry in M. Gilbert (ed.), *Winston S. Churchill: Vol. V, Companion, Part 2, The Wilderness Years, 1929–35* (London, 1981) p. 726.
3. 'Supplement on the Sino-Japanese Conflict' in *The New Statesman and Nation*, 8 October 1932.
4. C. Thorne, *The Limits of Foreign Policy: The West, the League and the Far Eastern Crisis of 1931–1933* (London, 1972), p. 216.
5. *Ibid.*, pp. 337–40.
6. See Streat diary entry for 6 October 1932 in M. Dupree (ed.), *Lancashire and Whitehall: The Diary of Sir Raymond Streat, Vol. 1, 1931–39* (Manchester: Manchester University Press, 1987) p. 186.
7. A. Trotter, *Britain and East Asia, 1933–1937* (Cambridge, 1975), pp. 30–1.
8. See Nish, *Japan's Struggle with Internationalism*, pp. 242–6, and C. Hosoya, 'Britain and the United States in Japan's View of the International System, 1919–37' in I. Nish (ed.), *Anglo-Japanese Alienation, 1919–1952* (Cambridge, 1982), p. 18.
9. On the Amau statement, see T. Shimada, 'Designs on North China, 1933–1937', in J.W. Morley (ed.), *The China Quagmire: Japan's Expansion on the Asian Continent, 1933–1941* (New York, 1983), pp. 79–91. On Shigemitsu, see T. Sakai, '"Ei-Bei Kenkyu" to "Nichi-Chu Teikei"' (Cooperation with the West or Collaboration with China: An Interpretative Essay on Early Showa Diplomacy), in *Kindai Nihon Kenkyu* (Journal of Modern Japanese Studies) No. 11 (1989), p. 85.
10. K. Matsui, 'Anglo-Japanese Relations', in *The Fortnightly Review*, November 1935.
11. M. Shigemitsu, *Gaiko Kaisoroku* (Diplomatic Memoirs) (Tokyo, 1978), pp. 203–5.
12. See Hosoya, 'Britain and the United States, pp. 18–19. See also Y. Watanabe and T. Ito (eds), *Shigemitsu Mamoru Shuki* (Shigemitsu Memoirs), Vol. 1 (Tokyo, 1993), p. 100. On Edwardes and Gwynne, see I. Nish, 'Anglo-Japanese Alienation Revisited', in S. Dockrill (ed.), *From Pearl Harbor to Hiroshima: The Second World War in Asia and the Pacific, 1941–5* (Basingstoke, 1994), pp. 19–24. For the right-wing journals, see for example, the views expressed in 'R', 'Anglo-Japanese Relations', *The English Review* (December 1933), and that journal's regular 'Foreign Affairs' column written by the former diplomat Sir Charles Petrie.
13. See for example Hosoya, 'Britain and the United States...', pp. 18–23, Sakai, '"Gi-Bei Kenkyu" to "Nichi-Chu Teikei"', p. 85, and S. Akita, 'British Informal Empire in East Asia 1880s–1930s: A Japanese Perspective', in J. Hunter (ed.), *Japanese Perspectives on Imperialism in Asia*, LSE STICERD International Studies pamphlet (1995), pp. 19–22.
14. See S. Endicott, *Diplomacy and Enterprise: British China Policy, 1933–1937* (Manchester, 1975); Trotter, *Britain and East Asia, 1933–1937*, pp. 213–7, and I. Nish, 'Japan in Britain's View of the International System, 1919–37' in Nish (ed.), *Anglo-Japanese Alienation*, pp. 44–53.
15. See, for example, W. Watkin Davies, 'The Long Designs of Japan', *The Fortnightly Review*, August 1933, J. Parmenter, 'Japan's Coming Crisis', *The Contemporary Review*, April 1934, and 'Japan's Monroe Doctrine', *New Statesman and Nation*, 28 April 1934.

16. W. Churchill, 'Germany and Japan', *Evening Standard*, 27 November 1936, in M. Gilbert (ed.), *Winston S. Churchill, Vol. V, Companion, Part 3, The Coming of War, 1936–1939* (London, 1982), p. 437, footnote 1.
17. For balanced contemporary assessments of the Japanese economy, see T.E. Gregory, 'Japanese Competition in World Markets', *International Affairs* (May 1934), and G.C. Allen, 'The Political and Economic Position of Japan', *International Affairs* (July 1934).
18. See the letters entered in the files MSS200 F/3/E1/15/13-16 in Federation of British Industry (FBI) papers, Modern Record Centre, University of Warwick.
19. Minutes of Extraordinary General Meeting, Manchester Chamber of Commerce, 29 Jan. 1934, FBI papers, MSS200 F/3/E1/15/16.
20. Trotter, *Britain and East Asia 1933–1937*, p. 73.
21. Cadogan (Foreign Office) to Chatfield (Admiralty) 1 January 1937, FO800/395, (Public Record Office, Kew).
22. See P. Bell, *Chamberlain, Germany and Japan, 1933–4* (London, 1996), pp. 95–6.
23. See A. Best, *Britain, Japan and Pearl Harbor: Avoiding War in East Asia, 1936–41* (London, 1995), pp. 11–12, and S. Bourett-Knowles, 'The Global Micawber: Sir Robert Vansittart, the Treasury and the Global Balance of Power, 1933–35', *Diplomacy and Statecraft*, Vol. 6, No. 1 (1995), pp. 92–121.
24. Orde note 28 August 1934, *Documents on British Foreign Policy*, Second Series, Vol. XIII, doc. 8, appendix II, pp. 19–20.
25. See A. Best, 'Constructing An Image: British Intelligence and Whitehall's Perception of Japan, 1931–1939', *Intelligence and National Security*, Vol. 11, No. 3 (1996), pp. 403–23.
26. See Trotter, *Britain and East Asia, 1933–1937*, pp. 97–109.
27. For standard accounts of the Leith-Ross mission, see *ibid.*, pp. 143–67, and Endicott, *Diplomacy and Enterprise*, pp. 82–139.
28. See Sakai, '"Gi-bei Kenkyu"', p. 85, and Akita, 'British Informal Empire in East Asia', p. 20.
29. N. Chamberlain to Hilda, 6 April 1935, N. Chamberlain papers, Birmingham University Library, NC 18/1/712. See also Trotter, *Britain and East Asia, 1933–1937*, pp. 142–7.
30. See P. Cain, 'British Economic Imperialism in China in the 1930s', *Bulletin of Asia-Pacific Studies*, Vol. VII (1997), pp. 23–34.
31. Nish, 'Japan in Britain's View', p. 47.
32. See, for example, S. Gwynn, 'The Price of Peace', *The Fortnightly Review*, September 1935, and the speeches in the House of Commons by P. Loftus (C. Lowestoft) on 11 July 1935, *Hansard*, 5th ser., DIII. 599–601, and F. Messer (Lab. S. Tottenham) on 5 December 1935, *Hansard*, 5th ser., DVII. 412–4.
33. Eden to Chamberlain 24 March 1937, W6363/5/50, FO371/21215.
34. Chamberlain to Eden 25 August 1936, T172/2111.
35. Cabinet Foreign Policy Committee 12th meeting, 11 June 1937, CAB27/622.
36. See S. Hatano, 'Yoshida Junetsushi no Shuhen' (Ambassador Yoshida's Tour), in *Ningen Yoshida Shigeru* (Yoshida Shigeru: The Man) (Tokyo, 1991), pp. 314–25, and J. Dower, *Empire and Aftermath: Yoshida Shigeru and the Japanese Experience, 1878–1954* (Cambridge, Mass., 1979), pp. 123–83.

37. Dower, *Empire and Aftermath*, pp. 112–13.
38. For the link in the 'liberal' mind between the bombing in China and Guernica, see the editorial in the *New Statesman and Nation*, 4 September 1937, and F. Acland, 'The International Situation', *The Contemporary Review*, December 1937. On public opinion in Britain, see also B. Lee, *Britain and the Sino-Japanese War, 1937–1939: A Study in the Dilemmas of British Decline* (Stanford, 1973), pp. 50–1.
39. Halifax to Eden 27 September 1937, Avon papers, Birmingham University Library, AP20/5/21. See also Stanhope to Eden 29 August 1937, Avon papers, and De La Warr to Eden 28 September 1937, FO954/6.
40. Edwardes to Amau 29 December 1937, Amau papers, National Diet Library, Tokyo, No. 848.
41. See K. Usui, 'A Consideration of Anglo-Japanese Relations: Japanese Views of Britain, 1937–41', in Nish (ed.), *Anglo-Japanese Alienation*, pp. 83–4.
42. T. Ohata, 'The Anti-Comintern Pact, 1935–1939', in J.W. Morley (ed.), *Deterrent Diplomacy: Japan, Germany and the USSR, 1935–1940* (New York, 1976), pp. 44–5.
43. See P. Lowe, *Great Britain and the Origins of the Pacific War: A Study in British Policy in East Asia, 1937–1941* (Oxford, 1977), pp. 25–37, Best, *Britain, Japan and Pearl Harbor*, pp. 42–8, and Lee, *Britain and the Sino-Japanese War*, pp. 54–104.
44. On Craigie and Piggott, see P. Lowe, 'The Dilemmas of an Ambassador: Sir Robert Craigie in Tokyo, 1937–1941', *Proceedings of the British Association of Japanese Studies*, vol. 2 (1977), pp. 34–56, and A. Best, 'Sir Robert Craigie as Ambassador to Japan, 1937–41', in I. Nish (ed.), *Britain and Japan: Biographical Portraits* (Folkestone, 1994), pp. 238–51.
45. S. Murashima, 'Yoshida Shigeru Chuei Taishi to Myunhen Kaidan' (Ambassador to Great Britain, Yoshida Shigeru, and the Munich Conference), in *Ningen Yoshida Shigeru*, pp. 326–45.
46. See Best, 'Sir Robert Craigie as Ambassador to Japan', pp. 48–60, and Lowe, Great Britain and the Origins of the Pacific War, pp. 45–9.
47. On Shigemitsu's appointment see Y. Watanabe, *Shigemitsu Mamoru: Shanghai Jihen Kara Kokuren Kamei Made* (Shigemitsu Mamoru: From the Shanghai Incident to the United Nations) (Tokyo, 1996), pp. 67–74.
48. See A. Best, 'Shigemitsu Mamoru as Ambassador to Great Britain, 1938–1941', in I. Nish (ed.), *Shigemitsu Studies*, LSE STICERD International Studies, 1990, IS/90/219.
49. Y. Watanabe and T. Ito (eds), *Shigemitsu Mamoru Shuki*, pp. 100–4.
50. See for example the regular column 'Episodes of the Month', in *The National Review* for November 1937 and July 1939.
51. Edwardes to Amau 10 January 1938, and Edwardes to Amau 22 January 1938, Amau papers, Nos. 850 and 852. For the expression of similar opinions by Shigemitsu see M. Shigemitsu, *Gaiko Kaisoroku*, p. 204.
52. See Best, *Britain, Japan and Pearl Harbor*, pp. 62–6, and Lee, *Britain and the Sino-Japanese War*, pp. 148–64.
53. See Best, 'Constructing an Image', pp. 412–21.
54. On Tientsin, see R.J. Pritchard, *Far Eastern Influences upon British Strategy Towards the Great Powers, 1937–1939* (New York, 1987), pp. 154–69; Best, *Britain, Japan and Pearl Harbor*, pp. 71–86; and Lowe, *Great Britain*, pp. 72–102.

55. Best, *Britain, Japan and Pearl Harbor*, pp. 92–5 and 102–8.
56. On the Burma Road crisis, see *ibid.*, pp. 112–20, and Lowe, *Great Britain*, pp. 136–51.
57. See Best, *Britain, Japan and Pearl Harbour*, pp. 122–31, and Lowe, *Great Britain*, pp. 167–75.
58. Best, *Britain, Japan and Pearl Harbour*, pp. 133–6 and 138–53.
59. See A. Best, '"This Probably Over-Valued Military Power": British Intelligence and Whitehall's Perception of Japan, 1939–1941', *Intelligence and National Security*, vol. 12, no. 3 (1997), pp. 77–91.
60. S. Hatano and S. Asada, 'The Japanese Decision to Move South (1939–1941)', in R. Boyce and E.M. Robertson (eds), *Paths to War: New Essays on the Origins of the Second World War* (Basingstoke, 1989), pp. 393–4.
61. On Craigie's efforts see Lowe, 'Dilemmas of an Ambassador', pp. 50–4, and Best, 'Sir Robert Craigie', pp. 247–51.

3
Markets and Diplomacy: the Anglo-Japanese Rivalries over Cotton Goods Markets, 1930–36

Ishii Osamu

In the Great Depression years Japan's rapid trade expansion created serious trade frictions with many countries and territories. Great Britain, along with the British Commonwealth countries, the British colonies, as well as the United States, the Philippines and France, among others were faced with the problem of the influx of cheap Japanese goods. In the history of Anglo-Japanese relations of the 1930s, commercial rivalries and the resultant worsening of mutual images between the two countries played no small part.[1] The Great Depression, the Ottawa Imperial Conference (1932), the failed World Economic Conference in London (1933), the Manchurian Incident (1931) together with Japan's subsequent withdrawal from the League of Nations (1933), Japan's renunciation of the Washington Naval Treaty (1934) and its decision to walk out of the London Naval Conference (1936) were the events that provided the backdrop against which the trade wars – in the form of currency devaluation, quota systems, reciprocity, abrogation of commercial treaties, trade limitation and upward adjustment of import duties – took place.

The Anglo-Japanese commercial rivalries – especially over cotton textiles – were so fierce that even in the post-war period the textile industry in Lancashire, still smarting from the pre-war Japanese competition, remained very concerned about the revival of Japan's textile export. The British shipbuilding industry was also fearful of Japan's economic recovery. Great Britain, France, Australia and some other countries discriminated against Japanese goods throughout much of the 1950s and after.[2]

52 *Ishii Osamu*

In the 1930s although light industry was giving way to heavy industry in the major industrial countries, cotton piece goods were still a prime export item for such countries as Great Britain and Japan. Thus, Japan's trade competition with Great Britain was the fiercest of all. The problem was compounded by the relative ease with which such countries as India and China could enter cotton manufacturing, and the shrinking purchasing power of world consumers due to the world-wide depression.

Rising nationalism and the growth of home industry in general, and in particular China's recently obtained tariff autonomy and recurrent anti-foreign boycotts, added another difficult dimension to the problem.

While, on the one hand, Lancashire, the home of the 'Industrial Revolution', was rapidly losing a competitive edge in the interwar years, Osaka, the centre of cotton manufacturing in Japan, on the other hand, had enhanced its productivity through rigorous 'rationalization' during the 1920s. Thus, Osaka was very much on the offensive in the world market. It is symbolic that in 1933 the volume of Japanese cotton goods export exceeded that of British exports for the first time in history.

This chapter takes a look at the major trade talks between the two countries and some other aspects of the commercial rivalries of the decade. Although the episodes covered in this chapter are limited in scope and, possibly, in significance, they do make up an integral part of overall Anglo-Japanese relations during the decade, as the role of psychological factors in the bilateral relations should not be ignored. By the middle of the decade mutual perceptions had deteriorated, and there was, on the part of the Japanese, a sense that they had been victimized and encircled by the 'Anglo-Saxon' powers.

Japan's trade expansion

As world trade (especially in value) dramatically dropped in the midst of the Great Depression, Japan's export (in value) also dropped: in 1931 by 47 per cent as compared with 1929. However, it soon recovered: after hitting the bottom the volume of the Japanese exports reached the level of 1929. This recovery contributed significantly to Japan's overcoming the Great Depression.

In his forecast of the economy for 1935, Finance Minister Takahashi Korekiyo, remarked: 'our foreign trade should be the determining factor in business conditions'.[3] He deliberately allowed the yen to depreciate against the US dollar and sterling. Takahashi adopted a proto-Keynesian policy of deficit finance and public spending. This, together with the cheap yen, helped Japan get out of the Depression exceptionally well. According to a study done in 1971, the increase in government spending and trade expansion were responsible for creating a large effective demand at home and maintaining an 8.8 per cent annual growth in GNP between 1933 and 1935.[4]

The cheap yen aside, what contributed to Japan's trade expansion in the longer term was high productivity and low wages. In the cotton industry many female workers who were recruited from the rural areas handled high-speed spindles. As Japan's exports came into conflict with the exports of other industrialized countries, these countries charged that Japan was engaged in 'social dumping'.

In response, Japanese employers emphasized cultural differences: they contended that the cost of living was lower in Japan, and therefore, wages were, in comparison, lower than those in the United States and the European countries. A personnel manager at a Kanegafuchi textile mill in Osaka boasted: 'We don't need any trade union. We are just one big family, working for the good of the enterprise'. Fujiwara Ginjiro, president of the Oji Paper Company, in his book published in English, even attributed Japan's industrial development to what he called the 'spiritual element' or the 'mental discipline cultured by the Japanese for centuries'.[5]

Behind the extraordinary eagerness of the Japanese to export we see psychological pressures. One source of this pressure was population growth. Japanese population, which had been static at approximately 28 million until the Meiji Restoration of 1868, shot up immediately thereafter: from the end of the first World War it had been increasing at a rate of 1 million a year. By the early 1930s Japan's population stood at 68 million and ranked fifth after China, India, the Soviet Union, and the United States. The restrictions on Japanese immigration imposed by such countries as the United States, Canada and Australia during the 1920s, and later by South American countries, not only wounded Japanese national pride and racial sensitivity, but also generated tremendous psychological pressure. A prominent Japanese economist asserted in 1934 that since emigration had not provided an answer to Japan's population problem during the preceding decade, it must be solved by the expansion of foreign trade. Western observers too recognized the problem.[6] Frank T.A. Ashton-Gwatkin at the British Foreign Office noted in a memorandum: 'Japan must either reduce her already low standard of living or develop her industries and her export trade'.[7]

Increasing imports were another factor that made the Japanese more export-minded. Japan's chronic adverse balance of trade, accentuated by the sharp decline in the price of raw silk following the Great Depression, was not corrected by the marked improvement in the export trade since the reimposition of the gold embargo in 1931. The expanding population and, more importantly, the growing textile industry and development of heavy industry (including the armaments industry) necessitated larger imports. Japan also had to pay some $20 million in interest annually on prior financial obligations. These factors put heavy pressures on Japan's balance of international payments whose precarious situation was only kept under control by the receipts from the shipping industry.

There was a political or psychological element in Japan's urge for trade expansion. Foreign Minister Uchida Yasuya remarked that 'it has become imperative for our imperial economic diplomacy to enable this Empire to champion world trade since we withdrew from the League of Nations'.[8] Some in Japanese business circles reasoned that, since Japan had withdrawn from the League and had become 'a political orphan of the world', Japan had no other option but to strengthen economic ties with other countries and overcome its problems. Japan's leading newspaper expressed its concern lest the Japanese might become 'a dropout from the international society'. In the minds of many Japanese their country's political isolation had to be resolved by economic expansion.

Britain's secret pledge to India – the Simla Conference of 1933–34

Tension first mounted in early 1930 with the announcement by the Indian government of its intention to raise tariffs on cotton goods. This was the first such tariff to differentiate between British and non-British products. From then on the gap widened with each tariff increase introduced by the government in Delhi. Then, in April 1933, the Indian government, through the British government, announced the abrogation of the Indo-Japanese commercial treaty of 1904. This act, as we shall see later, coincided with the British decision to exclude West Africa from the Anglo-Japanese commercial treaty of 1911.

In May the British embassy in Tokyo reported to the Foreign Office in London that the 'margin of safety' in Anglo-Japanese relations had 'fallen dangerously low' and that relations had reached 'a crucial turning-point'. George B. Sansom, Commercial Counsellor at the embassy, who had been living in Japan for 30 years, could remember 'no time when so strong angry anti-British feelings [had] been current'.[9]

In June the Indian government – with the consent of the British government – announced an increase in the duty on foreign cotton goods to 75 per cent, as compared with 25 per cent duty levied on imports from Britain.

Osaka's response was swift. The cotton manufacturers adopted a resolution of non-importation of Indian raw cotton. The Japanese anticipated that, in so far as Japan bought more cotton from India than Britain did, the boycott would soon hurt the majority of Indian cotton growers. Moreover, India's trade balance with Japan had been exceedingly favourable, whereas the balance with Britain was unfavourable. Some Japanese even went so far as to suggest a boycott of all Empire products – including Canadian wheat and lumber, Australian meat and wool, Indian pig iron and British machinery. Even the possibility of war with Great Britain was openly voiced.

Against this background, a meeting to conclude a new treaty was held in the autumn of 1933. In view of the deteriorating relations between Great Britain and Japan, the Japanese government desired an amicable settlement. When received in a farewell audience by the Emperor, the chief negotiator, Sawada Setsuzo, was reminded by Count Makino Nobuaki, the Lord Privy Seal, that 'his task in India was not merely the negotiation of a trade agreement', but 'a mission of first-class political importance', because the Japanese were 'at a turning-point in relations between Japan and Great Britain'.[10]

The Indian government, too, was eager to bring the conference to a successful conclusion, partly because this was the first international conference that India had ever hosted, but largely because Delhi was hard pressed to prevent the Japanese boycott.

The forthcoming conference was characterized by the (London) *Economist* as 'a triangular fight for trade – Japan to maintain her export trade, India to preserve her home market, and Lancashire to recapture part of her lost trade'.[11] The conference opened in September and lasted about three months. It is often referred to as the 'Simla Conference' because the early sessions were held at the mountain resort of Simla, the summer capital of India.

At the beginning of the conference negotiations were conducted at both the industrial and governmental level. Meetings were held separately between the Indian and Japanese delegates and between the British and Japanese industrial delegates. Negotiations between the Lancashire and Bombay industrialists had already been in progress in

Bombay. These would produce the 'Lees–Mody Pact' of October 1933. The industrial meetings soon broke down, and the task of negotiation fell to the governmental delegates of India and Japan. The official negotiations turned out to be very difficult and long drawn-out, lasting seven months. The Japanese delegates refused to 'link', as the Indian delegation proposed, Japan's export of cotton goods to India with Japan's purchase of a fixed amount of Indian raw cotton.

Another snag in the negotiations was the problem of the optional transfer (or 'tolerance') between categories of cotton piece goods. If for any reason the quota under any particular category was not required, a certain percentage of transfer was to be permitted into another category. It was the trade in bleached goods that had the greatest bearing on Lancashire, whereas in this category too, the Japanese had been increasing its exports to India. The disagreement over tolerance remained a stumbling block until the end of the negotiations.

The Indian negotiators were in a most unenviable position. They were under heavy pressure from every direction – not only from the Japanese who were holding the boycott like 'a pistol at [their] head', but also from domestic millowners and London. It was harvest time for cotton in India. With the prospect of Japan's continuing boycott of Indian cotton in the event of a breakdown in the negotiations, the Indian delegates were inclined to submit to the Japanese demands.[12]

Sensing in London that India was thinking of 'giving way' on the transfer issue, the President of the Board of Trade, Walter Runciman, through the Secretary of State for India, Samuel Hoare, told the Indians to 'stand firm'.[13] The Prime Minister, Ramsay MacDonald, called a special cabinet meeting in late November to discuss the means by which the British government could have the Indians withhold their concessions to Japan. After the cabinet meeting, Hoare immediately sent a telegram to the Viceroy, Lord Willingdon, stating that a concession to the Japanese demand for a tolerance of 10 per cent in bleached goods would 'injure seriously relations between Great Britain and India' because of the 'relentless opposition' of the Lancashire Members of Parliament. He even hinted that it would affect India's political future.[14]

In response to Hoare's telegram, the Viceroy gave vent to his indignation. London appeared to Delhi to be 'ready to push matters to a crisis and risk breakdown for what [it] still believe[d] to be issues of comparatively secondary importance'. Concessions to Japan would mean, at the worst, the loss of only about 25 million yards of bleached goods to Lancashire. India, however, would have to suffer not only from the surplus new crop due to Japan's continued boycott but, even worse, from a 'very unpleasant and costly tariff war' which would surely follow. As it happened, that year India was expecting to send 250,000 tons of pig iron to Japan. The consequences of a breakdown thus appeared to Delhi to be 'wholly out of proportion to the gains'.[15]

As a way out of this dispute, the Viceroy suggested that in the event of a breakdown the British government should purchase Indian crops. The exportable new cotton crop was estimated at 2.5 million bales if an agreement with Japan was reached.

In early December the Committee on Indian Cotton, set up by the British cabinet and composed of five cabinet members, deliberated on the Viceroy's cotton purchasing scheme. The Committee decided to give a definite guarantee against any loss which might be incurred by India by taking off the market up to 1.5 million bales. It took this step in the hope that India would 'display a determination not to move from the existing position'. It was thus confident that Japan would be deprived of its powerful weapon 'hanging over India's head' – the boycott. It also assured India that it would use every means available to bring pressure to bear on Japan in the event of a tariff war. The Viceroy in his response thanked the British government, offering 'cooperation in every way'.[16]

Fortified by the new scheme, Sir Joseph Bhore, the chief Indian negotiator, told Sawada that all the terms previously put forward by the Japanese were unacceptable. To make his answer sound more definite, Bhore said that the Indian government was determined to give the cotton growers financial support by all available means in case they needed it – without, of course, disclosing the British guarantee.

In the meantime, cotton importers, spinners and exporters gathered in Osaka in early December and expressed their indignation by passing a resolution (not for the first time) ordering the withdrawal of non-official delegates in India. The most vociferous and influential among them was Tsuda Shingo, president of Kanegafuchi Boseki. At the government–business talks, Nakajima Kumakichi, the Minister of Commerce and Industry, among others, made a desperate attempt to persuade the businessmen to move from their position and accept the general terms laid down by the Indians. He pointed out the international importance of an amicable settlement to Japanese foreign policy. The Japanese government's efforts finally paid off. The business representatives reluctantly promised to leave the final decision in the hands of the government negotiators at Delhi.

Late in December, Bhore told Sawada that India was offering slight concessions, which Japan needed to save face, if the Japanese government secured within ten days the withdrawal of the boycott of Indian cotton from the Osaka millowners. While the Indian side still insisted on the quota figure of 8 per cent for bleached goods, it offered to increase the tolerance for bleached goods and bordered greys from 10 per cent to 20 per cent. Bhore was, in effect, telling Sawada to take it or leave it.

After some last-minute efforts by the Japanese government officials to induce the industrialists to accept the final terms bore fruit in early January 1934, the Japanese government issued a communiqué to the effect that it would accept India's terms. The boycott was lifted, and a new trade agreement was formally agreed. Its details however remained to be worked out. On 19 April the new agreement, which was effective until 31 March 1937, was initialled, and on 12 July, signed in London. Lancashire interests were expected to be happy with the treaty, but they were not. They resented the tariff reduction given to Japanese goods. Some felt that there would be no room for British goods after the Indian textile market was supplied by Indian home products and Japanese imports.

The political significance of the settlement of the dispute are clear. It helped relieve the accumulated tension between India and Britain on the one hand, and Japan on the other. In the summer of 1933 relations were deteriorating rapidly because of the Indo-Japanese trade war. The Japanese public also believed that Britain was behind the League decision to condemn Japan for her aggression in Manchuria. Their belief was strengthened by Matsuoka Yosuke – who as head of the special Japanese delegation to the League had dramatically walked out of a League conference – who rather impolitically accused Great Britain of having abruptly changed her position at Geneva because of the fear of an anti-British boycott in China. 'The opening of the negotiations in Simla did a good deal to relieve the situation,' said the British chargé d'affaires to Japan, who had earlier observed that relations between the two countries had reached 'a crucial turning-point'.[17]

All in all, the conference strengthened the Japanese image of Great Britain as a status quo power holding desperately to its share by creating an economic bloc. During the conference, Sansom, who was at the conference as an adviser to the Indian delegation, noted 'the present difficult and suspicious temper of the Japanese, their somewhat bellicose mood, and their perhaps unnatural fear that the British Empire, and possibly other countries as well, desired to subject them to a kind of economic encirclement'. He then warned strongly against 'any movement which gave the Japanese grounds for feeling that they were bottled up'.[18]

Britain's failed attempts to divide the world cotton textile export market

In 1930, 1932 and again in 1934, Great Britain took the initiative to divide the cotton textile export market between herself and Japan on a global scale. These attempts to stem the tide of Japan's rapidly expanding export trade ended in abject failure, and this was all but a foregone conclusion. Nevertheless, the episode seems important in showing not only the distress in which the British cotton goods manufacturers found themselves, but also the delicate balance Whitehall had to strike between diplomatic considerations towards Japan on the one hand, and its need to respond to the outcries coming from Lancashire on the other.

The first initiative

By the interwar period Britain's cotton industry had come to be characterized as 'fantastically backward both in technique and in organization'. The historian A.J.P. Taylor summarized the conditions of the textile industry along with such 'depressed' exporting industries as coal: 'British economic life relied to a dangerous extent on a few industries, themselves often antiquated, the share of which was declining on the world market, and which catered mainly for the primary producing countries – themselves impoverished'.[19]

Since about 80 per cent of the goods manufactured in the British textile industry (as compared with the world's average of 20 per cent) were sold abroad, international conditions during the interwar decades had an important bearing on the decline of the industry. Because cotton textiles were the very things that other countries could produce with relative ease, after the First World War countries such as British India and China developed their own textile industries, thus reducing the demand for foreign textiles. Furthermore, they began to resort increasingly to protectionist measures. The recurrence of anti-British boycotts by the Chinese and the Indians during the 1920s as an expression of heightened nationalism also played a part in this decline.

Another important factor was Japanese competition. Not only did Japan cease to be a good customer for British products, it also became a formidable competitor in foreign trade during this period. Consequently, British textile exports to Far Eastern markets fell sharply.

Purchases of British textiles by India, China, Japan and Hong Kong, which in l913 took 54 per cent of the total export of British textiles, showed a 91 per cent decline between 1913 and 1937.

Great Britain's difficulties in textile exports, however, were not confined to Asia: in the Balkans and the Near East Italian textiles were making great advances, while in Central and South America the United States had become a leading supplier. In this situation, Lancashire's share (in value) of world markets dropped from 54.6 to 44.2 per cent between 1924 and 1929, whereas in the same period Japan and the United States increased theirs from 10.8 to 17.5 per cent and 6.3 to 7.0 per cent, respectively.

Since the cotton textile industry in England was 'dependent to an extraordinary degree upon foreign markets', the slump seriously affected the industry. After the war boom came to a sudden end in 1920, Lancashire remained stagnant for the rest of the decade. Aside from this external problem, however, there was a plethora of internal problems: over-capitalization and indebtedness, antiquated techniques and high labour costs as well as high middlemen's charges. But above all, subdivision of the industry into many small sections and also into many small units of production hindered the industry from modernizing itself.[20]

Subsequently, a number of combines were created under the auspices of the Joint Committee. The most important was the Lancashire Cotton Corporation, which was formed under the strong influence of the banks in 1929. It controlled nearly 10 million spindles – about one-fifth of the capacity of the spinning section – as well as about 30,000 looms. By 1931 the Corporation had acquired 107 mills and had nearly completed the first phase of rationalization, which included upgrading mills, scrapping obsolete plants and producing standardized yarns and cloths. In order to reduce production in proportion to demand, the Corporation proposed to operate about two-thirds of the spindles it had acquired. In influence, however, the Corporation was no match for its Japanese counterpart, the Japan Spinners' Association which controlled 97 per cent of all cotton spindles in the country and about half of the power-driven looms.[21]

While the Lancashire Cotton Corporation worked toward rationalization of the industry in order to meet foreign competition successfully, it made an overture to open cartel negotiations with the Japanese textile industry. In February 1930, a proposal was made by the British consul at Osaka, on behalf of the Lancashire interests, to open talks between the Lancashire industrialists and the Japan Cotton Spinners'

Association. Though the contents were not disclosed, it was widely understood that the proposal was in line with an article in the Trade Supplement of *The Times* (London) of 18 January, written by the chairman of the Lancashire Cotton Corporation, Sir Kenneth D. Stewart. In this article proposals were made to divide sales districts – in China, British India, the South Seas, Africa and the Near East – between Lancashire and Osaka, and to change the quality of products between Lancashire and Osaka in order to avoid exporting the same kind of products to the same districts.[22] Negotiations never took place, however. As it developed, the new Indian duties on cotton textiles imposed in the spring of 1930 created a furore among the Osaka industrialists. Japan was in the throes of the Great Depression, and business circles reacted vigorously to such a move.

The Japanese Ministry of Foreign Affairs, for its part, was still interested in discussing a cartel agreement. In October, the Deputy Minister for Foreign Affairs suggested that agreement would be 'possible, if Great Britain would curtail exports of cotton goods to China, Japan in return might be prepared to take similar action in regard to her exports of cotton goods to Australia and India …' At about the same time, Great Britain was sending an economic mission to the Far East with the chief purpose of investigating the Chinese market for British products. Before its departure, the British ambassador to Tokyo urged the Department of Overseas Trade and the Foreign Office in London that the mission 'come prepared with some definite ideas on the subject'.[23]

Obviously, the trade mission did not come to Japan with concrete proposals. There is no evidence that the delegates actually took up the matter. For one thing, it was very difficult for the British to give up something in return for possible Japanese concessions. In the Chinese market, for instance, the British were still unwilling to make substantial concessions despite the increasing difficulties that British exports encountered there. For the Japanese, the new Indian tariffs ruined whatever chance the cartel proposal had because 'it was hopeless to talk co-operation between Manchester and Osaka if the Japanese cotton industry was to be at the mercy of sudden attacks from the Indian government such as the prohibitive tariff rates on cotton goods now proposed'.[24]

By the time the British delegates arrived in Japan, the Japanese textile industry showed no desire to co-operate with Lancashire in regard to a cartel arrangement. The British Cotton sub-mission received a cool reception from the Osaka industrialists when it visited the mills in Osaka on its fact-finding tour. Considering the warm hospitality traditionally extended to foreign visitors to the mills by the Japanese, this was indicative that a change had taken place in the attitudes of the Japanese textile industry.[25] Two more years of economic crisis and Japanese competition for Lancashire, and a great deal of pressure from foreign competitors for Osaka, were necessary before the two sides were brought to the negotiating table.

The second initiative

In 1932 the British embassy in Tokyo noted a new trend in Japanese foreign trade: the names of countries like British Borneo, Aden, Greece, the Panama Canal Zone and El Salvador appeared for the first time in the monthly Japanese customs returns for 1930 and 1931.[26] Though temporarily dampened by the Great Depression, a strong urge to expand commercially continued to exist during the 1930s. After the Manchurian Incident, this commercial expansion into other areas was further accelerated by the anti-Japanese boycotts in China and by India's repeated tariff increases. Finance Minister Takahashi Korekiyo's new economic policy also reinforced this tendency.

By 1932 the Manchester Chamber of Commerce began to single out Japanese competition as the chief source of their predicament, and to ask the government to discriminate against Japan in the Empire market. Towards the end of the year high-ranking government officials, such as the President of the Board of Trade, Walter Runciman, and the Colonial Secretary, Sir Philip Cunliffe-Lister, were receiving 'constant' representations about Japanese competition from the Lancashire interests. These officials agreed that some measures were needed to check Japanese encroachments, but they were undecided what these measures should be.[27] As in 1930, an international cartel appeared to be the most desirable remedy, but its feasibility was much in doubt.

The attempt to reach an agreement in 1930 failed primarily because the Japanese cotton industrialists were not interested in it, even though the Japanese Foreign Ministry was eager to negotiate on a quid pro quo basis. In September 1932 the Foreign Ministry again expressed its interest in an agreement in such regions as India and China. But British officials were themselves doubtful of success because they felt that they had little to offer in exchange for Japan's concessions, except a threat of retaliatory duties against Japanese products. They feared, however, antagonizing Japan by enforcing this threat. For, as one Foreign Office official had observed earlier, 'from a material point of view we have nothing to gain and much to lose by antagonizing Japan'.[28]

The tariff increases in India had already aroused a great deal of hostility in Japan. The Japanese also resented Great Britain's role at

Geneva in condemning their policy in Manchuria. It was known that Japan was likely to leave the League of Nations in the near future. If she did, it would make relations between the two countries more uncertain than ever. In these circumstances, in the eyes of Foreign Office officials, it was 'an unfortunate time' to make such threats of retaliatory duties. They were, therefore, reluctant to take the initiative for a cartel negotiation, no matter how desirable. On the other hand, the Manchester Chamber of Commerce felt that 'it was quite useless for any direct approaches to be made by the industry ... in view both of the extreme state of opinion in Lancashire on this question, and of the attitude of the Japanese', and hoped that the initiatives would come from government.[29]

Meanwhile, commercial skirmishes in Empire markets were under way: Japan's advance into the South African market was blocked by the anti-currency depreciation tariff of 1932 and by the Ottawa Agreement; in Ceylon and Malaya 10 per cent preferences were granted to British cotton goods at the end of 1932. But in March 1933 the Manchester Chamber of Commerce declared that 10 per cent was not enough to check Japanese competition. Manchester businessmen later made three proposals: discrimination against Japanese goods throughout the colonial empire; a division of markets with Japan; and subsidies on the export of cotton goods.[30]

The third initiative

During March the cabinet discussed possible measures to be applied to Japan. Early in this month Runciman had proposed to the cabinet that Japan be told that Britain would abrogate the Anglo-Japanese Commercial Treaty and impose quotas unless Japan would agree to quantitative controls. The threat of outright denunciation of the treaty of 1911 would, however, be drastic enough to provoke indignation in Japan. A few days later Runciman suggested that the colonies in West Africa and the West Indies be excluded from the scope of the treaty without abrogating it entirely. Cunliffe-Lister supported the suggestion.[31]

Sir John Simon, the Foreign Secretary, approached the question more cautiously. When he asked the embassy in Tokyo about the feasibility of withdrawing West Africa from the treaty, Ambassador Francis O. Lindley urged delay, stating that it was 'most undesirable' at the moment because it was most likely to be interpreted by Tokyo as a British 'desire to make disapprobation of Japanese policy in China'. Thus, at a cabinet meeting on 8 March, Simon told his colleagues that 'the present time was singularly inopportune for raising the question'. He still held that the best way to deal with Japan was a limited cartel agreement, although he did not know if it was at all feasible.[32]

The issue was brought up again on 29 March. Runciman told the cabinet that 'the situation [of trade competition] had become much more acute' even in this short period. He expressed his belief that it was desirable 'eventually [to] arrive at a position where cartel agreements might be discussed with the Japanese', but he argued that 'these must be preceded by action such as he had proposed'. At this juncture, the cabinet agreed with Runciman. The same cabinet meeting also approved India's proposal to abrogate her commercial treaty of 1904 with Japan. On 16 May the British government announced that it would denounce the treaty as far as it concerned West Africa and the West Indies. Since this would not take effect for another year, the British government thought that there was still time to negotiate a market agreement with Japan. On 25 April, Runciman met the Japanese ambassador and made a proposal for industrial negotiations. On 24 May, the Japanese government consented.[33]

Later that year Runciman felt that the idea of having the businessmen themselves negotiate to solve the problem of international commercial competition was justified by their performance at the Anglo–Indian conference, which had resulted in the Lees–Mody Pact of 28 October. Government officials in Tokyo, such as Nakashima Kumakichi, the Minister of Commerce and Industry, and Kurusu Saburo, the Chief of the Bureau of Commercial Affairs of the Foreign Ministry, for their part, were also disposed towards the same idea for a different reason. Since they were greatly annoyed by the highly critical and militant attitudes of the Osaka industrialists during the Simla Conference, these officials wanted them to take responsibility for the outcome of the negotiations.[34]

The two governments, nevertheless, did not agree on certain points. The Japanese government, which was merely acting as a spokesman for the Japan Cotton Spinners' Association, proposed to limit the negotiation to the problem of cotton textiles and to exclude the Commonwealth nations and foreign (i.e. third) countries from the geographical scope of the discussion. At Britain's insistence, however, Japan agreed to add rayon to the agenda, but refused to yield on the second point. The Japanese would not agree to discuss Commonwealth markets unless some guarantee of a tariff truce in these areas was given in advance. They reasoned that the Dominions, which were autonomous, might interfere with a new agreement between Britain and Japan whenever they so desired. In view of the new trend towards economic nationalism and increasing emphasis on absolute trade reciprocity between two nations, it was likely that not only in third countries but also in the Dominions such measures as higher tariffs, import quotas and exchange control would be adopted, regardless of an Anglo-Japanese agreement. The Japanese, therefore, thought that these areas should be approached directly.[35]

Possibly, during the preliminary talks, each side might have mistakenly thought that the other had accepted its point of view in regard to the geographic scope. But more likely, both sides proceeded on the deliberate calculation that the other would concede at the conference table. At any rate, the Japanese cotton industry finally sent five delegates to England. The Japanese Rayon Federation saw in the scheme of the British industrialists to discuss rayon concurrently with cotton an attempt to curtail the future development of the Japanese rayon industry.

As soon as the Japanese delegates arrived in England in September, they started informal talks with Lancashire industrialists in London and Manchester. It soon became apparent that since the preliminary talks neither side had moved an inch from their original position: the British still demanded a limit on Japanese textile exports in world markets, whereas the Japanese were willing to consider only restrictions applied to exports going to the United Kingdom and the Crown Colonies.

As the informal exchanges were conducted simultaneously with the Simla Conference in India, they were necessarily inconclusive pending the outcome of the latter. Meanwhile, the Japanese rayon industry finally responded to the plea of Okada Gentaro, the leader of the Japanese delegation, and instructed the London branch manager of the Mitsui Bussan Kaisha to represent the industry at the conference. In Tokyo, five organizations – three cotton organizations, including the Japan Cotton Spinners' Association, and two rayon organizations – formed a policy formulating body for the negotiations in London. In Lancashire, the Special Committee on Japanese Competition, made up of 20 members, was set up to instruct and assist Lancashire's negotiating sub-committee.[37]

The announcement on 16 May 1933 of the withdrawal of West Africa from the Anglo-Japanese Commercial Treaty did not allay domestic dissatisfaction in England. Pressures within and outside of Parliament continued to buildup. Criticism of governmental policy vis-à-vis Japanese competition was led by several Conservative MPs representing Lancashire and its neighbouring districts, and also by the Cotton Trade

League in London. In regard to the methods to be applied to the problem, these critics took a more radical stance than the Manchester Chamber of Commerce, and pressed the Board of Trade to follow the example of the Indian government by abrogating the Anglo-Japanese Commercial Treaty of 1911, in order to enable the British government to restrict Japanese imports into all the Empire markets.[38]

Late in 1933 half the 50 million spindles in the Lancashire cotton mills were reported to be idle. As 1934 began anti-government pressure gathered momentum. On the evening of 23 January, seven Conservative MPs, who soon came to be known as a 'ginger group', sponsored a protest rally at (ironically enough) the Free Trade Hall in Manchester. The audience was delighted to hear one Member of Parliament declare that 'unless the Government dealt with this question there would be such a deluge in the north of England at the next election as would sweep every Cabinet Minister off the Treasury bench'. Some Members of Parliament appealed to workers: 'we are fighting the battle of the standard of life of the British worker in almost all our exporting trades'. The rally ended by adopting a resolution calling for government action: to abrogate all commercial treaties between England and Japan containing the most favoured nation clause; to take more drastic steps for the protection of the domestic market; and to use its influence to persuade the Dominions and colonies to take similar action.[39]

Whether it was a mere coincidence or not, the day after the rally, the President of the Board of Trade came to Manchester, accompanied by Sir Horace Wilson, Chief Industrial Adviser to the government, and other high-ranking officials in the Board of Trade. They had two exhausting days in this textile city, discussing the problems of the industry with representatives of various industrial and labour organizations. Runciman also met Sir Thomas D. Barlow, the chief negotiator for the Anglo-Japanese conference, and the other members of the negotiating sub-committee of the Special Committee on Japanese Competition. Before they left for London, Runciman assured them that the government would 'step in' if negotiations failed, and he made his view clear: 'no market will satisfy us except the world market; and all we ask is fair play in all the world markets'. Runciman expressed some hope for the successful conclusion of an agreement, and said that the Anglo-Japanese discussions were 'the only hopeful way of escape he had been able to see from the present difficulties'.[40]

A little note of optimism was also sounded in a diplomatic observation by Sir Francis Lindley, the British ambassador in Tokyo. The Japanese sense of international isolation had been strengthened recently by Washington's recognition of the Soviet government. Lindley thought that Japan was anxious about the Soviet Union and would be willing to make concessions in the trade discussions. Whatever optimism the British might have felt, however, dissipated in early February when British newspapers reported that they had learned that the Japan Cotton Spinners' Association in Osaka had adopted four basic guidelines for the Japanese delegation in London, which would never be accepted by Lancashire: the 1933 exports should be the basis of agreement; negotiations would not cover price arrangements; negotiations on cotton and rayon should be held separately; and negotiations would not include other markets. Though these were not official instructions from the committee in Tokyo, they did much to dampen hope in Great Britain.[41]

Formal negotiations began in London on 14 February, after the Simla Conference in India had reached an agreement in general terms. Both sides immediately found their disagreement over geographic scope to be a major stumbling block. On the following day the British delegation handed the Japanese a note making a firm demand for an agreement in all world markets. It proposed that Japan reduce exports in proportion to the diminished trades of other industrial nations for the next three years, and thereafter adjust the volume of her exports every year according to world conditions. A week later the Japanese delegation returned a stiff reply. The Japanese note contended that the British demand was 'one-sided, unfair and unacceptable to a country as efficient and progressive as Japan' and insisted on discussing only the limited Empire market. The note was in line with the opinion of the Osaka industrialists who at a meeting four days before had passed a resolution which showed that they had not moved from the position reported in the press on 3 February. Unless either side made some concessions by the time of the next meeting, a deadlock was unavoidable. Okada Gentaro, the chief negotiator, may have expected some change in the attitudes of the Osaka industrialists, but this did not materialize.[42]

Although the government in Tokyo was anxious to see an agreement, the Osaka cotton interests remained adamant. On 3 March, the Japan Cotton Spinners' Association and the Cotton Yarn and Cloth Exporters' Association held a meeting and formally resolved that the Lancashire proposal regarding the geographical scope of the negotiation was unacceptable.

As for the Lancashire delegates, their stance at the negotiations was unanimously endorsed by the special committee meeting held at the Manchester Chamber of Commerce on 26 February. The committee reasserted that a world-wide scope for the discussions was essential. The Lancashire industrialists incorrectly assumed that the Japanese delegates had come to England on the understanding that they would discuss a world market arrangement, and that they were now trying to 'evade' it. Only three weeks after the conference began, a breakdown appeared imminent. There was no sign of change in the Osaka policy. About this time Walter Runciman hinted at retaliation through the coastal shipping lines in the event of a breakdown. Although this threat made the government in Tokyo more cautious, it did not succeed in wresting any concession from Osaka.[43]

Suddenly it appeared that a breakthrough had come on the morning of 8 March. The British press reported, without disclosing the content, that Lancashire had made a new offer to Japan. What 'Lancashire's Fresh Conciliation Effort' turned out to be was a slightly changed formula based probably on the suggestion of Sir Horace Wilson, the governmental observer at the conference. The Lancashire delegates proposed a piecemeal discussion of the subject on a regional basis, by dividing world markets into six zones (i.e. Africa, Asia, the Middle East, Europe, South America and Central America) with Japan's voluntary quotas apportioned to each zone. Japan would, of course, face substantial reduction in her cotton textile exports.[44]

From the Japanese point of view, this was no compromise at all. Unable to see any significant change in the new proposal, the Japanese delegates said that they would refuse to consider it at the sixth session held on 14 March. They defended their refusal by pointing out that the proposal was not feasible and that Japan was already contemplating holding direct negotiations with such countries as the Netherlands, Turkey, Egypt and South Africa. The British finally concluded that the Japanese delegation did not intend to broaden the scope of discussion beyond the United Kingdom and the Crown Colonies. The negotiations collapsed.[45]

The cartel negotiations failed. They failed because of Lancashire's unrealistic proposals and because of Osaka's intransigence. Given the energetic, ambitious drive of the Osaka industrialists at the time, there was little chance of success in reaching a global agreement. Similar attempts were never made afterwards.

The British colonial quota system

Five days after the London Conference collapsed, the cabinet (following Runciman's suggestion) created a committee on Japanese trade competition, with the objective of dealing with the 'serious economic and political consequences' of complete termination of the negotiations.⁴⁶ Though the conference failed, the British wished the negotiations to be resumed in the future. But any new proposal had to come from Tokyo. As April wore on and no proposals came from Tokyo, patience ran out in London. Government officials thought that they could no longer postpone action to safeguard British trade, for it was felt that the Japanese were continuously expanding their exports in the Empire market while British hands remained tied.

In the meantime, the British embassy in Tokyo became increasingly pessimistic. George Sansom reported that he had become 'less and less hopeful on any concessions from the Japanese'. 'Until lately there was some hope of getting the government to persuade the industrialists to give way, on general grounds of Anglo-Japanese friendship', Sansom went on, 'but now even the [Japanese] Ministry of Foreign Affairs seem to be stiffening rather than relaxing'. Ambassador Lindley was much less optimistic than he had been a few weeks before and wrote in a similar vein: 'very little importance [was] attached by Japanese government to arguments based on general consideration of "ordered progress" and "stability" in the world market'.⁴⁷

At this juncture, the cabinet committee, meeting on 12 April, finally reached a decision; it recommended to the full cabinet that it inform Tokyo in the near future that it intended to terminate the negotiations and 'resume liberty of action' unless a real breakthrough came from Japan. Yet the committee decided not to denounce the Anglo-Japanese Commercial Treaty of 1911 because denunciation would serve no useful purpose and would entail substantial economic and political damage.⁴⁸

Meanwhile, voices demanding governmental action were becoming more shrill. The London *Observer* exclaimed: 'an ounce of retaliation is equal to a pound of negotiation in these matters'.⁴⁹ The 'ginger group' had regained some influence and started pressing the government to take action in the colonies. More importantly, the business leaders who had discreetly remained silent since the breakdown of the negotiations, began speaking up. In early May, the leaders of the Joint Committee of Cotton Trade Organizations and the Federation of Master Cotton Spinners' Associations called for definite action. The latter explained: 'Japan has been playing for time until she could make further headway.'⁵⁰

In this atmosphere, on 3 May 1934 Runciman gave Ambassador Matsudaira Tsuneo an ultimatum: the British government would take action unless Tokyo offered a proposal. On 7 May, he finally announced that his government would apply the quota system to cotton and rayon goods from all foreign countries in British protectorates and colonies. The quotas were to be based on average imports between 1927 and 1931. Since this was the period before the rapid increase in Japanese trade began to be felt, the quotas would discriminate against Japanese goods, while they would not be to the detriment of such countries as the Netherlands, Germany, Italy and the United States.[51]

Anglo-Dutch collaboration?

Lancashire's attempt to block the Japanese commercial advance in the British Empire was thus limited to the colonial market. There Great Britain succeeded in maintaining the status quo of 1931, the year before Japanese competition made itself felt. With the Japanese threat removed from the markets of the Crown Colonies, British attention shifted to the Dutch East Indies where Great Britain, along with the Netherlands, traditionally held commercial hegemony.

Lancashire interests had been urging the government to exert its influence to make the Iraqi and Egyptian governments take some action against Japanese trade for the purpose of restoring Lancashire's position in these regions. At the same time, Lancashire cotton industrialists had also been holding conversations with their Dutch and French counterparts to secure their cooperation in efforts to reduce Japanese imports into their colonies. Cooperation with foreign countries, the memorandum recommended, should be conducted subtly so that Japanese opinion would not be roused. Great Britain should avoid laying herself open to the Japanese accusation that she was attempting to form an economic bloc. The danger of concerted economic action against Japan had been repeatedly impressed upon Whitehall by the embassy in Tokyo.[52]

Outside the British Empire, one of the severest commercial contests between Britain and Japan had been under way in Dutch East Indies. While Japan's share of cotton textile imports expanded, Britain's and the Netherlands' own share fell drastically. It appeared that only the imposition of quotas on Japanese goods could check this trend. For Japan, the Dutch Indies was a very important market for cotton textiles and other goods. In the Indies cheap Japanese goods were eagerly sought by the local population. Now that British India had become less hospitable to Japanese exports, many Japanese began to consider the Dutch Indies as the 'life-line to be defended to the last'.[53]

Since 1933 British and Dutch cotton industrialists had been holding talks on these matters. In April and July 1933, Dutch missions visited London and Manchester, where it was agreed that quotas should be imposed in the Indies to restore British trade there to its 1928–29 position. In return the Dutch wished to revive their exports to Britain which had been severely damaged by the adoption of protection in 1932. In December a delegation from the Federation of British Industries visited the Hague. These exchanges were so conspicuous that the Japanese government suspected Anglo-Dutch 'collusion' against Japanese commerce in the Dutch Indies.[54]

As 1934 began, the British government became more concerned about the situation in the Indies, especially after the Anglo-Japanese negotiations collapsed in early March. The Dutch government, which had seen a decline in domestic textile exports to its own colony, was willing to co-operate with the British, but at the same time, wanted to avoid antagonizing Japan unnecessarily. Late in March a Lancashire delegation was again despatched to the Hague. In this instance the Dutch delegates agreed to increase the British textile quota in the Indies in exchange for Britain's expanded purchase of Javanese sugar. The Board of Trade in London did not act quickly enough on the agreement, and the Hague imposed quotas on all foreign goods to meet the demands of the Dutch textile industry. But these quotas would hurt Japan more than Britain.[55]

Japan's historical turning-point

In historical hindsight the year 1936 was a turning-point. In January Japan withdrew from the London Naval Limitation Talks and at the year's end the Naval Treaty was nullified. Japan was further drifting into international isolation. Domestically, in February of the same year an abortive military coup resulted in the assassination of several members of the Japanese cabinet, including the Finance Minister, Takahashi Korekiyo. This removed whatever restraints the Ministry of Finance had on military spending. The coup resulted in strengthening the hand of the military. In such an atmosphere the measures taken by Washington and Canberra successively in late May produced strong nationalistic reactions in Japan.

Trade negotiations between Australia and Japan had been under way in Canberra for more than a year. From the outset the Australians conducted the talks with a view to obtaining a voluntary limit on textile shipments from Japan to Australia, whereas the Japanese expressed their desire to have some tariff reductions on Japanese cotton textiles.

The Australians fully understood that Lancashire would boycott Australian butter and other products if the dominion did anything prejudicial to Lancashire's interests. At the same time Sir Henry Gullett, the Australian Minister for Trade Treaties, was conducting trade talks with the Japanese, he was also involved in meat problems in the British market. Prime Minister Joseph A. Lyons and Gullett spent some time in England during 1935 to discuss Australian meat exports. While in England they met heavy pressure from Lancashire interests. They were reminded of the rapid increase in Japanese textile shipments to the dominion and the resultant loss of market share suffered by Lancashire.

In early March 1936 a Lancashire trade mission arrived in Australia. It was led by Sir Ernest Thompson, who had headed a mission to the Far East in 1930. The mission was financed by the Manchester Chamber of Commerce and supported by all the cotton manufacturers' organizations. While in Australia, Thompson was gratified to see the dominion's 'intense loyalty to the Empire'.[56]

Probably emboldened by the pro-British sentiments in Australia, the trade mission later made highly inflammatory statements. On several occasions in early May, the delegates asserted that allowing imports of Japanese goods in such large quantities was tantamount to a departure from the 'White Australia' policy because 'the free admission of the product of coloured labour was equivalent to the free admission of the coloured races themselves'.[57]

These statements embarrassed the officials in both Canberra and London, and led the Japanese to believe that there was 'collusion' between the governments of Australia and Britain. The Japanese perceptions are substantiated in part by a letter to the British Prime Minister Stanley Baldwin from the Australian Prime Minister, J.A. Lyons, dated 18 May, in which the latter claimed that the Commonwealth government was taking action because of repeated requests from Britain.[58]

On 22 May Gullett announced to the Australian Parliament a 'Trade Diversion Policy'. In the case of Japan, the licensing system was applied to Japanese products and tariff revision struck a serious blow at textile imports from Japan. The old ad valorem duties on textiles were replaced by higher specific duties, under which the margin of preference given British textiles was greatly increased.

Although the Japanese market was valuable for Australian goods, the British market was even more so. Canberra thus decided to sacrifice a 'good customer' in order to please its 'best customer'. As it happened, on 21 May the US government raised tariffs on Japanese cotton goods too.

Coming as it did almost simultaneously with the US tariff action against Japan, Canberra's new trade policy of 22 May sent Japan into panic. The *Osaka Mainichi Shimbun* headlined its editorial 'Britain and

America Declare Economic War against Japan', while the *Osaka Asahi Shimbun*'s caption read, 'Head-on Collision Between Japan and England'. Since the Japanese expected both Americans and Australians to be grateful for Japan's bulk purchases of their cotton and wool, respectively, the 'reckless acts' of the two governments dealt a severe psychological blow to the Japanese. Immediately, a sense of crisis set in. The *Asahi* described the situation in the following words: 'we are surrounded by enemies on all sides'. 'We are moving towards the precipice,' argued the *Mainichi*.

In Japanese eyes Great Britain was the most menacing power because of its enormous influence and network of imperial trade. About the same time as these events in Australia, the Japanese saw evidence of what they considered British manipulation in Malaya, Iraq and Egypt.

Some observations

1. One special interest group – the cotton textile industry – in each country played a disproportionately large part in heightening the tension between the two countries. The cotton textile industry cannot be said to be the most important industry by any measure in Britain. Nevertheless, it was still able to exert influence on the British government, especially the Board of Trade, the Colonial Office and the Dominion Office. In Japan, the cotton textile industry was still an important industry although light industry was gradually being replaced by heavy industry by the mid-1930s.

    Some jingoistic individuals played a certain role in inflaming the mass media and the public. An MP from Lancashire named S.S. Hammersley, for example, uttered a pessimistic, even though exaggerated, sentiment, which was prevalent in certain circles, when he declared Japanese competition to be 'a new and extremely grave menace to the civilization of Western Europe'.[59] The 'ginger group' was vociferous in calling on the government for strong action against Japan. On the Japanese side too there is no difficulty in finding Japanese counterparts. Tsuda Shingo, president of the Kanegafuchi Spinning Company in Osaka, for instance, was virulently anti-British. The leading national newspapers in Japan such as the *Asahi* and the *Mainichi* often overreacted to economic measures by foreign governments and printed inflammatory headlines.

2. Both Britain and Japan were resource-poor island nations which largely depended on international trade. Thus, the British advocated 'free trade' in the nineteenth century and the early decades

of the twentieth century. In a similar manner Japan took every occasion to emphasize the importance of the free flow of goods. The Great Depression of the 1930s shattered the very basis upon which 'free trade' was made possible. With shrinking world trade, countries raised tariffs and imposed quotas. They demanded bilateral balancing of trade or 'linking' export of certain items with import of certain items. Great Britain created a preferential trade bloc. Japan, while resisting this trend, made adjustments to this new trend. At the same time, in the second half of the 1930s, it attempted to create a yen zone in East Asia, and this fact was partly responsible for creating friction with Great Britain in China.

3. It is interesting to note that during the Indo-Japanese conference as well as in the course of discussion to end the Anglo-Japanese negotiations in 1933, Neville Chamberlain, the Chancellor of the Exchequer, and Sir John Simon, the Foreign Secretary, took a conciliatory position, while Walter Runciman, the President of Board of Trade, and Sir Philip Cunliffe-Lister, the Colonial Secretary, took a hard line towards Japan.

4. In the process of trade negotiations which Japan conducted with Great Britain as well as other countries, the Japanese increasingly felt a sense of isolation economically, while they were already feeling a sense of isolation politically following Japan's withdrawal from the League of Nations. At the same time, the Japanese also suspected, rightly or wrongly, that there was a kind of 'collusion' between the United States and Great Britain – the two English-speaking nations – against Japan. The sheer coincidence in which Washington and Canberra announced their respective measures to limit Japanese exports in May 1936 strengthened this suspicion. And the Japanese suffered from a 'siege mentality' or a sense of being 'victimized' or 'encircled' from that time on, and presumably it affected Japan's external attitudes towards Great Britain and the United States in the coming years.

Notes

1. Professor Hosoya Chihiro suggests that the economic conflicts between Great Britain and Japan in the 1930s may have had a significant bearing on the political and military conflicts of the same decade. Hosoya Chihiro (ed.), *Nichi-Ei kankei-shi, 1917–1949* (History of Japanese–British Relations, 1917–1949) (Tokyo Daigaku Shuppankai, 1982), p. 299.

2. For instance, see Kibata Yoichi, *Teikoku no tasogare* (The Twilight of an Empire) (Tokyo Daigaku Shuppankai, 1996), pp. 33, 50, and Peter Lowe, *Containing the Cold War in East Asia* (Manchester: Manchester University Press, 1997), p. 60.
3. Quoted in *Nihon keizai nenpo* (Japan Annual Economic Report) (hereafter NKN) (Toyo Keizai Shimposha) no. 19 (1934), 202–3.
4. Nakamura Takafusa, *Senzenki Nihon keizai seicho no bunseki* (An Analysis of Economic Development in Prewar Japan) (Iwanami Shoten, 1971), pp. 205, 213.
5. John G. Roberts, *Mitsui* (New York: Weatherhill, 1973), p. 246; William Henry Chamberlain, *Japan over Asia* (Boston: Little, Brown and Co., 1937), p. 206; Fujihara Ginjiro, *The Spirit of Japanese Industry* (The Hokuseido Press, 1936), p. 61.
6. Uyeda Teijiro, 'Nihon no jinko mondai to keizai gaiko (Japan's Population Problem and Economic Diplomacy), *Gaiko jiho* (Revue Diplomatique) (hereafter GJ), no. 707 (15 May 1934), 153.
7. Memorandum by Ashton-Gwatkin, 5 December 1933, FO 371/17166 (F6674).
8. Quoted in NKN no. 14 (1933), 229.
9. Snow to Wellesley, 13 May 1933, FO 371/17152 (F5080). Sir Robert Vansittart of the Foreign Office sent a copy of the memorandum to Sir Horace Wilson at the Treasury on 12 August 1933. See also Ann Trotter, *Britain and East Asia, 1933–1937* (London: Cambridge University Press, 1975), p. 31.
10. Sansom's memorandum, 21 August 1933, BT 11/219.
11. *The Economist* (London), 5 August 1933, p. 276.
12. Viceroy to Hoare, 28 November 1933, CAB 27/556.
13. Hoare to Viceroy, 23 November 1933, CAB 27/556; Memorandum by Runciman, 27 November 1933, CAB 27/556 C.P. 283 (33).
14. Hoare to Viceroy, 28 November 1933, CAB 27/556.
15. Viceroy to Hoare, 30 November and 1 December 1933, CAB 27/556.
16. CAB 27/556 IC (33) Series, 1 December 1933; Hoare to Viceroy, 1 December 1933, CAB 27/556; Viceroy to Hoare, 28 November and 3 December 1933, CAB 27/556; CAB 23/77, 68 (33) 12, 6 December 1933, p. 351.
17. Snow to Orde, 22 December 1933, FO 371/18184 (F591).
18. Sansom to Simon, 20 November 1933, BT 11/219 (F7934/1203/23).
19. Noreen Branson and Margot Heinemann, *Britain in the 1930s* (New York: Praeger Publishers, 1971), p. 92; A.J.P. Taylor, *English History, 1914–1945* (New York: Oxford University Press, 1965), p. 182.
20. Alfred E. Kahn, *Great Britain in the World Economy* (New York: Columbia University Press, 1946), pp. 92–3; Charles F. Remer, *Foreign Investments in China* (New York: Macmillan Company, 1933), p. 368; Freda Utley, *Lancashire and the Far East* (London: George Allen & Unwin, 1931), pp. 13–14; L.H.C. Tippett, *A Portrait of the Lancashire Textile Industry* (London: Oxford University Press, 1969), p. 8.
21. G.E. Hubbard, *Eastern Industrialization and its Effect on the West, with Special Reference to Great Britain and Japan* (London: Oxford University Press, 1935), pp. 81, 328; Tippett, *A Portrait of the Lancashire Textile Industry*; Utley, *Lancashire and the Far East*, pp. 55–6.

76 Ishii Osamu

22. DOT copy of FO 321/14753 (F1966 and F2287); DOT copy of FO 371/14754 (F2493 and F2604).
23. 'Mission to the Far East' Tilley (Tokyo) 10 September 1930, BT 59/2 (1930)/DC 62.
24. DOT copy (5 May 1930) of FO 371/14754 (F2493).
25. Runciman to Simon, 19 December 1932, FO 371/16250 (F8773).
26. Memorandum by the Acting Economic Counsellor to the Embassy in Tokyo, 12 March 1932, FO 371/16241 (F2469) DOT copy.
27. Arthur Redford, *Manchester Merchants and Foreign Trade*, Vol. II 1850–1939 (Manchester: University Press, 1956), p. 252; Runciman to Simon, 19 December 1932, FO 371/16250 (F8773).
28. *Documents on British Foreign Policy* (hereafter *DBFP*) Ser. 2, Vol. 9 (no. 239) (HM Stationery Office), Memorandum by Wellesley, 1 February 1932.
29. Cunliffe-Lister to Runciman, 18 November 1932 and Runciman to Simon, 19 December 1932, FO 371/16250 (F8773).
30. Hubbard, *Eastern Industrialization*, p. 16; Redford, *Manchester Merchants*, pp. 252–3.
31. CAB 24/239, C.P. 54 (33). 3, 6, and 8 March 1933. Also Ian M. Drummond, *British Economic Policy and the Empire, 1919–1939* (London: George Allen & Unwin Ltd, 1972), p. 133.
32. *DBFP* Ser. 2, Vol. 2 (no. 396); CAB 23/75, 8 March 1933 (p. 218).
33. Drummond, *British Economic Policy*, p. 134.
34. CAB 23/77 p. 306, 29 November 1933. Also see Drummond, *British Economic Policy*; Ando Yoshio (ed.), *Showa seiji-keizai-shi eno shogen* (Oral History of Japanese Politics and Economy during the Showa Period) (Mainichi Shimbunsha, 1965) Vol. I, p. 300.
35. The Japanese Ministry of Foreign Affairs, Press Release, 'Nichi-Ei tsusho mondai ni kansuru kosho keika' (The Progress Report on the Anglo-Japanese Commercial Conference) 12 May 1934, in *Kokusai hyoron* (June 1934), 173; Obama Toshiye, 'Nichi-Ei kaigi no zento' (The Prospect of the Anglo-Japanese Conference) *Chuo koron* (April 1934), 75.
36. Kurusu Saburo, 'Nichi-Ei kaisho ni tsuite' (The Anglo-Japanese Conference) GJ (1 March 1934), 99; Ando, *Showa seiji-keizai-shi eno-shogen*, p. 295; *The Manchester Guardian* 28 December 1933 and 25 January 1934.
37. Kurusu, 'Nichi-Ei kaisho ni tsuite'; NKN no. 15 (1933), 230 and no. 16 (1934), 229–30; *The Manchester Guardian*, 6 and 25 January 1934; T.A. Bisson, 'Japan's Trade Expansion', *Foreign Policy Reports* (10 October 1934), 203.
38. See, for example, Hansard's Parliamentary Debates (hereafter H.C.Deb.) fifth series, House of Commons 5s. Vol. 277, Cols 648–9 (2 May 1933) and Vol. 278, Col. 914 (23 May 1933).
39. Dai-Nippon Boseki Rengokai Geppo (The Monthly Report of the Japan Cotton Spinners' Association) (Osaka), 496; *The Manchester Guardian*, 24 January and 17 February 1934; NKN no. 15 (1933), 231.
40. *The Manchester Guardian*, 25 and 26 January 1934; NKN no. 15 (1933), 231; CAB 23/78, 3 (34) 26. 31 January 1934, p. 90.
41. Lindley to Simon, 22 January 1934, FO 371/18166 (F731), in Trotter, *Britain and East Asia*, p. 32; Matsudaira to Hirota, 4 February 1934, Japan, Ministry of Finance Papers, Showa zaisei-shi shiryo (Materials on the History of Finance during the Showa Era) 8/42 (552); NKN no. 15 (1933), 230; *The Manchester Guardian* and *The Times* (London), 3 February 1934.

42. Kurusu, 'Nichi–Ei kaisho ni tsuite'; NKN no. 15 (1933), 230 and no.16 (1934), 229–30; Ando, *Showa seiji keizai-shi eno shogen*, pp. 298–300; Obama, 'Nichi–Ei kaigi no zento', p. 76; *The Manchester Guardian* 16 and 22 February 1934.
43. *The Manchester Guardian*, 5 March 1934.
44. *The Manchester Guardian*, 8 and 10 March 1934; Ando, *Showa seiji keizai-shi eno shogen*, pp. 298–300; Obama, 'Nichi–Ei kaigi no zento', p. 76; Minutes of the First Meeting of the Cabinet Committee on Japanese Competition, 27 March 1934, CAB 27/568; Oliver L. Lawrence, 'Competition in the World Textile Market', *Pacific Affairs*, Vol. VII, no. 2 (June 1934), 177.
45. Ando, *Showa seiji keizai-shi eno shogen*; Obama, 'Nichi–Ei kaigi no zento'; Beer (BT) 14 March 1934, FO 371/18178 (F1464); *The Manchester Guardian*, 15 March 1934.
46. CAB 23/78, 10 (34) 6, 19 March 1934; CAB 27/568 JTC (34) Series; CAB 24/248, C.P. 106 (34).
47. Sansom to Crowe (DOT) 30 March 1934, FO 371/18178 (F2753) DOT copy (9 May 1934); Lindley to Simon, 6 April 1934, FO 371/18178 (F1938); CAB 27/568, JTC (34) Series.
48. Report, 12 April 1934, CAB 24/248.
49. Quoted in Whitney H. Shepardson, 'Nationalism and American Trade', *Foreign Affairs* (April 1934), 406.
50. *The Manchester Guardian*, 5 May 1934.
51. H.C. Deb. 5s. Vol. 289, Col. 717, 7 May 1934; Drummond, *British Economic Policy*, p. 136; Ethel B. Dietrich, 'British Commercial Policy at the Crossroads', *Far Eastern Survey* (New York) (23 March 1938), 62; *The Manchester Guardian*, 9 May 1934.
52. Memorandum by Runciman, 20 March 1934, CAB 24/248, C.P. 81 (34); Minutes of the First Meeting, the Cabinet Committee on Japanese Trade Competition, 27 March 1934, CAB 27/568.
53. NKN no. 16 (1934), 243.
54. Redford, *Manchester Merchants*, pp. 255–6; *The Manchester Guardian*, 4 and 16 December 1933; the Japanese Foreign Minister's report to the cabinet meeting, 5 December 1933, Japan, Ministry of Foreign Affairs Papers, Teikoku boeki kankei zakken (Documents Pertaining to Japanese Foreign Trade).
55. Memorandum by Runciman, 20 March 1934, CAB 24/248, C.P. 81 (34); Minutes of Second Meeting of the Cabinet Committee on Japanese Competition, 11 April 1934, CAB 27/568; *The Manchester Guardian*, 16 February and 24 March 1934; NKN no. 16 (1934), 235; Redford, *Manchester Merchants*, p. 256.
56. Joint Committee of Cotton Trade Organizations (Manchester) to A.E. Overton (BT) 21 October 1935, BT 11/299 (CRT 6164/34); DOT 5 May 1936, UK Senior Trade Commissioner (Sydney) FO 371/20281 (F2552); Appendix to Minutes of the Fortieth Meeting of the Overseas Trade Development Council, 29 July 1936, BT 59/28, DC/misc. no. 4.
57. DOT to FO 5 May 1936, Minute by Orde (9 May 1936) and Henderson (8 May 1936), FO 371/20281 (F2552).
58. Lyons to Baldwin 18 May 1936, DO 35/278/9279/112, quoted in Drummond, *British Economic Policy*, p. 485, footnote 36.
59. H.C. Deb. 5s. Vol. 289, Col. 718, 7 May 1934; *The Manchester Guardian*, 12 May 1934.

4
Economic Diplomacy in Anglo-Japanese Relations, 1931–41

John Sharkey

In the 1930s, British perspectives on economic questions in Anglo-Japanese relations centred on the legitimacy of Japan's 'have-not' or 'late-starter' economic critique. Derived from self-evident economic imperatives, the 'have-not' argument ran that as an overpopulated and resource-poor island, Japan's economic development was further hindered by the status quo powers. After carving up the world's markets and resources amongst themselves, these powers now denied access – or an equitable redistribution – to those who were unfortunate not to be in on the initial grab for colonies: a situation which, according to the argument, legitimized any attempt at a redistribution by force. In fact, throughout the 1930s this proved a powerful argument as many Britons readily subscribed to an economic interpretation of Japan's recent behaviour. Frank Ashton-Gwatkin, the economic expert at the Foreign Office, cautioned that: 'To provide for the growing population, Japan must either reduce her already low standard of living, or develop her industries and export trade.' Given these circumstances, he argued that to hinder this expansion could court a violent Japanese reaction, which was especially dangerous with a country 'which is armed to the teeth'.[1]

However, for the British the economic causes of Japanese aggression was not a mere academic debate as it had important implications as to how British interests could be reconciled with the ambitions of this 'materialist' power. The argument ranged between those who believed that by a process of 'economic diplomacy', political tensions in East Asia could be reduced through economic adjustments with Japan: and those who did not.[2] The so-called 'Treasury Group' led by Neville

Chamberlain, who served as Chancellor of the Exchequer and then Prime Minister, and Sir Warren Fisher, the Permanent Secretary at the Treasury, saw political and economic co-operation as a means of improving Anglo-Japanese relations, which would free limited British resources to focus on the unstable situation in Europe. This was not simply a case of economic appeasement, as many believed that a still economically weak Japan would welcome offers of British assistance, although it was also argued that political cooperation would improve Britain's trade prospects with Japan. However, the opposite conclusion was drawn by a group of officials in the Foreign Office whose intellectual driving force was George Sansom, the British Commercial Counsellor in Tokyo. These officials argued that, while economic questions required careful management, they did not in themselves offer a solution to Anglo-Japanese tensions. From the perspective of British national interest, cooperation with Japan could not be bought at the price of unilateral political or economic concessions to Japan. This stemmed from a conviction that a combination of the internal economic dynamic and ultra-nationalism meant Japan was indifferent to political compromise and incapable of adjusting to the requirements of British-defined economic multilateralism. The difference between these two groups was not over the need for improved Anglo-Japanese relations, but whether or not the economic and political circumstances of Japan made it a practicable project.

Despite the importance attached to economic questions in the 1930s, there is a significant lament that such issues have received insufficient attention in Anglo-Japanese history.[3] In part this reflects the dissociation of Anglo-Japanese political and economic rivalries in China,[4] from the more commercial rivalries – those not directly linked to political and strategic issues – outside the region. However, those 'traditional' diplomatic historians who have addressed these commercial questions have tended to dismiss them as an issue that affected British attitudes to Japan, but did not influence British policy.[5] This view has been challenged by those who feel that the preoccupation of such histories with military and political events has led them to ignore the question of commercial friction in Anglo-Japanese relations.[6] Indeed, this is not simply a question of mere academic oversight, but of how British commercial policies contributed to Japanese suspicions of Britain, and legitimized Japanese aggression in East Asia.[7] This viewpoint sees commercial relations as central to Anglo-Japanese political relations, and also represents a reworking of the 'have-not' critique, in which economic mismanagement by status quo powers like Britain is held partly responsible for Japanese policy choices. The prescriptive argument is that, since British national interest was best served by unconditional economic internationalism, Britain's failure to foster such conditions as epitomized by the imperial preference agreements of the Ottawa Conference of August 1932, left other countries with little choice but to pursue aggressive economic nationalism.

However, if economic factors were of such critical importance, then it is important to clarify how Anglo-Japanese economic relations fitted in with Britain's own economic and political strategies in the 1930s. First, in an emotive sense British economic nationalism was self-justified by the conviction that it was reacting to the failure of others to implement the internationalist economic agenda of the 1920s.[8] Second, Britain's economic policies were resented in countries such as America and France, which were seen as Britain's natural allies. It is argued that these economic tensions impeded friendship amongst the 'democratic' powers and undermined attempts to resuscitate the multilateral economic system.[9] Still, if this economic diplomacy proved impossible between countries that had fewer areas of direct confrontation, then how much more difficult must it have been for Britain and Japan to improve relations through economic diplomacy. Not only did Britain and Japan have some acute non-economic suspicions, but Japanese criticisms of British economic bloc building were matched by British perceptions that Japan was inimical to any effort to rebuild the multilateral economic system.[10] The lack of a common economic ideology meant that political improvements through economic understandings had to be conducted through a narrow range of issues which ignored many of the substantive economic questions that were central to their respective political economies. This does not mean that Anglo-Japanese economic understandings were impossible, but simply that their very piecemeal nature meant that confidence-building would be a long drawn-out process.[11]

Furthermore, while British protectionism had its own internal dynamic, even in an era of economic nationalism, external economic conditions still circumscribed policy options, so that the application of British economic preponderance in a tangible form was not a foregone conclusion.[12] First, in the summer of 1932 British officials rejected radical overseas trade initiatives because the potential benefits to Britain were more than outweighed by the potential drawbacks of the universal adoption of such measures. The need to export amongst divergent sectoral interests ensured that Britain could not propound an isolationist economic policy. Second, the more limited bilateral arrangements practised by Britain in the 1930s – which include the Ottawa arrangements – did not increase Britain's exports but simply shifted a finite amount of British trade from one trade partner to another. Third, the rise of protectionism amongst the industrial nations encouraged economic nationalism throughout the British Empire and in other 'client states', so that Ottawa revealed the desire of the Dominions to protect their infant industries and not provide Britain with secure export markets. Finally, even in areas of direct rule, British officials had to consider the impact of self-serving economic policies on the indigenous populations. Thus the parameters for British economic discrimination against Japan, based on domestic and imperial economic exclusivity, were circumscribed by Britain's need to maintain access to the world market and the economic nationalism amongst third parties. However, while Japan would be offended by any discriminatory practices, it does serve to remind us that from the outset commercial and economic imperatives limited the scope for British economic discrimination, and by extension, the political impact of such discrimination.

Markets: 1931–37

Trade friction over market access emerged in the 1930s as one of the critical economic issues, not only in Anglo-Japanese relations, but within international relations in general. With the collapse of international trade from 1929, and the failure of attempts to revive an open global trading order as a means of supporting their own industries, successive countries turned first to domestic, and then if possible to imperial, trade protection. For Japan these 'beggar my neighbour' trade policies were a major cause of anxiety because as a 'late-starter' on the road to industrialization, her limited range of export commodities appeared highly vulnerable to trade discrimination, and as a 'have-not' power she lacked the colonial base from which to form her own exclusive trading bloc. If the 'have' colonial powers deprived Japan of export markets which were vital to pay for raw materials and capital goods, then Japan, as Frank Ashton-Gwatkin implied, would have to starve or seize them by force.

The major trade friction between Britain and Japan in the 1930s was over cotton textile markets, a result of the bitter commercial rivalry between the Lancashire and Japanese cotton industries. Lancashire had been the world's leading exporter of cotton textiles since the mid-nineteenth century, but due to a mixture of economic inefficiency, structural disadvantages and cultural complacency, witnessed a huge decline in export volumes from 1929. Between 1930 and 1931, at the height of the world depression, the Manchester Chamber of Commerce – the main representative body of the Lancashire cotton industry – abandoned free trade and endorsed both protectionism and imperial preference.[13] In this difficult environment Japanese competition emerged as Lancashire's overriding concern, particularly following the abortive revival of Lancashire's exports between 1932 and 1933, at a time when Japanese exports continued to expand, most notably in many Empire markets. This clearly pointed to the failure of Ottawa and other measures of trade preference, especially in India. The possibility of an industry-level solution was discounted given the Japanese rejection of a proposed Lancashire–Osaka cotton cartel in August 1930.[14] Indeed Lancashire was so bewildered by the competitiveness of Japanese cotton goods that it became difficult to view it in rational terms, and so entrenched was the fear of Japanese competition that few believed claims that industrial reform could enable Lancashire to compete against Japan.[15] However, more important for Lancashire was the fact that this perception was widely held amongst British industrialists and politicians,[16] easing resistance when the Chamber demanded anti-Japanese trade measures.

In late 1932 under intense pressure from the newly organized Cotton Trade League, the Chamber abandoned its earlier public moderation and joined in demands for firmer anti-Japanese measures. Resentment focused on Japanese penetration of Empire markets with demands made for tougher anti-Japanese measures or increased British trade preferences. The specific demand was for the immediate denunciation of the 1911 Anglo-Japanese Trade Treaty – or the most-favoured-nation clause – as a prelude to anti-Japanese measures in Britain's East and West African colonies.[17] Still while Lancashire railed at government indifference, as early as November 1932 concerns over the economic situation in Lancashire had already propelled the President of the Board of Trade, the pro-free trade Sir Walter Runciman, and the Colonial Secretary, the arch-protectionist Sir Philip Cunliffe-Lister, into considering measures to placate Lancashire.[18] Concerns were now so widespread that, despite criticism of the 'supine' Lancashire cotton industry, they were shared by pro-free-trade officials in the Foreign Office.[19]

Although pressure from the cotton interests had succeeded in forcing the issue, from the outset and in keeping with the established desire to avoid trade radicalism, Whitehall was determined to limit the scope of any anti-Japanese measure. In early March 1933, both Runciman and Cunliffe-Lister submitted to cabinet schemes of trade discrimination against Japanese goods in the British colonies. In practice neither minister envisaged the denunciation of the 1911 Trade Treaty. The primary difference was that Cunliffe-Lister sought to impose his quota scheme (favourable to Lancashire and highly unfavourable to Japan) throughout the British colonies. In contrast Runciman only desired, after one year's formal notification, to discriminate against Japanese goods in Britain's West African colonies, which accounted for a minuscule 6.9 per cent of Lancashire's exports in 1932. The Board of Trade's concern was that any significant measure of trade discrimination against Japan could lead to a more damaging retaliation against British and Empire trade. The chances of Japanese retaliation were considerably reduced by the fact that West Africa accounted for under 1 per cent of Japanese cotton piece good exports. The East African colonies were not included because they had already been captured by cheaper Japanese cotton piece goods, and the levels of discrimination required to return Lancashire to its former pre-eminence would be unacceptable to the indigenous population.[20]

To an extent the Board of Trade's rejection of excessive trade discrimination allayed Foreign Office fears that the measures envisaged would be inordinately provocative to Japan. However, officials were also worried about the impact a mistimed announcement could have on an already excitable and xenophobic Japan, which particularly resented Britain's singular participation in a recent, but short-lived, League of Nations-inspired arms embargo against China and Japan.[21] These concerns had already led Runciman to delay his presentation to cabinet for two months.[22] Subsequently, when debating the two proposals in cabinet, there was no objection to the insistence of Sir John Simon, the Foreign Secretary, that questions of timing should still take precedence. Despite intense pressure from Lancashire the decision was deferred until the end of March, following a clarification by the British Ambassador in Japan, Sir Francis Lindley, on the current political situation. It was Lindley's confirmation that the situation in Japan had improved and West Africa alone would not cause undue resentment which allowed the cabinet to endorse Runciman's West African scheme. This was announced in April 1933.[23] Lindley proved an accurate judge, as the muted Japanese reaction was totally overshadowed by events in India.[24] Still, what is important to note is that, even for such a modest scheme, fears of commercial retaliation together with colonial economic realities were sufficient to limit Britain's room for manoeuvre. In effect, foreign policy considerations focused mainly upon questions of timing.

It was obvious that the West African measures alone would not placate Lancashire and it was the desire to defuse this trade radicalism – and by extension foreign policy tension – that led Runciman to insist that any further anti-Japanese measures (that is, colonial quotas) would be dependent on an attempt by Lancashire to negotiate a cartel agreement with Osaka. Given past failures Runciman was initially somewhat sceptical of Cunliffe-Lister's interest in the matter, but soon accepted that the best hope for Lancashire lay with voluntary trade restraint by the Japanese cotton industry. It was only Runciman's insistence that trade discrimination would not be extended unless the attempt was made that induced a thoroughly suspicious Lancashire into participation. Similarly, while the Japanese government welcomed the idea of cotton trade talks in London, the Japanese cotton industrialists indicated their disinterest as they had nothing to gain from the talks or to fear from Lancashire.[25] However, not only was the centre piece of Runciman's trade strategy spoiled from the outset by industry-level sparring, it was now also increasingly secondary to events in India.

Parallel with Lancashire's demand for colonial trade discrimination was the demand for increased trade preference in the 'vital' Indian cotton market, the world's largest importer of cotton textiles. However, not only did Lancashire face severe Japanese competition, it also had to contend with the commercial challenge of the assertive Indian cotton textile industry. The growth of Indian nationalism coupled with changing economic priorities meant that the British authorities were increasingly willing to subsume Lancashire's demands into wider imperial interests.[26] Although a measure of tariff preference had been introduced which exceeded the provisions of the Ottawa agreements, Lancashire regarded its protectionist intent as unacceptable.[27] Still in this precarious situation Lancashire also recognized the limits of its leverage on India: demands for increased preference could be met by counter-demands for its total abolition, while attempts to gain leverage through the sabotage of Indian constitutional reform were half-hearted and proved unworkable.[28] Such was the political and economic waning of Lancashire's influence on Indian tariff policy that Thomas Ainscough, the Senior British Trade Commissioner in India, argued that it was no longer the role of the British and Indian governments to preserve Lancashire's access. Instead, it was simply to avoid any further Anglo-Indian political complications by ensuring that Lancashire's demise was 'as gradual a process as possible'.[29] In contrast it was the

Indian millowners who were the driving force behind trade discrimination against Japanese goods in the 1930s. Fearful of Japanese competition and yet recognizing the dead hand of Lancashire on tariff policy, the Indian millowners were still able, by acquiescing in 'face-saving' imperial preference, to push up tariff rates on both the preferential British and non-preferential tariffs between 1930 and 1932.[30] Furthermore, despite Japanese resentment over tariff discrimination, they did not indicate before 1932 that they would retaliate against the actions of the Indian government.[31]

Despite the recent tariff increases, the relatively faster growth of Japanese imports in 1932 and early 1933 indicated their continued threat to Indian manufacturers as Japanese goods increasingly competed more directly with Indian goods.[32] Indian millowners again pressed for further anti-Japanese measures. However, when implemented in September 1932, these measures failed to have the desired effect.[33] Under intense but divergent pressure from Indian and Lancastrian millowners the Indian government recognized that it could no longer avoid Japanese resentment by again using the expedient of raising the preferential tariff in proportion to the non-preferential tariff. Only the abrogation of the 1904 Indo-Japanese Trade Convention – or merely the suspension of the most favoured nation clause – would allow for further discrimination solely against Japanese goods. To meet Indian demands on 29 March 1933 with the minimum of debate, the British cabinet approved the Indian government's denunciation of the Trade Convention as a prelude to further anti-Japanese measures, which was accompanied by an invitation for trade negotiations with the Indian government. Then in early June 1933 it increased the non-preferential tariff on cotton piece-goods from a 50 per cent to a 75 per cent ad valorem rate.[34] Despite the importance of the Indian market to the Japanese cotton industry, and in contrast with the West African measures, Foreign Office concerns were marginal to these decisions. In part it was because the Foreign Office believed that the stabilization of Japanese foreign policy since late March 1933 meant that Japanese anger would not be matched by any dramatic counter-measures. However, even if the Foreign Office had raised objections they were unlikely to have had any effect, because in this commercial context the British and Indian governments placed the mollification of Indian nationalism above the perceived needs of Anglo-Japanese relations.[35]

Unfortunately for the British, these less than careful calculations were shattered when the outraged Japanese industrialists responded on

14 June 1933 by initiating a boycott on Indian raw cotton. In this tense atmosphere both Lancashire and Osaka were reluctant to appoint delegates for a separate round of trade talks in India to discuss the Indian market, particularly since the Japanese industrialists were convinced that Lancashire was behind the Trade Convention denunciation. Both sides recognized that their mutual talks would be meaningless and what mattered would be their respective negotiations with the Indian government and/or millowners. As expected, Lancashire's attempt in September 1933 to wring concessions out of the Indian millowners – essentially a reduction in the preferential tariff – proved inconclusive. Contrary to Japanese perceptions, Lancashire had neither the competitive drive nor the political clout to intimidate the Indian millowners into making concessions. Similarly, the talks with the Japanese delegates in the following month proved even more fruitless and acrimonious, as the same weaknesses foiled Lancashire's attempt to extract concessions from the Japanese cotton delegation.[36]

However, the cotton trade talks did provide scope for the airing in private of the cotton question in the wider context of Anglo-Japanese relations: discussions which indicated how tangential the cotton question was to Anglo-Japanese relations. Prior to the departure of the Lancashire delegation, interviews with various officials mainly revealed the emptiness of Lancashire's hand, a point acknowledged by Sir William Clare-Lees, the head of the delegation and a former president of the Manchester Chamber of Commerce. Clare-Lees' personal view, linking trade and political questions, was that Lancashire's position would be helped by concessions to Japan in the China market and the recognition of Manchukuo. The insignificance of the talks in foreign policy terms can be judged by the fact that no one seriously considered making such an offer to Japan on behalf of Lancashire. The main concern was that enunciating statements which were at variance with official policy could make the delegation very difficult to handle.[37] Similarly, while British officials did raise the wider foreign policy implications of the cotton trade talks with the delegates, no one suggested that Lancashire should take this into account during the talks. On 24 August 1933 Sir Horace Wilson, the chief industrial adviser to the British cabinet and a member of the 'Treasury Group', informed the delegates that, while Britain did want to improve relations with Japan, the government was prepared for the failure of the talks and even accepted that the talks would fail. Clearly at variance with 'Treasury Group' logic – gaining political concessions through economic understandings – Wilson stated that the delegates' interpretation of Lancashire's interests remained paramount, as the government preferred the talks to end in failure rather than witness the signing of a botched agreement that was not in Lancashire's interest.[38] No foreign policy goals were loaded onto, or bargaining chips provided for, the Lancashire delegates because, so long as Britain did not escalate the encounter, it was clear that the cotton trade talks could not be an important factor in Anglo-Japanese relations without Japanese cooperation. In this regard British officials appeared to have made a fair assessment of Japanese policy as Japanese officials made only one belated effort to link trade and political questions: Japanese trade cooperation in return for British concessions to China and Manchukuo.[39]

Formal Indo-Japanese trade negotiations began on 23 September 1933, again revealing how marginal Lancashire's influence was over Indian commercial policy, and how tenuous the links were between commercial and foreign policy. The eventual Indo-Japanese Trade Convention of early 1934 limited Japanese cotton piece-good imports to 400 million yards (subdivided into four quality categories), and linked to Japanese purchases of Indian raw cotton. In return the non-preferential tariff was reduced to the former 50 per cent ad valorem rate. The agreement represented a 30 per cent reduction on Japan's 1932 exports to India, or some 8–9 per cent of total exports for 1932. However, more importantly it created a ceiling for Japanese goods in the premier market for imported cotton piece goods. Still Lancashire's interests were almost totally ignored by the Indian government. Only the vehement opposition of Runciman and to a lesser extent of Sir Samuel Hoare, the Secretary of State for India and admirer of Chamberlain, stymied the further sacrifice of Lancashire's interest in the bleached goods subdivision, by halting the intended increase in Japan's allotment where it competed more directly with Lancashire's goods. The Indian government's willingness to concede this point for the sake of a settlement with Japan in late November to early December 1933, was contained by the intervention of Chamberlain, who placed support for Lancashire above the perceived needs of Anglo-Japanese relations.[40] This did not represent an abdication of 'Treasury Group' logic but reflected an indifference to the impact of such minor commercial wangling upon the overall structure of Anglo-Japanese relations. Similarly the Foreign Office had little interest in the Anglo-Indian skirmish, again believing that such minor details were of little consequence. This attitude derived from the ongoing conviction that the stabilization of Japan's foreign policy had significantly reduced the prospects of an extreme Japanese reaction, even to the more substantive Indian trade discrimination. Such assessments appeared correct as by late December 1933 the Japanese government proved determined to accept the Indian terms and was strenuous in its efforts to stand down attempts by its own industrialists to press the Indian government for more concessions.[41] Thus the British desire to divorce commercial from political questions appeared to have been mirrored by similar attempts in Japan.

The conclusion of the Indo-Japanese cotton negotiations allowed for the Anglo-Japanese trade talks to proceed in London. However, these talks were virtually doomed from the start because of the prior inability of Lancashire and Osaka to establish any ground rules over geographical scope. Osaka insisted that only those markets in which Britain had formal commercial jurisdiction, essentially the Crown Colonies, should be discussed. Lancashire, however, insisted that there should be no geographical limitations since displaced goods would then compete with Lancashire's goods in other markets. Formal talks began in mid-February 1934 and were effectively terminated by mid-March amid much rancour, as the question of geographical scope remained insoluble. The fundamental problem was that Lancashire saw the cartel agreement in terms of reduced Japanese exports while the Japanese found this suggestion totally unacceptable. Meanwhile, neither government was prepared to pressure their respective industrialists to back down. The final Japanese offer to kick-start the talks by linking Japanese commercial concessions to British political concessions appeared so late in the day as to be meaningless. In response the British government introduced Colonial Quotas in May 1934, a measure it had been preparing since November 1933. When discussing these measures, Chamberlain's concerns about the negative impact of this 'pinprick' strategy of trade containment was either superfluous or indicative of future intent, as he had not displayed such an attitude during the course of the various cotton trade talks. However, for Runciman this signalled the end of the active pursuit of anti-Japanese measures, not only because of fears of Japanese political and economic retaliation, but also because of the limited amount of commercial leverage and influence available to the British government in the wider world.[42]

However, what was also clear to the British government was that, while the Japanese government remained alarmed by the implications of global trade restraint, it was less concerned about discrimination in the British Crown Colonies.[43] Raymond Streat, the respected secretary of the Manchester Chamber of Commerce, stated that 'The Japs will almost certainly take it very rough'[44] – a view which proved incorrect.

The introduction of Colonial Quotas led to no overt strain in Anglo-Japanese relations, in part because of the trifling volumes involved. The cabinet committee dealing with the matter estimated it would reduce Japan's exports by 100 million yards, which constituted under 5 per cent of its cotton piece-good exports in 1933.[45] Also, as George Sansom speculated, it meant that the Japanese cotton industrialists could no longer be forced into an unwelcome cartel agreement by the Japanese government, and displaced goods could now seek other outlets.[46] In effect the British government had introduced a measure of anti-Japanese trade discrimination which effectively killed off trade radicalism in Lancashire,[47] and without significantly increasing tensions with Japan. The principal reason was the moderation of the measure themselves, created in part out of a desire not to provoke Japan, but also because of the limits of British commercial leverage and influence in the wider world: a point implicitly recognized by the Japanese in their refusal to discuss markets outside areas of formal British commercial jurisdiction.

The events of 1933–34 did not mark the end of Anglo-Japanese trade friction since the continuation of trade discrimination meant that the 'have' versus 'have-not' nexus remained unchanged. Equally, as the political situation in Europe and East Asia had not improved, Britain's reasons for the economic appeasement of Japan had not abated. Furthermore, the desire to ease Anglo-Japanese economic tensions tied in with British concerns that trade barriers were an impediment to both domestic and international economic recovery. Britain's commitment to this process can be seen in the economic understandings reached with America and France in the late 1930s, in which limited attempts were made to stabilize the franc and improve multilateral trading arrangements, although the political objective of demonstrating Anglo-American solidarity appears less clear cut.[48] However, what prevented economic liberalization in Anglo-Japanese relations were the mutual suspicions of Lancashire and Osaka, and the relative disinterest of the Japanese.

In the case of Colonial Quotas, by late 1935 officials in the Colonial Office realized that the net effect had been to replace Japanese goods with those of other countries, and that a modified system would allow for the increase of Japanese exports which would not be at Lancashire's expense. However, Whitehall recognized that hostility from Lancashire would not permit any modification to Colonial Quotas. Similarly Sir Frederick Leith-Ross, the Chief Economic Adviser to the British government, made a rather desperate plea in March

1936 for concessions in textiles to get Japan on board for his proposed Chinese currency reform, which floundered as the Board of Trade and India Office insisted that Lancashire and India would not tolerate any interference in existing arrangements. Lancashire made it perfectly clear that the experience of the 1933–34 trade talks made them willing only to consider a trade agreement that originated from Osaka and which would incorporate the global market.[49] Vested interests in Lancashire and India prevented unilateral British concessions to Japan which might have resolved Anglo-Japanese trade difficulties, and continued to do so for the remainder of the 1930s.[50]

However, what was also clear to the British government was that the Japanese government remained uninterested in pursuing a political understanding based on the easing of trade friction. On questions of the political aspect of economic issues, it was clear that Japan placed the resolution of Sino-Japanese relations on Japanese terms above all other considerations. Leith-Ross failed to gain Japanese support for Chinese currency reform because of fears over the impact it would have on Japanese interests, and not because he was unable to offer concessions in cotton textiles.[51] This point was borne out when Yoshida Shigeru, the Anglophile Japanese ambassador to Britain, made a rather dubious offer for an Anglo-Japanese cotton understanding. The agreement would be limited to British colonial and Dominion markets, but more importantly was predicated on British acquiescence in a Sino-Japanese accord that one British official stated would turn China into 'a vassal state of Japan'.[52] Even an old-fashioned internationalist going out on a limb had no doubt what Tokyo's priorities were, and consequently placed Japan's concerns about China above Anglo-Japanese trade friction.

On a different level, the acceptance by the Japanese cotton industry that trade restraint was an unwelcome but inevitable response to Japan's export success, increasingly neutered trade discrimination as a foreign policy issue. The healthy export performance of cotton textiles until 1935–36, indicated that, despite various trade restrictions, Japanese exports could still prosper in the world market.[53] Even with the post-1936 downturn in cotton textile exports many prominent industrialists now accepted that their blind opposition to earlier anti-Japanese trade measures was ill-conceived.[54] Given this moderation, the British found that the renewal of the Indo-Japanese Trade Convention in 1937 was a modest affair, which led to no surge in animosity towards Britain.[55] Similarly, in a tough series of trade negotiations between 1934 and 1937, as Japan sought to optimize her access to the Australian and various Middle Eastern markets in the face of fluctuating British trade preferences, fewer complaints were directly levelled against British interference. Japan merely sought to negotiate the best possible bilateral arrangements in a fight that was aided by British recognition that it would be a major error to deny certain populations cheaper Japanese cotton textiles.[56] The process was continued by the 1937 Kadono Mission, a Japanese attempt to foster economic understandings with Britain, America and Germany. The Foreign Office readily welcomed the proposal because of fears that the post-1936 downturn in Japan's export performance would be blamed on British Empire trade restrictions and so increase Anglo-Japanese tension. Given Lancashire–Osaka suspicions, it remained difficult for officials to see how the cotton question could be resolved. However, the Kadono Mission proved something of a success principally because there was no intention to discuss anything of substance.[57] Thus at an industry level a status quo had been achieved which, despite obvious imperfections, neither side had any immediate incentive to disturb.

The departure of the Kadono Mission in July 1937 marked the end of trade friction as a substantive issue in Anglo-Japanese relations. Its recall reflected changed Japanese priorities due to the outbreak of the Sino-Japanese War and served as a foretaste of how from 1937 to 1941 economic priorities would be subsumed by the need to prosecute the war with China. Therefore, while market access remained critical to pay for imported war material, export expansion for commercial advantage was no longer a key policy requirement. The net result was a progressive curtailment in Japanese exports, so that after 1937 Japan struggled to attain the maximum amount allowed by the Indian import quota.[58] Thus, as Japanese export pressure eased, so did Anglo-Japanese commercial tension.

Raw materials: 1933–41

In many ways the raw material question should have been the central issue in the diplomacy between the 'have' and 'have-not' powers, as it was the 'have-nots' who pressed the question in the international arena. An importance which is all the more significant given the role which the American, British and Dutch oil embargo played in Japan's decision for war in 1941. However, even prior to this event the disproportionate control of the world's resources by the status quo powers was already perceived as an incalculable threat to Japan's economic development and security. The argument ran that Britain's excessive control of raw materials, through both the formal and informal empire, allowed for the manipulation of raw material supplies, if not for the benefit of the British economy then at least to the detriment of the Japanese economy. Second, and of far more critical weight, Britain's control of vital strategic resources, e.g. oil, meant that Japan's access to such materials was dependent on the goodwill of other powers. Even ignoring the fact that control of overseas resources did not guarantee security of supply, if such control was deemed vital for Britain then it was equally vital for Japan.

Although it was only in the 1930s that the raw material question emerged centre stage, the 'have' versus 'have-not' structural relationship existed in the 1920s and yet remained an important, if partially obscured, question. The lessons of the First World War, coupled with technological change, left few in doubt that any future war would be an economic as much as a military conflict, and that in terms of raw material supplies Japan was poorly placed to wage such a conflict. For example, the post-1919 conversion of the Japanese fleet to oil-fired boilers meant that the Imperial Japanese Navy would remain largely dependent on foreign-controlled supplies. However, these critical military concerns did not form a central plank of Japan's foreign policy.[59] With regard to commercial supplies, there is no evidence or sustained charge from the Japanese that foreign raw material control impeded Japan's economic development. Overproduction of raw materials, due to wartime expansion, had in many cases undermined producer incomes, and led to output restriction schemes aimed at price support. However, while such schemes were severely criticized, mainly by the Americans, for their negative impact on the world economy, there was no suggestion that these producer cartels were intended to discriminate against any one country.[60] Oil is as illuminating an example as any, in that, despite the formation of an Anglo-American production cartel in 1928, and Japanese concerns over price instability and foreign competition in the domestic market, the year-on-year increases in imports indicated that there was no impediment to Japan's access to crude or refined oil supplies.[61] Finally, Japanese commercial ambitions to own and manage raw material production in various Southeast Asian colonies were not systematically hindered by respective European colonial authorities, nor did Japanese firms object to operating within the existing colonial structures.[62] Indeed, the fact that the raw material issue was contained by the internationalism of the 1920s suggests that it was the breakdown of common political norms, and not the emergence of a new economic dynamic, that propelled the issue to the centre of world affairs in the following decade.

Like manufacturing industry, the 1929 depression had a major impact on raw material producers, as decreased industrial demand on top of existing oversupply problems further diminished producer incomes. However, while the depression-induced price collapse stimulated attempts to form producer cartels, there can be little doubt that the raw material producers had no incentive to use respective economic blocs as an exclusive supply region. The converse of the attempt to gain trade preferences for British manufactured goods through the Ottawa agreements was the desire of Empire raw material producers to gain preferential access to the British market. Naturally such preferential access was obtained at the expense of competing non-Empire producers via tariffs or quota arrangements. Still the logic of these arrangements, and certainly to the British, was that there was no intention to impede the export of raw materials outside of Britain or Empire markets. Indeed Empire governments and raw material producers would not have tolerated such limitations, nor would Britain have sought to undermine Dominion or colonial export incomes.[63] Thus the Ottawa preferences in the British market did not mean the restriction of raw material exports to third countries like Japan. In contrast, due to a mixture of strategic and political reasons, from the mid-1930s Japanese commercial exploitation of raw materials was undoubtedly hindered by the administrative measures of various colonial authorities. However, given the undoubted military-strategic dimension to many of these Japanese investments, not only was the rationale for such restrictions understandable, it is equally clear that there was no overall intention to undermine the competitiveness of the Japanese economy through a squeeze on raw materials.[64]

Indeed, despite the linkage between the control of strategic raw materials and Japan's conquest of Manchuria, in the early 1930s the overall raw material question remained only a poorly articulated grudge against the 'have' powers. Many commentators who complained of monetary instability, tariff protection and putative economic blocs, paid no attention to the actual or potential economic impact of foreign-imposed restrictions on raw material exports to Japan.[65] However, others increasingly argued that 'the nation would sink deeper into economic adversity', in part because the 'natural movements of raw materials [had been] artificially stopped',[66] or that certain countries, i.e. Japan, were disadvantaged due to 'inequalities in natural resources'.[67] This line of argument gained further international respectability as the 1933 Banff Conference on problems in the Pacific – sponsored by the Institute of Pacific Relations – accepted that resource deficiencies and overpopulation was a critical source of conflict in the Pacific region. Still in this conference the contrast between the market and raw material questions could not be more revealing. The actual examples of tariff discrimination were not matched by examples of raw material exclusion, but by tedious lists of Japanese raw material deficiencies.[68] So even though the 'have-not' critique was gaining momentum and international respectability, the proof of the thesis remained somewhat weak.

Surprisingly even as the Japanese articulated a deep-seated belief in the invidiousness of their situation, many were equally aware that numerous raw material producers were far more dependent on Japanese industrial demand than Japan was on them as individual raw material suppliers. In challenging Indian trade discrimination through the 1933 raw cotton boycott, the Japanese were consciously attempting to pressure the Indian government by exploiting the desperation of the Indian cotton growers. Nearly six months beforehand Kamisaka Seitaro, the general secretary of the Japan Cotton Spinners' Association, did not doubt the impact such a boycott would have on the Indian economy. 'If, therefore, we stop our purchases, there would naturally take place a big fall in the price of raw cotton, and this will inevitably work havoc on the general economic fabric of India'.[69] Once the boycott was underway, both Nakajima Kumakichi, the Minister of Commerce and Industry, and the more belligerent Tsuda Shingo, president of Kanegafuchi Spinning Company, believed that the boycott offered Japan an enormous amount of leverage in the forthcoming Indo-Japanese trade negotiations.[70] To an extent such views were borne out by events. The Indian government's willingness in late November 1933 to concede Japanese demands in the bleached goods subdivision arose out of the desire to ease the situation for the Indian raw cotton growers by ending the boycott. These demands were only resisted after the British government guaranteed the purchase of the crop, which enabled the Indian government to ignore the pressure of the raw cotton growers.[71] Similarly, Japan's hand in a couple of trade spats in 1934 and 1936 with Canada and Australia was considerably strengthened by actual or threatened tariff discrimination on raw material imports used by Japanese industry.[72] These strategies may not have eliminated tariff discrimination of Japanese manufactured exports, but the ability of Japan to use such leverage during the course of negotiations indicated that the various Empire producers were more dependent on the Japanese market than Japan was on them as individual suppliers. In the commercial field of raw material supply this was a total reversal of the structural dependency which the 'have-not' critique so condemned.

With strategic raw materials such as oil, there appears little to substantiate claims that in periods of normality Japanese supplies were threatened by its dependence on foreign suppliers. This is all the more surprising given the British desire to use raw material control as leverage in the Anglo-Japanese confrontation over Japan's treatment of British oil interests. The petroleum question emerged between March and October 1934 as the Japanese government sought a tighter regulation of its 'volatile' oil market, and then the Manchukuoan government decided to nationalize its oil industry.[73] Advocates of the policy argued that the intention was commercial, a response to the Anglo-American stranglehold on the Japanese and Manchukuoan refined oil markets, which resulted in massive price fluctuations that were detrimental to economic activity, and to increase domestic refining capacity.[74] None the less, despite some fears that Japan was in no position to deal with a retaliatory foreign oil boycott,[75] the Japanese were equally aware that, because of oversupply and supply diversity, the foreign oil companies had very little commercial leverage over the Japanese government. In June 1934 Taji Yasushi, who had a background in naval construction and business, taunted the foreign oil companies by arguing that a boycott of Japanese oil supplies would require the co-operation of all the major oil producers, a particularly difficult task even within America given the massive levels of overproduction.[76]

However, the giant Anglo-Dutch oil company Royal Dutch Shell and its American counterpart Stanvac had a lot to fear from industry regulation and nationalization. Both companies through their subsidiaries – for Royal Dutch Shell these were Rising Sun Petroleum in Japan and Asiatic Petroleum in Manchukuo – had strong market positions and in 1933 they jointly supplied over half of Japan's consumption of refined petroleum products.[77] However, both firms were highly vulnerable to import substitution as neither operated refining plants in Japan, and given the limitations of their oil cartel lacked a complete control over Japan's oil supplies.[78] The slow strangulation of both firms was confirmed when the government's market share quotas indicated a decline for the British and American companies and a rise for all but one of the four major Japanese oil companies. Discrimination against Asiatic Petroleum in Manchukuo, again with Stanvac and a smaller American oil company Texas Oil, was far more clear-cut once it was clarified that the government-sponsored Manchukuo Petroleum Company would be given monopoly privileges that violated the 'Open Door' principle. Although there were fears that the operation of the Petroleum Law was not discriminatory nor broke any international treaty, British officials were bullish in their support of Royal Dutch Shell and its determination to ameliorate the situation in Japan and Manchukuo.[79]

The lack of progress in talks with the Japanese and Manchukuoan governments led the two foreign oil companies from August 1934 to advocate using the threat of a commercially orchestrated oil embargo, or more likely sales restrictions, as leverage against the Japanese government. This proposal gained the immediate support of the Foreign Office, which saw it as a relatively risk-free method of putting pressure on Japan. However, both Royal Dutch Shell and the Foreign Office realized that, to ensure a comprehensive embargo, the support of the US government would be crucial. British officials and Royal Dutch Shell agreed that, despite the two oil companies' control of Middle Eastern and Dutch East Indies oil supplies,[80] without the participation of the independent American oil companies the oil embargo threat would be a fiasco. Furthermore it was agreed that these oil companies were extremely unlikely to participate in restricting supplies to Japan unless the measure had the strong backing of the US government. This was all the more imperative because in September 1934 Royal Dutch Shell had received reliable reports that a Los Angeles based oil company was seeking permission to export 30 million barrels of crude oil to Japan. This was the equivalent to three times the annual supplies to Japan and Manchukuo of the three threatened oil companies. Even more telling was the nullification of the oil companies' decision in October 1934 not to supply crude oil to the Manchukuo Petroleum Company, when two independent American oil companies immediately tendered for the same supply contract.[81]

However, approaches by the Foreign Office and the oil companies in September–October and then December 1934, revealed the limits of American participation. In the State Department, sympathy for the plight of the oil companies was tempered by concerns over the military response to any attempt, or threat, to curtail Japan's oil supplies. However, the main obstacle to US government participation was its inability to enforce the compliance of the independent oil companies in any supply restrictions against Japan. The American refusal meant that the oil embargo threat had to be abandoned and the Foreign Office left Royal Dutch Shell to fend for itself. Over the coming years Royal Dutch Shell witnessed the slow strangulation of its market share in Japan and gained no financial compensation for its losses in Manchukuo.[82] In contrast there was no abatement in the increases in Japanese crude oil imports, which more than doubled between 1933–34 and the first year of the Sino-Japanese War.[83]

The petroleum question has never been interpreted as one of commercial raw material supplies, but it clearly demonstrated the inability of Britain to modify Japanese economic policy through the control of raw materials. By extension this severely undermines the validity of the 'have-not' critique – though not its emotive appeal – that the unfair distribution of raw materials was to the detriment of Japan. Indeed from Taji's taunt, initial Japanese calculations appear to have been based on the fact that these limitations precluded effective retaliation. Even without discussing whether the British government would have allowed the use of the oil embargo threat against an 'armed to the teeth' nation outside of a national emergency,[84] Foreign Office policy floundered on the imperfect British control of oil supplies and the limits of Anglo-American political and economic co-operation. Again ignoring the political dimension, the Anglo-American front proved unworkable as American legislative limitations were compounded by the fact that the independent oil producers had every incentive to welcome difficulties amongst domestic and foreign competitors. Furthermore, if Stanvac and Texas Oil had not been involved or willing to co-operate with the Japanese and Manchukuoan governments as Royal Dutch Shell later feared,[85] then the oil embargo threat would have been ineffective as American cooperation would have been totally unforthcoming.

However, while there was little evidence that Japan was being denied access to raw materials, by the mid-1930s the Japanese had aligned themselves with the demands of the 'have-nots' for a redistribution of world resources. The Abyssinian crisis in the summer of 1935 provided the rallying point for those who insisted that only an equitable redistribution could remove the main source of international friction.[86] These demands received support in the West amongst those who accepted that Japan's self-evident raw material requirements had to be guaranteed by the status quo powers.[87] However, such sympathies were by no means universal as Hugh Byas, the Tokyo correspondent for *The Times* and *New York Times*, argued that Japan's booming economy was not hindered by access to raw materials. Concerns over the commercial implications of the distribution of raw materials amongst the territories of various imperial powers were meaningless because 'The markets for colonial raw materials are open to all. The British manufacturer pays the same price for Canadian nickel and Rhodesian copper and Malayan tin as the Japanese, and the Japanese pays the same price as everyone else'. In an era of massive overproduction, questions of raw material control based on worries over access and scarcity were irrelevant.[88] Still such narrow economic liberalism cut little ice in Japan as this emotive question was as much about political status and strategic security as about commercial practicalities.[89]

For British officials, Japan's espousal of the 'have-not' case was tied up with the claims of Italy, an issue which was soon broadened out into a wider discussion on how the raw materials question could be used to ease international tensions. The decisive British intervention into this question came when Sir Samuel Hoare, now the Foreign Secretary, informed the League of Nations Assembly in September 1935 that, out of 'enlightened self-interest', Britain had a desire to discuss a guarantee of equal access to all colonial raw materials. However, the Foreign Office was deeply divided over the implications of this policy primarily because of differing perceptions of the validity of the project. Those who supported the initiative like Sir George Mounsey, who oversaw the League of Nations department, argued that the 'have-not' powers did have a case. This view was qualified in a Foreign Office memorandum which stated more accurately that the problem was not one of inequitable access but stemmed from foreign exchange problems. In this case it was the result of imperial preference which denied Japan the capacity to earn sufficient sterling to pay for Empire-produced raw materials. Others were far more hostile, and leading figures in the main European departments argued that any investigation into the matter would prove that the British Empire already provided satisfactory access, 'thus revealing that the revisionist powers' cult of expansionism had no economic justification'. Britain's inability to move forward on this matter meant that, despite Hoare's public declaration, Anthony Eden, who had succeeded Hoare as Foreign Secretary, was able to ensure that the raw material question would await the resolution of the Abyssinian crisis. Although Britain was undoubtedly half-hearted in its approach, there is also little evidence at the diplomatic level to suggest any sustained interest in the matter from Japan.[90]

It was German demands for colonies that maintained British interest in the raw material question and led Eden to reiterate Hoare's call for an investigation into the question of access to colonial raw materials. Unlike the earlier proposal, not only did the League establish a Raw Materials Committee in March 1937, but Japan now showed its interest by appointing a representative. Still, in discussing Britain's attitude to Japan, it was clear that in the British colonies the problem was trade discrimination and not raw material access. Britain had no problem with a guarantee of equal access to colonial raw materials, save in cases of war or League-imposed sanctions, but could not concede to Japan equal access to colonial markets. Although the Japanese representative at Geneva pressed Britain for raw material concessions so that Prime Minister Hirota could stand up to the Japanese army, none was forthcoming. In essence the British position – as reflected in the final Committee report – was that, no matter how desperate Japan was for concessions, the fact remained that Japan was not being denied access to colonial raw materials. The more sophisticated position was that foreign exchange difficulties, in part due to trade discrimination but also to spending on armaments, undermined Japan's ability to purchase raw materials.[91] Thus raw material access was not a problem in itself while the removal of foreign exchange problems would have required as many adjustments in Japan as in other countries.

The outbreak of the Sino-Japanese War in July 1937 had important implications for the raw materials question. As the scale of the conflict increased, Japan's progressive moves towards an economy geared for total war meant that raw material supplies to the military economy took precedence over commercial industries.[92] The net effect was that Japan increasingly focused on the immediate implications of foreign-imposed restrictions on specific raw materials for its overall strategic position.[93] In contrast, the question of a general adjustment was left in abeyance. For Britain the fighting in East Asia also complicated Anglo-Japanese affairs. Officials who were prepared to consider a settlement which met some Japanese grievances now had to temper such proposals with a broad-ranging assessment of the overall situation in East Asia. In various discussions between August 1937 and September 1938, no official argued that a one-dimensional economic understanding – in raw materials or any other economic field – would lead to a settlement in China, and ease Britain's strategic dilemmas.[94] Once fighting had broken out the strategic aspect of raw material procurement obliterated the previous commercial aspect of the 'have-not' critique, and limited the political impact of any Anglo-Japanese economic understanding.

Just as the Sino-Japanese war changed Japanese attitudes to raw materials so too did Britain's decision for war in September 1939. Britain, like Japan, could no longer afford to view raw materials in anything other than a military perspective, and had to balance its own material requirements with those of Japan, whilst ensuring that Japan did not become a raw material conduit, via the Soviet Union, to Germany. Increasingly, British concerns that excessive restrictions could heighten Anglo-Japanese tensions and distract Britain from winning the war in Europe, were superseded by the need for a single-minded prosecution of the war in Europe. From late September 1939 British officials were aware of Japanese concerns over possible restrictions on the supply of Empire raw materials. The initial British response was positive as there was no desire to increase political tensions by unnecessary restrictions on raw material exports to Japan, or access to Empire markets. However, by December 1939 this gentlemanly approach was rejected as it simply failed to take account of Britain's wartime needs. For the Treasury, excessive Japanese exports to Empire markets would have a deleterious effect on sterling, which would undermine British purchasing power in America. Meanwhile the Board of Trade insisted that it was impossible to reach any agreement with Japan on raw materials since Britain's own wartime requirements were as yet unknown. Furthermore Britain's desire to tighten the economic blockade in November 1939 aroused Japanese anger when Britain insisted that it would interdict third party trade with Germany. Still throughout the Phoney War, Britain's diminishing interest in minimizing restrictions on trade with Japan did not lead to a serious breach in Anglo-Japanese relations. Indeed the main Japanese complaint was about British interference in German-manufactured exports to Japan, and not over the war-related raw material restrictions in the British Empire.[95]

The abrupt end to the Phoney War in May 1940 had a significant impact on the raw materials question in East Asia, as the control of raw materials was increasingly seen only in terms of respective war potential. Military defeat on the continent left Britain in straitened circumstances, and exposed the Southeast Asian colonies of the defeated European countries to Japanese depredations. However, this strategic 'revolution' also exposed US prevarication as the United States could no longer remain indifferent to the possible impact of Japanese incursions into Southeast Asia upon American strategic interests, which included raw material supplies.[96] None the less the initial British response to the events of May 1940 focused on the questions of German contraband and Japanese raw material requirements, and negotiations between May and June made little progress as the demands of the British and Japanese war economies proved incompatible.[97] Furthermore, in private discussions over the summer of 1940, British officials were explicit that the economic aspect of any general settlement in East Asia had to be predicated on the prior settlement of outstanding political and military questions. This attitude was more than matched by Japanese initiatives up to late February 1941, which placed the resolution of the China conflict at the forefront of its diplomatic agenda.[98]

However, it was the increase in Anglo-Japanese tensions following the June–July 1940 Burma Road crisis, with the parallel escalation in US–Japan tensions, that transformed British perspectives on the raw material question. Although there were no formal political and military arrangements overall, British strategic requirements in both Europe and East Asia more than dovetailed with the new American agenda. For Britain, the desperation to be tied in with America meant that the adoption of the latter's containment of Japan through economic sanctions was a foregone conclusion: this was as much part of the political choice for the United States as a means of hindering Japan. Since the outbreak of the Sino-Japanese War, Britain without full American support had eschewed economic sanctions against Japan. However, as US–Japan tensions escalated, the US's tightening of the screw on Japan, particularly with the imposition of full-scale economic sanctions from July 1941, was more than welcomed by Britain. For Britain the risks of Japanese military retaliation was more than outweighed by the need to keep in step with the US.[99] The impact of these economic sanctions on Japan was profound, as the oil embargo certainly affected Japan's timing for war, if not her actual decision,[100] which ironically enough proved the validity of the strategic aspect of the 'have-not' critique. Still, for Britain such ironies were now of only academic importance, as the embargo with all its economic implications was simply a means towards an overwhelming political end.

Conclusion

In looking at the economic aspect of Anglo-Japanese relations the central question was whether economic factors drove policy choices, and if so, whether they formed a basis for cooperation or confrontation. From a British perspective it is clear that, while domestic economic demands did affect the foreign policy agenda, these influences were more than counterbalanced by the intermixing of internal and external economic pressures. British economic leverage was limited not only by the threat of Japanese economic retaliation, but also by the concrete fear of the disproportionate impact on British trade of the non-Japanese response to further British trade radicalism. These economic pressures impelled such a toning-down of the various anti-Japanese trade measures that the Foreign Office did not have to lecture other ministries on the political consequences in Japan of any extreme action. In this regard from 1933 onwards the British government consistently sought to minimize anti-Japanese trade measures, and in effect bludgeoned a dissolute Lancashire into acquiescence. Indeed, the most acute case of anti-Japanese protectionism was in practice the result of Indian, and not British, pressure. Similarly, due to external political circumstance and market operations and despite the protestations of the 'have-not' critique, Britain did not deny Japan access to vital raw materials such as oil. It was only after the start of the 1939 European War that Britain placed its own strategic requirements above those of Japan. Likewise Britain's participation in the economic embargo of Japan was a political choice in which the embargo was clearly the tool for a distinct political objective: solidarity with America and the containment of Japan. Thus, outside of war, British-inspired economic discrimination against Japan was not the product of untrammelled domestic forces, and consequently not as severe as its reputation would suggest.

However, if Britain's anti-Japanese measures were so mild, then given the economic interpretation of Japanese behaviour, why did relations between the two countries continue to drift throughout the 1930s? Unfortunately this is the wrong approach since an historic assessment of economic factors in Japanese motivations has by definition no place in a study of British policy-making. Furthermore those who place the 'have-not' critique at the centre of Anglo-Japanese relations should bear in mind the converse question, why did Japan – driven by economic forces and so strident in denouncing the illiberalism of others – not fight harder to resuscitate the liberal international economic order?[101] Still what mattered to British policy-makers was their interpretation of Japanese motivations, which was ultimately defined by how Japan presented itself as viewed through the prism of British interests. In this regard it is clear that after the initial pre-1934 skirmishing, Japanese officials and industrialists accepted that trade discrimination was not a critical priority in foreign policy. Similarly the raw material question never emerged at the fulcrum of Anglo-Japanese relations, because, despite intense hectoring, Japan's episodic interest at the diplomatic level precluded a thorough discussion of the issue. Finally it was the changed economic priorities following the outbreak of the Sino-Japanese War that virtually ended overt Japanese interest in the two matters. Thus the neutralization of economic questions resulted from the convergence of two trends: British moderation and the palpable Japanese acceptance of this moderation. This status quo was not perfect but no one displayed any incentive to disturb it.

Furthermore Japan's perceived rejection of the subordination of political to economic factors goes a long way to explain why British economic diplomacy was so ineffectual. On the one hand, British interest in using markets and raw materials as a positive tool in Anglo-Japanese relations was certainly half-hearted, yet on the other hand, Japan showed an equal disinterest. In a different context, in regard to the possibilities of an Anglo-Japanese non-aggression pact in October 1934, Chamberlain noted: 'I hope I too shall not be finally bowled out by the duplicity of the foreigner'.[102] This was a clear recognition that any British initiative intended to improve Anglo-Japanese relations was dependent on the Japanese response. However, it turned out that the 'duplicitous foreigner' was, as George Sansom argued, more than capable of ordering its own political and economic priorities, which did not match British perceptions of what motivated Japan. So long as Japan did not put the improvement of political and economic relations with Britain at the centre of its foreign policy agenda, then even unilateral British economic concessions to Japan could not improve Anglo-Japanese relations. Concessions which Japan delineated as peripheral could not address the core motivation of Japan's foreign policy.

Indeed, given the mildness of British economic discrimination, the level-headed Japanese response and the failure of economic diplomacy, it is clear that, while economic questions occasionally strained Anglo-Japanese relations, they did not define the Anglo-Japanese confrontation in the decade before the Pacific war. In essence this confrontation was the product of political and military instability, as British weakness faced an armed and ambitious Japan. Ultimately, it was only the resolution of the political and military aspect of this crisis that could stabilize Anglo-Japanese relations, as the political goodwill of any piecemeal economic understanding could easily be swept aside by political and military events both inside and outside East Asia. Until this question was resolved, the need not to escalate tensions through the mismanagement of divergent economic agendas proved a mutual priority. However, the aim of alleviating Anglo-Japanese political tension through economic diplomacy remained a fallacy.

Notes

1. Minutes by Ashton-Gwatkin, 7 March and 5 December 1933, FO371/17166, F1571, F6774/1571/23.
2. G. Bennett, 'British Policy in the Far East: Treasury and Foreign Office, 1933–1936', *Modern Asian Studies*, 26:3 (1992); A. Trotter, *Britain and East Asia, 1933–1937* (London: Cambridge University Press, 1975); S.L. Endicott,

Diplomacy and Enterprise: British China Policy, 1933–1937 (Manchester: Manchester University Press, 1975); W.R. Louis, British Strategy in the Far East, 1919–1939 (Oxford: Clarendon Press, 1971).

3. C. Hosoya, 'Some Reflections of the Conference from the Japanese Side', and D.C. Watt, 'Work completed and Work as Yet Unknown', both in I.H. Nish (ed.), Anglo-Japanese Alienation, 1919–1952: Papers of the Anglo-Japanese Conference on the History of the Second World War (Cambridge: Cambridge University Press, 1982), pp. 281–2, 294–5.

4. Bennett, 'British Policy'; W.R. Louis, 'The Road to Singapore', in W.J. Mommsen and L. Kettenacker (eds), The Fascist Challenge and the Policy of Appeasement (London: George Allen & Unwin, 1983); I.H. Nish, 'Japan in Britain's View of the International System', in Nish (ed.), 'Anglo-Japanese Alienation'; P. Lowe, Great Britain and the Origins of the Pacific War: A Study of British Policy in East Asia, 1937–1941 (Oxford: Clarendon Press, 1977); Trotter, Britain and East Asia; Endicott, Diplomacy and Enterprise; W.R. Louis, British Strategy in the Far East.

5. I.H. Nish, 'Japan in Britain's View of the International System', p. 53.

6. C. Wurm, Business, Politics and International Relations: Steel, Cotton and International Cartels in British Politics, 1924–1939 (Cambridge: Cambridge University Press, 1993); H. Shimizu, Anglo-Japanese Trade Rivalry in the Middle East in the Inter-War Period (London: Ithica Press, 1986); O. Ishii, 'Cotton Textile Diplomacy: Japan, Great Britain, and the United States, 1930–1936' (Rutgers University: unpublished PhD, 1977).

7. A. Best, Britain, Japan and Pearl Harbor: Avoiding War in East Asia (London: Routledge, 1995), pp. 3, 18, 119–201; Wurm, Business, Politics and International Relations, pp. 286–7; Shimizu, Anglo-Japanese Trade Rivalry, pp. 27–8; Ishii, 'Cotton Textile Diplomacy', pp. 1–2.

8. The Manchester Chamber of Commerce, Monthly Record: Annual Report of the Board of Directors and Trade Sections, 1928, p. xviii (hereafter, MCC: ARBDTS); A. Marrison, British Business and Protection, 1903–1932 (Oxford: Clarendon Press, 1996), pp. 393–6, 399–400; F. Capie, Depression and Protectionism: Britain between the Wars (London: George Allen & Unwin, 1983), pp. 2–5, 7, 26–7, 40–1, 46–9, 51, 64–5, 74.

9. Tom Ireland, for example, argued that economic rivalries would prevent Anglo-American military co-operation against Japan, T. Ireland, War Clouds in the Skies of the Far East (London: G.P. Putnam's Sons, 1935), p. 434; P. Clavin, The Failure of Economic Diplomacy: Britain, Germany, France and the United States, 1931–1936 (London: Macmillan, 1996); R. Boyce, 'World War, World Depression: Some Economic Origins of the Second World War', in R. Boyce and E. Robertson (eds), Paths to War: New Essays on the Origins of the Second World War (London: Macmillan, 1989).

10. Clavin, The Failure of Economic Diplomacy, pp. 100–1, 140, 145, 148; M. Ito, 'Senkyuhyakusanjusan Nen Rondon Kokusai Keizai Kaigi to Nippon' [Japan and the 1933 London International Economic Conference], in Y. Goto (ed.), Nippon Teikoku Shugi no Keizai Seisaku (The Economic Policy of Japanese Imperialism) (Tokyo: Kashiwa Shobo, 1991), pp. 141, 148–58; W.M. Fletcher, The Japanese Business Community and National Trade Policy, 1920–1942 (London: The University of North Carolina Press, 1989), pp. 89–92.

11. It should be remembered that the various German–Japan economic accords of the late 1930s were the consequence of their spurious political cooperation, and that they did not significantly improve mutual economic relations, E. Pauer, 'Lots of Friendship, but Few Orders: German–Japanese Commercial Relations in the Late 1930s', *International Studies*, 3 (1986); J. Dulffer, 'The Tripartite Pact of 27th September 1940: Fascist Alliance or Propaganda Trick?', *International Studies*, III (1984); J.P. Fox, *Germany and the Far Eastern Crisis, 1931–1938: A Study in Diplomacy and Ideology* (Oxford: Clarendon Press, 1982).
12. T. Rooth, *British Protectionism and the International Economy: Overseas Commercial Policy in the 1930s* (Cambridge: Cambridge University Press, 1993), pp. 81–3, 87–8, 111, 309–12; P.J. Cain and A.G. Hopkins, *British Imperialism: Crisis and Deconstruction, 1914–1990* (London: Longmans, 1993), pp. 84–6, 88, 123, 125, 217; R.J. Skidelsky, 'Retreat from Leadership: the Evolution of British Economic Foreign Policy, 1870–1930', in B.M. Rowland (ed.), *Balance of Power or Hegemony?: the Interwar Monetary System* (New York: 1976), pp. 178–83; I.M. Drummond, *Imperial Economic Policy, 1917–1939: Studies in Expansion and Protection* (London: George Allen & Unwin, 1974).
13. Wurm, *Business, Politics and International Relations*, pp. 193–203; A.J. Robertson, 'Lancashire and the Rise of Japan, 1910–1937', in M.B. Rose (ed.), *International Competition and Strategic Response in the Textile Industries since 1870* (London: Frank Cass, 1991), pp. 88–96; J.H. Goodwin, 'The Politics of the Manchester Chamber of Commerce, 1921 to 1951', (University of Manchester: unpublished PhD, 1982), pp. 185, 196, 280–1; A. Redford, *Manchester Merchants and Foreign Trade, 1850–1939*, vol. II (Manchester: Manchester University Press, 1956), pp. 235–45, 247–8, 299–300.
14. Wurm, *Business Politics and International Relations*, pp. 209–10; Ishii, 'Cotton Textile Diplomacy', pp. 65–6.
15. *The Economist*, 10 March 1934, p. 512; Robertson, 'Lancashire and the Rise of Japan', pp. 97–8, 102–3.
16. Cabinet Conclusions, 29 Mar. 1933, CAB 23 22(33)4; Wurm, *Business, Politics and International Relations*, pp. 258–9; G.E. Hubbard, *Eastern Industrialisation and its Effect on the West* (London: Oxford University Press, 1935), p. 97.
17. Wurm, *Business, Politics and International Relations*, pp. 204–14; Redford, *Manchester Merchants*, p. 250.
18. Wurm, *Business, Politics and International Relations*, pp. 216–7, 219–20.
19. Minute by Orde, 28 February 1933, FO371/17153, F1256/583/23.
20. Wurm, *Business, Politics and International Relations*, pp. 220–1, 226; M. Havinden and D. Meredith, *Colonialism and Development: Britain and its Tropical Colonies, 1850–1960* (London: Routledge, 1993), pp. 188–9.
21. Cabinet Conclusions, 8 March 1933, CAB 23 15(33)3; Lindley (Tokyo) to the Foreign Office, 2 March 1933, FO371/17153, F1437/583/23; minute by Ashton-Gwatkin, 27 February 1933, FO371/17153, F1256/583/23; C. Thorne, *The Limits of Foreign Policy: The West, the League and the Far Eastern Crisis of 1931–1933* (London: Macmillan, 1972), pp. 337–42, and 'The Quest for Arms Embargoes: Failure in 1933', *Journal of Contemporary History*, 5:4 (1970), pp. 129–49.

22. Simon to Runciman, 20 January 1933, FO371/16250, F8773/8773/23.
23. Streat diary entry, 8 March 1933, in M. Dupree (ed.), *Lancashire and Whitehall. The Diary of Sir Raymond Streat, 1931–1939*, vol. 1 (Manchester: Manchester University Press, 1987), p. 220; Wurm, *Business, Politics and International Relations*, pp. 221–2.
24. Snow (Tokyo) to the Foreign Office, 7 May 1933, FO371/17153, F3025/583/23.
25. Wurm, *Business, Politics and International Relations*, pp. 215–7, 222–4, 256, 269–70.
26. B.R. Tomlinson, *The Economy of Modern India, 1860–1970* (Cambridge: Cambridge University Press, 1993), pp. 112, 132–3, 149–52; B. Chatterji, *Trade, Tariffs, and Empire: Lancashire and British Policy in India, 1919–1939* (Delhi: Oxford University Press, 1992), pp. 14–15, 17–18, 20–2, 199, 202–4, 209–11, 238–60, 318, 333–47; A.C. Fearnley, 'The Manchester Chamber of Commerce, Lancashire Textiles and British Imperial Trade, 1919–1939' (Oxford University; unpublished MLitt., 1986), pp. 184–6, 201–2, 205–7; P. Harnetty, 'The Indian Cotton Duties Controversy, 1894–6', *English History Review*, 77 (1962); Redford, *Manchester Merchants*, pp. 278–80, 282–3.
27. *MCC: ARBDTS, 1932*, pp. xii-xiv; *The Manchester Chamber of Commerce, Monthly Record*, March 1930, p. 83 (hereafter, *MCC, MR*).
28. *MCC, MR*, March 1930, pp. 83–4; Chatterji, *Trade, Tariffs, and Empire*, pp. 387–8; S.C. Ghosch, 'Decision-making and Power in the British Conservative Party: A Case Study of the Indian Problem, 1930–1934', *Political Studies*, 13 (1965), pp. 205–12, and 'Pressure and Privilege: The Manchester Chamber of Commerce and the Indian Problem, 1930–1934', *Parliamentary Affairs*, 18 (1964–65), pp. 201–5; Redford, *Manchester Merchants*, pp. 282, 286–7.
29. Ainscough to Edgcumbe (Board of Trade), 27 October 1933, FO371/17164, F7065/1203/23.
30. Tomlinson, *The Economy of Modern India*, pp. 133–4; Chatterji, *Trade, Tariffs, and Empire*, pp. 19, 320, 323, 333–8; C. Markovits, *Indian Business and Nationalist Politics, 1931–1939* (London: Cambridge University Press, 1985), pp. 68, 70–1, 88–9.
31. H. Nishikawa, *Nippon Teikoku Shugi to Mengyo* [Japanese Imperialism and the Cotton Industry] (Kyoto: Minerva Shobo, 1987), pp. 316–17.
32. F.A. Mehta, 'Price-Competition between India, Japan and the UK in the Indian Cotton Textile Market during the Nineteen-Thirties', *The Review of Economics and Statistics*, 39 (1957), pp. 76–7.
33. Chatterji, *Trade, Tariffs, and Empire*, p. 378.
34. Wurm, *Business, Politics and International Relations*, pp. 233–4; Chatterji, *Trade, Tariffs, and Empire*, pp. 377–9.
35. Wurm, *Business, Politics and International Relations*, p. 234.
36. Streat diary entry, 11 October 1933, in Dupree (ed.), *Lancashire and Whitehall* p. 256; Wurm, *Business, Politics and International Relations*, pp. 234–5, 238–40, 241–4; Chatterji, *Trade, Tariffs, and Empire*, pp. 384–9.
37. Memorandum of an interview between Clare-Lees and Crowe, 16 August 1933, FO371/17162, F1203/23.
38. Meeting of the Manchester Chamber of Commerce's cotton textile delegation to India with Wilson, 24 August 1933, FO371/17162, F5839/1203/23.

39. Kadono to Sansom, 11 October 1933, FO371/171163, F5839/1203/23.
40. J. Sharkey, 'The influence of British business interests on Anglo-Japanese relations, 1933–1937' (University of London: unpublished PhD, 1994), pp. 171–80, 182, 184.
41. Minute by Orde, 27 November 1933, FO371/17165, F7450/1203/23; Sharkey, 'The influence of British business interests', pp. 181, 183–4.
42. Wurm, *Business, Politics and International Relations*, pp. 226–9, 256–70, 275–83.
43. *Ibid.*, pp. 277–8, 281.
44. Streat diary entry, 4 May 1934, in Dupree (ed.), *Lancashire and Whitehall*, p. 325.
45. 'Report of the Committee of Japanese Trade Competition', 27 March 1934, CAB 27/568.
46. Dodds (Tokyo) to the Foreign Office, 19 May 1934, FO371/18178, F2929/347/23.
47. MCC, MR, June 1934, p. 167; Wurm, *Business, Politics and International Relations*, pp. 280–1.
48. Clavin, *The Failure of Economic Diplomacy*, pp. 185–94; Cain and Hopkins, *British Imperialism*, pp. 94, 99–102; C.A. MacDonald, 'The United States, Appeasement and the Open Door', in Mommsen and Kettenacker (eds), *The Fascist Challenge*, pp. 400–10.
49. Streat diary entry, 28 January 1937, in Dupree (ed.), *Lancashire and Whitehall*, p. 473; minute by Ashton-Gwatkin, 27 August 1936, FO371/20290, F4978/1391/23; Overton (Board of Trade) to the Foreign Office, 5 May 1936, FO371/20290, F2572/89/23; minute by Orde, 4 April 1936, FO371/20290, F1563/1391/23; Colonial Office Memorandum, 'Memorandum on Japan's trade with the Colonial Empire', undated *c*. 1936, FO371/20279, F7639/89/23; Havinden and Meredith, *Colonialism and Development*, pp. 190–1.
50. Best, *Britain, Japan and Pearl Harbour*, pp. 33–5.
51. *Ibid.*, p. 22; Endicott, *Diplomacy and Enterprise*, chs 5 and 6; Trotter., *Britain and East Asia*, pp. 151–3, 177–85.
52. J. Dower, *Empire and Aftermath: Yoshida Shigeru and the Japanese Experience, 1878–1954* (Cambridge, Mass.: Harvard University Press, 1988), pp. 149–60; Trotter, *Britain in East Asia*, pp. 191–5, 197–8.
53. Minute by Orde, 19 March 1935, FO371/19361, F1116/116/23.
54. N. Komutani, 'Nitchu Sensozen no Nippon Keizai Gaiko – Dainiji 'Nichi-In Kaisho' (1936–37 Nen) o jirei ni' (Japan's Economic Diplomacy before the Sino-Japanese War – the Second 'Japan–India Trade Conference' (1936–37) as an example), *Jinbun Gakuho*, 77 (1996), pp. 106–7; Fletcher, *The Japanese Business Community*, pp. 111–13.
55. Komutani, 'Nitchu Sensozen', pp. 100, 113–33; Sharkey, 'The influence of British business interests', pp. 189–95.
56. Shimizu, *Anglo-Japanese Trade Rivalry*, chs V, VI, VIII, and IX; Ishii, 'Cotton Textile Diplomacy', pp. 371–7, 394, 406–8; J. Shepherd, *Australia's Interests and Policies in the Far East* (New York: Institute of Pacific Relations, 1940), pp. 24–9, 34–5, 60–4; Hubbard, *Eastern Industrialization*, pp. 352–4.
57. MCC, MR, August 1937, pp. 347–52; White (Osaka) to Tokyo, 19 April 1937, FO371/21039, F2859/277/23; minute by Ashton-Gwatkin, 12 March 1937, FO371/21039, F277/277/23; Streat to Brown (Board of Trade), 4 February

1937, FO371/21039, F277/277/23; Crowe (Department of Overseas Trade) to the Foreign Office, 13 Aug. 1936, FO371/20290, F4978/1391/23.
58. T. Nakamura, 'Depression, Recovery, and War, 1920–1945', in K. Yamamura (ed.), *The Emergence of Modern Japan* (Cambridge: Cambridge University Press, 1997), pp. 145–7, 154; Sharkey, 'The influence of British business interests', pp. 194–5, 198; Fletcher, *The Japanese Business Community*, pp. 128–43; M.A. Barnhart, *Japan Prepares for Total War: The Search for Economic Security, 1919–1941* (Ithaca: Cornell University Press, 1987, ch. 5, and pp. 137–8; R. Holland, 'The Federation of British Industries and the International Economy, 1929–1939', *Economic History Review*, 34 (1981), p. 296.
59. Barnhart, *Japan Prepares*, pp. 23, 25–9; R. J. Samuels, *The Business of the Japanese State: Energy Markets in Comparative and Historical Perspective* (London: Cornell University Press, 1987), pp. 170–3; T. Inokuchi, *Gendai Nippon Sangyo Hattatsushi* II, *Sekiyu* (History of the Development of Modern Japanese Industries II, Petroleum Industry) (Tokyo: Gendai Nippon Sangyo Hattatsushi Kenkyukai, 1963), p. 55.
60. S. Lee, 'Kokusai Genryo Mondai' (The International Problems of Raw Materials), in H. Fujise (ed.), *Sekai Daifukyo to Kokusai Renmei* (The Great Depression and the League of Nations) (Nagoya: Nagoya Daigaku Shuppankai, 1994), pp. 287–96; Havinden and Meredith, *Colonialism and Development*, pp. 148–59; J. Foreman-Peck, *A History of the World Economy: International Economic Relations since 1850* (London: Harvester Wheatsheaf, 1983), pp. 198–201, 205–7.
61. Samuels, *The Business of the Japanese State*, pp. 173–4; Inokuchi, *Gendai Nippon*, pp. 245–6; Mitsubishi Economic Research Bureau, *Japanese Trade and Industry: Present and Future* (London: Macmillan, 1936), pp. 211–14.
62. M.R. Peattie, '*Nanshin*: The "Southward Advance," 1931–1941, as a Prelude to the Japanese Occupation of Southeast Asia', in P. Duus, R.H. Myers and M.R. Peattie (eds), *The Japanese Wartime Empire, 1931–1945* (Princeton: Princeton University Press, 1996), pp. 195–6; Y. Yasuba, 'Hiroichiro Ishihara and the Stable Supply of Iron Ore', in S. Shiraishi and T. Shiraishi (eds), *The Japanese in Colonial Southeast Asia*, vol. III (Ithaca: Cornell Southeast Asia Program, 1993), pp. 139–42, 146; H.P. Frei, *Japan's Southward Advance and Australia: From the Sixteenth Century to World War II* (Honolulu: University of Hawaii Press, 1991), p. 123; H. Dick, 'Japan's Economic Expansion in the Netherlands Indies Between the First and Second World Wars', *Journal of Southeast Asian Studies*, 20:2 (1989), pp. 248–9, 250, 258–9, 263, 268; W.L. Swan, 'Aspects of Japan's Prewar Economic Relations with Thailand', in C. Khamchoo and E.B. Reynolds (eds), *Thai–Japanese Relations in Historical Perspective* (Bangkok: Innomedia, 1988), pp. 91–2; T. Morris-Suzuki, 'The South Seas Empire of Ishihara Hiroichiro: A Case Study in Japan's Economic Relations with Southeast Asia, 1914–41', in R. Mouer and A. Rix (eds), *Japan's Impact on the World* (Nathan: Japanese Studies Association of Australia, 1984), pp. 155–7; Y. Choy-Leng, 'Japanese Rubber and Iron Investments in Malaya, 1900–1941', *Journal of Southeast Asian Studies*, 5:1 (1974), pp. 18–27.
63. Lee, 'Kokusai Genryo Mondai', pp. 296–7; Havinden and Meredith, *Colonialism and Development*, pp. 167–88; Rooth, *British Protectionism*,

pp. 78–9, 81, 83–5, 89–94, 97–8; Cain and Hopkins, *British Imperialism*, pp. 84–5, 125–6, 223–4, 226; D. Anderson and D. Throup, 'The Agrarian Economy of Central Province, Kenya, 1918 to 1939', in I. Brown (ed.), *The Economies of Africa and Asia in the Inter-War Depression* (London: 1989), pp. 8–19; R.F. Holland, *Britain and the Commonwealth Alliance, 1918–1939* (London: Macmillan, 1981), ch. 8; Drummond, chs 5–8.

64. Peattie, 'Nanshin', p. 203; Yasuba, 'Hiroichiro Ishichiro', pp. 146–7; Frei, *Japan's Southward Advance*, pp. 151–3; Dick, 'Japan's Economic Expansion', pp. 251, 259–63, 267–71; Swan, 'Aspects of Japan's Postwar Economic Relations with Thailand', pp. 87–90; Morris-Suzuki, 'The South Seas Empire', pp. 151–61; W.R. Purcell, 'The Nature and Extent of Japanese Commercial and Economic Interest in Australia, 1932–1941', *Australia-Japan Economic Research Project* (Canberra: Australia National University, 1978), pp. 33–41; Choy-Leng, 'Japanese Rubber and Iron', pp. 27–33.
65. K. Kodama, 'The Trade Outlook', *Contemporary Japan*, 1:1 (June 1932); Y. Sobun, 'Economic Depression and the Gold Embargo', *Contemporary Japan*, 1:1 (June 1932), pp. 52–61.
66. H. Kamikawa, 'Japan's Diplomacy at the Crossroads', *The Diplomatic Review* (1 April 1932), translated in *Contemporary Japan*, 1:1 (June 1932), p. 138.
67. S. Sayegusa, 'A Practicable World Order', *Contemporary Japan*, 2:1 (June 1933), pp. 65–6.
68. E. Green, 'The Fifth Biennial Conference of the Institute of Pacific Relations: A Survey', *Pacific Affairs*, 6 (October 1933), pp. 456–64; 'Japanese Expansion', in W.L. Holland and B. Lasker (eds), *Problems of the Pacific, 1933: Economic Conflict and Control – Proceedings of the Fifth Conference of the Institute of Pacific Relations, Banff, Canada, 14–26 August, 1933* (London: Oxford University Press, 1934), pp. 136–7, 147–53.
69. S. Kamisaka, 'India's Tariff Policy', *Contemporary Japan*, 1:3, (December 1932), pp. 428–9.
70. K. Nakajima, 'Japan's Trade with India: An Official View', *Contemporary Japan*, 2:2 (September 1933), pp. 218–20; S. Tsuda, 'Japan's Trade with India: Britain's Folly', *Contemporary Japan*, 2:2 (September 1933), pp. 220–4.
71. Sharkey, 'The influence of British business interests', pp. 180–2.
72. Fletcher, *The Japanese Business Community*, pp. 99–103; Ishii, 'Cotton Textile Diplomacy', pp. 364–77, 394, 406–8; Shepherd, *Australia's Interests*, pp. 24–9, 34–5, 60–4; Hubbard, *Eastern Industrialization*, pp. 349–54, 357–8.
73. Samuels, *Business of the Japanese State*, pp. 176–7; I.H. Anderson, *The Standard Vacuum Company and United States East Asian Policy, 1933–1941* (Princeton: Princeton University Press, 1975), pp. 750–76; Inokuchi, *Gendai Nippon*, pp. 250–2.
74. Clive (Tokyo) to the Foreign Office, 7 November 1933, FO371/18190, F6670/1659/23; Anderson, *The Standard Vacuum Company*, p. 78; K. Shiraishi, 'Problems of Oil Industry Control', *Contemporary Japan*, 4:4 (March 1936), pp. 536–8; Y. Taji, 'The Manchukuo Oil Problem', *Contemporary Japan*, 3:1 (June 1934), pp. 596–8.
75. Inokuchi, *Gendai Nippon*, p. 252.
76. Taji, 'The Manchuria Oil Problem', pp. 604–5.
77. Royal Dutch Shell (London) to Rising Sun Petroleum (Yokohama), 29 January 1937, FO371/21032, F710/66/23; T. Kikkawa, 'Business Activities of

the Standard-Vacuum Oil Co. in Japan Prior to World War II', *Japanese Yearbook on Business History*, 7, (1990), pp. 32–3, 36, 39–40; M. Udagawa, 'Business Management and Foreign-Affiliated Companies in Japan Before World War II', in M. Udagawa and T. Yuzama (eds), *Foreign Business in Japan Before World War II* (Tokyo: University of Tokyo Press, 1990), p. 23; Samuels, *Business of the Japanese State*, pp. 169–70.
78. Kikkawa, 'Business Activities', pp. 36–8, 40–1; Inokuchi, *Gendar Nippon*, pp. 137, 141.
79. Anderson, *The Standard Vacuum Company*, pp. 51–6, 75–9.
80. Soviet oil supplies were considered too inelastic to meet Japan's short-term needs, meeting between Coleman (Petroleum Department) and Agnew (Royal Dutch Shell), 20 August 1934, FO371/181189, F5104/1659/23.
81. Royal Dutch Shell (New York) to Royal Dutch Shell (London), 17 September 1934, FO371/18189, F5661/1659/23; Butler (Mukden) to Cadogan (Peking), 6 October 1934, FO371/18110, F6270/142/10; Anderson, *The Standard Vacuum Company*, pp. 56–62.
82. Anderson, *The Standard Vacuum Company*, pp. 64–70, 79–83, 86–91, 93–102.
83. GHQ SCAP, *Japanese Economic Statistics* (GHQ SCAP Economic and Scientific Section Programs and Statistics Division, Bulletin No. 60, Section 1 – Industrial Production, August 1951), pp. 19–20.
84. Cabinet support was limited to seeing if the oil embargo threat was feasible, i.e. if America would participate and on what terms. However, it is unclear that unless there was American military backing the use of the oil embargo threat would have passed Admiralty opposition, who feared a Japanese seizure of the Dutch East Indies oil fields, and the Board of Trade, who feared major Japanese economic retaliation, Foreign Office Memorandum, 'The Japanese Petroleum Law an the Threatened oil Monopoly in Manchukuo', 30 October 1934, FO371/18190, F6426/1659/23; Foreign Office Memorandum, 26 October 1934, FO371/18190, F6312/1659/23.
85. Anderson, *The Standard Vacuum Company*, p. 99.
86. K. Sugimori, 'World Government and National Policy', *Contemporary Japan*, 4:3, (December 1935), pp. 323–30; Lee, 'Kokusai Genryo Mondai', p. 301.
87. M.D. Kennedy, *The Problem of Japan* (London: Nisbet, 1935), p. 257.
88. H. Byas, 'The Great Colonial Illusion', *Contemporary Japan*, 4:4 (March 1936), pp. 496–502.
89. K. Sugimori, 'On the Colonial Illusion', *Contemporary Japan*, 5:1 (June 1936); Peattie, *Nanshin*, pp. 207–11; Morris-Suzuki, 'The South Seas Empire', p. 161.
90. Best, *Britain, Japan and Pearl Harbour*, pp. 18–20; Lee, 'Kokusai Genryo Mondai', p. 302; Havinden and Meredith, *Colonialism and Development*, pp. 191–2.
91. Best, *Britain, Japan and Pearl Harbour*, pp. 33–5; Lee, 'Kokusai Genryo Mondai', pp. 303–9; Havinden and Meredith, *Colonialism and Development*, pp. 192–3; K. Usui, 'Japanese Approaches to China in the 1930s: Two Alternatives', in A. Iriye and W. Cohen (eds), *American, Chinese, and Japanese Perspectives on Wartime Asia, 1919–1949* (Wilmington: Scholarly Resources, 1990), pp. 105–6; Barnhart, *Japan Prepares for Total War*, p. 95.
92. Barnhart, *Japan Prepares for Total War*, ch. 5, and pp. 137–8.

93. Peattie, *Nanshin*, pp. 204, 217–18, 220; Frei, *Japan's Southward Advance*, pp. 152–6; Swan, 'Aspect', pp. 93–4, 96–9; A. Watanabe, 'Tekkoseki Kinyu Mondai o Meguru Nichi-Osu Funso (1938–1939)' [Looking at the iron ore embargo problem in Japan-Australia friction (1938–1939)], in C. Hosoya (ed.), *Taiheiyo-Ajiamaki no Kokusai Keizai Funsoshi* [History of international economic friction in the Asia-Pacific region] (Tokyo: Tokyo Daigaku Shuppankai, 1983).
94. Best, *Britain, Japan and Pearl Harbour*, pp. 47–88; Lowe, *Great Britain*, pp. 23–4, 38–9, 46–50.
95. T. Makino, 'Japan's Wartime Economy', *Contemporary Japan*, 8:3 (December 1939), pp. 119–20; Best, *Britain, Japan and Pearl Harbour*, pp. 92–4, 97–100, 102–7; Barnhart, *Japan Prepares for Total War*, ch. 8; K. Sato, *Japan and Britain at the Crossroads, 1939–1941: A Study in the Dilemmas of Japanese Diplomacy* (Tokyo: Senshu University Press, 1986), ch. 1, and pp. 41–56; Lowe, *Great Britain*, pp. 105–19; W.N. Medlicott, *The Economic Blockade*, vol. 1 (London: HMSO, 1952), pp. 389, 393–5.
96. J. Marshall, *To Have and Have Not: Southeast Asian Raw Materials and the Origins of the Pacific War* (Berkeley: University of California Press, 1995).
97. Best, *Britain, Japan and Pearl Harbour*, pp. 107–9.
98. Sato, *Japan and Britain*, pp. 56–60; Lowe, *Great Britain*, pp. 145–6, 153–60, 216–20, 224–8.
99. Lowe, *Great Britain*, pp. 236–42, 261–3.
100. Barnhart, *Japan Prepares for Total War*, ch. 13.
101. Hosoya Chihiro has argued that from the mid-1930s economic questions were subordinate to political questions in Japanese foreign policy. Furthermore he has speculated that British trade discrimination against Japan could have ameliorated Anglo-Japanese political tensions because, in order to improve Japan's trade prospects, from the late-1930s some Japanese officials began to view political co-operation as an economic necessity, C. Hosoya, 'Britain and the United States in Japan's view of the International System, 1919–1941', in I.H. Nish (ed.), *Anglo-Japanese Alienation*, pp. 22–3, and 'Retrogression in Japan's Foreign Policy Decision-Making Process', in J.W. Morley (ed.), *Dilemmas of Growth in PreWar Japan* (Princeton: Princeton University Press, 1971), p. 88.
102. Chamberlain papers, NC 18/1/891, quoted in Bennett, 'British Policy in the Far East', p. 555.

5
Anglo-Japanese Relations, 1941–45
Ikeda Kiyoshi

Following Japan's surrender, former General Tojo Hideki, Prime Minister at the outbreak of hostilities, and former Foreign Minister Shigemitsu Mamoru (April 1943–April 1945) were incarcerated, along with other suspected war criminals in Sugamo Prison. During their captivity, Tojo is reported to have reminisced to Shigemitsu:

> It all boils down to sheer lack of co-ordination. Could you in all honesty visualise a country that does not allow her prime minister, the keeper of her destiny, any say in the command of her armed forces, actually winning a war? That command was furthermore cursed by a serious split between the army and navy which effectively precluded any concerted action by the two arms. Indeed, it was over a month after the event when it finally occurred to the navy to inform me of their defeat off Midway, and they never got around to giving me the details. Down to the very end, the possibility of truly joint operations remained sadly elusive to our military.[1]

After the Marco Polo Bridge incident of July 1937, armed clashes between China and Japan tended to increase. Under these conditions, Prime Minister Konoe Fumimaro, driven by determination to co-ordinate Japan's political and military leadership better, planned the establishment of the Imperial Headquarters (IHQ). However, while the IHQ was indeed realized in November of the same year, it fell short of overcoming the split between the political and the military, turning out to be a purely military command structure. Accordingly, the government and the military command agreed to hold a periodic IHQ and Government Liaison Conference (LC), to adjust political (especially diplomatic and economic) and military strategies. The IHQ itself was prone to chronic bickering between the Army and Navy Staff, which legally should have been arbitrated by the Conference of Military Councillors (Gunji Sanjikan Kaigi); such a function in actuality was scarcely performed at all throughout the course of the Sino-Japanese war and the war in the Pacific.

Under the Meiji constitution, the Emperor nominally had supreme authority in affairs of state and military command. In deference to this authority, all decisions of note made by the LC were duly reported to the Emperor by the Prime Minister and the Chiefs of Staff of the army and navy, and were subject to his approval. Particularly weighty decisions were discussed at an Imperial Conference. In practice, however, the Imperial Conferences were mere formalities, with the Emperor customarily granting approval without question to measures which had already been effectively decided upon at regular LCs. If the Emperor could be said to have exercised any influence over Japan's conduct of war, it was in the most indirect and subtle way, by hinting at his preferences through questions and expressions of doubt made to his Prime Minister and Chiefs of Staff when they reported at private audiences.[2]

Japan's war preparations and objectives

On 5 November 1941, the Imperial Conference concluded that war was unavoidable. The Army and Navy Staff and the diplomatic corps had been busying themselves over the preparation of 'Guidelines for the conduct of war against Great Britain, the Netherlands, and the United States' since the Imperial Conference of 6 September. These guidelines laid out Japan's general war strategy, including basic military strategy, objectives, occupation policies, justification for initiating hostilities and diplomatic strategy. Parts of these guidelines were approved at successive Imperial Conferences and became the basis of Japan's war plans; namely, 'Plans for a successful outcome of hostilities with Great Britain, the Netherlands, and the United States' (15 November), along with 'Basic wartime economic policy' (10 November), 'Guidelines for the administration of occupied Southeast Asia' (20 November) and 'The Tripartite Agreement' (11 December).

However, latent discord between the Army and Navy Staff over Japan's war aims and strategy existed during the discussions on the overall guidelines. Namely, while the navy's objectives were limited to the attainment of self-sufficiency on Japan's part in strategic terms, the army concentrated on the building of a 'Greater East Asian Co-prosperity

Sphere'.[3] At a cabinet meeting on 12 December, Japan's planned war (perceived as one with the Sino-Japanese war) was formally named the 'Greater East Asian war', with the Cabinet Information Agency adding that this 'did not signal an intent to limit the theatre of operations to Greater East Asia'.[4] Behind the Information Agency's footnote lay the desire to highlight Axis solidarity, given expression in the commitment of the Axis Powers in the 'Pact Renouncing a Separate Peace' (10 December) to the construction of a 'New Order'. The actual shape such a New Order would take was a matter as yet undiscussed either between the Axis powers or within the Japanese government.[5]

The fundamental reason for the difference of opinion between the army and navy was that the army's basic scenario for a war with Great Britain and the United States was a drawn-out war of attrition, whereas the navy's was one of a swift and overwhelming first strike. While both agreed that their main opponent was the United States, the crux was that Japan did not have the means to force the United States into submission. The army's scenario was expressed thus:

> our strategy against the United States should be limited to the acquisition of bases on the Pacific Front which would enable us to stalemate them, and any forces released by the achievement of the said stalemate would be better employed on a front where there are realistic prospects of dealing decisive blows to the opposition, leading step by step to a successful conclusion of hostilities; for instance a Japanese-Nazi pincer operation in Western Asia and the Indian Ocean, or an advance on Chungking.[6]

IHQ favoured an attack in the relatively vulnerable Western theatre against British territories and Chungking in the hope that an early British defeat would crush the American will to carry on fighting. The aforementioned 'Plans for a successful conclusion of hostilities with Great Britain, the Netherlands, and the United States' explicitly outlined Japanese intentions to 'speedily overrun allied centres of resistance in the Far East area, thus gaining a position of strategic self-sufficiency, proceeding to further active measures to topple the Chiang government and defeat Britain, with German and Italian support, thereby undermining US morale'.[7]

Specific Japanese plans for Britain were: that Japan would cut off India and Australia from Britain by political intrigue and the destruction of communication lines; that Japan would promote Burmese independence, with an eye to encouraging similar efforts in India; and that the Germans and Italians would advance into the Near East, North Africa and the Suez Canal zone, eventually linking up with the Japanese westward advance. The blockade of Britain would be strengthened, and, given favourable circumstances, a landing on Britain's home territories would be attempted.

Parallel to these plans, Japan would attempt to sap the US will to fight by: keeping the current Filipino government in power and enlisting it in bringing about an end to hostilities; disrupting US supply lines by decimation of its merchant fleet; stepping up the propaganda campaign against the US and inducing defeatism among the population; and poisoning US–Australian relations.

Japan perceived the following as windows of opportunity for ending hostilities on favourable terms:

(a) the consolidation of Japan's planned gains in Southeast Asia;
(b) the successful military operations in China, especially the fall of the Chiang government;
(c) Axis progress in the European theatre, a German victory over Russia, a Japanese-engineered overthrow of colonial rule in India.[8]

IHQ had no effective means at its disposal for toppling the Chiang regime. On the contrary, since the occupation of Hankou in October 1938, Japan's stance on the China issue had been aggressive politically (as seen in Prime Minister Konoe's proclamation of the Greater East Asian Co-prosperity Sphere of 3 November 1938), but it had been defensive militarily, avoiding attrition on the Western front. Navy Chief of Staff Admiral Nagano Osami stated at a Conference of Military Councillors on 4 November:

> The weaker partner is Great Britain. Should the sea lanes to her colonies be disrupted, her capacity to carry on the war will surely be greatly reduced. Our foremost goal should be to starve Britain into defeat. A successful German landing on British home territories would render the Axis position yet more favourable. Hamstringing the allied war effort by striking at its weakest link is the wisest way to go, and an agreement to this effect with our German counterparts could hardly be detrimental to our prospects.[9]

The LC, along with their designs for striking at the allies' weak link, as they saw it, had plans for drawing the Soviet Union, which was still a neutral power vis-à-vis Japan at that point, into the Axis cause.

'German and Soviet intentions permitting, we could facilitate an armistice between them, bring the Soviet Union into the Axis, shelve our differences for the moment, and perchance even a Soviet strike into India and Iran could be contemplated.'[10] Alongside this somewhat wishful thinking on the part of the Staff, Foreign Minister Togo Shigenori had plans for conditional peace through Soviet arbitration on his mind from the very start of hostilities. Behind this lay a sense of familiarity with, and confidence in, Soviet affairs, stemming from his personal experience as ambassador to the Soviet Union, in which capacity he had negotiated a very good deal for Japan after the Nomonhan Incident.[11] In addition, many among the High Command considered the general power-balancing dynamics of international relations as a substantial argument in favour of the possibility of a conditional peace.[12] In sum, it could be said that Japan's initial war aims depended to a large extent on exogenous factors, namely Germany's supremacy or at least her non-defeat in the European theatre, and offered little in the way of independent plans for the cessation of hostilities.

Japan thwarted in her occupation policies and westward pincer strategy

On 8 December 1941, Japan attacked Great Britain's colony of Malaya, commencing approximately 1 hour and 40 minutes before the attack on Pearl Harbor; the real driving force behind the events leading up to the war in the Pacific was Anglo-Japanese rivalry in China. The first phase of Japan's advance into Southeast Asia exceeded all expectations in its effortless smoothness and success. Hong Kong fell on 25 December, likewise Manila on 3 January 1942, and Singapore, the bastion of the British Empire in the Far East, on 15 February. The seemingly unstoppable Japanese progress extended to Rangoon on 8 March and Java the following day, with the Dutch colonial government fleeing into exile in Australia. In truly lightning fashion, Japanese forces had secured all the resource-rich areas of Southeast Asia.

Japanese policies towards the newly occupied territories had already been laid out in the 'Guidelines for the administration of occupied Southeast Asia', but Prime Minister Tojo had further instructions to add on 21 January at the 79th Diet. These were:

> Considering that Hong Kong and the Malay Peninsula, long standing colonies of Britain, had been bulwarks of oppression in Asia, the

Japanese Empire should not stop at rooting out any remnants of colonial oppression, but should fortify them in turn for the defence of Greater East Asia.

Should the Filipino population prove itself co-operative to the vision of a Greater East Asian Co-prosperity Sphere, the Japanese Empire would grant the Philippines independence.

The Japanese Empire would give Australia and the Dutch East Indies no quarter as long as they resisted the Japanese advance, but would be willing to be considerate to their citizens' welfare should they come to understand and accept Japan's benevolent intentions.[13]

Furthermore, Tojo publicly appealed to Burma and India in a Diet speech on 16 February, when he stated that 'the Japanese Empire stands steadfastly by the Burmese people in their long-standing aspirations to build a nation of their own' and that 'India now has a golden opportunity to rise from her state of barbaric enslavement and march as comrades-in-arms towards Greater East Asian Co-prosperity; the Japanese Empire shall spare no effort to assist the peoples of India in their patriotic endeavours to regain their rightful independence'.[14]

As these examples illustrate, Japan's wartime leadership pinned unrealistically high hopes on anti-British sentiment in India, as embodied in Gandhi and Nehru, then active in the Indian National Congress. The LC's 'Assessment of the International Situation' of 7 March saw the possibility that 'the enlargement of Axis operations, in particular the occupation of Burma and a Japanese–German encirclement of India, in conjunction with intelligence operations, would invigorate the anti-British movement in India'.[15] Admittedly, there were instances of Indian military personnel taking up the Japanese call to join the anti-British Indian National Army (INA), and Rash Behari Bose organized the Indian Independence League (IIL). However, on the whole, the Indian people, while resentful of British rule, were no less suspicious of Japanese intentions, fearing a Japanese assault on India and its subsequent transformation into a Japanese puppet-state.

Japan's Britain-first strategy depended on cutting off India from Britain, and isolating Australia from Britain and the United States. The navy's Fiji–Samoa operation aimed to accomplish the latter objective, but was cancelled owing to the defeats in the Battle of the Coral Sea and the Battle of Midway. As to the Indian Ocean, although some small-scale forays there were attempted from 14 March to early April, the navy's strength was simply not up to establishing supremacy over the region. The combined fleet's main objective was the United States' naval power in the Pacific. Fleet Commander Admiral Yamamoto Isoroku, decidedly an advocate of a blitzkrieg-style war, saw little importance in diverting efforts to the Indian Ocean.

The 'Guidelines for further conduct of war' approved by the IHQ on 7 March, although not devoid of schizophrenic tendencies between the navy's haste to settle its showdown with the US Navy in the Pacific and the army's desire to entrench its position in Southeast Asia, in preparation for a drawn-out war, still reaffirmed the defeat of Britain as Japan's basic objective. A joint advance by the Japanese westwards, and by the Germans into the Middle East, especially the Suez Canal Zone, would serve to isolate India from Britain. However, Germany, engaged in a life-and-death struggle with the Soviet Union, was cool about the idea. The Tripartite Military Agreement of 18 January did indeed demarcate German–Italian and Japanese theatres of responsibility along the latitude 70° East, and commit the Germans and Italians to 'strike at and occupy British and American bases of power in the Near and Middle East, the Mediterranean, and the Atlantic',[16] in response to Japanese gains in Southeast Asia and the Pacific. The agreement notwithstanding, German energies in early 1942 were mostly funnelled into preparation for the planned assault on the Caucasus.[17]

The Germans were not only unresponsive to Japanese hopes for their co-operation in a pincer manoeuvre; they pressed Japan to take on the Soviet Union. Their reasoning was that 'the Soviet threat would cast a permanent shadow' on any Japanese advance on India, and that 'the presently precarious Soviet situation brought about by our all-out assault should render any Japanese move against them relatively easy'.[18] A wait-and-see attitude towards the Soviet Union being Japan's basic strategy, Tokyo declined.[19] The army pressed on with its plans to occupy Burma, thus pressuring India and cutting off aid to Chungking.[20] The grand pincer operation was not to be.

Occupied Southeast Asia and Japanese intelligence operations in Burma and India

Despite proclaiming the liberation of Asia as their ostensible war aim, Japanese leadership, the military in particular, were generally unsympathetic to indigenous independence movements. The IHQ Army Section's 'Occupation policies for the Southeast Asia Operation', issued on 25 November 1941 on the eve of war, bluntly instructed Japanese forces to 'avoid igniting a premature conflagration of independence movements, but rather harness the native population to assist our military operations, commandeer supplies, and mop up hostile European elements'.[21] A certain form of 'independence' was tolerated in so far as it served the purpose of securing resources and extinguishing remaining pockets of allied resistance, but even this was martial law in all but name. Foreign Ministry exhortations to move on to self-government fell on deaf ears, with the military claiming that security concerns precluded any such possibility. Burma may be cited as a typical example of Japanese occupation policy.[22]

Japanese intelligence operations in Burma were conducted by so-called 'Minami Corps', organized in February 1942 and led by Colonel Suzuki Keishi. Plans in the early stages of the war were to infiltrate Burma with sympathetic Burmese volunteers who would attempt to incite demands for independence. The Minami Corps followed the 15th Army into Bangkok and proceeded to form the Burmese Independence Army (BIA). Japan was faced with a choice on the fall of Bangkok on 8 March 1942: whether to impose martial law, or to grant Burmese independence. The Minami Corps argued for immediate independence, but 15th Army Command dismissed its suggestions, intending to have an initial period of martial law while preparations for Burmese independence were made. Colonel Suzuki responded by jumping the gun and proclaiming the establishment of the Burma Ba Maw Government.[23]

IHQ denounced the Burma Ba Maw Government of Suzuki on 3 June, and imposed martial law. The Minami Corps and the BIA were dissolved, with the remnants of the BIA being placed under Japanese command as the Burmese Defence Force. Tojo's 'Burma for the Burmese' declarations of January 1942 were starting to ring hollow. Burma, far from becoming a launching pad for Japanese operations geared towards independence in India, was fast being transformed into a strategic western outpost of the Greater East Asian Co-prosperity Sphere. From July on, Ba Maw (Mo), head of Burma's civilian administration, would answer to 15th Army Command. As Burmese independence faded into the background, and the Burmese economy went into a downhill slide, Burmese scepticism about Japanese intentions grew, as also happened in the Philippines. Ba Maw recounts: 'It did not take me long to notice that the Japanese themselves were unsure whether they were fighting to reclaim Burma from the British, or to claim Burma for their own ends. Most of them, if uncertain how, ultimately wanted to colonize Burma effectively, just like Korea and Manchuria.'[24]

The lightning Japanese conquest of Southeast Asia came as a shock to the complacent British colonial regime in India. Taking into account Roosevelt's and Chiang's critical attitude towards British rule in India, the British War Cabinet dispatched a delegation under Sir Stafford Cripps to negotiate with the Indian National Congress, which was promoting a 'Quit India' movement, but without success.[25] This agitation in the home country induced many Indians abroad in Asia to commit themselves to the anti-British movement. Large numbers of British Indian Army personnel taken prisoner by the Japanese were sympathetic to the cause of Indian independence. The Japanese, with a view initially to mobilizing their support against Britain, organized the 'Fujihara Corps' (*Fujihara Kikan*) under Major Fujihara Iwaichi.[26]

Mohan Singh, a pure volunteer, formed the INA. The INA's ranks swelled rapidly, reaching by some accounts 42,000 in August 1942.[27] To co-ordinate the independence movement, the Army General Staff held the Tokyo Conference with Rash Behari Bose as chairman, and P. Singh of the IIL and Mohan Singh of the INA attending. The IIL was formally recognized at this forum. The League proceeded to demand a commitment from the Japanese government to respect Indian sovereignty and guarantee Indian independence. The Japanese government, however, was wary of making binding future commitments, and avoided a direct response. The General Staff enlarged the Fujihara Corps, forming the Iwakuro Corps under the command of Colonel Iwakuro Hideo. The new Corps' mission was to have been the dissemination of propaganda aimed at India, and the bolstering of the INA. The Corps, however, became mired in bureaucracy after its expansion, turning in effect into a mere branch of the 15th Army occupation administration.[28]

The outpouring of anti-British sentiment in India rekindled Japanese intentions to carry the war westwards. On 22 August the Army General Staff ordered the 15th Army to prepare for 'Operation 21', an advance into eastern India in mid-October. 'Operation 21', however, was called off for logistical reasons, as the Japanese were taking heavy losses in the Pacific, particularly in shipping, since the Americans had started their counter-offensive with a landing on Guadalcanal in early August.

Earlier, in June 1942 in Bangkok, the IIL convention had formally affirmed the League and the INA as its military arm. The convention resolved that the National Congress was the 'sole legitimate political representative of the Indian people' and requested that the Japanese government recognize their non-violent independence movement. The Bangkok resolution at the same time expressed hopes that Japan would invite Subhas Chandra Bose, advocate of an armed push for independence, from Germany. However, growing discord between the Iwakuro Corps and the IIL and INA led the independence movement to falter.

This would not be reversed until spring 1943, when Chandra Bose, transported by German and Japanese submarines, arrived in Singapore.[30]

Retrenchment and the core defence zone

1943 was a turning point in the war; the Axis was on the defensive in East and West. The Germans abandoned Tripoli in January, the Japanese retreat from Guadalcanal starting in February. The Japanese conduct of the war from the beginning had lacked an awareness of the shortage of overall national resources, giving priority to purely military considerations. The allied counter-offensive commenced a year earlier than Japanese expectations; Japanese forces, drawn into an epic war of attrition on land, sea and in the air, were quick to run short of supplies and naval tonnage. Control of the skies was also lost as aircraft were shot down at a frightening rate even after the retreat from Guadalcanal, in hard-fought battles in the Solomons and northern New Guinea. Increasing production of aircraft and shipping became a pressing concern, and the strain of the discrepancy between operational needs and available national resources suddenly became glaringly apparent. In November 1943 the Ministry of Munitions was established and concentrated especially on aircraft production, but rivalry between the separate air arms of the Army and Navy was a fatal impediment to the achievement of true efficiency.[31]

Coordination between civilian government and the military command should have been essential under total war, but the LC sank into paralysis. To break out of this internal impasse, Prime Minister Tojo from February 1944 served concurrently as Minister of War and Chief of Army Staff, while Naval Minister Shimada Shigetaro was also appointed Chief of Naval Staff. Thus in an organizational sense, Prime Minister Tojo at last held both supreme civilian and military authority in his hands, but circumstances were already far too desperate for him to exercise any effective leadership. On the contrary, criticism of Tojo's 'dictatorial' government mounted,[32] and his increasingly unpopular cabinet was forced into resignation in July 1944, and was succeeded by Koiso Kuniaki's government.

In May 1943, US forces landed on Attu in the North Pacific, wiping out the Japanese garrison. Their counterparts on Kiska were more fortunate, making good their escape in July. Japan's gains in the South Pacific were meanwhile being regained one by one by the allies. We have already dwelt upon Japan's heavy losses in the area, and its effects on the overall Japanese war effort. Meanwhile in the European theatre, Field Marshal Badoglio's government in Italy, with no consultation with either Germany or Japan, surrendered unconditionally. One pillar of the planned three-pronged assault on the British Empire had crumbled.

Under these disadvantageous conditions, IHQ and the government thoroughly revamped Japan's war plans, with the revised policy being approved at the Imperial Conference on 30 September. The new emphasis was on withdrawal from the exhausting engagement with the allies in the Pacific. Japan would retrench her position, contracting the front to dimensions more appropriate to her resources; this core defence zone was defined as the area within the Kurile Islands, Ogasawara Islands, the middle and western parts of the South Seas, western New Guinea, Sunda and Burma.[33] Within this core defence zone, Japan would contain the allies, particularly through reinforced air power. IHQ was quite frank in admitting that the disparity between allied and Japanese strength rendered holding on to Japanese acquisitions in the Southeast Pacific unfeasible. IHQ and the government, after analysis of the last two years of war and additionally the general global situation in its political, economic and industrial aspects, concluded that Germany could hardly be relied upon for assistance and resolved to carry on fighting self-sufficiently.[34]

Japan expected to be able to reorganize herself along these lines by mid-1944. Meanwhile, it was essential at least to avoid war with the Soviet Union and hopefully improve Russo-Japanese relations and, should the chance present itself, to arbitrate between the Soviet Union and Germany. Pressure would be kept up on China, partly to ward off aerial attacks on Japan and harassment of her maritime supply lines from the mainland, and any opportunities to put Chinese issues to rest should not be overlooked. As for Germany, efforts for closer co-operation would be made, but not so much as to antagonize the Soviet Union.[35] These new 'Guidelines for the Conduct of War' signalled a shift from Japan's initial intentions of undermining American morale through defeating the British first, to aiming at negotiating peace through the Soviet Union. Foreign Minister Shigemitsu, however, was deeply suspicious of Soviet sincerity in her non-aggression pact with Japan, and was pessimistic about any possibility of peace between the Soviet Union and Germany.[36]

The Naval Command reorganized the fleet around the carrier force in April 1943, in accordance with the new priority of air units. The core defence zone itself had been defined from the viewpoint of sustainable supply lines and control of the skies. The army and navy initially requested an aggregate 55,000 aircraft for fiscal 1944, but annual production at that point being only 17,000–18,000, targets for 1944 were set at 40,000.[37]

IHQ was none the less not fully confident of its ability to hold the 8,000 mile front which enclosed the core defence zone. Furthermore, in their view, the allies had several choices: they could attack from the north of Australia (western New Guinea, Celebes, Timor), in the Central Pacific (the Carolines and Marianas), or in the southeast (Burma, the Andaman and Nicobar Islands). IHQ, however, did not get around to analysing the possibilities of each route in depth. In addition, although the aim of the core defence zone concept had in the first place been to rectify Japan's overextended positions, the navy, and most conspicuously the combined fleet, had yet to shake off its outdated duelling mentality, with the result that they developed a fixation on holding on to Truk in the central Carolines, which in turn led to the perceived necessity of maintaining a forward presence in the Marshalls and Rabaul, which lay outside the zone, turning the whole concept into a rather nebulous one. At any rate, it was decided that prime responsibility for dealing with north Australia and the Southwest Pacific area would devolve on the army while the Central Pacific would come under the navy.

The Greater East Asian joint declaration as a diplomatic offensive

The core defence zone concept meant the abandonment of westward expansion and a trial by endurance, with the main battleground being the Pacific. Accordingly, political unity and stability in Japanese-occupied Asia was urgently called for. The Greater East Asian Conference held on the 5–6 November 1943 in Tokyo should be seen in this light.

The Nanking government had declared war on the Allies on 9 January. The Japanese government, convinced that this was a 'major turning point', renounced its extraterritorial rights and concessions, shelved its plans to transform Shansi and Inner Mongolia into special regions, and revised the 1940 Treaty, in a bid to improve Chinese relations. Behind this new China policy was ex-ambassador to China Shigemitsu. Shigemitsu reflected Japan's former brazen pursuit of its interests in China, and with that in mind sought to strengthen the Nanking regime.[38]

In the cabinet reshuffle of April 1943, Shigemitsu was appointed Foreign Minister and Greater East Asian Minister, and consequently presided over the Greater East Asian Conference and Joint Declaration. Prior to the conference, Burma under Premier Ba Maw on 1 August, and the Philippines under President Jose P. Laurel on 14 October were granted independence with the caveat that they would remain 'under the tutelage of the Japanese Empire'. Additionally, the Provisional Free Indian Government, with nominal jurisdiction over the Nicobar and Andaman Islands under Subhas Chandra Bose, was established on 21 October in Singapore. The Japanese and Nanking governments formally signed an alliance treaty on 30 October.

The representatives at the Greater East Asian Conference were Prime Minister Tojo for Japan, Wang Chao-Ming for the Nanking regime, Wan Waithayakorn for Siam, Chang Ching-Hui for Manchuria, Jose P. Laurel for the Philippines, and Ba Maw for Burma, with Chandra Bose attending as an observer. They endorsed the Greater East Asian Joint Declaration which lacked the exclusionist tones of the earlier Greater East Asian Co-prosperity Sphere concept. The revised war aims were:

> cooperation in stabilizing Greater East Asia and building a just and mutually beneficial order;
> mutual respect for sovereignty and Greater East Asian brotherhood;
> mutual respect for traditions and national development, leading to cultural rejuvenation;
> mutually beneficial cooperation in the economic sphere, leading to prosperity;
> maintenance of a spirit of generosity towards all nations, together with the abolition of racism, promotion of cultural exchange, and sharing of natural resources in the cause of global progress.[39]

Two motives on Shigemitsu's part lay behind the declaration. First, he wished to apply the ideals of the declaration to all Asia, and in effect to rein in the military domestically. Second, he was trying to redefine Japan's war aims along universal values. Of course, the overall declaration still saw the war as a struggle for liberation from western chains. In this sense, it was directly descended from traditional theories on the liberation of Asia and was regional in nature. However, Shigemitsu, by incorporating in it universal elements reminiscent of the Atlantic Charter, was laying the groundwork for a postwar order. It was on this point that Shigemitsu and the military, along with Prime Minister Tojo, differed in their understanding of the conference and the joint declaration. While Shigemitsu had his eyes on the allies' response, Tojo and the military were concerned with Asian unity in the face of a difficult military situation.[40]

In response to the conference and declaration, Churchill, Roosevelt and Chiang Kai-Shek convened in Cairo on 22 November to discuss postwar policies. The resulting declaration announced on the 27th was the first explicit statement of the allies' intentions concerning post-war Japan. The allies would:

> deprive Japan of all territories gained since the beginning of the first world war;
> return all properties seized by the Japanese from the Chinese in Manchuria, Taiwan, the Pescadores, and other areas;
> expel Japan from all other regions she had occupied by force;
> recognize the enslavement of the Korean people and resolve to facilitate their future freedom and independence.

The declaration ended on the note that the United States, Britain and China, in concert with other nations hostile to Japan, would take extraordinary and long-term measures necessary to bring about Japan's unconditional surrender.[41]

At the following Teheran Conference, Churchill and Roosevelt promised Stalin to open a second front in Europe. In return, Stalin committed himself to join the war on Japan pending German surrender. Stalin claimed that Soviet strength in the Far East was adequate for defensive purposes, but fell short of the 3:1 superiority he deemed necessary for any offensive action. In addition, the Soviets demanded the Kurile Islands, southern Sakhalin, recognition of their predominant interests in Dairen and concessions on the Manchurian railways.[42] Japan, blissfully unaware of these events, saw the Soviet position as 'basically unchanged'.[43]

The collapse of the core defence zone

Churchill and Roosevelt had met in Vancouver in August 1943, before the Cairo Conference, and approved the Anglo-American Joint Chiefs of Staff's plans for operations against Japan. This involved a two-pronged attack on Japanese-held areas, with the Central Pacific Fleet under Admiral Nimitz advancing westwards through the Gilberts, Marshalls and the Carolines, and with General MacArthur moving northwards from New Guinea. The Joint Chiefs of Staff also planned large-scale bombings against Japan from the Chinese mainland, and to that end required the British to reopen a land route to China. The newly established Southeast Asian Command (SEAC) initially found the reconquest of Burma a daunting task, and recommended the recovery of Singapore and Sumatra, but plans were finalised for the invasion of Burma.[44]

As early as the beginning of 1943, the allies had started preparing for a counter-attack in the Chindwin River region in north-western Burma, the Hukwang Valley and Yunnan. In February, approximately 3,000 troops under the command of Colonel Wingate penetrated central Burma, taking the Japanese by surprise. In October, a joint US–Chinese force commanded by General Stilwell invaded northern Burma. IHQ, judging that the allies would eventually commence an all-out offensive in western and central Burma, cleared preparations for an active defence of the area in September. As Chandra Bose's independence movement was proceeding under Japanese protection, IHQ planned to promote the movement to the point that the INA could advance into India, depriving the allies of India as a base from which to launch operations against Japanese occupying forces. Japan's 'Operation U' was hatched under such circumstances. Its objectives were to advance the Japanese line of defence across the Chindwin River to Imphal and Kohima, and simultaneously to cut off lines of support to Chiang that ran from Ledo to Yunnan.[45]

In March 1943, the Japanese Army Group in Burma was newly organized under the command of General Kawabe, while Lieutenant-General Mutaguchi, an outspoken advocate of 'Operation U' (popularly known as 'Operation Imphal'), was promoted to lead the 15th Army. Under these commanders the Japanese embarked on their assault on Imphal. The operation basically required Japanese forces to remain on the defensive in the Salween River and Hukwang Valley area, while the 15th Army would be the core of the offensive in the Kohima-Imphal region. Aggressive by nature, Mutaguchi relied on surprise in his planning; his estimate for the time required for the capture of Imphal was a very optimistic 20 days. He sent out his men lightly equipped, with little regard for logistics, and insufficient information on climate and terrain in the battle zone. In mid-April, the 31st Division did indeed succeed in occupying Kohima and laying siege to Imphal, but the resistance of the defending British and Indians, supplied from the air, proved stubborn. Supplies on the Japanese side were in contrast running out, and bad weather, combined with bickering between commanders in the rear and in the field, led to a collapse of the

Japanese offensive. IHQ was forced to call off the operation on 4 July.[46] Japanese army strength in Burma was decimated as a result; the pursuing British and Chinese units even threatened Japanese forces in Akyab and on the border of Yunnan. Japanese casualties amounted to a staggering 190,000 dead. Japanese forces had no option but to retreat to southern Burma and adopt a wholly defensive stance. Chandra Bose's INA played a supporting role in the operation and at one point advanced into India, but was routed along with the Japanese, never to return to its former strength.[47]

In June, as the Japanese were retreating in Burma, Nimitz's Pacific Fleet was at the gates of Japan's core defence zone, nearing the Mariana Islands, and arrived at Saipan on the 15th. A Japanese task force attempted a naval air attack on the American operation, but was repulsed with the loss of three aircraft carriers. Inexperienced pilots and inferior equipment were the main culprits.[48] MacArthur's force, meanwhile, was following its stepping stones, awaiting an opportunity to advance on the Philippines. With the loss of the Marianas, the Japanese mainland fell within the range of B-29 bombings.

In these dire straits, criticism of the leadership of the Tojo cabinet and IHQ was rampant and, as mentioned before, the Tojo cabinet resigned, giving way to the Koiso cabinet, sworn in on 22 July, with Shigemitsu as its Foreign Minister. IHQ was also overhauled, General Umezu becoming Chief of the General Staff, and Admiral Oikawa as Chief of Naval Staff. Prime Minister Koiso was also mindful of the necessity for closer co-ordination between the administrative, diplomatic and military branches, and reorganized the LC as the Supreme War Conference (*Saiko Senso Shido Kaigi*). The new conference was to prove yet another failure at overcoming differences between the army and navy.[49]

The Supreme War Conference predicted that the next allied attack would be on the Philippines and the Ogasawara Islands, and that it could be expected around October. On the Burmese front and in the Indian Ocean, the allies were likely to open an India–China route, land on the Andaman and Nicobar Islands, and bomb the Sumatran oil fields. Under these premises, on 19 August 1944, the Council announced its 'Guidelines for the further conduct of war', dwelling on strategic, domestic, and diplomatic factors. On the strategic side, Japan should:

> shatter the attacking US forces in the Pacific; secure resources in the south and at all costs keep up the flow of maritime transport; keep

to the status quo in the Indian Ocean; deter as far as possible bombing and disruption of maritime routes from the Chinese mainland.

On the domestic front, measures had been stepped up especially for increasing the production of aircraft and developing and securing self-sufficiency at home and in Manchukuo, China and territories in the south. In the diplomatic area, Japan should:

> maintain a state of neutrality with the Soviet Union, seek opportunities to improve relations, and engineer a German-Soviet peace; aim for a speedy resolution of the China issue by diplomatic manoeuvring directed at the Chungking regime, preferably with Soviet assistance; endeavour to co-operate closely with the Germans, in so far as it would not spark hostilities with the Soviet Union. In the event of a German collapse or surrender, swiftly search for means to utilize the Soviet Union to secure favourable terms; recruit the Philippines in the war to resist the Americans and the British; and declare as soon as possible its intentions to bring about Indian independence in future.[50]

The Koiso cabinet's leadership ran into trouble almost immediately. Diplomatic energies were centred on negotiating a German–Soviet peace and overtures to the Chungking regime; but the Germans replied that they had no plans for peace on 14 September, and the Soviets declined in talks with a Japanese special envoy, former Prime Minister Hirota Kohki. As for the Chungking regime, Koiso placed his hopes on the mediation of the Nanking regime's Miao Bin, about which Foreign Minister Shigemitsu, among others, was dubious. The mediations were fruitless – no surprise as Miao was a dishonest broker, doubling for Nanking and Chungking. Industrial policy to increase aircraft production ran into difficulties, with little hope of avoiding heavy losses of merchant shipping to allied submarine attacks in future.[51]

In October 1944, US task forces hit the Ogasawara Islands and Taiwan, providing covering fire for MacArthur's Philippines offensive. MacArthur's troops landed on Leyte on the 20th. The Japanese combined fleet mounted a counter-attack with all the determination and resources at its disposal, but was repulsed by an American task force and submarines; 30 vessels, including aircraft carriers, were sunk – a devastating blow. MacArthur's forces moved on to Luzon the following January, the outgunned and outnumbered Japanese defenders retreated into the mountains, to put up a passive defence. With the loss of the Philippines, Japan was cut off from her southern resources and bombing raids from Saipan and the Chinese mainland detracted greatly from Japan's productive capabilities.[52] In January 1945, the Army and Navy High Command issued directives for 'Operation Ketsu', in essence a last-ditch defence of the Japanese home islands, Manchuria and occupied areas in China. However, the allies' offensive was swift and massive, with the Americans landing on Iwo Jima on 19 February, and Okinawa on 1 April. Faced with overwhelming seaborne support, numbers, and firepower, the Japanese ground forces were completely annihilated by 21 June. Okinawa suffered 110,000 military, and 100,000 civilian, casualties.[53]

Suzuki cabinet and the search for a way to peace

The assessment of the General Staff in the first quarter of 1945 was that the Soviet Union would in all likelihood not agree to an extension of the Neutrality Act in April, but would not launch hostilities against Japan immediately. However, as it could not be hoped that the Germans would hold out beyond mid-1945, a Soviet assault would become a probability after that. In this case the Soviets could be expected to let the Japanese, Americans and British wear themselves down, then step in to bring the war to an end on their own initiative. The General Staff, therefore, still hoped for an opportunity after the cessation of hostilities in the European theatre to negotiate terms through the Soviet Union.[54] In addition, the Koiso cabinet in its last days in March attempted to employ Widar Bagge, the Swedish minister to Japan, in a private capacity to sound out the Americans and British. Shigemitsu displayed some interest, but Togo, who succeeded him as Foreign Minister, was sceptical and terminated the overtures.[55]

The Koiso cabinet, deadlocked in its leadership, resigned on 5 April. On the same day, just before the formation of the Suzuki cabinet on the 7th, the Soviets sent notification that they would not extend the Neutrality Pact. The army, still intent on a fight to the last over the home islands, would have to find ways to stave off the Russians for as long as possible.

The new Foreign Minister, Togo, believing that a negotiated peace was feasible as long as Japan had some resources still at her disposal, decided to move swiftly towards this end by playing on the army's desire to avoid a Soviet conflict. Navy Minister Yonai was of a like mind.[56] Togo first limited access to the Supreme War Conference to the heads of the Cabinet, the Army Ministry, the Navy Ministry, the Foreign Ministry, the General Staff and the Naval Staff exclusively, thereby enabling a consensus to be reached in the search for peace. Regarding the Soviets, Japan should prevent a Soviet attack on Japan and try to bring relations to a friendly neutrality.[57] The Supreme War Conference and the Imperial Conference of 8 June approved the army's plans for a fight to the finish, but, contrary to the army's expectations, this served to strengthen the government's resolve to seek for peace. The Supreme Conference on 12 July agreed to request the Soviets to act as a go-between, and the Soviets were asked to accept Prince Konoe as a special envoy.[58] Some discussion took place over what price Japan might have to pay the Soviet Union for these services, but was inconclusive as Soviet intentions were at that point unknown.[59]

On 26 July, the Potsdam Declaration was announced in the name of the President of the United States, the Premier of China and the Prime Minister of Great Britain. Togo and the Foreign Ministry understood this as having Soviet support, and considered that it could provide the basis for peace with the US and Britain. The government, however, elected to await a reply from the Soviet government to the proposal of Konoe as envoy, and avoid any comment on the declaration for the time being. When the government's intentions were misrepresented as 'purposeful disregard' (*mokusatsu*) in a newspaper article on the 28th,[60] this became a perfect excuse for the Soviet Union to initiate hostilities against Japan. On 6 and 9 August, the Americans dropped atomic bombs on Hiroshima and Nagasaki. Togo reported on their devastating effects to the Emperor, and was instructed to end the war with all possible haste, words which naturally further strengthened his resolve to seek peace.[61]

The Soviet Union launched a broad offensive over its entire frontier with Japanese territories on 9 August. The Soviet attack and its endorsement of the Potsdam Declaration dashed all hopes of a negotiated peace being negotiated with America and Britain through the Soviet Union. That Japan had no option other than to negotiate directly with them on the Potsdam terms had become an unavoidable fact in the view of the majority of the cabinet. It could be said that the Soviet entry into the war against Japan was the final push that brought about the Japanese decision to surrender, as it extinguished the army's last hopes for avoiding a Soviet conflict and defending the home islands.

From this day on, the issue for the Supreme War Conference was not whether to carry on with the war, but what modifications would be acceptable in the basic Potsdam Declaration. Togo and Yonai had only the right of the Emperor to rule on their minds. War Minister Anami and Chief of General Staff Umezu were strongly in favour of voluntary disarmament, avoidance of Allied occupation of the Japanese home islands and Japanese jurisdiction over war criminals. At the first Imperial Conference on 9 August, the Emperor pointed out that preparations for the defence of the home islands were inadequate and agreed to Togo's proposals for an immediate acceptance of the Potsdam terms. On the next day, the Japanese government notified the allies of their acceptance, with the understanding that the terms did not entail any demands for a change in Imperial rule.[62]

Doubts as to whether Japan should carry on fighting resurfaced from the 12th to the 14th, as the reference in the twelfth article in the Potsdam Declaration to a polity chosen by the freely expressed will of the Japanese people raised concerns about the future of the Emperor and the Imperial family. Chief of Naval Staff Toyoda shared this concern, and opposition to its acceptance grew, along with demands for querying the Americans about its meaning. However, the Emperor, Prime Minister, Foreign Minister and Naval Minister firmly decided on peace.[63] At the second Imperial Conference which was convened by the Emperor himself, he issued his divine judgement – a highly irregular procedure under the Meiji Constitution – and the national intent to surrender was realized. At noon on the 15th the Emperor issued an edict on the cessation of war to his subjects.

Looking back on the Anglo-Japanese confrontation of 1941–45, Japan's initial victories, especially the sinking of the state-of-the-art HMS *Prince of Wales* and HMS *Repulse* on the third day of the war, made a powerful impression on the British nation, and Churchill in particular. Further blows to Britain's prestige in the Far East followed. Japan swiftly overran the Malay Peninsula and occupied Singapore, the symbol of Britain's colonial presence, on 15 February 1942. As C. Thorne points out, the fall of Singapore seemed to many Japanese to validate the 'decline of the West'. Many in Asia also came to harbour doubts about Western superiority.[64]

Although the British went on the counter-offensive in the last stages of the war, they played only a complementary role to the United States and were unable to recover Singapore unaided. Although the British were stubborn in their desire to regain their Asian colonies, the framework of strategy and postwar policies in the Asian-Pacific region being hammered out in US–Soviet negotiations was already in place by mid-1944. The fall of Singapore was indeed a symbolic event, announcing a turning point in history: the retreat of the British Empire from Asia.

Notes

1. Shigemitsu Mamoru, *Showa no doran* (Upheaval in the Showa Era) (Chuo Koron Sha, 1952), p. 135.
2. Hattori Takushiro, *Daitoa senso zenshi* (Complete History of the Great Asian War) (Hara Shobo, 1975), pp. 141–3.
3. Boeicho Boeikenshujo (ed.), *Senshi sosho: Daihonei rikugun-bu, Daitoa senso kaisen keii* (IHQ, Chief of Army Staff, Origins of the Outbreak of War), Vol. 3 (Asagumo Shinbunsha, 1974), p. 192.
4. Hatano Sumio, *Taiheiyo senso to Ajia gaiko* (Pacific War and Japanese Foreign Policies to Asia) (Tokyo Daigaku Shuppankai, 1996), p. 8.
5. *Ibid.*, p. 9.
6. Boeicho Boeikenshujo (ed.), *Senshi sosho: Daihon'ei-Rikugunbu*, p. 193.
7. Sanbo-Honbu (ed.), *Sugiyama memo* (The Memoirs of General Sugiyama), Vol. 2 (Hara Shobo, 1967), p. 529.
8. *Ibid.*, p. 624.
9. *Ibid.*, p. 396.
10. *Ibid.*, p. 524.
11. Togo Shigenori, *Jidai no ichimen* (One Aspect of Our Time) (Hara Shobo, 1985), pp. 139–41.
12. Tomioka Sadatoshi, *Kaisen to shusen* (Beginning and Ending of the War) (Mainichi Shinbun Sha, 1968), p. 56.
13. *Kanpo gogai* (Government Gazette), 22 January 1942 (Shugiin Sokkiroku, No.3), p. 16.
14. *Ibid.*, 17 February 1942, No. 16, p. 232.
15. Sanbo-Honbu, *Sugiyama-Memo*, Vol. 2, p. 68.
16. *Ibid.*, p. 6.
17. Oshima Hiroshi (Military Attaché in Berlin) to the Chief of Army Staff, 17 February 1942 (Boei Kenshujo, Telegram Collection from the Military Attaché in Berlin).
18. Milan Hauner, *India in Axis Strategy: Germany, Japan, and Indian Nationalists in the Second World War* (Stuttgart: Klett-Cotta, 1981), pp. 503–4.
19. Togo, *Jidai no ichimen*, pp. 229–30.
20. Boeicho Boeikenshujo (ed.), *Senshi sosho: Biruma kosei sakusen* (Offensive Operations in Burma), pp. 71–5.
21. Boeicho Boeikenshujo (ed.), *Senshi sosho: Nanpo no gunsei* (The Military Administration in the South), pp. 94–5.
22. Ota Jozo, *Biruma ni okeru Nihon gunsei no kenkyu* (Historical Studies of Japanese Military Administration in Burma) (Yoshikawa Kobunkan, 1967), pp. 47–8.

23. Ba Maw, *Breakthrough in Burma: Memoirs of a Revolution, 1939–1945* (Yale University Press, 1968); Japanese edition: *Biruma no yoake* (translated by Yokobori Yoichi, Taiyo Shobo, 1973), p. 275.
24. Izumiya Takuro, *Sono na wa Minami boryaku kikan* (Minami Secret Service) (Taiyo Shobo, 1967), pp. 191–5.
25. Peter Lowe, *Britain in the Far East* (London: Longman, 1981), pp. 184–5.
26. Fujihara Iwaichi, *F-Kikan* (F Secret Service) (Hara Shobo, 1966), pp. 75–7.
27. Maruyama Shizuo, *Indo kokumin gun* (Indian National Army) (Iwanami Shoten, 1985), p. 37.
28. Hauner, *India in Axis Strategy*, p. 597.
29. Nagasaki Nobuko, 'Indo kokumin gun no keisei', in Nagasaki Nobuko (ed.), *Minami Ajia no minzoku undo to Nihon* (Nationalist Movements in South Asia and Japan) (Asian Economic Research Centre, 1980), pp. 54–5.
30. Shinobu Seizaburo, *Taiheiyo senso to 'mohitotsu' no Taiheiyo senso* (The Pacific War and 'Another' Pacific War) (Keiso Shobo, 1989), pp. 124–6.
31. Sanbo-Honbu, *Sugiyama-Memo*, Vol. 2, pp. 420–2.
32. Ito Takashi and Watanabe Yukio (eds.), *Shigemitsu Mamoru shuki* (Diaries of Shigemitsu Mamoru) (Chuo Koron Sha, 1988), pp. 433–5.
33. Sanbo-Honbu, *Sugiyama-Memo*, Vol. 2, p. 473.
34. *Ibid.*, p. 472.
35. *Ibid.*, pp. 482–3.
36. Shigemitsu, *Showa no doran*, pp. 182–3.
37. Sanbo-Honbu, *Sugiyama-Memo*, Vol. 2, p. 485.
38. Shigemitsu, *Showa no doran*, pp. 158–72.
39. *Nihon gaiko nenpyo narabi ni shuyo bunsho* (Chronology of Japanese Diplomacy and Major Documents), Vol. 2 (Hara Shobo, 1955), p. 594.
40. Hatano, *Taiheiyo senso to Ajia gaiko*, pp. 239–40; Shigemitsu, *Showa no doran*, p. 179.
41. *Nihon gaiko nenpyo narabi ni shuyo bunsho*, Vol. 2, pp. 594–5.
42. Robert Dallek, *Franklin D. Roosevelt and American Foreign Policy, 1932–1945* (Oxford: Oxford University Press, 1995), p. 487; Lowe, *Britain in the Far East*, p. 191.
43. Sanbo-Honbu, *Sugiyama-Memo*, Vol. 2, p. 519.
44. Lowe, *Britain in the Far East*, p. 190.
45. Boeicho Boeikenshujo (ed.), *Senshi sosho: Imphal sakusen* (Battle in Imphal), pp. 157–62.
46. *Ibid.*, pp. 615–20.
47. *Ibid.*, p. 614.
48. E.B. Potter and C.W. Nimitz, *The Great Sea War* (1960); Japanese translation: *Nimitz no Taiheiyo senso* (Kobunsha, 1962), p. 257.
49. Ito and Watanabe, *Shigemitsu Mamoru shuki*, 3 March 1945, pp. 439–41.
50. Sanbo-Honbu (ed.), *Haisen no kiroku* (Reflections on the Defeat of Japan) (Hara Shobo, 1967), pp. 50–6.
51. Ito and Watanabe, *Shigemitsu Mamoru shuki*, pp. 461–74.
52. Hattori, *Daitoa senso*, pp. 870–2.
53. *Ibid.*, p. 808.
54. Hatano Sumio, *Daitoa senso no jidai* (The Era of the Great East Asian War) (Asahi Shuppansha, 1988), p. 287.

55. Matsumoto Shun'ichi and Ando Yoshio (eds), *Daitoa senso shusen gaiko* (Diplomacy of Ending the Great East Asian War) (Kajima Shuppankai, 1972), pp. 79–84.
56. Togo, *Jidai no ichimen*, pp. 337–8.
57. *Ibid.*, pp. 331–2.
58. *Ibid.*, p. 346; Kido Koichi, *Kido Koichi nikki* (Diaries of Kido Koichi), Vol. 2 (Tokyo Daigaku Shuppankai, 1974), p. 1217.
59. Togo, *Jidai no ichimen*, p. 332.
60. Matsumoto and Ando, *Daitoa senso shusen gaiko*, p. 214.
61. Togo, *Jidai no ichimen*, p. 356.
62. Matsumoto and Ando, *Daitoa senso shusen gaiko*, pp. 225–34.
63. Takagi Sokichi and Sanematsu Yuzuru (eds), *Kaigun taisho Yonai Mitsumasa oboegaki* (Memoirs of Admiral Yonai Mitsumasa) (Kojin Sha, 1978), pp. 149–54.
64. Christopher Thorne, 'Racial Aspect of the Far Eastern War of 1941–1945', in *Proceedings of the British Academy*, Vol. LXVI (Oxford: Oxford University Press, 1980), pp. 342–3.

6
From Singapore to Tokyo Bay, 1941–45
Peter Lowe and Ian Nish

There were virtually no political or diplomatic relations between Britain and Japan from December 1941 until the end of the war. The relationship between the two countries was defined by the military and naval encounters in the Asia-Pacific war. An historical distinction has to be drawn between the Pacific war, which was a naval and island-hopping war, and the Asian war, which originated with Japan's China campaigns in 1937 and spread to Indochina, Malaya, Indonesia and Burma. In the first the Americans carried the overwhelming burden, while in the Asian campaigns Britain and India shared the major role with the Chinese and the Americans.[1] There were inevitably points of tension between the two war zones; and the degree of Anglo-American cooperation which existed was an important factor in British policy towards Japan at the time. The greatest contribution to our understanding in this field has been the distinguished work of the late Professor Christopher Thorne.[2] But Britain also had diplomatic relations with China throughout the war and it is possible to deduce from these and other sources how British policy-makers viewed the progress of the war with Japan and how they saw the future of the East after the tide of war had turned.

In the absence of direct communications between Britain and Japan, it is the object of this chapter to indicate British attitudes to the various phases of the war.

The fall of Singapore, 1942

The British Empire suffered devastating blows in consequence of the dramatic Japanese victories in the first part of the war. Hong Kong, British Borneo and Malaya were swiftly captured. The sinking of the battleship *Prince of Wales* and the battle cruiser *Repulse* was a great national disaster and evidence of the failure of Britain's naval strategy in Southeast Asian waters. Malaya had been deprived by Whitehall of the necessary reinforcements and given a lower priority than other operational zones like the Middle East and Russia. Local officials were not faultless and the command structure was deeply flawed. But it appears to have been the leadership in London who, in the fraught atmosphere of global conflict, seriously underestimated the threat of a Japanese invasion of the Malayan peninsula.[3]

The fall of Singapore was a natural consequence of failures in Malaya. Instead of the main fleet which had been promised for its defence, only a small fleet was sent to the area. There was insufficient artillery, no tanks and some 16 battalions missing. The 158 aircraft available were fewer than half of those deemed essential to cater for the island's defence. The surrender by General Percival at Singapore on 15 February 1942 was the most humiliating single feature of the whole campaign since it emphasized starkly the collapse of Prime Minister Winston Churchill's strategy for containing the Japanese advance; and it was the greatest reverse experienced by the British Empire since the loss of the American colonies in the eighteenth century.

There was therefore a great outcry and the demand for guilty parties to be named. Recent research has discredited the myth that the British were taken by surprise by Japan's landward invasion down the Malayan peninsula and over the causeway while the guns of the Singapore naval base pointed fruitlessly out to sea. On the contrary, Singapore strategists did expect the Japanese to attack the island from the rear. Military thinking was well aware of the necessity of reinforcing the defence of the Malayan hinterland and precautions had been taken. But they proved inadequate.[4]

Retreat from Burma

The British position in Burma disintegrated rapidly after Singapore fell. Following Japan's major offensive, Rangoon was taken on 8 March. The governor since 1941, Sir Reginald Dorman-Smith, retreated to Simla to form the Burmese administration in exile. The British Burmese forces were helped in their resistance by Chinese forces who were involved in order to keep open their vital supply-lines from Burmese ports to the Chinese hinterland. The Chinese came under the command of General Joseph W. Stilwell, chief of staff China and commander-in-chief of the

Chinese expeditionary force. In spite of these combined forces, a fighting retreat towards India took place, which was completed in May.[5]

In the context of withdrawal, collaboration inevitably led to Anglo-Chinese and Anglo-American tensions. The Americans were imbued with tremendous confidence and regarded the British as handicapped by their colonial mentality from which situation Americans had escaped with the creation of the United States (the American occupation of the Philippines was conveniently put on one side). For their part the British regarded themselves as possessing a breadth of experience and expertise in South and Southeast Asia lacking in their American colleagues. The incongruity of the relationship was fittingly symbolized in the personalities of Lt-Gen. Archibald Wavell and General Joseph Stilwell.[6]

British hopes of launching a counter-attack centred on Burma, but no significant advances were made during 1943. Much was expected of General Orde Wingate's operations behind enemy lines in February and his concepts of long-range penetration probably came as a shock to the Japanese army but did not secure the degree of success Churchill hoped for when he decided to support Wingate's ideas. Burma was the only area where Britain could hope to turn the tide; the Pacific campaigns were dominated by the United States, which intended to maintain a firm grip in the theatre.[7]

The Japanese came close to the Burmese frontier with India. But, though India was bombed, she was not occupied by Japan. Indian troops had been much involved in the retreat from Burma and had made a great contribution to the British Empire war effort. On the other hand, this had taken place against the background of the Quit India movement waged by the Indian National Congress from 1942 onwards. Moreover, recruits to the Indian National Army, organized by Subhas Chandra Bose and the Japanese in Singapore, were taking part in operations in Burma. These continued to go in Japan's favour, though attempts at landing in the Arakan continued to be made.

Wartime conferences

Among Anglo-American differences of opinion on the war, it seems that the American public was inclined to favour dealing with Japan first while Britain wanted to concentrate on Europe. While the European war came first in their priorities, the leaders of the Conservative, Labour and Liberal Parties who made up Churchill's wartime coalition cabinet were agreed that Britain must restore her role as an Asian power, and that necessitated playing as vigorous a part as possible both in the wartime conferences and in the later stages of the fighting.

Following Germany's attack on the Soviet Union, the eastern campaigns had to be seen as part of a global struggle and therefore part of the agenda of the wartime summit conferences. These were primarily the meetings of President Franklin Roosevelt, Joseph Stalin and Winston Churchill. In the middle and later stages of the war Roosevelt attached more importance to cultivating his relationship with Stalin, while his relationship with Churchill underwent more tension. Stalin was urged to consider joining the war against Japan from the aftermath of Pearl Harbor onwards. At the Moscow conference of Foreign Ministers in October 1943, Stalin stated that the Soviet Union would enter the Far Eastern conflict three months after the termination of the European war – a promise he was to keep. Stalin reiterated his determination to Roosevelt and Churchill at the Teheran conference (EUREKA) the following month.[8] American–Soviet exchanges developed in 1944 in the form of discussions between respective representatives in Moscow on the terms for Soviet entry. Stalin told the American ambassador, Averell Harriman, that the Kuril islands and lower Sakhalin should be taken over by the Soviet Union and that Russia should develop strategic and economic interests in Manchuria.[9] Roosevelt believed that the savage nature of the war in Asia and the Pacific, which was likely to last well into 1946, if not 1947, required Soviet intervention as soon as was practicable and that concessions made to Russia were justified. The project to create an atomic bomb was proceeding satisfactorily but it was impossible, at the beginning of 1945, to forecast with accuracy when this could be used against Japan.

Britain was not consulted over east Asian issues during the Yalta conference in February 1945 at which Roosevelt, Stalin and Churchill were present. Roosevelt reached agreement with Stalin on the terms for Soviet entry and notified the British afterwards. Anthony Eden, the British Foreign Secretary, was most indignant and believed that the concessions were excessive because the Soviet Union would have moved against Japan at the appropriate moment for its own reasons.[10] Churchill was by now accustomed to Roosevelt's approach and did not deem it wise to embark on a dispute with Washington. The episode confirmed the marginalization of Britain in key policy decisions over the war against Japan.

Creation of SEAC and the fightback

While a Grand Alliance for the global war was being negotiated – more by the United States than by Britain – the management of the eastern war effort was being rearranged. Britain was invited by the Combined Chiefs of Staff at the first Quebec conference in August 1943 to organize Southeast Asia Command based on Ceylon and to supply the Supreme Allied Commander (SACSEA). Rear-Admiral Lord Louis Mountbatten was promoted to the command, which he took up in October. General Stilwell was made deputy commander. The original remit of SEAC was to defeat the Japanese armies in Burma, Malaya, Sumatra, Siam and other appropriate parts of the area.[11]

From 1944 Britain contributed decisively to forcing the Japanese back. The war in Burma turned dramatically against Japan following the withdrawal from Kohima (in Assam, India) and the failure of her offensive at Imphal (July). The British were assisted by superior intelligence achievements and by a decline in Japanese morale amidst military setbacks and disease. Equally serious was her defeat in the north with the capture of Myitkina by Stilwell in August. This was followed by Britain's asking for the recall of Stilwell from Burma. In any case American assistance to SEAC ended with the completion in January 1945 of the Ledo route into China.

With the capture of Rangoon on 2 May, the first part of Mountbatten's remit – the recovery of Burma – was accomplished. Rangoon could now serve as the base for further campaigns against Malaya and Singapore and as a conduit for sending allied supplies into the Chinese hinterland.[12]

On 11 July Mountbatten left Ceylon for Manila to discuss coordination with General MacArthur as Supreme Commander South Pacific. As MacArthur's troops moved northward in the Pacific, he appeared to be less interested south of the equator. As a result the purview of SEAC was increased by the Combined Chiefs to take in Java, Celebes, Borneo and Indochina south of the 16th parallel – a tremendous expansion in area – while the Southwest Pacific command was made over to General T.A. Blamey, an Australian general. This vast extension of the territorial coverage of the command was one for which manpower was in fact lacking. But London was content that Britain's role was being recognized and American suspicions over SEAC were being dissolved by the sheer needs of the campaign. This was surely an historic turning-point as the United States which had made use of Britain's colonial bases and highways in its campaigns to relieve China, now turned away from its anti-colonial preoccupations.[13]

The Royal Navy reappeared significantly in the Pacific from the end of 1944 in accordance with Churchill's determination that a British naval presence should accompany the military advance in Burma. It was hoped that these developments would assist in promoting British influence in allied policy-making. This was not borne out to the extent hoped for by Churchill. The British Pacific fleet became involved with the Americans in their attack on Okinawa; and the Chiefs of Staff in London were reluctant to weaken that role which was 'deemed so important to the British cause'.[14]

With the war in Europe ended, Britain was asked and offered to take part in operations leading to the invasion of Japan's main islands. Britain obtained the agreement of her Dominions to taking part in the assault on Japan and was able to offer in August a British Commonwealth force, including Australia, New Zealand, India and (it was originally hoped) Canada.[15]

Planning for peace

It is generally agreed that Britain was less well prepared for the end of the war than the United States. First, she had given priority to obtaining Germany's surrender and working out an accommodation with the Soviet Union. Second, there was the expectation of a long war continuing until 1947 at least. While Britain had many experts on East Asian matters, they were generally preoccupied elsewhere. One of the exceptions was Sir George Sansom who after retirement from the diplomatic service had been appointed to a professorship at Columbia University and who, when war broke out, offered his services to the Washington embassy. From 14 September 1942 he had served as minister plenipotentiary with special responsibility for the war with Japan under Lord Halifax as ambassador. It appears to have been Sansom whose reports prodded the officials in the Foreign Office to think ahead as the Americans were doing under Grew through the various advisory committees of the State Department.[16] Professor Thorne's researches have indicated that, while there were of course disagreements between the British officials, they had remarkably liberal attitudes over the future of Japan. Thus, they tended to agree that the Japanese should not be humiliated and should be brought back speedily within the community of nations. They favoured a 'hands-off' approach towards Japan's internal affairs, largely because outside interference might encourage the emergence of a communist-type government. Then there was the question of a military occupation of the Japanese islands which Britain accepted, provided it was kept short. They appear to have been sceptical of the comprehensive plans for reform of Japan being promoted by American New Dealers. It is important, of course, not to assume that the broadly liberal views of officials are necessarily shared in a democracy by politicians who have to bear in mind the excited state of public opinion.

One minor issue which Britain stressed was that China should be consulted over all matters pertaining to Japan. Thorne draws attention to the fact 'that it was British rather than American officials who throughout these final stages of the war bore in mind the desirability of involving China in major decisions regarding Japan'. He observes that it 'serves as yet another ironic comment upon the myths woven around the subject of US/British/Chinese relations by Americans at the time and American historians since'.[17]

In the summer of 1945 the British approach to the existing policy of unconditional surrender changed. This policy had been adopted by Roosevelt and Churchill at the Casablanca conference in January 1943. The peculiar horror and barbarism shown by Nazi Germany and Japan appeared to justify the adoption of such a policy. But it complicated the task of securing surrender immensely and this was particularly significant in dealing with Japan. While it was clear by 1945 that Japan would lose the war, it was difficult to estimate when she would surrender. Japanese forces were continuing to fight with their customary zeal and tenacity even though forced ever more on to the defensive; they had occupied vast tracts of China and Southeast Asia and the challenge of obtaining their surrender was formidable. Japanese loyalty to the Emperor was potent and rendered Japanese resistance to unconditional surrender all the stronger.

Not until 29 May was an indication given informally to Sansom in Washington of the State Department's thinking on ending the war. Grew, by this time Under-Secretary of State, had only discussed matters with President Truman on 28 May, urging that there should be a specific declaration about the future of the emperor. Truman was new; and his cabinet thought it was not advisable for the president to make any declaration, with fighting still going on in Okinawa.[18] Thus, the fact that Britain was not informed earlier showed that the United States was undecided over its policy, not reluctant to consult its ally.

In a lengthy memorandum to London, Sansom advocated the preservation of the monarchy. But officials in the Foreign Office, bearing in mind the imminent summit conference between Truman, Stalin and Churchill at Potsdam, had reservations about this. Foreign Secretary Anthony Eden came down against Britain taking any initiative while being 'very chary of dropping unconditional surrender'. Britain was clearly reluctant to take a lead over the monarchy issue or to influence the Americans. The British military view, as expressed by General Sir Hastings Ismay, was significant. He took the view that, if unconditional surrender involved the dissolution of the imperial dynasty, 'there would be no-one to order the cease-fire in outlying areas, and fighting might continue in various British and Dutch territories and also in China for many months or even years. Thus from a military point of view there was a good deal to be said for the retention in Japan of some central authority who would command obedience'.[19] There is an implication that the continuation of the present emperor on the throne would serve a strategic purpose for the allied forces, especially in areas where Britain had been given the responsibility for taking Japan's surrender. Over this surrender issue the position of the British, Dutch and Chinese armies differed from that of the Americans.

Even allowing for the fact that there was some degree of consensus over this in policy-making circles, the British leaders were by no means sure how far to push their views on a subject so sensitive to public opinion on both sides of the Atlantic as the future of the Japanese emperor. Later Eden on 19 July stated firmly: 'I do not wish to recommend to the Americans that the Emperor should be preserved. They would no doubt like to get such advice and then say they had reluctantly concurred with us'.[20] Eden was perhaps reflecting anxieties about the outcome of the forthcoming general election, and the fact that he was a 'lame duck' Foreign Secretary. He was even more cautious than before in trying to influence American policy.

On 5 July polling took place in the first general election for a decade but it took time for overseas service votes to be counted. When the results were known, the Labour Party emerged with a substantial majority and supplied the government from the end of the month. This affected the representation at the Potsdam conference being held at this time, with Churchill leading the delegation at first, followed by Clement Attlee from 28 July.

Churchill considered dropping the policy of unconditional surrender during the Potsdam conference and was encouraged by the knowledge that American joint chiefs of staff were reflecting along similar lines. He raised the issue with Truman and spoke of the American and British casualties likely to be incurred through adhesion to unconditional surrender. Truman's response was essentially negative and the exchange confirmed his tough attitude towards Japan. Churchill hoped for a modification in policy but this did not occur.[21]

The successful testing of an atomic bomb in New Mexico in July 1945 meant that it was no longer necessary for the United States to encourage Soviet participation in the war. Stalin was conversant with the evolution of the atomic project through his various spies, and was resolute in his determination to intervene before Japan surrendered. Britain had agreed in principle to the use of an atomic bomb against Japan in the Hyde Park agreement, signed by Churchill and Roosevelt in September 1944.[22] During the Potsdam conference, the new Prime Minister, Attlee, was equally prepared to consent to the use of the atomic weapon in order to bring the war with Japan to a more rapid conclusion. The Far Eastern department of the Foreign Office was not consulted on the decision to use the atomic bomb but approval had already been granted at a much higher level.[23] The main justification for using the atomic bomb was the saving of allied lives resulting from the earlier termination of the war. Japan was certainly defeated; but it was feared that the large numbers of Japanese troops in China and Southeast Asia could cause a great deal of difficulty unless the war was ended in a clear-cut way with the acceptance of the allied terms by the Showa Emperor himself.

It was at Potsdam on 24 July that the SEAC commander-in-chief, Lord Mountbatten, heard confidentially for the first time of the availability of the atomic bomb for potential use against Japan. The implications of this for him were that, if its use were to be authorized, the amphibious operations which SEAC was planning, e.g. Operation Zipper against Malaya due in August and Operation Mailfist against Singapore due in September, might become redundant. In any case the pace of operations was likely to become more rapid and the need for urgent decision-making greater. The obligations which were likely to be thrust on SEAC, already suffering from slender resources and especially shortage of shipping, were therefore unexpectedly increased.

The dropping of the atomic bombs on 6 and 9 August, together with the intervention of the Soviet Union, led to the Emperor Hirohito's announcement of Japan's acceptance of the allied terms on 15 August. SEAC's military campaigns had to be suspended but there was a period of uncertainty as to whether the Japanese armies overseas would indeed lay down their arms. Sporadic fighting did continue in Burma until the end of August as local Japanese commanders tried to find consensus over the approach to surrender. There were also moves to convince Field Marshal Terauchi Hisaichi, the commander in chief of the Southern armies in Saigon, to defy the announcement from Tokyo. But Terauchi held firm to Tokyo's line; and the surrender went ahead.[24]

There were many uncertainties associated with the surrender. General MacArthur was appointed on 15 August to the new role of Supreme Commander Allied Powers (SCAP). Mountbatten wrote congratulating him the following day but warned:

> The fact that you have been prevented from inflicting a crushing defeat will, I fear, enable Japanese leaders to delude their people into thinking they were defeated only by scientists and not in battle.[25]

SCAP laid down that local commanders like Mountbatten should not approach Japanese-occupied territories until the overall surrender had been signed. Whatever the reason for this gap of two weeks, the delay played into the hands of the nationalist movements and was an embarrassment to Britain, whose forces were entrusted with the task of disarming the Japanese and restoring law and order in the face of nationalist disturbances.

Britain's problem had changed radically from one of invasion of these territories to one of takeover. On 2 September a surrender document was signed at Penang. The naval task force reached Singapore the following day. Terauchi in Saigon on 12 September deputed General Itagaki Seishiro, commander of the 7th Area army, to make the formal surrender. This was accepted on the steps of the Old Municipal Buildings (now the City Hall) when the surrender of Japanese forces, numbering 50,118 army and airforce personnel and 26,872 navy men, took place. Mountbatten later accepted the Field Marshal's personal surrender in Saigon on 30 November.[26]

Although there was no longer any need for the Allies to invade Japan, Britain renewed her willingness to take part in the occupation of Japan. It was still uncertain what the reception would be like and what that commitment would entail. Esler Dening, the Chief Political Adviser to SACSEA since 1943, was well aware of the difficult choice that had to be made. He was worried about merely walking back into territories like Burma, Malaya and Singapore 'for which we might have expected to fight' at short notice without adequate resources, including food. He thought that it was of paramount political importance that SEAC 'should make the best possible showing in our re-occupation of territories which the Japanese have over-run'. But in general the British government's decision to take part in an allied occupation of Japan was a political rather than a military one. Dening, while recognizing the importance of Britain being part of the occupying force, concluded that 'a token representation in the occupation of Japan is politically far less important to us than showing the flag in South East Asia'.[27]

The problem of Britain's motivation should be touched on at this stage. For Britain there was a strong national sense that the fall of Singapore in 1942 and the sinking of the *Prince of Wales* and the *Repulse* had been a great national disaster and humiliation. Singapore, which had been one of the jewels in the British colonial crown, was, in Dening's words, a territory 'for which we might have expected to fight' but did not now have to.

Apart from these matters of national prestige, there were important and urgent objectives laid down for the SEAC, many of them matters of intense political difficulty well beyond Japan. The first task for the British in SEAC was to rescue and repatriate their own prisoners-of-war with the limited shipping available. The second was to go beyond former British territories and deal with kindred problems in Indochina, Indonesia and Thailand. It was estimated that some 123,000 British and allied prisoners of war and 120,000 internees were located in Thailand, Indochina, Malaya, Singapore, Java and Sumatra (though the numbers fluctuated from time to time). Large numbers of prisoners of war were held in Japanese camps, and reports suggested that they had been subjected to inhumane, sadistic treatment. Anxiety over the fate of the POWs and determination to free them were important political issues, furthered by relatives and friends.[28]

These proved to be serious problems because there were acute shortages of shipping for the purpose of repatriating troops and distinct shortages of food for the area at large. This also affected the related task of disarming the Japanese troops who had surrendered, estimated at 630,000, and repatriating them. Repatriation of the Japanese dragged on for several years, and the armies on duty in Indonesia were not shipped back until the summer of 1947.[29]

Some concluding thoughts

The Asia-Pacific war of 1941–45, like all wars, ended in chaos and confusion. It ended with the surrender statement of the Japanese emperor on 15 August which was confirmed by the official ceremony on board the *Missouri* on 2 September for signing the general surrender. Although the allied victory in Europe had had a long gestation period, there had been confusion. The allied victory over Japan came upon those involved like a thunderbolt; and, despite the simplicities of the surrender ceremony, the confusion was widespread.

It has been the argument of this chapter that Britain had a major role at the end of the war in Asia and a much more modest role in the ending of the separate war in the Pacific. Her role in Southeast Asia after August 1945 was thrust upon her by the decision of allied military authorities. It was widely recognized that Britain in 1945 was an imperial power in decline in the sense that her resources no longer allowed her to control a global empire. But she still had a strong voice in world affairs and wanted to continue to exert an influence in Asian affairs when peace conferences took place. By reason of her being the only military power in the Southeast Asian region in 1945, she was instantaneously confronted by the problems created by the transformation of empire or decolonization. She saw her prime task as being to deal with the Japanese armies, and to re-establish law and order and restore stability.

Britain's prestige had been badly dented by the Japanese since 1941; and Mountbatten wrote to the Foreign Secretary in 1944 that the failure of Britain to reconquer at least one colony would 'irretrievably impair our prestige in the Far East'.[30] That reconquest did not take place in the form that Mountbatten envisaged. Yet Britain, like Mountbatten, squared up to the new situation in which she was cast in these territories : reform, independence and decolonization.

Notes

1. Useful general accounts are given in Goto Kenichi, *Kindai Nihon to Tonan Ajia* (Tokyo: Iwanami, 1995); I.C.B. Dear (ed.), *Oxford Companion to the Second World War* (Oxford: University Press, 1995); Hosoya Chihiro et al., *Taiheiyo senso* (Tokyo: Todai shuppankai, 1993); S.W. Kirby, *War against Japan*, 5 vols. (London: HMSO, 1957–69). On the failure of British defence policy, see Peter Lowe, *Great Britain and the Origins of the Pacific War* (Oxford: Clarendon, 1977); Paul Haggie, *Britannia at Bay* (Oxford: Clarendon, 1981); Antony Best, *Britain, Japan and Pearl Harbor: Avoiding War in East Asia, 1936–41* (London: Routledge, 1995); Nicholas Tarling, *Britain, Southeast Asia and the Onset of the Pacific War* (Cambridge: Cambridge University Press, 1996); Ian Cowman, *Dominion or Decline: Anglo-American Naval Relations in the Pacific, 1937–41* (Oxford: Berg, 1996).
2. Christopher Thorne, *Allies of a Kind: The United States, Britain and the War against Japan, 1941–5* (Oxford: Oxford University Press, 1978).
3. Andrew Gilchrist, *Malaya, 1941: Fall of a Fighting Empire* (London: Hale, 1992); Richard Aldrich, *Key to the South: Britain, the United States and Thailand during the Approach of the Pacific War, 1929–42* (Kuala Lumpur:

Oxford University Press, 1993); Alfred Duff Cooper, *Old Men Forget* (London: Hart-Davis, 1953).
4. Ong Chitchung, *Operation Matador: Britain's War Plans against the Japanese, 1918–41* (Singapore: Times Academic Press, 1997); S. Woodburn Kirby, *Singapore: The Chain of Disaster* (London: Cassell, 1971); Louis Allen, *Singapore, 1941–2* (London: Davis-Poynter, 1977).
5. Kirby, *War against Japan*, vol. V; John Ehrman, *Grand Strategy*, vol. VI (London: HMSO, 1956); Louis Allen, *Burma: The Longest War, 1941–5* (London: Dent, 1984).
6. On Stilwell, see Barbara Tuchman, *Sand against Wind: Stilwell and the American Experience of China, 1911–45* (London: Macmillan, 1970), chs 11–12; Wesley M. Bagby, *Eagle-Dragon Alliance: America's Relations with China in World War II* (Newark: University of Delaware, 1992).
7. On Wingate, see Derek Tulloch, *Wingate in Peace and War* (London: Macdonald, 1972); Trevor Royle, *Orde Wingate* (London: Weidenfeld, 1995).
8. On the Moscow conference, see Keith Sainsbury, *The Turning Point: Roosevelt, Stalin, Churchill and Chiang Kai-shek, 1943, The Moscow, Cairo and Tehran Conferences* (Oxford: Oxford University Press, 1985), pp. 110, 241–2.
9. Harriman to Roosevelt, 17 October 1944 in *Foreign Relations of the United States, 1945, The Conferences at Malta and Yalta*, pp. 370–1. (hereafter *FRUS*).
10. On the Yalta conference, see David Dilks (ed.), *The Diaries of Sir Alexander Cadogan, 1938–45* (London: Cassell, 1971), p. 715; Peter Dennis, '*Troubled days of peace': Mountbatten and Southeast Asia Command, 1945–6* (Manchester: University Press, 1987).
11. Philip Ziegler, *Mountbatten: the Official Biography* (London: Collins, 1985), pp. 216–22. Also Ziegler, *Personal Diary of Admiral the Lord Louis Mountbatten, 1943–6* (London: Collins, 1988).
12. Ziegler, *Mountbatten*, pp. 290–2. *The Times*, 3 May 1945. On SEAC, see the *Report to the Combined Chiefs of Staff by SACSEA, 1943–5* (New York: Philosophical Library, 1951).
13. Dennis, *Troubled days of peace*, p. 5; Ziegler, *Mountbatten*, pp. 296–7.
14. A.J. Marder, M. Jacobsen and J. Horsfield, *Old Friends, New Enemies: Royal Navy and Imperial Japanese Navy*, vol. II, 'The Pacific War, 1942–5' (Oxford: Clarendon, 1990), p. 344ff; R. Humble, *Fraser of North Cape* (London: Routledge, 1983), p. 246; Ministry of Defence (Navy), *War with Japan*, vols IV–V (London: HMSO, 1995–8).
15. Ian Nish, 'British Commonwealth and the Occupation of Japan', in *International Studies* (STICERD, LSE), 83/78, pp. 69ff.
16. Katharine Sansom, *Sir George Sansom and Japan* (Tallahassee: Diplomatic Press, 1972), pp. 139–40; Roger Buckley, *Occupation Diplomacy: Britain, the United States and Japan, 1945–52* (Cambridge: Cambridge University Press, 1982), pp. 10–13.
17. Thorne, *Allies of a Kind*, p. 531fn.
18. Buckley, *Occupation Diplomacy*, p. 13.
19. Nish, foreword to Kiyoko Takeda, *The Dual Image of the Japanese Emperor* (London: Macmillan, 1988), p. xii.
20. R. Bullen and M.E. Pelly (eds), *Documents on British Policy Overseas*, first series, vol. I (London: HMSO, 1984), no. 304, note 4 (hereafter *DBPO*).
21. Summarized note of conversation between Churchill and Stalin, 18 July 1945 in *DBPO*, I(i), no. 181.

22. Churchill to Stimson, 18 July 1945, enclosing aide-mémoire of conversation between Roosevelt and Churchill, Hyde Park, 18 September 1944 in *FRUS, The Conference at Berlin (Potsdam), 1945*, II, no. 1306, pp. 1370–1
23. Thorne, *Allies of a Kind*, pp. 533–4.
24. 'Terauchi Hisaichi', in Dear (ed.), *Oxford Companion*, pp. 1105–6; E. Bruce Reynolds, *Thailand and Japan's Southern Advance, 1940–5* (London: Macmillan, 1994), pp. 223–7; Tillman Remme, *Britain and Regional Cooperation in South-East Asia, 1945–9* (London: Routledge, 1995), pp. 28–9.
25. Quoted in Ziegler, *Mountbatten*, p. 302.
26. Remme, *Britain and Regional Cooperation*, pp. 29–33; F.S.V. Donnison, *British Military Administration in the Far East, 1943–6* (London: HMSO, 1956), chs 3 and 22.
27. Dening to Sterndale-Bennett, 2 Aug. 1945 in *DBPO*, I/i, no. 599
28. Donnison, *British Military Administration*, pp. 283–5; Dear, *Oxford Companion*
29. Goto Kenichi, *Returning to Asia: Japan-Indonesia Relations, 1930s–1942* (Tokyo: Ryukei Shyosha, 1997); Goto in Hosoya et al., *Taiheiyo senso*, p. 486ff; Oba Sadao, *Java haisen yokuryu nisshi, 1946–7* (Tokyo: Ryukei Shyosha, 1996).
30. Mountbatten to Eden, 10 October 1944, quoted in Ziegler, *Mountbatten*, p. 282.

7
British Prisoners of War of the Japanese, 1941–45

Sybilla Jane Flower

The first British servicemen to be captured by the Japanese, only hours after the outbreak of hostilities on 8 December 1941, were the few survivors of the gunboat HMS *Peterel* sunk at Shanghai, and a British Army officer seized on the airfield at Kota Bahru (northeast Malaysia). By the end of Japan's 'Hundred Days' there were approximately 67,000 British prisoners of war in Japanese hands.[1] Of this number over 40,000 entered captivity after the surrender of Singapore, the remainder were taken principally in Hong Kong, the Dutch East Indies and at the Battle of the Java Sea. During the course of the war, their number came to include participants in the Burma Campaign, aircrews, naval personnel and members of the Special Forces. Their dispersal began within weeks of capture, drafted as labour forces to Japan and to the Japanese-occupied territories, and in 1945 British POWs were recovered from all over the Asia-Pacific region – from the Tenasserim peninsula to Hokkaido, from the Celebes to the edge of the Gobi Desert.

More than 30,000 British POWs (drawn from camps in Singapore, Kuala Lumpur and the Dutch East Indies) were employed on the building of the Thailand–Burma Railway. The evidence concerning the conditions in which they laboured on this project was a prominent feature of the case for the Prosecution at the International Military Tribunal for the Far East (the Tokyo War Crimes Trial). Their story, since familiarized in book and film, has overshadowed the experiences of other British POWs who worked in equally harrowing circumstances in the mines, steelworks, docks and factories of Japan, on the railway built between Moearo and Pakanbaroe in Sumatra (Indonesia), in the copper mine at Kinkaseki (now Quinkashee) in Formosa (Taiwan), on coral islands in the Moluccas, on the Mergui Road and elsewhere. The manner in which some met their deaths is only now being revealed from newly released documents which detail investigations in the immediate postwar period. These throw light on the fate, for instance, of 500 men of the Royal Artillery who perished on Ballale Island (south of Bougainville) and the POWs who were held in the camp at Sandakan in British North Borneo (Sabah) and either died during forced marches (the Sandakan 'Death Marches') or were eliminated.

Attitudes to the act of surrender

Nothing in the Japanese military or naval code had prepared their invasion forces for the surrender of fighting men. The combatant's code issued on 8 January 1941 by the Army Ministry stated that a soldier should not survive to suffer the dishonour of capture. To the British servicemen, no personal sense of shame accompanied the act of surrender on the battlefield or indeed elsewhere; and care of a wounded comrade was a basic tenet of service life.

Until the invasion of Hong Kong, little had been anticipated about the manner in which the Japanese would treat white surrendered personnel and prisoners of war. But the policy towards both soon became apparent. In tracing the routes of three infantry regiments of the 38th Division which invaded Hong Kong Island, that of the 229th Regiment (Tanaka) which landed at Shaukiwan on the night of 18–19 December 1941, 'was littered with corpses of murdered men, men bound, then bayoneted or shot'. And a similar examination of the movements of the 228th Regiment (Doi) and the 230th (Shoji) provided similar evidence: 'at San Wai, the Salesian Mission, Eucliffe and Stanley Gap, the men were first questioned and searched and then executed. Bodies were found all along the line of march with their hands tied behind them.... There is ... every evidence of a set policy to dispose of prisoners'.[2] At his trial in 1948 the commander of 38th Infantry Group, Lieutenant General Ito Takeo, clarified this issue. Once the invasion had begun he had not expected 'any tough resistance'. Army orders, he explained, stipulated that POWs were to be sent immediately to divisional headquarters 'only for the purpose of information'. But, Ito added, 'in the Hong Kong operation there was not much need for information once the operation had commenced'.[3]

The atrocities against surrendered personnel and prisoners of war occurred wherever Japanese fighting troops were in action. At the Mulo

School in Palembang at the end of March 1942, an Australian nursing sister, Vivian Bullwinkel, was able to give Air Commodore C.O.F. Modin, RAF, an account of the massacre of 21 Australian nurses on 16 February, of which group she was the only survivor, and the fate of 15 or 20 British servicemen who were dispatched by bayonet within earshot of the nurses by the same Japanese patrol.[4] In the long Burma campaigns where, as Louis Allen commented, 'It was often better to be killed outright than to be taken prisoner',[5] the knowledge of Japanese behaviour in the field had a significant effect on the British and Indian Armies. A senior staff officer of the 14th Army cited as one explanation of the low morale of the troops in the first Burma campaign, 'the current stories and rumours, most of them unfortunately only too accurate, on the subject of Japanese brutalities to wounded and prisoners of war'.[6]

Interrogation of POWs

POWs taken in the field were assessed by the infantry officers into whose hands they fell. As the taking of POWs in such numbers had not been anticipated, little provision appears to have been made for their interrogation other than by the divisional staff officers in charge of intelligence. Reference has already been made to the opinion of Lieutenant General Ito Takeo that the interrogation of POWs was unnecessary during the invasion of Hong Kong. There the fighting was over in 17 days and advance knowledge of defensive positions was thorough and accurate. In Malaya, circumstances were different. The greatest need was for regular information on troop positions and the most up-to-date intelligence about the defences of Singapore. But many of the officers of the Indian Army captured in the early fighting had never been to the island and had difficulty convincing the Japanese staff officers that their ignorance was genuine. On the other hand, the officer caught at Kota Bahru, Captain J.C. Close, 'Capture No. 1', commanded an anti-aircraft battery of the Hong Kong and Singapore Royal Artillery and his severe interrogation at the hands of the *kenpei-tai* at the headquarters of the Southern Expeditionary Army in Saigon lasted until after the surrender of Singapore.[7] Other POWs who endured similar treatment at Saigon included the crew of a Blenheim of 60 Squadron, RAF, shot down on 9 December during a bombing raid on the Japanese invasion force at Singora, and four officers of the RAF from Hong Kong, including Wing Commander H.G. Sullivan, senior officer at Kai Tak.

In Java, where there was a concentration of senior officers of the RAF, Air Commodore W.E. Staton was interrogated at Japanese headquarters in Bandoeng in front of a large map, and severe efforts were made to extract information.[8] The British commandant at the airfield camp at Tasikmalaja, Wing Commander E.B. Steedman, was ordered in 1942 to hand to aircraft pilots a form for them to complete. The questions ranged widely over RAF practice from reactions to high altitude flying, to diet and to whether RAF pilots were given drugs or injections before flights. When Steedman refused categorically to distribute the forms, he was removed from the camp.[9] Postwar investigations concluded he had died under interrogation. The pilots at Semarang when posed similar questions realised that a matter of particular interest to the Japanese was the ability to pull out of a long vertical dive without losing consciousness.[10]

Those who experienced the fighting in Hong Kong, Malaya, the Netherlands East Indies and Burma began their lives as POWs with no illusions about the extent of the Japanese capacity for mercy on a fallen foe; others who had not set eyes on a Japanese before surrender were more sanguine. In the shocked aftermath of the discovery of what had occurred in Hong Kong, efforts were made by the Western governments to censor the details in an attempt to maintain morale; these failed, and the Foreign Secretary Anthony Eden made a candid statement to the British House of Commons on 10 March. *The Times* commented, 'Rarely has any Minister of the Crown had to make ... a statement more terrible'.[11] Pressure was brought on the Japanese to make their position clear as regards adherence to the provisions of the Geneva Convention, which Japan had signed but never ratified.[12]

Japanese policy on POWs

The surrender of so many POWs presented the Japanese with a dilemma. There was the international problem of how to present their capture and subsequent treatment to the Allies, and the practical problem of how to confine them. In Tokyo two bureaux were set up to handle matters concerning POWs: the POW Information Bureau, established in December 1941, was intended to act as a registry and clearing-house in line with the requirements of Article 77 of the Geneva Convention; and the POW Control Bureau, formed at the end of March 1942 by the Army Ministry, had charge of administrative matters relating to POWs.[13] Until the end of the war every detail relating to the housing, employment, feeding and transport of POWs was regulated from the Control Bureau; but from the beginning of 1944 much responsibility was devolved upon the commanders in each area who were merely obliged to submit reports to the bureau.[14] The two bureaux appeared to be separate, but were in fact run by the same personnel, most of whom were drawn from the retired list of the Army.

The advantages to be derived from holding so many POWs were quickly assessed by the Army Ministry. These were two-fold: the potential to acquire information on every aspect of Allied warfare by interrogation; and the possession of a substantial pool of labour which could be incorporated *en bloc* into the Japanese war machine. General Tojo Hideki, the Prime Minister, suggested a third possible benefit when the question of using the POWs for forced labour was discussed. Tojo described the propaganda value of using white POWs in the occupied territories in a way which he believed would help banish any sense of racial inferiority among the people, and thereby instil 'a feeling of trust towards Japan'.[15]

Both Tojo and Lieutenant General Uemura Mikio, first director of the Control Bureau, took a hard line on the subject of POWs, the latter writing, 'In the war with Russia, we gave them excellent treatment in order to gain recognition as a civilized country. To-day such need no longer applies'.[16] At a meeting in Tokyo on 7 and 8 July 1942 the senior officers selected to run the POW administrations were given their orders. Tojo's address to them insisted that the POWs should not remain idle 'even for a single day, so as to utilize most effectively their manpower and technical ability for the expansion of our industries and to contribute to the execution of the great East Asia War'.[17] The administrations appointed to manage the POWs in each area did not take over until August 1942 (except in Hong Kong where one was largely in place by January). Thus the majority of POWs were in the hands of fighting troops for the first six months and treatment varied, some POWs enjoying relatively benign conditions. But the advent of the administrations with their strict Army Ministry instructions reflecting the attitudes of Tojo and Uemura inaugurated uniformly harsh regimes.

Changi military camp, Singapore

Most British POWs began their captivity on 17–18 February 1942 in Changi Military Camp in the northeast corner of Singapore island, formerly the cantonment of the British garrison. Here Lieutenant

General A.E. Percival (GOC Malaya Command) and Major General C.A. Callaghan, the Australian commander, organized the POWs into six areas in each of which the senior officer had a more or less peacetime staff organization. For the first few weeks Changi was commanded by Lieutenant Colonel Sugita Ichiji, intelligence chief of the 25th Army. An early order directed all officers to take down insignia of rank and wear only one star on the left breast. On 19 February Sugita read to the senior POW officers a special Order of the Day issued by Lieutenant General Yamashita Tomoyuki which insisted that any question posed by the Japanese must be answered 'without evasion' and that opposition to this demand would not be tolerated.[18] Thereafter interrogations were carried out, particularly directed at identifying skilled technicians, artificers, radio specialists and engineers, those with knowledge of signals and cyphers, also radio announcers and journalists. On 23 March further Japanese orders were issued including threats of punishment 'without mercy' and the cutting of rations.[19]

As the Japanese were imposing their rule on the camp the POWs had to contend with serious health problems. When they arrived there were present all the predisposing factors for a major epidemic of dysentery: low morale, inertia, gross overcrowding, swarms of flies, lack of water and no sewerage system. Within two days the outbreak had begun; it spread rapidly and reached its peak in March when 1,196 cases were admitted to hospital in one week.[20] From April the symptoms of nutritional deficiencies became apparent, a distressing feature of POW existence throughout the captivity.

In August 1942 POWs at Changi of the rank of colonel and above were removed to Formosa leaving Lieutenant Colonel E.B. Holmes (1st Bn, Manchester Regiment) and Lieutenant Colonel F.G. Galleghan (2/30th Bn, Australian Imperial Force) in command of the British and the Australians. On 30 August the two were informed by the new GOC POW Camps, Malaya, Major General Fukui Shinpei, that all POWs were to be given 'an opportunity' to sign a pledge not to escape. Holmes pointed out that 'by the laws and usages of war' a POW cannot be required by the power holding him to give his parole.[21] Lieutenant Okasaki Akira, Fukui's staff officer, quoted to Holmes the section of the Hague Convention (1907), ratified by Japan, which, Okasaki explained, summarized the position of the Imperial Japanese Army (IJA) with regard to the POWs: 'POWs shall be subject to the laws, regulations and orders in force in the army of the state in the power of which they are. Any act of insubordination justifies the adoption towards them of such measures of severity as may be considered necessary'.[22]

'Such measures of severity' included the execution in the presence of Holmes and others on the following day of four POWs (two British and two Australian) who, the Japanese claimed, had attempted to escape. The Japanese, informed by Holmes that the POWs would not sign, ordered the 15,400 POWs then in Changi to move to the Australian area, Selarang, where they were packed into the seven barrack blocks, in the square and on the roofs. Negotiations continued for three days and, on Fukui's written order to sign, Holmes agreed to do so under duress. Faced with the prospect of an epidemic and the Japanese threat that the sick would be brought in from the hospital, Holmes had no other option but to comply.

Confrontations over the signing of the pledges occurred in most Japanese POW camps. The Japanese reason for forcing the issue had been made clear to the officers of the new POW administrations gathered on 7–8 July at the conference in Tokyo: manpower to police the POWs would be limited, and the POWs would be widely dispersed, working in open conditions in ports, on road and rail construction, on airfields and in mines and factories.[23] The prisoners' signatures were obtained under duress and their declaration was therefore invalid: their duty, clearly defined in British service law, was to escape where possible. Percival at Changi and later senior British officers in camps throughout the Asia-Pacific region warned POWs not to escape unless the attempt stood a reasonable chance of success. In most areas this chance was nil.

Apart from the threat of execution, the most powerful weapon the Japanese had in controlling POWs was the rationing or withholding of food. Lieutenant General Percival wrote: 'Their trump card, of course, was always food'.[24] On this point Brigadier K.S. Torrance commented: 'There is little doubt that the food issued was very carefully calculated, and that by persons with some scientific dietetic knowledge, to just maintain life at a very low energy level'.[25] Another method of control was developed when the Japanese became aware of the fundamental nature of the POWs' sense of obligation towards the sick and the wounded. Repeatedly, throughout the captivity, the sick were used by the Japanese as bargaining counters, or as hostages to good behaviour.

The POWs were forced to accept that the letter and the spirit of the conventions formulated in 1907 and 1929 would offer no protection. If the Japanese government chose to ignore the fact that the forced labour carried out by POWs in the Asia-Pacific region to further the Japanese war effort was, by international standards, unacceptable, it was optimistic to expect that the average Japanese captor would abide by conventions unknown to him. In Java, Major General

H.D.W. Sitwell succeeded in incorporating into the surrender terms agreed between the Japanese and the Allied commanders, a clause which stated that the POWs would be treated according to the Geneva Convention. At his interrogation Sitwell was informed crisply by a staff officer who had attended these negotiations, 'Japan – as Great Britain – only stuck to the Geneva Convention when it suited her'.[26]

Japanese and officer POWs

The Japanese required the officer POWs to run the camps and to keep order; thus the majority of officers and men were kept together until the last year of the war, except in Hong Kong, Borneo and Java where security dictated otherwise. The POWs' officer status, within limitations, was accepted by the Japanese with the result that much better provision was made for them than for the men. When officers and men were separated at Sham Shui Po Camp in Hong Kong, the 300 officers were sent into their new camp accompanied by 180 batmen even though these officers had been sent there as a punishment. At the Officers' Camp formed early in 1945 at Kanchanaburi in Thailand when the threat of an Allied invasion necessitated the strictest security, the 3,000 officers, confined in close quarters, were allowed a staff of 200 to carry out the menial tasks such as latrine digging and fetching water.

Though the decision to pay officers in August 1942 at IJA rates in the appropriate local currency clearly reflected Article 23 of the Geneva Convention which directed that 'officers ... who are prisoners of war shall receive from the detaining Power the same pay as officers of corresponding rank in the armed forces of that Power', the actual amount handed over was only a fraction of their entitlement. But the possession of these legitimate Japanese funds, however meagre, gave the officers a degree of economic freedom which enabled them to buy extra food or assist in the funding of camp hospitals. The men, on the other hand, were paid a pittance, and this only if they worked. To remain alive extra money could be earned from camp duties, but it was more often derived from trading, both licit and illicit, the latter inevitably running the risk of discovery and punishment by beating, burning or even death.

Many of the POW officers – camp commanders, medical officers, interpreters, adjutants and junior officers in charge of work parties – bore onerous and exhausting responsibilities in that every aspect of life and labour had to be negotiated and renegotiated on a daily basis. The medical officers were required to improvise a primitive form of medicine with the minimum of supplies, and partake in the daily tragedy enacted in the formation of the labour force. Although the younger British officers on the Thailand–Burma Railway were forced to work on the track (many at the point of bayonet or machine-gun), the majority of officer POWs in Japanese hands were not required to carry out hard manual labour. Instead, the officers were engaged in camp administration and duties such as hut-building and repairing, grave and latrine-digging, and the cultivation of vegetables and livestock.

Very few POWs had any knowledge of the Japanese language and of the customs and manners of Japan; the Japanese themselves provided English speaking interpreters only to their senior officers. In Singapore most of the expert linguists were evacuated just before the surrender, leaving behind a small group of men most of whom had learnt their Japanese in commerce, in the Christian missions or as children brought up in Japan. The interpreter's task was an unenviable one as he was inevitably the first casualty of Japanese, Korean or Formosan rage. Of necessity, communication was carried out in the smaller camps and in the work parties in the lingua franca of captivity – a mixture of languages and signs – with its limitless scope for misunderstanding. Generally speaking, a refusal to learn Japanese, other than the numerals and the most basic commands, became a symbol of POW defiance.

The Japanese often overestimated the ability of the POW officers to maintain control, particularly from 1943 onwards when some units had been divided and subdivided. Lieutenant Colonel C.R. Holmes described his difficulties as the senior British officer at the airfield camp of Pangkalin Balai, near Palembang, Sumatra.[27] Primarily a Dutch camp, the British numbered approximately 400, but these were men of mixed provenance – Royal Navy, Merchant Navy, Army, Royal Air Force – an impossible mixture to regulate in a camp where anarchy reigned through the abdication of all responsibility by the Japanese camp commandant, Captain Hojo Kanemitsu, to his subordinates, including the Korean guards. The degree of perversity among some POWs disenchanted with their officers surprised the Japanese whose own system would not have tolerated such behaviour. But the options available to senior POWs to discipline the men was strictly limited; courts martial were held on occasions with permission of the IJA, but it was considered unacceptable to hand over an errant POW to the Japanese for punishment.

In many areas a system of successful camp government gradually evolved, forged by men of adaptability, firmness and patience, in contrast to those whose tendency was to acquiesce at once, or to say 'No' to anything demanded by the Japanese, an action which was seldom helpful, caused the captors loss of face and negated any chance of improvement in conditions. In some labour forces senior officers evolved policies of 'limited co-operation' with the Japanese working with realism and imagination within the extreme limitations of their circumstances. It was clearly important for the running of a camp that there should be some rapport between the Japanese commandant and the senior POW officer.

Japanese POW administrations

Many of the Japanese officers in the POW administrations had been recalled from the reserve or from retirement; some of the junior officers and NCOs seconded had patently failed for one reason or another to advance in fighting units. Alcoholism was a common fault, exacerbated no doubt by the unpleasing task of managing POWs. As camp guards the Japanese raised two corps of youths in Korea and Formosa whose lowly rank as civilian auxiliaries of the IJA was senior only to the POWs. The ability or willingness of the Japanese camp staff to control these guards became a major factor and excesses were to be expected when, as in some camps, these guards were in sole charge. Initially some of the senior Japanese officers were not unreasonable. The POW administration in Sumatra was commanded at first by a major of the Matsudaira family; by 1944, Captain Hachisuka Kunifusa had taken over. Revealing no gentlemanly qualities to the POWs, he took no interest in them, refused to permit the senior British officer to approach him and allowed the Korean guards to terrorize the camp at will.

The example of Palembang mirrors the brutalization of many of the POW administrations. The corruption and racketeering among the Japanese camp staff and the guards who had access to stores and Red Cross issues became steadily more blatant as local supplies became scarcer and inflation took hold. Although Colonel Nakamura Shigeo, head of the POW administration in Thailand, believed that his dismissal from that posting in July 1944 was due to resentment at his clumsy handling of an incident in which a Japanese officer had ordered the shooting of a POW with cholera, the senior British officers were convinced that the outrageous scale of his profiteering was at least a contributory factor.[28]

Reference has been made to the fact that the senior officers were separated, leaving the POWs in the charge of their unit commanders. In removing these men the Japanese both eliminated the need to negotiate with any officers other than those in direct command of labour, and nullified possible threats to security in the way of organized resistance. Accordingly, officers above the rank of colonel, senior civilians and their staff, including Lieutenant General Percival, Sir Shenton Thomas (Governor of Singapore), Major General B.W. Key, Brigadier Torrance and Air Commodore Modin, left Singapore on 20 August 1942, in the hold of a Japanese transport, *Kanjong Maru*. Nothwithstanding their status before captivity, they were subjected to the most distressing treatment. After 11 days of infernal conditions they disembarked at the port of Takau in southern Formosa. Given no time to recover from the journey, 'bearded, unkempt, weary and thoroughly disreputable',[29] carrying hand baggage and with the stronger men assisting those who were too weak to walk unaided, the party was marched four abreast through the streets for over three miles to a transit camp at Heito. Dense crowds including schoolchildren had been marshalled to line the route. Very few of the Formosans showed open hostility; a few laughed. Brigadier Torrance was forcibly reminded of a scene from classical antiquity, 'a Roman triumph'.[30]

The dispersal of POWs throughout the Asia-Pacific region entailed long journeys in the holds of Japanese transports, such as the *Kanjong Maru*, with no consideration given to their welfare or safety. The ships were unmarked, and many of them sailed in convoys carrying troops and munitions. It has been estimated that more than 68,000 Allied POWs were carried in these 'hell-ships' in the period 1942–45, of whom over 22,000 died after the ships were attacked and sunk by planes and submarines.[31] Some of the ships were scarcely seaworthy. The *Maros Maru*, a ferry boat of about 500 tons, left Ambon island on a voyage to Java on 17 September 1944 and was delayed in the Makassar roads for 40 days because of mechanical trouble, not arriving until 23 November at Sourabaya. The result was the death of 305 of the 638 POWs, including some who died on deck of dehydration within sight of the Japanese and Koreans bathing and washing their clothes.[32]

The greatest British tragedy was the loss of the *Lisbon Maru* which left Hong Kong for Japan on 27 September 1942, with 1,816 POWs on board, over 750 Japanese troops and a cargo of bombs, detonators and petrol. After being torpedoed by an American submarine, the Japanese ordered the POWs into the holds, put on the hatches and fastened tarpaulins over them in an attempt to cut off the supply of air.

160 Sybilla Jane Flower

Eventually the POWs were able to fight their way out, to discover that the ship had already been abandoned. Some of the POWs were rescued, others in the water were shot at by the Japanese: the death toll was 846.[33]

Hong Kong

The history of the POWs in Hong Kong is to a large extent determined by the links – geographical and political – with China. As a neutral enclave during the Sino-Japanese war, Hong Kong harboured by the end of 1941 numerous undercover bureaux, some loosely controlled from Chungking, others working on their own. The POWs who went into captivity included men who had lived and worked in Hong Kong and who, because of their enlistment in the Volunteer Forces, went into captivity as POWs rather than as civilian internees. Some senior British civilians, including officials of the Hong Kong and Shanghai Bank and the medical profession, remained 'free' on parole until 1943 and beyond, as the bankers were required to sign the Japanese 'duress' banknotes and the doctors were needed to work in the city hospitals. There was thus far more opportunity for productive collusion in Hong Kong between POWs and outside sources than, for example, in the POW camp at Changi.

At the end of December 1941, the POWs in Hong Kong were assembled at Sham Shui Po Barracks, three miles north of Kowloon which, although a hutted camp, was totally inadequate in size to house the initial arrivals who numbered 8,000. The escape attempts began at once. On 9 January, Lieutenant Colonel L.T. Ride, the Australian-born commanding officer of the Hong Kong Field Ambulance, left with three other POWs, arriving at Waichow on 18 January, from whence Ride journeyed on to Chungking. Here Ride formulated the proposals which led to the foundation of the British Army Aid Group (BAAG) which successfully infiltrated into the camps in Hong Kong for a short period between 1942 and early 1943, supplies of medicine, information and materials to aid escape.[34]

But it was not aid for escapes that the average POW was in need of in 1942; morale was at a low ebb, and a further infliction of collective punishment could not be contemplated. This state of affairs did not prevent another party of POWs, led by Lieutenant J.D. Clague, from leaving Sham Shui Po on 11 April, thereby increasing the Japanese fear of a mass outbreak. Their reaction was to take punitive action against the officers, moving them all at the end of that month, except a selected handful kept behind to administer Sham Shui Po, to a camp in Argyle Street, Hong Kong, where their rations were reduced to the minimum required to sustain life. From Sham Shui Po work parties were sent to clear up war damage and repair the airfield at Kai Tak. The Japanese soon began to raid the camp for labour to send to Japan; between September 1942 and April 1944, a total of 4,800 POWs left Sham Shui Po for labour camps in Tokyo, Yokohama, Kobe, Osaka and other destinations.[35]

In May 1944, those officers who had not been sent to Japan were returned from Argyle Street to Sham Shui Po, but to an area separated from the men. The departure of these officers had occasioned hardship in the men's camp, particularly during a diphtheria epidemic in late 1942, because their funds had earlier enabled the camp to buy extra medical supplies and food. Furthermore, the men at Sham Shui Po were at a tragic disadvantage because of the presence as British camp commander of Major Cecil Boon (Royal Army Service Corps), who is alleged to have collaborated with the Japanese. It seemed obvious to the POWs that he had come to an understanding with the senior Japanese officer, Colonel Tokunaga Isao; and they were only too well acquainted with the major's defeatist sentiments and admiration for Japan, as well as his positioning of spies in the work parties, which rendered the chances of trading most hazardous.[36] Every effort made by the medical officer, Major T.S. Ashton-Rose (Indian Medical Service), to improve conditions was sabotaged.[37] The BAAG discovered that Boon had written to Tokunaga after the departure of the first and second drafts of POWs to Japan (in 1942), informing him that the camp had been purged of 'undesirable' elements and that 'he was 100% satisfied'.[38]

It was Wing Commander Sullivan's view that possibly the worst feature of the Hong Kong camps was 'the complete lack of interest, amounting to criminal neglect' shown by Captain Saito Shunkichi, the medical officer in charge.[39] Saito had graduated in 1940 from the Kyoto Prefecture Medical College, but his plans for a career were interrupted by military service. He stated (as did other medical officers attached to POW administrations) that he had general medical duties on the Japanese side but that, as far as the POWs were concerned, he was required only 'to assist the Camp Commandant concerning sanitation'.[40] Saito did not consider that his duties extended to preserving the health of the POWs, an attitude clearly shared by his superiors and manifested in their refusal to accept the assistance offered by the International Committee of the Red Cross (ICRC).

The Japanese recognized officially only three delegations of the ICRC during the Pacific war: those of Tokyo, Shanghai and Hong Kong.[41] The others were refused accreditation on the grounds that they lay within zones of military operations; accordingly, the POW Information Bureau in Tokyo handed over to the Allies full details of the POWs they were holding in, for instance, Hong Kong, but refused to do so in respect of the POWs in areas such as Thailand, Singapore and Borneo, where the receipt of such information would be useful for strategic planning. The ICRC made numerous, but unsuccessful, attempts to persuade the Japanese government to recognize the delegates appointed, before the occupation, in Singapore, Java, Sumatra and Borneo, eventually concluding that the elderly officers of the POW Information Bureau 'distrusted' foreigners.[42] But it is clear that this distrust was rooted in the conviction that the ICRC was an instrument of espionage. In December 1943, the ICRC delegate in Borneo, Dr Carl Matthäus Vischer, a medical missionary, was executed with his wife and others, charged with conspiracy against the Japanese government.[43] The Japanese were, on the other hand, prepared to use the ICRC for propaganda purposes, such as the orchestrated publicity surrounding the carefully arranged 'show' POW camp at Zentsuji, on the island of Shikoku.

The severity of the experience of POWs in Japanese hands varied considerably. Whereas the POWs in Sham Shui Po endured famine, lack of medical attention, the unpredictability of their captors and a constant sense of apprehension over the formation of the overseas drafts (the loss of the *Lisbon Maru* was announced to the camp), their conditions compared favourably with, for example, those POWs engaged in hard manual labour in camps in Southeast Asia, or in the industries of Japan. Even on the Thailand–Burma Railway the POWs in the base camps or in one of the small specialist parties were far better off than those in the jungle camps during the worst months of 1943.

Thailand–Burma Railway

The Thailand–Burma Railway was planned by the Japanese to ensure an overland supply route for their forces in Burma. Strategically, this was the most important project in which POWs of the Japanese were involved, and its completion was given the highest priority. The starting point was Nong Pladuk, near Banpong on the Thai National Railway system, which linked Bangkok ultimately with Singapore, and the terminus was 260 miles north at Thanbyuzayat, about 30 miles from Moulmein. The terrain was virgin jungle, mountains rising to 1,300 feet above sea level, and rivers; the annual rainfall was among the heaviest in the world. A total of approximately 64,000 Allied POWs worked on the railway, including nearly 30,000 British who started at the Thai end in June 1942, reinforced in early 1943 by Australians and Dutch. On the Burma stretch the POWs were primarily Australians and Dutch. The two tracks met on 17 October 1943. There was also a substantial Asian labour force, which is difficult to quantify, but possibly numbered over 300,000. The Japanese construction team comprised initially a railway headquarters, two railway regiments – the 5th and 9th – each of four battalions, a railway materials depot and some ancillary units. Labour was specified from the outset as POW and Asian, the POWs being the responsibility of the POW administrations of either Burma, Thailand or Malaya and the Asian labourers coming under the direction of the engineers.

The failure of the POW administrations to provide equipment and supplies for the POWs aggravated their plight because the skilled engineers for whom they were sent out to work expected far more of them that they were in a position to carry out. This accounts in no small part for the ensuing mistreatment. The officers and men of the 9th Railway Regiment, who were responsible for the Thailand section of the railway, were commanded by Colonel Imai Itaru and most of them belonged either to the regular army or had been drafted in from the administrative or technical divisions of the Japan National Railways. Imai himself and all his company commanders were graduates in engineering, some from the most elite institutions, and among the technicians were those who would later play a role in the successful development of the *Shinkansen*. Imai, an ambitious officer whose men regarded him with a combination of awe and devotion, was deeply conscious of the importance attached to the completion of the railway by the highest authorities in Tokyo. Thus, when the construction began to fall behind schedule in 1943, his rallying call to the regiment contributed to the climate in which the worst excesses of the 'speedo' period took place when the POWs and Asian labourers in the jungle camps, including the sick, were driven out to work by the most inhumane means.

For most of the construction period the railway engineers had no formal jurisdiction within the POW camps which were the sole responsibility of the POW administration. There was constant but predictable friction between these two Japanese commands. Thus the POWs were the victims of, on the one hand, a random assemblage of elderly officers, misfits, arrogant adjutants and peasant guards who largely made up the administration responsible for the camps; and, on the other, the ambitious professionals with careers to further. The total manpower of the POW administration for the entire Burma–Thailand Railway at the start (August 1942) was only 40 officers, 85 NCOs and 1,280 Korean Guards which, given the distances and the number of camps, had the effect of devolving considerable authority on to individuals of lowly rank.[44] In June 1943 when conditions were at their worst, the headquarters of the Thailand POW administration in Kanchanaburi which had responsibility for camps up to the Burma border, consisted of only Colonel Nakamura who was then nearing 60 years of age, 10 officers, 15 NCOs and forty Korean guards, who were increased in number to 80 before the railway was completed in October.[45]

The medical section of the POW administration was negligible, and clearly reflected the Japanese disregard for physical frailty. Lieutenant Muraoka Shigeo, medical officer of the principal British group of POWs in the jungle camps (Group IV), had qualified as a doctor in 1935; but his job on the railway was, he said (echoing Captain Saito in Hong Kong), solely 'to forward opinions concerning the sanitary conditions'.[46] This neglect and maladministration of the POWs by the Japanese partially explains the tragedy enacted in Burma and Thailand in 1943: POWs were sent into the virgin jungle to build camps and to work during the monsoon season, equipped with neither adequate cooking pots nor medical supplies, provided only with axes, picks, hoes and shovels of the most primitive variety, and food which was barely edible.

But it would be wrong to include all the Japanese of the POW administration in this condemnation. There were a few Japanese who exercised restraint in their approach to the POWs. It is also fair to point out that, after the completion of the railway, drafts of younger, fitter POWs were sent to Japan and most of the remaining POWs in Thailand experienced over 12 months of comparatively reasonable conditions apart from the lack of food and medical supplies, but with freedom of association and some leisure to pursue intellectual interests. On the other hand, the Japanese used POWs as human shields to protect the railway installations round the base camps after the Allied bombing raids began in late 1944.

POWs in the islands

Much of the work carried out by POWs in Java and Sumatra was the repair and extension of airfields, or the loading of fuel and ammunition at the docks of Sourabaya and the port of Batavia. The drafts which left Java in April 1943 included two large British parties sent to construct airfields in the Molucca islands as part of a strategic plan to provide refuelling bases across the islands between the Indian Ocean and the Pacific.

Of these drafts, 1,700 British POWs were landed on 4 May in torrential rain on the island of Haruku, east of Ambon. No arrangements had been made by the Japanese for accommodation, feeding or medical care; the POWs found some rough huts, but efforts to establish a camp were delayed after five days when the POWs were organized into two shifts to start work on the airfield. Food for the entire camp on the first working day consisted of 20 1 lb cans of meat, a few vegetables and some ill-cooked rice which half filled each billycan.[47] There was no adequate supply of water. The Japanese officer, Captain Kurashima Hideichi, relinquished control to the camp staff, headed by Sergeant-Major Mori Masao and his Korean second, Kasayama Yoshikichi. The conditions and the brutality of these two rendered the situation by the end of May 'beyond human control',[48] causing work on the airfield to be temporarily suspended. Four months later, the senior British officer, Squadron Leader W.C. Pitts, RAF, could do little more than contemplate '[the] pitiable, emaciated, blinded, twisted, maggot-eaten wrecks of human beings ... giving up their staggering hold on human life'.[49] An appeal to Captain Shimada who made periodical visits from his base on Ambon, was turned down with the words: 'As a doctor I understand, but not as an officer'.[50]

It was probably Shimada (though no names are given in the official Japanese report) who arranged to have carried out on the POWs during the worst period at Haruku, a series of medical experiments, purportedly to discover means to combat deficiency disease. The experiments involved 18 British POWs including the medical officer, Flight Lieutenant F.A. Forbes, RAFVR, who received painful injections of coconut milk in varying doses, both sterilized and unsterilized, in their thighs, over the period 5–11 October 1943. The Japanese report indicates that the results were 'meagre'.[51] Whereas this report survives and Flight Lieutenant Forbes was able to furnish the British government with full details after the war, the experiments apparently carried out on British POWs from the camp at Mukden (Manchuria) are more difficult to determine as some of the evidence is circumstantial.[52] The diary of the senior British officer, Major Robert Peaty, RAOC, refers to tests and details the extent of the interest in the POWs by the senior medical figures in the IJA.[53]

The problems encountered by the Japanese in organizing a POW labour force in a remote zone of combat was described by Lieutenant Commander Ozaki Norihiko, the commanding officer of a naval construction unit sent in late November 1942 to build an airfield on Ballale Island.[54] Having arrived with only 800 labourers, Ozaki pressed his superiors for reinforcements. At the end of the year, without warning, a draft of 500 British POWs disembarked from a Japanese transport, watched with dismay by Ozaki because some were barely able to walk. As the POWs could be put to little more than gathering ballast from the beach, and with air raids intensifying, construction of the airfield fell behind schedule. With a rapid build-up of troops on the island, the atmosphere among the Japanese (and no doubt the POWs) became increasingly tense, with problems of supply worsening by the day. In the unhealthy climate, both Japanese and POWs fell ill; no funeral pyres could be lit because the smoke would attract Allied attention. Shortly after a major air raid in March which caused widespread casualties, Ozaki was notified of the imminent arrival of an Allied invasion force. In the 'extreme excitement' of that moment, Ozaki carried out the plan which had been drawn up by the garrison commander on the island in the event of such a threat, and ordered the execution of the remaining POWs.[55]

Lieutenant Commander Ozaki and the garrison commander on Ballale Island were forced to make a rapid decision about the fate of the POWs in the light of the intelligence presented to them (although there was, in fact, no Allied assault on the island at that point). The naval officers at the headquarters of the 23rd Special Naval Base Force at Makassar (South Celebes) had longer to formulate a policy towards the POWs who were captured in action in 1942, at a time when the Imperial Japanese Navy (IJN) rescued Allied naval personnel from stricken ships.

To quarter these POWs, a camp was established in 1942 under naval auspices in the infantry barracks at the naval base at Makassar, with branch camps at the airfield at Maros and at Pomolaa. Most of the POWs here were Dutch, but initially the camp housed 934 British naval personnel who, apart from a few merchant navy seamen, were survivors of *Exeter, Encounter, Stronghold, Anking* and the oil tanker, *Francol*. The IJN camp commandant entrusted the internal discipline of the camp and the formation of the work parties to Yoshida Tomonao, a seaman first class promoted in 1943 to petty officer. He was unsupervised, beginning his reign of terror in April 1942 by the maltreatment of POWs which resulted in broken arms and ribs, and continuing until

1945.[56] The senior naval officer, Lieutenant Commander G.T. Cooper, RN, reported: 'He ran the camp on a policy of fear with collective reprisals on the innocent and the sick'.[57] The work at Makassar was mostly of a military nature: loading and unloading ships, constructing foundations for anti-aircraft guns, making armaments which involved the powdering of lyddite by hand without any protective measures, and later building air-raid shelters. Medicines were issued in minute quantities and, after 1943, rations deteriorated, being sharply reduced in September 1944 – a reduction which was followed by a serious dysentery epidemic.

Captain Sakurai Yoshifumi, senior IJN physician at Makassar from November 1943 until the end of the war, was supplied with weekly data about the health of the POWs including analyses of the causes of death and regular requests for medical supplies; in the dysentery epidemic of late 1944 and early 1945, this information was passed to him on a daily basis. At a court martial held by the Dutch authorities in 1947, Sakurai did not deny his lack of interest in the POWs, and he agreed 'that a single word ... put in with the authorities at Naval HQ on behalf of the Ps.O.W. would have been sufficient to effect considerable improvement of their conditions'.[58]

Many of the POWs who were drafted to civilian companies found themselves at the mercy of two regimes. The 500 British POWs from Singapore who arrived at the copper mine at Kinkaseki (Quinkashee) in Formosa in November 1942, were in the awkward position of being under civilian foremen in the mine and IJA control in the camp, with the jurisdiction of the POW administration ending (at least through 1942 and 1943) at the mine entrance. The senior foreman were Japanese, the remainder Formosan; together they directed the forced labour gangs, consisting of POWs, Chinese transported from Shanghai and Hong Kong, and even some children. After the two-hour march to the mine, the POWs had to climb down about 1,000 steps to reach their work face, and walk along dangerous passages whose roofs were unstable. In some shafts there was an incessant drip of ice-cold caustic water: WO I J.O. Edwards, RCOS, who was one of the 60-odd POWs who worked at Kinkaseki for the whole period from 1942 until 1945, described to War Crimes Courts in 1946 the effect this water had as it ran into his eyes and onto his skin.[59] The heat in other shafts was so suffocating (temperatures of 184° F were recorded) that the men could work for short periods only before losing consciousness. The foremen did not hesitate to beat with hammers those they felt had not worked hard enough. The mining company (Nippon Kogyo) failed to provide boots and carbide for the lamps, thus forcing the POWs to work barefoot by the light of oil lamps.[60]

The Imperial Japanese Navy and POWs

There were instances as the war progressed of a POW's service role rendering him liable to harsher treatment, such as naval personnel, aircrews and members of the Special Forces. When in late 1943 an operation was planned by the Japanese South-west Area Fleet with the purpose of disrupting Allied communications in the Indian Ocean, specific orders were given to the naval officer commanding, Rear Admiral Sakonju Naomasa, that enemy ships should be captured if possible and the lives of only specified members of the crew saved for interrogation. The remainder were to be executed without delay. By eliminating most of the crew, the Japanese reasoned that they could avoid the threat posed by a large group of POWs on board a ship that was subsequently engaged in action, and the possibility of naval intelligence being disseminated by POWs in camps to enemy agents.

Most of the Allied naval officers captured during the Pacific War were taken to the interrogation camp set up in 1942 by the IJN at Ofuna, near Yokohama. The methods employed at Ofuna have been described by Lieutenant D.C. Douglas, RN, of HM Submarine *Stratagem* which was depth-charged and sunk on 22 November 1944 by a Japanese destroyer off Malacca. The Japanese spared three of the eight survivors, Douglas and two ratings, who were kept together for a time at Ofuna where there were no divisions between officers and men. At Ofuna, Douglas was subjected to months of interrogation. 'The treatment ... was particularly brutal and at times almost beyond endurance', he reported after his release. 'Our food ... was never sufficient to keep us in health .... We were not permitted the use of ... anything which might have helped our morale'.[61]

The senior POW administrations throughout the Asia-Pacific area were summoned in late 1943 to a conference in Tokyo.[62] It is conceivable that the matter of security was high on the agenda. In 1942 the Japanese were confident enough to take the risk of stationing large groups of POWs in the occupied territories, reasoning that the lethargy induced by shortage of food and the threats of execution would deter any organized resistance. But contacts between POWs and anti-Japanese elements, particularly Chinese, in these territories were less easy to police. The extent of the conspiracies involving both POWs and civilian internees with sympathizers outside their camps or with Allied intelligence operatives became apparent as a result of extensive *kenpei-tai* investigations from May 1943 onwards. First in Dutch Borneo, then in Hong Kong (where the link with Waichow was uncovered between May and July), at Sandakan in British North Borneo, and later at Kanchanaburi in Thailand, and in Singapore, exchanges of intelligence, funds and occasionally arms were uncovered.

POWs after 1943

Although these conspiracies were independent of one another, they were exposed over a short period of about six months, and together offered a serious challenge to Japanese (particularly *kenpei-tai*) authority. As a result of their investigations, many of which resulted in executions, only one major intelligence chain was by the end of 1943 still operational: that set up with Chinese assistance in Thailand within months of the arrival of the first British POWs in June 1942, and which continued to operate into 1944. By late 1944 new intelligence links had been forged by the POWs with Allied organizations, but the investigations and resulting persecutions of 1943 effectively removed the cumulative threats for at least a year.

The events of 1943 resulted in heightened security, including the scrutiny of all previously sanctioned outside connections. Repressive measures were taken in some camps in 1944–45, such as the ban on assemblies (religious, sporting or educational) and the confiscation of pens, pencils and paper, which occurred in Thailand. Food rations were steadily reduced and POW efforts to grow vegetables and raise livestock were often disrupted. Most of the atrocities against POWs which occurred in 1944–45 took place in isolated garrisons, such as those in British North Borneo, as Allied bombing increased, and supplies and communications were interrupted; others were the result of the necessary shoring up of military defences. In Thailand, Lieutenant General Nakamura Aketo raided the POW hospital at Nakhon Pathom in April 1945, and sent 1,000 patients (most of whom were convalescent) to complete and maintain a road between Prachuab Kherikan (S. Thailand) and Mergui which had been hurriedly constructed for strategic reasons. Of the 546 British POWs in that party, 178 died; the condition of the others was so bad that, when they were rescued in August, some were unable to give their names.[63]

There is no doubt that those POWs on the Mergui Road who survived until the end of the war were recovered just in time. They were clearly considered by the Japanese to be expendable contributions to the war machine and there is no reason to believe that any of them would have emerged alive had the war lasted longer. The parlous physical and mental condition of the POWs when they were released from camps all over the Asia-Pacific region understandably caused shock followed by outrage when the details and the photographs were published in 1945. For three and a half years these men had endured a form of continuous mental torture. Brutality, venom, the lack of sustenance and medical supplies, combined with frequent false promises of better conditions, had sapped the morale and the energies of the majority. Some of the POWs were fortunate in receiving mail (even though the letters were a year or more out of date); others were deprived of any news from home for the entire period of their captivity. The information which the POWs were permitted to include on the printed postcards issued to them on rare occasions was strictly controlled. The Japanese refusal to send complete nominal rolls to the Allied governments was one reason why some POWs suffered in this way even though the camp records, both nominal and financial, were kept meticulously by the Japanese administrative staff. News derived from clandestine radios had of necessity to be distributed with care in the camps so that by the time this reached the average POW it was generally discounted. These deprivations severely tested the morale of the POWs some of whom gave up the struggle to remain alive; but in the majority they evoked determined efforts to survive and to return home.

Notes

There is no published history of British POWs of the Japanese. A brief survey appears in a volume of the official war history: S. Woodburn Kirby, *The War Against Japan*, volume V (London, 1969), appendix 30, pp. 532–41. The Australian and New Zealand official histories explore the subject of their own POWs in detail if not in depth. But extensive research on the experience of British POWs was carried out by Miss M.M. Baird in preparation for a section in the official history; the project was abandoned in the 1960s. Miss Baird's substantial, but incomplete, typescript history is in the Public Record Office, Kew (Cabinet Office Papers, hereafter CAB, 101/199). This forms the basis as far as it goes of any study of British POWs (it does not, for instance, consider the POWs in Thailand or Japan), but some of the details require modification in the light of later research. Her narrative is frank, which may have influenced the decision to exclude it from the official publication.

1. The figure of 67,000 is based on the work of Miss Baird (see note above, hereafter Baird). The International Military Tribunal for the Far East (hereafter IMTFE) gave figures of 62,449 United Kingdom POWs of whom 12,433 died.

2. Public Record Office, Kew (hereafter PRO), War Office Papers (hereafter WO), 235/1107. Military Court, Hong Kong, Jan.-Feb. 1948. Trial of Lieutenant General Ito Takeo: prosecution's closing address, exhibit 'MM', pp. 1, 5.
3. *Ibid*. Cross-examination by Prosecutor, Lieutenant General Ito, 29 January 1948, p. 173.
4. PRO AIR 20/9164. Statement by Air Commodore C.O.F. Modin, Appendix 'K', 1946, pp. 1–2.
5. Louis Allen, *Burma, The Longest War, 1941–45* (London, corrected edition, 1986), p. xv.
6. PRO CAB 101/172. Major General H.L. Davies, 'A Background to the First Burma Campaign 1941–42', typescript memorandum, to the official historian, Major General Kirby.
7. *Lieutenant John Christopher Close MC, Royal Artillery*, privately printed (1946). Royal Artillery Institution. An account of Close's incarceration at Saigon was given to the author by Wing Commander P. N. Kingwill who was present.
8. PRO WO/14550. Report by Air Commodore W. E. Staton, Mukden, 23 August 1945.
9. PRO WO 32/14550. Report by Flying Officer D. B. Mason, n.d. (1946).
10. Anthony Cowling, *My Life with the Samurai* (Kenthurst, 1996), p. 63.
11. *The Times*, 11 March 1942, pp. 4–5.
12. For a discussion of the Japanese attitude to the Geneva Convention, see Ikuhiko Hata, 'From Consideration to Contempt: The Changing Nature of Japanese Military and Popular Perceptions of Prisoners of War Through the Ages', in Bob Moore and Kent Fedorowich (eds), *Prisoners of War and their Captors in World War II* (Oxford, 1996), pp. 264–5.
13. Aiko Utsumi, 'Prisoners of War in the Pacific War: Japan's Policy', in Gavan McCormack and Hank Nelson (eds), *The Burma–Thailand Railway: Memory and History* (St Leonards, 1993), pp. 69–74.
14. PRO WO 235/952. Military Court, Singapore. Examination in chief of Major General Saito Masatoshi, witness for defence, 8 July 1946, p. 299.
15. Quoted in Utsumi, 'Prisoners of War', p. 73.
16. Quoted in Hata, 'From Consideration to Contempt, p. 266.
17. IMTFE. Exhibit No. 1963. Instructions of War Minister Hideki Tojo to the Newly-Appointed Commanders of the Prisoner of War Camps, 7 July 1942.
18. Baird, p. 16.
19. PRO WO 32/14550. Brigadier K.S. Torrance, 'Major Events at Changi, from 17 Feb to 16 Aug 42', typescript, dated 24 Aug. 1945, p. 2.
20. Baird, p. 19.
21. PRO WO 32/14550. Lieutenant Colonel E. B. Holmes, Report, typescript.
22. Holmes, *ibid*., Appendix 4A. Letter of Lieutenant Okasaki to Holmes, 31 August 1942.
23. Sibylla Jane Flower, 'Captors and Captives on the Burma–Thailand Railway', in Moore and Fedorowich, *Prisoners of War*, pp. 234–5.
24. A.E. Percival, *The War in Malaya* (London, 1949), p. 308.
25. Torrance 'Major Events at Changi, p. 2.
26. PRO WO 32/14550. Major General H. D. W. Sitwell, Report (1945), pp. 2–3.
27. PRO WO 235/946. Lieutenant Colonel C. R. Holmes, Report.

28. Interview, author with Colonel H. Cary Owtram, Newland, October 1992. Owtram was a camp commander at Chungkai Camp, Thailand.
29. Modin, Appendix 'K', p. 6.
30. Torrance, 'Major Events at Changi', p. 1.
31. Van Waterford, *Prisoners of the Japanese in World War II* (Jefferson, 1994), pp. 167–8.
32. PRO WO 235/886. Military Court, Singapore, July 1946. Examination in chief of Flight Lieutenant W.M. Blackwood, pp. 47–8.
33. Baird, p. 113.
34. Edwin Ride, *BAAG, Hong Kong Resistance, 1942–1945* (Hong Kong, 1981), chapter vii.
35. Baird, pp. 113–14.
36. See, for example, Imperial War Museum, IWM 66/228/1, diary of Captain the Revd H.L.O. Davies, CF.
37. PRO WO 32/14550. Major T.S. Ashton-Rose, IMS, Report, Hong Kong, 8 September 1945.
38. PRO WO 208/3809. Captain J.L.C. Pearce, RA, BAAG, letter to HBM Military Attaché, British Embassy, Chungking, 24 December 1944.
39. PRO WO 32/14550. Report by Wing Commander H.G. Sullivan, 1946.
40. PRO WO 235/1012. Military Court, Hong Kong, October 1946–February 1947. Examination of Dr Saito, 13 January 1947, p. 568.
41. André Durand, *From Sarajevo to Hiroshima. History of the International Committee of the Red Cross* (Geneva, 1984), p. 524.
42. *Report of the International Committee of the Red Cross and its Activities during the Second World War* (Geneva, 1948), p. 446.
43. See 'Die Affäre Vischer', in David Borja, *Schweizer in Südostasien während des Zweiten Weltkriegs*, thesis, University of Basle (1994), pp. 72–6.
44. Flower, 'Captors and Captives', p. 236.
45. PRO WO 235/963. Examination-in-chief of Colonel Nakamura Shigeo, Military Court, Singapore, November 1946.
46. Shimada graduated in 1941 from the medical department, Tohoku Teikoku University, Sendai.
47. Cowling, *My Life with the Samurai*, p. 90.
48. IWM 81/32/1. LAC J.F. Chandler, RAF, War Memoir, typescript, p. 234.
49. Quoted in Baird, p. 84, from Squadron Leader W.C. Pitts's report [of 17 October 1945].
50. Leslie J. Audus, *Spice Island Slaves: A History of Japanese Prisoner-of-War Camps in Eastern Indonesia May 1943–August 1945* (Richmond, 1996), p. 82.
51. Charles G. Roland, 'Human Vivisection: The Intoxication of Limitless Power in Wartime', in Moore and Fedorowich, *Prisoners of War*, pp. 165–6.
52. Peter Williams and David Wallace, *Unit 731. The Japanese Army's Secret of Secrets* (London 1989), pp. 51–62; for a discussion of the testimony of Colonel Odajima Tadashi of the POW Control Bureau, see p. 216.
53. IWM 96/14/1. [Major Robert Peaty], 'Report on conditions while a Prisoner-of-war in Manchuria'.
54. IMTFE. Exhibit No. 21,943. 'Statement Concerning the English Prisoners on Ballale Island', by Ozaki, typescript dated 8 August 1946.
55. Ozaki states that 90 POWs were executed. The mass grave disinterred by the Australians after the war was said to contain the remains of approximately

430 sets of human bones. These are buried in the Bomana War Cemetery, Papua New Guinea.
56. PRO WO 325/78. Proceedings of the temporary court martial at Makassar against Sakurai Yoshifumi, verdict, 25 January 1947, pp. 16, 18.
57. Baird, p. 103.
58. PRO WO 325/78. Proceedings ... against Sakurai Yoshifumi, p. 10.
59. PRO WO 235/905. Military Court, Hong Kong. Examination of WO I J.O. Edwards, 5 October 1946.
60. Baird, pp. 124–8.
61. *Submarine Operations*, Vol. 3, Appendix III. Report on the Loss of HM Submarine *Stratagem*, by Lieutenant D.C. Douglas, 1945, pp. 119–24.
62. Saito, PRO WO 235/952, p. 299.
63. PRO WO 235/981. Trial of Lieutenant General Watari Sakon and others, the 'Mergui Road' case.

8
Uneasy Readjustment, 1945–58
Peter Lowe

The central theme of the issues discussed in this chapter relates to the allied occupation of Japan. This constituted an enormous challenge to Britain, for on its success hinged the future stability of Japan, East Asia and the western Pacific. The Attlee government hoped to exert considerable influence in the occupation. For most of the twentieth century, to the start of the war in December 1941, Britain had been far more closely involved than the United States in dealing with Japan. This was the product of British primacy in the nineteenth century and of the warm relationship resulting from the Anglo-Japanese alliance, followed by the decline in the relationship in the course of the growth of Japanese militarism. British officials in 1945 worked on the assumption that Britain would have a great deal to contribute to the reshaping of Japan.[1] The new Foreign Secretary, Ernest Bevin, shared this outlook. However, it soon became clear that the occupation, although 'allied' in name, would be essentially *American* in character.

President Truman had no particular interest in Japan and, prior to the outbreak of the Korean war, most of his time was devoted to domestic and European matters. Truman did not want unnecessary complications in the administration of Japan and did not favour active involvement by the allies.[2] In the initial years of the occupation, the Truman administration did not interfere unduly with the conduct of the occupation by the Supreme Commander, Allied Powers (SCAP), General Douglas MacArthur. He was the most obvious man for the appointment in the light of his prominence in directing the military campaigns in the Pacific from 1942 to 1945. MacArthur was a 'political' general, possessing valuable contacts in the Republican Party in the United States and entertaining an ambition to be a presidential candidate. MacArthur was a man of diverse positive and negative characteristics: bold, courageous, far-sighted in certain respects, yet vain, arrogant and histrionic. The man who headed the British liaison mission in Tokyo for most of the occupation, Sir Alvary Gascoigne, commented that, before he left London to assume his new responsibilities in Tokyo, he had been told 'that I might find General MacArthur a difficult man to deal with as he was inclined to be Anglophobe'.[3] He added that MacArthur in fact greeted him 'with the utmost friendliness and kindness'.[4] It was possible when he arrived to pursue with MacArthur vital matters concerning the administration 'with the certainty that he would, at least, lend an interested ear to the suggestions made without displaying the fits of temper which invariably occurred in the years to come'.[5] In the main Gascoigne and the officials in the Foreign Office believed MacArthur was a hardworking, capable and successful head of the occupation. It was necessary to recognize the general's ego and to tolerate his theatrical mannerisms and stage management of meetings. Some SCAP officials from a 'New Deal' background were deemed to be excessively optimistic about transforming Japanese society; they endeavoured to implement changes too swiftly. As time passed MacArthur appeared, in British eyes, to be adopting too lenient an approach to the running of Japan. Nevertheless, all aspects considered, he discharged a most challenging task vigorously and ably.

Gascoigne's relations with MacArthur were occasionally strained, as over British complaints concerning the National Public Service Law in September 1948, when Gascoigne reported that his interview with MacArthur was 'the most painful one which I have yet had with him during my duty in Japan'.[6] SCAP resented strongly British Commonwealth criticisms over this issue. Gascoigne's relations with him were mostly of a cordial nature until the beginning of the Korean war in June 1950, when differences intensified in consequence of the pressures facing MacArthur in Korea and when the British government became more critical of him.[7]

Once the immediate challenges of establishing a positive American presence and of combating famine conditions in parts of Japan had been surmounted, the principal problem was to secure greater democratization within Japan. This was tackled on the basis of political, social and educational reforms consisting of the introduction of a new constitution, land reform, extension of the vote to women, encouragement of trade unions and a new educational structure with emphasis on civic responsibility. The character of the constitution was fundamental. Disenchanted with the Shidehara cabinet's reluctance to proceed with sweeping changes, MacArthur's officials produced a radical constitution of American rather than Japanese outlook, but including some features from British constitutional procedure. The British reaction, as summarized by Gascoigne, was that: 'To our way of thinking it was too severely Western in tone and effect to be entirely suitable for Japanese use'.[8] The most striking article of the constitution was Article 9, renouncing war and the threat of using force. The emperor was defined unambiguously as a Western-style constitutional monarch, thus eliminating State Shinto, which had been central to the ideology of the state. Therefore, British officials regarded the constitution as too idealistic and unlikely to survive unchanged, once the occupation receded following Japanese resumption of sovereignty. As the British perceived the position, the right wing retained too much power and this could again become dangerous. The extreme right had been purged (but not comprehensively) and, for the time being at least, did not represent a danger. However, the attempt to encourage a moderate centre-left party as an alternative to a moderate centre-right party, had not succeeded. Katayama Tetsu was the sole left-wing Prime Minister during the occupation and he survived tenuously in a coalition government in 1947–48. (His resignation may have been due to his being a Christian.) Democratic socialism was handicapped by the bitter divisions between left and right factions and by the antagonism of the Communist Party (JCP). The latter was well organized and made the most of the electoral opportunities opened by MacArthur in 1945.

British officials believed that communism connoted a serious potential problem and welcomed the tough line adopted by MacArthur in cracking down on militant trade unions and on the JCP, as in a purge of the party's central committee applied by MacArthur just before the start of the Korean war.[9] The most prominent politician during the occupation was Yoshida Shigeru, a former diplomat of pronounced conservative opinions but who was firmly opposed to old-style militarism. British officials in London underestimated him, seeing Yoshida as lacking the requisite skills for building democratic conservatism successfully: he was regarded as well meaning but inept. MacArthur had regretted the resignation of Katayama and regarded Yoshida as lightweight in their early dealings. According to Gascoigne, MacArthur lamented his inability 'to unearth a first class politician and statesman'.[10] Gascoigne was more sympathetic to Yoshida: he had known him since 1923 and possessed a better understanding of his merits.[11] Yoshida was Prime Minister twice, in 1946–47 and from 1948 to 1954. He revealed considerable guile and dexterity, allied with growing authoritarianism in directing his administration. Yoshida worked to consolidate the hold of the right wing, while eschewing the extreme right, and aimed to prevent the socialists from obtaining power. He wished to see the occupation ended as soon as was feasible; Japan must accept American foreign and defence priorities, which suited Yoshida, since he wanted to avoid a revival of militarism. Japan could concentrate on developing its economy and ensuring the continued dominance of conservatism domestically.[12] Yoshida's role will be discussed further later in this chapter in the context of post-1952 developments.

The redefinition of the purpose of the monarchy was axiomatic to the immediate and longer-term objectives of the occupation. In each allied country divisions of opinion existed between those who favoured retaining the monarchy and using it to assist allied reforms and those who regarded it as an impediment and who wished to depose Emperor Hirohito, if not to abolish the monarchy. The Emperor's role was strengthened symbolically according to the tenets of State Shinto, as interpreted by the militarists and their supporters in the 1930s and early 1940s. His contribution to the functioning of the government remains opaque in a number of respects: it would probably be fair to conclude that the emperor was not a principal figure in decision-making, but that he contributed rather more than his defenders have sought to argue.[13] Some politicians and officials in allied states urged a more radical approach, advocating the removal of the emperor. 'Old Japan hands' usually supported the retention of the monarchy, seeing it as a pillar which could not be removed without causing a great deal of trouble for SCAP. The British Foreign Office reached the conclusion that it was best to keep both the monarchy and the ruling monarch. Gascoigne believed firmly that MacArthur acted wisely in retaining the monarchy and reshaping it as he did:

> It will be recalled that the Allied Powers had, before the surrender, decided to use the Emperor to bring about the cease fire. This decision was undoubtedly a wise one, for if the Emperor had not instructed his people to lay down their arms, there is no doubt that the war might well have continued in outlying parts of Asia for many months or even for years. MacArthur's policy was from the first to respect the Emperor and the Royal Family, and to attempt to bring about the democratisation of the monarch's position *vis-à-vis* his people. This process has undoubtedly been to some degree successful, in great measure owing to the willingness of Hirohito to submit himself to the new democratic regime. Thus, the emperor

has, under MacArthur's advice, made himself more available to his people; this is shown by the tours throughout the country which he has undertaken each year since 1946.[14]

Gascoigne then commented more critically over MacArthur's refusal to allow Crown Prince Akihito to be taught by an English tutor:

> MacArthur has proved very jealous of his prerogatives where the Palace is concerned, and I regret to record that an excellent offer made by His Majesty's Government in the United Kingdom to furnish an Englishman who, it was thought, might have been of great use to the Imperial Household by tendering advice to them on questions pertaining to the relationship between a democratic monarch and his people, was refused out of hand, and this in spite of the fact that to our certain knowledge the appointment would have been more than welcomed by the Emperor himself, his household, and by Mr. Yoshida.[15]

Gascoigne continued that Japan's successful evolution into a full democracy would require skill in dealing with the monarchy:

> All through my $4^1/_2$ years service in Japan, the majority of the Japanese people have demonstrated by their attitude towards the Emperor how profoundly they still revere him. But when, after the peace, Japan is left to herself, that reverence might conceivably translate itself into a demand for the restoration of the sacerdotal monarchy, if little is done in the meantime to foster the idea of the Emperor as a genuinely popular monarch in a dignified and fatherly relationship to this people. We might have helped in this; but MacArthur, purely for reasons of his jealousy, has prevented us from doing so. It is by no means the least important item, I feel, on the debit side of the ledger of his achievements in Japan.[16]

Ironically, given the emphasis placed by the British government on the emperor's fully constitutional position, Britain itself proposed deviating from this line on one occasion. This arose in connection with the conclusion of a peace treaty with Japan in 1951. The Foreign Secretary, Herbert Morrison, was anxious to claim as much credit as possible for Britain's part in negotiating the treaty (and, in turn, ardently desired recognition for himself). Exchanges between the Foreign Office and the State Department occurred in July and August 1951. George Clutton, the acting head of UKLIM, discussed the subject with William Sebald: the latter conveyed the lack of enthusiasm felt by the government section of SCAP. Morrison believed that the Emperor should state his personal support for a peace treaty so as to ensure that all Japanese understood that the treaty received total endorsement in Tokyo.[17] Despite negative reactions from Sebald, Morrison pressed the issue in a telegram sent to Tokyo on 2 August:

> I still attach great importance to securing the Emperor's public endorsement of the Treaty. It had certainly not been my intention to suggest that the Emperor should issue anything except on the advice and with the consent of his Government in accordance with the constitution. An Imperial rescript would no doubt carry the most weight in view of its traditional prestige in Japan. An alternative method would be for the Emperor to broadcast on the analogy of the broadcast in which he denied his divine origin. I can see no reason why some such means could not be found by democratic and constitutional channels for him to exhort his people to carry out the provisions of the Treaty. This could and would have an important effect, particularly in the more traditionally minded circles.[18]

The British proposal was rejected by the State Department, and the Yoshida government decided that the Emperor should not act as suggested.[19] The Emperor personally notified the British government of his appreciation for its help in obtaining the peace treaty which was 'of non-punitive character' and 'unique in history'.[20] This episode is interesting for revealing how Britain was willing to bend the provisions of the 1947 constitution so as to achieve the ulterior purpose of ensuring that intransigent Japanese right-wingers did not endeavour to undermine the treaty in the future.

One of the most sensitive aspects of the occupation concerned the revival of the Japanese economy and intensified competition with British exports. From the British viewpoint two features were important. The Attlee government was faced with enormous problems in seeking to regalvanize the British economy after the huge strains of war, including the disposal of British assets, and to implement an ambitious domestic reform programme. It was essential to stimulate British exports and, accordingly, the prospect of encountering renewed Japanese competition in significant markets was not welcome. Such a threat was not, of course, an immediate one in the post-1945 situation.

The Japanese economy was devastated by war and occupation policy aimed at holding it back in 1945–46. However, the cost to the American taxpayer of subsidizing the occupation – according to Gascoigne, approximately $2,000 million were spent by the United States from 1946 to the start of 1951[21] – was such that pressures to restore the economy grew from the 'Japan lobby' in Washington in 1947–48. In addition, the extension of the Cold War in Asia in the later 1940s strengthened the case for Japan to be rebuilt more rapidly. The period of inflation was addressed through the methods introduced by the Dodge mission in April–May 1949, comprising emphasis on a balanced budget, removal of export subsidies and a cut in import subsidies. British businessmen were allowed to return to Japan in August 1947 and the United Kingdom Chamber of Commerce was revived. Gascoigne remarked on the respect with which the British commercial community was met, which he attributed to 'the high standard of character and the ability of the senior members of the principal United Kingdom firms here'.[22] The pattern of Japanese trade in the early stages of the occupation consisted largely of transactions with the United States, but this was followed by a revival in Japanese markets in Southeast Asia and South Asia. Trade with China was very limited and was hindered by the communist victory in the Chinese civil war and then by the problems arising from China's entry into the Korean war. The Korean conflict acted as a powerful stimulus for Japanese recovery, so that MacArthur stated, early in 1951, that Japan was 'approaching complete economic viability' and that this could be realized in 1952.[23]

British views on the Japanese economy were defined in March 1948 as giving a qualified endorsement to recovery. Future reparations should incorporate industrial assets, shipping and shipbuilding capacity beyond what was essential; Japanese gold deposits and other external assets should be utilized for reparations. Low wages and poor working conditions in Japanese factories should be eliminated, as should undesirable commercial practices revealed in pre-war competition.[24] A trade agreement was reached between Japan and members of the British Commonwealth in November 1948, anticipating a substantial increase in trade between Japan and the sterling group. Goods exported would include cotton textiles, industrial machinery, raw silk, caustic soda plus other chemicals, rayon, paper and bunker coal. The sterling area would export raw materials including raw wool, iron ore, salt, raw cotton, cereals, rubber, tin, jute and manganese.[25] British anxiety centred particularly on potential Japanese threats to cotton textiles, shipbuilding and the Staffordshire potteries. Textiles were the most sensitive because of the attempts to revive the cotton industry in Lancashire and because of recollections of the success achieved by Japanese firms in pre-war competition. The lower costs in Japanese firms meant that Lancashire firms could not compete effectively. Sir Raymond Streat, chairman of the Cotton Board, visited Japan for discussions with SCAP officials in May 1950. He met MacArthur and was impressed with him as a personality and the general talked knowledgeably about textiles. However, it was clear that MacArthur was glossing Japanese competition as skilfully as he could and Streat was not convinced that unfair Japanese practices had been curbed to the extent claimed by MacArthur.[26] The best that could be hoped for was to use voluntary methods of persuasion to contain Japanese competition in the short term while endeavouring to improve the efficiency of the Lancashire industry. The latter was a forlorn hope. British officials concerned in representing their national British views over a peace treaty to the Truman administration recognized that it was not possible to include restrictions on textiles within a peace treaty with Japan. Apart from certain American opposition to such a proposal, the British textile industry could not meet the large demand, particularly in Southeast Asia.[27] With shipbuilding British concern revolved around excess Japanese capacity and the potential threat to British shipping this connoted. It was again accepted that this could not be included in the terms of a peace treaty but it was pursued with some vigour in discussions with the State Department in 1951. Morrison stated that Japanese capacity was excessive and that it should be reduced, although this would occur outside the treaty.[28]

Preparations for peace

The peace treaty was the biggest single area in which Britain contributed to the occupation but, even here, the United States determined the shape of the treaty. Britain advocated the conclusion of an early peace treaty and had not favoured prolongation of the occupation. The United States would not move on the subject for a lengthy period because of basic disagreement between the State Department and the Pentagon over the desirability of an early treaty: President Truman did not resolve the impasse until the appointment of John Foster Dulles as a special emissary, charged with negotiating a treaty. British officials argued that extending the occupation would cause growing discontent among Japanese: Gascoigne reported that a greater truculence could be seen in Japanese conduct in 1949–50.[29] What kind of treaty did Britain contemplate? British politicians were more critical of Japan than their American counterparts. They largely accepted that a peace treaty should have a broadly liberal character, since this would mark the culmination of an occupation distinguished by its magnanimity. Left to their own devices ministers in the Labour government would probably have opted for a tougher treaty with more restrictive provisions (the same would no doubt have obtained had the Conservatives held office). The British were more critical than the Americans for several reasons. Less than a decade before Japan had inflicted extremely humiliating blows on Britain of which the fall of Singapore was the most painful. The shocking treatment of POWs greatly compounded British ire. Therefore, Japan caused more suffering to Britain and accentuated British decline. American policy-makers were more generous because the United States carried most of the responsibility for administering Japan and Japanese friendship was essential as the Cold War intensified and as the conflict raged in Korea but a short distance from Japan. However, the peace treaty required the concurrence of a large number of countries so the United States could not adopt too dictatorial an approach. British cooperation was important, but the British had to realize that they must function within boundaries decided in Washington.

The vital personality in the whole process on the American side was John Foster Dulles. A capable international lawyer and negotiator, Dulles was simultaneously a leading member of the Republican Party and was closely involved in the Democratic administration of Harry Truman. Dulles possessed no particular expertise in Asian matters. Douglas MacArthur resented Dulles's appointment and complained that he knew little of Asia.[30] While this was true, Dulles possessed great diplomatic skill, which he deployed most successfully in his various visits and meetings with politicians in Britain, Australia and Japan.

Britain was concerned to maintain unity in the Commonwealth as far as possible. Canada and South Africa were not deeply involved. India evinced an ambivalent attitude and ultimately declined to sign the peace treaty in September 1951. Australia and New Zealand were chiefly involved and each harboured grave doubts about Japan in consequence of the havoc wreaked by Japanese militarism.[31] The only way in which Australia and New Zealand could be persuaded to acquiesce in a liberal treaty was for their defence to be underwritten by a powerful state. Britain could not offer such a guarantee and had indeed been unable to do so effectively since the early years of the twentieth century. Dulles knew that he must construct a viable Pacific defence treaty structure of integrated character through which the United States could dictate Japanese defence policy (thus obviating the dangers of a possible revival of Japanese militarism), while guaranteeing to protect Australia and New Zealand against aggression.[32] Of course, the Pacific dominions were also worried over a potential communist threat, particularly in the light of China's military role in Korea. Labour cabinet ministers viewed the predicament facing them with mixed feelings. For Britain to be excluded effectively from Commonwealth defence as dictated by the United States was embarrassing but none the less realistic; the Attlee cabinet and the chiefs of staff acquiesced reluctantly. Churchill, leader of the Conservative opposition and shortly to become prime minister again, was incandescent over the ANZUS Pact of 1951 and persevered for a lengthy period, in vain, to secure British admission.[33]

The development of British policy in the first few months of 1951 was marked by some disarray. This resulted in part from the heavy pressure of business in the Foreign Office, exacerbated by the physical decline of Ernest Bevin and the lack of experience of his successor, Herbert Morrison. Bevin was a sick man in 1950–51 and clung to office through a sense of dedication, although increasingly he lacked the energy or resilience to handle business. His deputy, Kenneth Younger, had to shoulder more responsibility without the status of his chief. At last Bevin resigned in March 1951 and was succeeded by Morrison. It was not one of Attlee's more inspired appointments. Morrison possessed great seniority in the Labour Party and was a major figure. He was essentially ignorant of foreign policy and showed a certain petulance in his conduct. For a brief period in March 1951 the cabinet decided to hold up further negotiations on a peace treaty, which marked the only occasion when Britain deviated from the advocacy of an early treaty. The divergence concerned policy towards China and Taiwan and the question as to which of the rival Chinese regimes (or neither) should sign a Japanese peace treaty.[34] Morrison soon realized his error and the cabinet reversed its decision when it met on 2 April.[35] Dulles was exasperated at British policy and felt for a short period that the United States might have to advance without Britain. However, political realities meant that the two countries had to cooperate. Separate British and American drafts were produced, the former being longer and more specific than the American. Questions relating to China and Taiwan were the most difficult. The British position was reserved in early May over Taiwan, the Antarctic, Ryukyu islands, war criminals, fisheries, UN property, Japanese gold deposits, assets in neutral and former enemy countries, and disputes. A number of issues relating to economic relations was also reserved. Anglo-American discussions in April and May 1951 clarified issues and produced better awareness of respective positions. Much remained to be decided during Dulles's visit to London at the beginning of June. The revised draft of a treaty, jointly agreed, was described by Morrison as 'fairly evenly balanced and in length the document is somewhere between the original United Kingdom and United States drafts'.[36] Morrison added that British light should not be hidden 'under a bushel' and the extent of Britain's contribution to the peace treaty should be made clear.

Concern was felt in the cabinet over Japanese rearmament. This had started in a very limited way in the late 1940s and was handled in a clandestine manner by General Willoughby.[37] The start of the Korean war stimulated American anxiety and rearmament was intensified. Members of the cabinet made clear on 28 May that they wished to see limitations on rearmament stipulated in the relevant paragraph in the treaty. It was decided the next day that a previous cabinet decision reached on 2 January 1951 should be modified and a further attempt should be made 'to persuade the United States government that the Peace Treaty should include some reference to the limitations which were to be placed upon Japanese rearmament'.[38] A spirited exchange of views took place between leading cabinet ministers and Dulles during his visit. Dulles demonstrated full mastery of the subjects handled and emerged with the upper hand from most of his encounters. On 4 June Morrison emphasised the strength of feeling in Britain at the savage treatment of POWs and civilian internees which in part explained British views regarding rearmament.[39] Dulles expressed understanding of British feelings but stressed the necessity to look ahead constructively and to avoid the wish for revenge discredited in the Versailles Treaty of 1919. The complex issues concerning Taiwan were reviewed. Dulles saw the various possibilities as embracing neither Chinese state signing; a series of bilateral peace treaties being signed instead of a multilateral one; or that it might be possible for governments other than the principal parties to adhere to a multilateral agreement before or after ratification, leaving the Japanese government to decide later with which China to conclude an agreement. Dulles maintained that he was not trying to bounce Britain into supporting Chiang Kai-shek's regime: rather he was motivated by the desire to minimize the problems he would face in securing ratification of the peace treaty in the American Senate.[40] The cabinet was unhappy at the failure to make more progress on China and was dubious of the alternatives suggested by Dulles. Eventually, Morrison suggested in cabinet that neither Chinese regime should sign the treaty and that the Japanese government should decide which regime to recognize after regaining sovereignty. Some of his colleagues feared, correctly, that the United States would lean on Japan to recognize Chiang Kai-shek's government.[41] However, it was not possible to obtain a more satisfactory formula and Dulles and Morrison agreed accordingly.

Hugh Gaitskell, the Chancellor of the Exchequer, firmly advocated the pursuit of a harsher line, underlining the vocal nature of anti-Japanese opinions in Britain. He believed that Japan should not receive back gold deposits which should instead be retained by the allies or, if the United States desired compensation for the cost of the occupation, kept by them.[42] British unease over Japanese rearmament was conveyed by several ministers in meetings with Dulles. They felt that Dulles underestimated the potency of the apprehension in Britain and in parts of the Commonwealth, notably Australia and New Zealand. It was also held that Dulles revealed excessive enthusiasm for rearming Japan owing to his zeal to strengthen western defences against communism. Dulles responded with a succinct and accurate definition of American aims towards Japan:

> The United States Government wanted to continue with the substance of the occupation but not the form. They wanted to maintain United States armed forces in Japan with the consent of the Japanese.[43]

Dulles conceded little and Morrison and Gaitskell were compelled to accept that nothing would be gained by pressing him further. The one area where Dulles did concede involved the Congo Basin treaties. Sir Hartley Shawcross, the President of the Board of Trade, argued that Japanese rights under the treaties should be forfeited formally on the grounds that Japan secured such rights originally because of participating in the Great War on the allied side between 1914 and 1918. The real British aim was to minimize Japanese competition in cotton textiles in the African market so as to assist Lancashire. At first Dulles sought to reject the British case, citing the precedent of Italy, where it had been decided not to cancel Italian rights as a signatory to the Saint-Germain convention.[44]

Subsequently Dulles accepted that Japan should lose its rights under the Congo Basin treaties. However, he rejected the British argument regarding Japanese gold deposits.[45] Dulles's visit to London ended amicably; he summarized his approach to Japan by drawing the analogy of Japan being admitted to a club comprising select members:

> They were people who liked conforming and doing what was correct. He thought we should capitalize on this quality by inviting them into their club but explaining the rules which they must keep, and that they would then keep them on a voluntary basis.[46]

The peace treaty was signed at a conference held in San Francisco in September 1951. The final deliberations went smoothly and the communist states present, led by the Soviet Union, caused no trouble or, at any rate, much less than had been feared. Dean Acheson chaired the conference with a certain panache. Herbert Morrison attended the closing part of the conference, having missed the early stages because he had been on a Scandinavian cruise. The main cause for regret as regards the Commonwealth was that India declined to attend or approve the treaty. Nehru was critical of American policy in Asia and believed that the Truman administration had given excessive encouragement to Japanese rearmament and that the Yoshida government was too closely identified with traditional conservative forces in Japanese society.[47] Yoshida attended the conference, reversing a provisional decision that he would not take part. He reciprocated British wishes for a better relationship, thus moving away from the acrimony and horror of war. Yoshida was an Anglophile and was fond of repeating his regret at the demise of the Anglo-Japanese alliance. According to Kenneth Younger, the Minister of State in the Foreign Office, who talked with him in San Francisco:

> Yoshida referred with some emotion to the long standing tradition of friendship between our two countries, a tradition unhappily broken by the war. The Japanese leaders before the war, he said, had gone 'crazy and lost common sense' and he hoped this would never recur.[48]

At the end of the conference Morrison met Yoshida and urged the adoption of progressive economic and social policies in Japan; this could then diminish the resentment caused in Britain by low wages and devious commercial practices. Yoshida replied positively – he wished to strengthen democracy in Japan and to maintain good relations with the United States and Britain.[49]

The Japanese peace treaty represented primarily the attainment of American objectives. The United States achieved all its priorities in bringing the occupation to a close. This was a remarkable triumph for Dulles: he demonstrated tremendous industry, dedication and skill with not a little deviousness. Britain was satisfied with the general character of the treaty but entertained doubts over rearmament, shipbuilding capacity and the return of gold deposits. The most difficult single aspect after the signing of the treaty concerned China and Dulles's pressure on Yoshida to recognize Chiang Kai-shek's government. Anthony Eden, now Foreign Secretary after the change of government, was irate at the behaviour of Acheson and Dulles and believed that his own officials should have kept him better informed. Eden conveyed his annoyance to the State Department and his resentment was shared by Herbert Morrison. It was not surprising that Dulles acted as he did: it was essential to obtain the requisite majority in the Senate to ensure ratification of the treaty and Dulles would not risk his considerable achievement by incurring trouble at the end of the lengthy process. In addition, Dulles wanted to succeed Acheson at the State Department, assuming the Republicans triumphed in the 1952 presidential campaign.[50] Sir Esler Dening, the last head of UKLIM and first postwar ambassador to Japan, commented on 28 April 1952, the day the occupation finished, that the most striking feature of the occupation had been the violent change in American policy, from preaching radical reform and disarmament to advocating rearmament and castigating all signs of weakness in combating communism:

> Much of the good which the Occupation has undoubtedly brought to Japan is vitiated by this. Until two years ago complete pacifism was the badge and sign of progress and international respectability: today it is evidence of susceptibility to Communist indoctrination. Doubt has thus come to be cast on democracy, parliamentary institutions and all the other new wonders which the Occupation brought in its train.[51]

A similar note was struck in the British press. Just before the occupation ended *The Economist* published a rather sombre assessment. The situation over rearmament was awkward because of the tergiversations in American policy. It was premature to search for changes in Japanese foreign policy. Questions regarding reparations affecting Indonesia and the Philippines had to be resolved; the policy of China towards Japan was unclear; the future pattern of trade in Southeast Asia required clarification. The one certainty was that Japanese foreign policy would be neither pro-West nor anti-West but 'exclusively pro-Japanese'.[52]

Dominance of trade considerations

British attitudes towards Japan were largely negative in the 1950s for reasons identified earlier: in essence these combined residual anger over wartime atrocities with resentment at Japan's contribution to Britain's decline. This was illustrated in the unhappy saga of Japan's application to join the General Agreement on Tariffs and Trade (GATT). The Labour President of the Board of Trade, Shawcross, had made clear in 1951 that Britain was not sympathetic 'bearing in mind the prewar record of Japanese competition, especially in the textile trades'.[53] The Conservative government followed the same approach, although differences existed within ministerial circles. Much of the British anxiety related to cotton textiles. The industry was significant in early postwar Japanese revival: in 1951 cotton textiles comprised 27.8 per cent of total exports with raw cotton comprising 22.9 per cent of total imports.[54] An international cotton textiles conference met in Britain in September 1952, meeting initially in London and then continuing in Buxton. This provided further evidence of the intensifying competition which now extended to include cheap textiles from southern Europe.[55] The omens were not encouraging for Lancashire textiles. Britain, France, Australia and New Zealand opposed Japanese adhesion to GATT but India, Pakistan and a number of other countries endorsed American sponsorship for Japan's application to join.

The Economist demonstrated its traditional preference for free trade when it criticised a speech by the Conservative President of the Board of Trade, Peter Thorneycroft, as being more than usually unconvincing: it was virtually certain that Japan would join GATT and the hostile British policy was foolish.[56] It went on, in October 1953, to state that the Japanese government was shocked at the 'implacable' character of British opposition. The British ambassador in Tokyo, Sir Esler Dening, had done his best, but was handicapped by the absence of a positive British post-occupation policy and because of the belief that he had been posted to Tokyo only because Communist China declined to accept a British ambassador.[57]

The Conservative cabinet discussed commercial relations with Japan on a number of occasions. In October 1954 Thorneycroft referred to unease among Conservative backbench MPs and industrialists regarding Japanese adhesion to GATT – 'widespread controversy would be aroused unless it could be shown that the trade of the United Kingdom had been safeguarded from the dangers of Japanese competition'.[58] The Minister of State at the Foreign Office, the Marquess of Reading, warned of the consequences of not reaching an understanding with Japan – it would be more difficult 'to secure the continued political alignment of Japan with the countries of the West'.[59] Reading continued that he did not object to the proposals put forward by the President of the Board of Trade, but he hoped that this would not be put to the Japanese in a manner which might seem tantamount to an ultimatum. The Prime Minister of Japan was coming to the United Kingdom on a visit of goodwill and it would be against British interests to weaken his political position in Japan, since no one who succeeded him was likely to be so well-disposed to the strengthening of Japanese relations with the West.[60]

In February 1955 the cabinet considered a memorandum on the problem of the cotton industry. Thorneycroft observed:

> The real difficulties of the cotton industry were due, not to competitive imports, but to the loss of export trade, especially in cheap cotton cloth, owing to Japanese and Indian competition, mainly in the Colonies. Colonial Governments had eased their restrictions on imports of Japanese textiles when Japan had an adverse balance of trade with the sterling area. Japan was now accumulating sterling balances, and it would be of great assistance to Lancashire if Colonial Governments could be persuaded to reduce their imports of Japanese textiles. He suggested that Colonial Governments should be warned to consider this now, not as a long-term policy, but on the ground that it was justified in view of the balance of trade between the sterling area and all Japan.[61]

The best course of action for the cotton industry was to specialize in the production of higher quality cloth, although the imposition of purchase tax was a complication. The Prime Minister, Winston Churchill, said that he had received an invitation to meet a delegation from Lancashire to discuss the region's problems. He thought he would do so, but it did not appear that much could be done to alleviate the difficulties facing the cotton industry.[62]

Eventually the British strategy of delaying Japan's adhesion to GATT terminated when Japan gained admission after three years of effort. It appeared, reported *The Economist*, that Britain and Australia, with the possible support of France and South Africa, would resort to article 35, meaning that there would be no necessity to give or receive Most Favoured Nation (MFN) treatment in mutual trade; however, Japan already received MFN treatment in Britain and the colonies as a concession resulting from the peace treaty. Japan should reconsider certain of its questionable trade practices, such as concealed export subsidies, which were contrary to the spirit of GATT and almost certainly did not comply with the terms of GATT. It was recognized in Whitehall that Britain should put its relationship with Japan on an improved basis and it was hoped to negotiate a long-term commercial treaty with Japan.[63]

Britain responds to changing Japanese politics

The evolution of Japanese politics was viewed with considerable fascination and underlying anxiety in Britain. After a lengthy period in power, Yoshida Shigeru came to be regarded favourably and was perceived as the most satisfactory leader Japan could produce from the perspective of Anglo-American interests. However, aspects of Yoshida's performance were criticized, as in May 1952, when Yoshida encountered strong opposition from a wide spectrum of opinion to his proposal to counter subversive activities. This was seen as redolent of legislation repealed during the occupation; Yoshida duly retreated. A partial revival of nationalism was discerned in 1952–53 and this was reflected in the growing rivalry between Yoshida and his challengers, Hatoyama Ichiro and Shigemitsu Mamoru. Yoshida revealed what *The Economist* described as an 'arrogant *daimyo*-like disdain for public opinion'.[64] Combined with the venom displayed by his rivals, Yoshida's hold on power, after six years as prime minister, was weakened. Ultimately he was compelled to resign in December 1954, and was succeeded by Hatoyama. The latter wished to improve relations with the Soviet Union and China, but without alienating the United States too far. The Liberal Democratic Party was created in 1955 as a fusion of right-wing parties promoted by Japanese business, so as to surmount the acrimonious confrontations of the latter part of Yoshida's tenure. The Liberal-Democratic Party (LDP) was quickly revealed as an umbrella beneath which bitter factionalism prevailed, particularly between those supporting Hatoyama and the ousted Yoshida.

In October 1956 Hatoyama reached Moscow in his mission to negotiate a peace treaty between Japan and Russia, based on the 'Adenauer formula', that is to say, that the thorny topic of the Kuril islands would be shelved for later discussion. Diplomatic relations between Tokyo and Moscow should be restored, POWs returned, the current fisheries agreement confirmed, and Soviet opposition to Japanese membership of the UN withdrawn. Hatoyama's wish to achieve reconciliation with Russia was regarded with vehement hostility by an appreciable number of LDP members. Hatoyama secured Diet ratification of the Russo-Japanese declaration which he negotiated in December 1956, thus ending the state of war and providing for the resumption of diplomatic relations.[65] Hatoyama and his successor, Ishibashi Tanzan, wished to improve relations with Russia further, but both were forced to relinquish office through ill-health.

Kishi Nobusuke then emerged as Prime Minister in March 1957. He was highly ambitious and had been identified closely with militarism in the 1930s and during the Pacific war. Kishi wished to work more closely with the United States and to develop a more assertive policy in Southeast Asia. *The Economist* saw Kishi as a leader of great vigour but one who probably wanted to achieve too much too quickly. This was illustrated in his departure, leading a large group of 33, to visit India, Burma and Ceylon plus Taiwan, Thailand and Pakistan. Kishi was keen to adopt a higher profile than preceding postwar prime ministers and he emphasized his *Asian* credentials. Japan was not viewed with enthusiasm in parts of East and Southeast Asia, as in South Korea, the Philippines and Indonesia: Kishi was deferring visiting these countries until he had been to Washington. He was quite outspoken by Japanese standards: it seemed doubtful whether much of Southeast Asia would react with enthusiasm to the news that Japan wanted to assume the lead in opening up the region.[66]

Rearmament was bound to be a highly sensitive issue for Britain and the Commonwealth. Some apprehension was felt in London because of American failure to consult fully over the subject during the latter part of the occupation. In August 1952 the newly created Pacific Defence Council met for its inaugural session without a British observer being present. *The Economist* observed:

> Although the mainspring of the Pacific Defence Council lies in Australian fears of a revival of aggressive Japanese militarism, this does not fully explain the reasons for its present limited membership. Nor does it quite account for the fact that the Council represents the nucleus of a Pacific defence structure which is more likely to have to oppose Communist than Japanese aggression.[67]

There were fears in November 1952 that Japanese rearmament could become more of a problem: army and navy officers were reported to be anxious to secure full self-sufficiency for Japan in defence which could then afford the basis of an independent foreign policy, rather than one dominated by the United States. Financial constraints would probably inhibit Japan from carrying rearmament too far.[68] The United States wanted Japan to contribute more powerfully to western defence, under American direction. As *The Economist* drily observed, 'The situation is heavy with paradox, rich in irony and pregnant with eaten words'.[69] John Foster Dulles's statement that the size of Japan's armed forces should be increased to 150,000 by March 1954 was regarded as confirming his reputation for saying the wrong thing at the right time. Anxiety was more vocal in 1952–53 as part of the speculation as to how Japan would act upon regaining its freedom. Subsequently it was felt to be unlikely that Japan would become a dangerous force in the near to medium term, although undercurrents of concern can be discerned in the reports of Kishi's ambitions.

The Economist's survey

In March 1958 *The Economist* published a substantial survey of Japan. This examined the nature of Japanese politics, society and economy. In the political sphere a greater degree of stability existed than had been forecast in 1951–52. This was the product of economic achievement and was accordingly brittle: if economic progress stalled or was reversed, turbulence might well occur. The foreign press tended to exaggerate occasional physical exchanges in the Diet: this was no worse than the experience of the Italian parliament. The reassuring feature was that the electorate eschewed extremist parties of the right and left. The extreme right lacked credibility and the extreme left was harried zealously by the police. But the established Japanese parties contained a wide variety of opinions, as demonstrated by the LDP and the Socialists: therefore, certain electors could indulge their liking for pronounced right-wing or left-wing views within the major parties. The general elections of 1952, 1953 and 1955 showed a gradual rise in support for the Socialists, but it would be some time before the latter challenged seriously for government. In the event of an economic crisis the electors might desert the democratic parties and move to the extremes. It was difficult to say which extreme would benefit, but the right was more likely to do so than the left. The inherent factionalism of Japanese parties could assist the emergence of extremism but, for the time being, the situation appeared satisfactory. The period of real test might occur in the middle to late 1960s when the economy might experience more pressure. A Constitution Revision Council, established by the LDP in 1956, had been considering proposals for changing the 1947 constitution. The principal aim was to amend article 9 so as to make it clear that Japan was committed to defending itself. Japanese public opinion was divided over the desirability of rearmament – 'The first and so far the only victims of atomic warfare, the Japanese tend to cherish Article 9 as if it were in itself a magic talisman against a repetition'.[70] It was unlikely that the required two-thirds majority necessary for changing the constitution could be secured. Labour relations had become more volatile under the Kishi government. Some trade unions were prepared to challenge the government. Kishi and his followers tended to use the term 'violence' as indicative of any criticism that was deemed too robust. *The Economist* adopted a cautious line in arguing that careful, limited constitutional reform might be salutary:

> It would be wrong to assume that Japan was poised on the brink of black reaction. Most European liberals would agree that some repairs and alterations are needed in the political structure that the Americans slapped together with such zestful improvisation after the war. In particular, the schools and universities were infected by some of the more dubious concepts of American education and in some places standards of higher education have sagged. If reform in education went no further than a tightening of standards, and a prohibition of the more outrageous forms of political proselytising by teachers, it would be respectable enough. A nominal change in the Emperor's status would do no harm if his prestige was not subsequently used for political purposes. Alterations in the system of local government are tolerable so long as they are chiefly designed to relieve the urgent financial difficulties in which local authorities have found themselves since the war.
>
> But there are so many ifs. The worrying thing is that the party which wants to make the changes has so many links with the politicians who permitted reaction before the war, and the party which opposes the changes is still largely committed to the academic forms of dogmatic Marxism. Fortunately, the central mass of moderate opinion among the electorate still seems to be strong enough to prevent any disastrous plunge to the right or left. But this moderating influence might well vanish if Japan subsided into a deep and prolonged economic crisis.[71]

The report surveyed population problems. It estimated that by 1990 the population would reach approximately 107 million, 'two-thirds of the population of the United States in a land less than one-twentieth of its size'.[72] Japan's death and birth rates were both relatively low;

Japan was therefore advancing towards the higher range of western attainments in these areas – 'Indeed the statisticians reckon that in a few years' time a Japanese will be no more apt to procreate than a Swede and no more prone to die than a New Zealander'.[73] The difficulties of the approaching three decades resulted from a fall in the death rate 20 years prior to birth control developing. Birth control was effected through abortion rather than contraception.

Japanese farmers were very efficient, producing a higher yield than in most other countries, but efficiency could not be pressed much further. The problems of agriculture would have to be solved by industry. The infrastructure required modernization. The financing of industry needed greater flexibility and diversification. The biggest challenge lay in the division of Japanese industry into two discrete types: highly modern enterprises and numerous small and inefficient family firms. Large firms proved most successful in the chemical and machinery industries. The old *zaibatsu* were reviving, as seen in the Mitsui and Mitsubishi empires. The economy had grown with remarkable success, partly through the stimulus provided by rebuilding, the Korean war and American assistance. But signs of overheating could be seen, as in capacity problems in the coal, steel, power and transport industries. Industry's demand for imported raw materials encountered Japan's inability to pay for them by selling enough exports. New, voracious overseas markets were vital for the future.[74] Businessmen looked towards China as an important trading partner, but this was prevented by the American embargo on trade.

A number of countries continued to castigate Japan for former commercial practices and for some current practices. This explained the delay in granting Japan membership of GATT until 1955. It then gained entry, but not on terms of equality:

> A staunch group of old members, led by Britain, still refuses to grant to Japan the full benefit of the 'most favoured nation' treatment which is the core of GATT. Yet many countries of the western world have gradually been opening their markets to Japanese goods. The United States, in particular, has been fairly generous to Japan since the war and was the first among the great trading powers to grant most-favoured-nation treatment.[75]

A very limited degree of progress had been achieved in penetrating European markets: Belgium and the Netherlands had been fairly positive and West Germany had adopted a more liberal approach. However, in very few European countries could Japan compete on a basis of equality. A new trade agreement was currently under negotiation with Britain. Japan's immediate aim lay in penetrating Afro-Asian markets.

The survey ended with a brief discussion of Japan's foreign policy. After a phase in which Japan cultivated relations with the Soviet Union and, to a lesser degree, with China, the policy of the Kishi government emphasized cooperation with the United States and exploitation of Southeast Asia. Kishi desired American finance for Japanese provision of capital goods and associated expertise in order to fulfil his scheme for 'cooperation'. Critics of the latter compared it with Japan's notorious Greater East Asia Co-Prosperity Sphere, *c.* 1940–45. Kishi sought to allay fears in Southeast Asia through emphasizing common administration of development funds with each country placed on an equal footing. Japan was seeking to depict its policy in a moral light, emulating the Asian moral lead given by India under Nehru's leadership – 'The difference – and the difficulty – is that Japan specifically eschews ideological neutrality and 1941 is still a little too recent for the halo to sit quite straight'.[76] The presence of American bases in the home islands and in Okinawa was criticized by the Socialists and the JCP. The Socialists would like to see an end to the alliance with the United States. Although the strength of the Self-Defence Forces had grown, ground forces would total only 180,000 men by 1960. Naval power had expanded a little, but air power was rudimentary. Economic success could lead Japan again to the pursuance of an active foreign policy:

> The Japanese fully expect to play once more a leading role in Asia and the world. Less than six years after the American occupation, they are cautiously, but with increasing confidence, making their voice heard again.[77]

The author of the survey might have been surprised to discover that nearly 40 years later similar arguments would be pursued over amending the constitution (but not so much over elevating the Emperor) and over whether or not Japan should follow a more active foreign policy. Great economic success and reliance on the United States paradoxically allowed Japan to persevere with a quiescent foreign policy.

Readjustment but unease

This chapter has examined the course of Anglo-Japanese relations from the savagery of total war to a position where Japan was re-establishing itself successfully, if rather gingerly, within the framework of international relations. War defined the relationship throughout, which explains why this chapter is entitled 'Uneasy Readjustment'. British politicians, civil servants, and the man and woman in the street, could not forget, even though some were prepared to forgive, the depredations and atrocities for which the Japanese armed forces were responsible. Japan destroyed the prestige of the British Empire with its devastating campaigns in 1941–42, as Winston Churchill admitted. Japan and its Axis partners were responsible for the liquidation of remaining British investments in order to support the British war effort. Britain found it far more difficult to come to terms with Japan after the end of the war in Asia and the Pacific than did the United States. John Foster Dulles remarked on this when he visited London in June 1951. The answer seems to lie in the onerous responsibility shouldered by the Truman administration and SCAP during the occupation. In essence it was an *American* rather than an allied occupation and Americans concerned with Japan developed a sense of mission to ensure that democratisation was advanced positively and that the occupation achieved its principal aims. However, we have to keep in mind that tensions remained on the American side, too, and were to be rekindled by the 50th anniversary of the outbreak and termination of the Pacific war: this is illustrated in the controversy associated with the character of the exhibition at the Smithsonian in 1995. The 50th anniversary of both events also rekindled controversy in Britain with the POWs lobby voicing more loudly the case for additional compensation for the horrors inflicted on the now elderly survivors. This was compounded by the revelations of the shocking experiences of the 'comfort women' in Korea and Southeast Asia. As we know, Japan's attitude towards responsibility for wartime evils has been ambiguous. During the 1990s two prime ministers made more open and candid statements of regret – Hosokawa Morihiro and Murayama Tomiichi. In January 1998 the then prime minister, Hashimoto Ryutaro, reiterated an apology for the suffering experienced by the victims of conflict, following a meeting in Tokyo with Britain's Prime Minister, Tony Blair. Hashimoto also published an article in a popular tabloid British newspaper, *The Sun*, expressing Japan's remorse. This may be seen as endeavouring to create a more favourable atmosphere for Emperor Akihito's state visit to Britain in May 1998. While acknowledging that responsibility for the outbreak of war is often complex and rarely straightforward, it has to be said that the reluctance of many Japanese leaders to recognize the scale of the atrocities committed during the war delayed full Anglo-Japanese reconciliation.

British cabinet ministers in the 1950s were prepared to compromise over the punishment of Japanese war criminals; they were conscious of the strength of public opinion over these matters. On 14 July 1955 the Conservative cabinet of Anthony Eden discussed a memorandum submitted by the Foreign Secretary, Harold Macmillan. This addressed the issue of clemency towards war criminals. Macmillan recommended that Britain should support the American proposal that major Japanese war criminals convicted at the International Military Tribunal in 1948, should be released after serving ten years' imprisonment. Macmillan thought it preferable that they should be released without qualification: however, if other countries involved favoured release on parole, he would concur. Macmillan then discussed the situation of convicted minor war criminals:

> The question of exercising similar clemency in favour of minor Japanese war criminals, for whom the United Kingdom Government had jurisdiction, was in a sense more difficult. There were eighty-one of these still in our custody, and the last of them would not be due for release until 1960. It would benefit Anglo-Japanese relations, and would bring our policy into line with the more lenient attitude adopted by other Powers, if we now reduced sentences of more than fifteen years to fifteen years. This would mean that, with one-third remission for good conduct, all these criminals would be released after serving ten years.[78]

The ensuing debate revealed that opinion was divided and emphasis was placed upon the shocking treatment of POWs:

> It was suggested that, if a more lenient policy was to be followed, it might be better to put it into effect gradually and unobtrusively. If the prisoners still in custody were all released at once, public opinion was more likely to be aroused. Many of these men had been personally responsible for barbarous treatment of British prisoners of war.[79]

British economic decline, as shown in the experiences of the cotton textile and shipping industries, accounted further for British resentment. These attitudes or prejudices were understandable but regrettable. Britain was too negative or carping in its approach to Japan in the later 1940s and 1950s. Perhaps this was accentuated by the fact that Britain did not carry more responsibility for the occupation. In many ways the period and the problems examined in this essay mark the end of a century of Anglo-Japanese relations rather than the start of a new era. Thus developments from 1945 to 1958 are best viewed as an appendix to a century embracing the vigorous British role in the opening of Japan, the flowering and decline of the Anglo-Japanese alliance, and descent into war. The readjustment was uneasy because it accompanied the rapid decline of the British Empire (this had largely disappeared in Asia by 1958) and the beginning of the process whereby Japan sought to redefine its role in the world. After 1958 a new era in Anglo-Japanese relations developed.

Acknowledgement

I am most grateful to those who participated in the Anglo-Japanese Workshop, held in Hayama in September 1997, for their constructive comments in the course of discussion.

Notes

1. See Roger Buckley, *Occupation Diplomacy: Britain, the United States and Japan, 1945–1952* (Cambridge, 1982), and *US-Japan Alliance Diplomacy, 1945–1990* (Cambridge, 1992).
2. See Roger Buckley, 'A Particularly Vital Issue?: Harry Truman and Japan', in T.G. Fraser and Peter Lowe (eds), *Conflict and Amity in East Asia: Essays in Honour of Ian Nish* (London, 1992), pp. 110–24.
3. 'Trend of Events in Japan from July 1946 to February 1951', despatch from Gascoigne to Bevin, 6 February 1951, FO 371/92521/5. For a helpful discussion of MacArthur's career from 1941 to 1945, see Michael Schaller, 'General Douglas MacArthur and the Politics of the Pacific War', in G. Bischof and R.L. Dupont (eds), *The Pacific War Revisited* (London, 1997), pp. 17–40.
4. *Ibid.*
5. *Ibid.*
6. Tokyo to Foreign Office, 1 September 1948, FO 371/69823/12111.
7. See Peter Lowe, 'An Ally and a Recalcitrant General: Great Britain, Douglas MacArthur and the Korean War', *English Historical Review*, vol. 105, no. 416 (1990), 624–53.
8. Gascoigne to Bevin, 6 February 1951, F 371/92521/5.
9. Gascoigne to Younger, 12 June 1950, FO 371/83831/93.
10. Gascoigne to Bevin, 13 February 1948, FO 371/69819/3508.
11. Peter Lowe, 'Sir Alvary Gascoigne in Japan, 1946–1951', in Ian Nish (ed.), *Britain and Japan, Biographical Portraits* Vol. I (Folkestone, 1994), p. 286.
12. See J.W. Dower, *Empire and Aftermath: Yoshida Shigeru and the Japanese Experience, 1878–1954* (London, 1979).
13. For a lucid discussion of the controversies surrounding the Showa emperor, see Stephen Large, *Emperor Hirohito and Showa Japan* (London, 1992).

14. Despatch from Gascoigne to Bevin, 6 February 1951, FO 371/92521/5.
15. *Ibid.*
16. *Ibid.*
17. See Peter Lowe, *Containing the Cold War in East Asia: British Policies towards Japan, China and Korea, 1948–1953* (Manchester, 1997), pp. 62–3.
18. Foreign Office to Tokyo, 2 August 1951, FO 371/92595/905.
19. Washington to Foreign Office, 13 August and Foreign Office to Washington, 11 August 1951, FO 371/92582/1039.
20. Tokyo to Foreign Office, 30 August 1951, FO 371/92590/1274.
21. Despatch from Gascoigne to Bevin, 6 February 1951, FO 371/92521/5.
22. *Ibid.*
23. *Ibid.*
24. Foreign Office to Tokyo, 18 March 1948, FO 371/69885/4043.
25. *The Economist*, 13 November 1948.
26. Peter Lowe, *The Origins of the Korean War*, second edition (London 1997), p. 86.
27. Notes by C.H. Johnston for Morrison, 6 April 1951, FO 371/92539/234.
28. Lowe, *Containing the Cold War in East Asia*, pp. 60–1.
29. Lowe, 'Gascoigne in Japan' in Nish (ed.), *Britain and Japan*, Vol. I, p. 287.
30. Lowe, *Containing the Cold War in East Asia*, p. 23.
31. *Ibid.*, pp. 34–7, for a discussion of Commonwealth views in 1950–51.
32. *Ibid.*, pp. 36, 48.
33. *Ibid.*, p. 5.
34. Cabinet minutes, 22(51)3, 22 March 1951, Cab. 128/19.
35. Cabinet minutes, 22(51)3, 2 April 1951, Cab. 128/19.
36. Memorandum by Morrison, CP(51)137, 23 May 1951, Cab. 129/45.
37. Lowe, *Origins of the Korean War*, second edition, pp. 87, 107.
38. Cabinet minutes, 38(51)2, 29 May 1951, Cab. 128/19.
39. Record of meeting between Morrison and Dulles, 4 June 1951, FO 371/92553/498.
40. Record of meeting held in House of Commons, 5 June 1951, FO 371/92554/513.
41. Cabinet minutes, 42(51)1, 11 June 1951, Cab. 128/19.
42. Treasury memorandum by A.J. Phelps, 6 June 1951, FO 371/92557/564A.
43. Record of meeting held in House of Commons, 6 June 1951, FO 371/92554/515.
44. Record of meeting held in House of Commons, 8 June 1951, FO 371/92552/516.
45. Cabinet minutes, 43(51)3, 14 June 1951, Cab. 128/19.
46. Record of meeting held in House of Commons, 14 June 1951, FO 371/92556/563.
47. Lowe, *Containing the Cold War*, p. 68.
48. San Francisco to Foreign Office, 5 September 1951, FO 371/92594/1348.
49. San Francisco to Foreign Office, 12 September 1951, FO 371/92616/5.
50. See Lowe, *Containing the Cold War*, pp. 74–7 for the acrimonious reactions of Eden.
51. Despatch from Dening to Eden, 28 April 1952, FO 371/99472/4.
52. *The Economist*, p. 32, 5 April 1952.
53. *Ibid.*, p. 252, 26 July 1952.
54. *Ibid.*, p. 712, 20 September 1952.

55. *Ibid.*, p. 43, 4 October 1952.
56. *Ibid.*, pp. 51–2, 3 October 1953.
57. *Ibid.*, p. 182, 17 October 1953.
58. Cabinet conclusions, CC68(54)8, 20 October 1954, Cab. 128/27.
59. *Ibid.*
60. *Ibid.*
61. Cabinet conclusions, CC16(55)5, 22 February 1955, Cab. 128/28.
62. *Ibid.*
63. *The Economist*, pp. 607–8, 20 August 1955.
64. *Ibid.*, p. 80, 11 April 1953.
65. *Ibid.*, p. 958, 15 December 1956.
66. *Ibid.*, pp. 603–4, 18 May 1957.
67. *Ibid.*, p. 321, 9 August 1952.
68. *Ibid.*, p. 442, 15 November 1952.
69. *Ibid.*, p. 459, 15 August 1953.
70. *Ibid.*, p. 14, 'Japan's Second Century', 8 March 1958.
71. *Ibid.*, p. 17.
72. *Ibid.*, p. 18.
73. *Ibid.*, p. 19.
74. *Ibid.*, pp. 20–2.
75. *Ibid.*, p. 28.
76. *Ibid.*, p. 32.
77. *Ibid.*
78. Cabinet minutes, CM23(55)10, Cab. 128/29.
79. *Ibid.*

9
Anglo-Japanese Relations in the 1950s: Cooperation, Friction and the Search for State Identity

Tanaka Takahiko

The Asia-Pacific war dramatically transformed the international political structure in the Far East. The devastation caused by the war compelled both Japan and Britain to retreat from their past status as leading imperial powers in the region and resulted in the expansion of US and Soviet influence in Far Eastern affairs. The Korean peninsula was divided by the superpowers, and China entered the turmoil of civil war between the Nationalists and the Communists. Although there are various views as to when and how the Cold War started in Asia, Britain and Japan were undeniably placed under the Cold War structure in the 1950s.

International relations in the Cold War structure were totally different from the pre-war ones. Britain and Japan were faced with the pressing necessity to adjust themselves to the totally new situation in the Far East generated by the Cold War. Both countries had to redefine their international roles, power and influence, as well as their behavioural codes. Anglo-Japanese relations had also to be redefined by both countries in adjusting to the changed international scene.

Looking at Anglo-Japanese relations in the 1950s, it is possible to point out that there were at least three interconnecting categories of issues that they had to cope with. First, the problems generated by the Cold War. Problems related to their political and economic relations with communist China are included in this category. Second, Britain and Japan had to cope with long-standing economic frictions, such as unfair commercial practices by some of the Japanese textile companies. These frictions were to develop into a prolonged period of Britain obstructing to Japan's admission to the GATT. Finally, both countries had to solve the problems generated by the Asia-Pacific war: the British POW issue and the treatment of war criminals, etc.

The leaders of each country tried to solve those problems basically through cooperative methods, though they did not hesitate to assert their national interests frankly. Sometimes one tried to use the other for the purpose of political leverage in their relations with the superpowers and sometimes they held back from asserting their own interests, under the Cold War bipolar structure.

This chapter is intended to outline the historical development of Anglo-Japanese diplomatic relations in the 1950s with reference to the three kinds of issues mentioned above, and to discuss its broad meaning.[1]

The Yoshida period: commencement of post-war Anglo-Japanese relations

After the occupation of Japan ended, Britain and Japan were faced with various crucial and difficult issues, which they did manage to solve by means of direct negotiations between themselves. The traumatic effect of the 'Yoshida letter' on British officials had to be overcome.[2] Trade frictions had become the main focus of concern for both governments, even before the end of the occupation. Compensation for the British POWs treated cruelly by the Japanese during the war was the intractable thorn between the two nations. It is not going too far to say that most of the questions the two countries had to contend with after the occupation were raised during the last two years of the Yoshida administration, and that Anglo-Japanese relations in the 1950s evolved as a result of those questions.

Obstacles and new policies

In March 1952, Sir Esler Dening, the British ambassador at Tokyo, observed that Anglo-Japanese relations were not good.[3] It was natural that the memories of wartime atrocities involving the British POWs could not be easily erased, even after a peace treaty had been concluded in September 1951. In addition, the revival of Japanese trade and unfair commercial practices threatening the British pottery and textile industries reminded many in Britain of the pre-war trade drive by the Japanese. Improving Anglo-Japanese relations was the imperative for both the British and the Japanese governments. It was also necessary for them to define what their relationship should be like.

It was Dening on the British side who took the initiative in redefining Anglo-Japanese relations. Concerned with the indifference to Japan in London, he urged the Foreign Office by means of observations and analyses to establish new policy guidelines towards Japan. What Dening suggested to Whitehall was that the British government should and could regain its influence over Japan. Stating that Japan was no longer a military 'menace', but was now an economic one, he suggested that Japan should be treated as a potential partner. The resentment that the Japanese felt about the American occupation, combined with the traditional respect Japan had for British culture and politico-social institutions, such as the monarchy, parliament, trade unions and social security, would, he assumed, give the British a solid grounding for renewed influence. Dening then recommended that the British government establish offices of the British Council in Japan and promote personal interactions by providing facilities for Japanese officials, trade union leaders and businessmen to visit the United Kingdom to study British institutions.[4] Thus, the new British ambassador regarded it as necessary and beneficial for Britain to improve Anglo-Japanese relations.

The logic of the Cold War also influenced Dening's view. In his opinion, if the British mishandled the Japanese and failed to improve relations, Japan would go in the direction of neutralism or join the communist bloc. What he most feared was Sino-Japanese rapprochement, which would, he believed, shift the world balance of power dramatically. On the other hand, if the British could keep on good terms with the Japanese, it could be expected that the British government would be able to exert considerable influence on the US government as an honest broker. It was predicted that the Japanese would become more self-assertive after Japan's independence and that the rather insensitive and over-reactive tendencies of American diplomacy would cause serious friction with the Japanese. Dening realized that such a situation would be a diplomatic asset for the British.[5]

Although it took rather a long time for Dening's recommendations to materialize as government policy, they gradually obtained wide support in the Foreign Office, whose officials started to prepare their guidelines based on Dening's proposals. On 23 February 1954, the Foreign Office completed a policy paper 'Policy towards Japan', which comprised the following two parts: analysis of present Anglo-Japanese relations and policy recommendations.

In the first part, the policy paper argued that antipathy towards Japan as expressed in the media and in Parliament was highly emotional and not based on sufficiently objective analysis. It went as far as to say that, while Japan was an economic threat, the US, Germany and India were greater threats with stronger economic competitiveness. The crucial and real problem was, it continued, the danger of a Sino-Japanese coalition, which would drastically change the world balance of power. The guidelines observed that a coalition was possible because the Japanese were not entirely hostile to communist or totalitarian regimes and that, if Japan was faced with economic hardship, the present conservative government could not survive. The policy paper concluded that the most important task for the British government was to prevent a potential Sino-Japanese coalition by letting the Japanese realize that they could gain more from cooperation with the West. It added that the British government should help the US, which had hitherto borne almost all the burdens.

Based on the above conclusions, 'Policy towards Japan' recommended that the following actions be taken:

1. The prevention of a possible Sino-Japanese rapprochement and to keep Japan in the western camp.
2. Promotion of trade between Japan and the sterling area to avoid economic distress in Japan.
3. Advantage to be taken of any opportunities to mitigate the existing anti-Japanese sentiments held by British public opinion.[6]

These guidelines suggest at least the following two shifts in British policy towards Japan. First, although the Foreign Office had been inclined to let the Japanese recognize communist China during the peace treaty negotiations, it now reversed its stance. The Foreign Office also changed its attitude towards relations between Japan and Southeast Asia. Its dominant view during the occupation period was that the Southeast Asian market should be protected from the Japanese economic drive.[7] But the end of the special procurement of the Korean war compelled the Japanese to search for a new market. China could not be a substitute because of the rigid restrictions imposed by the US on trade with China. As a result the Southeast Asian market was the only alternative. The Colombo powers, including many British Commonwealth countries, sought extensive financial and technological assistance, which Britain could no longer provide. But the British disliked the idea of obtaining financial support from the Americans.[8] If Japan as an Asian state could recover from the recession through expansion of trade with Southeast Asia and become powerful enough to offer the Colombo plan powers financial assistance, Britain could keep her influence over the Colombo countries without recourse to the financial resources needed for her own reconstruction. Thus, the British government started to give favourable consideration to the possibility of Japan entering the Colombo plan.

The Japanese were also eager to improve relations with Britain. The staff in the Foreign Ministry and Prime Minister Yoshida were well aware of anti-Japanese sentiments in Britain. Yoshida repeatedly referred to his anxiety over trade frictions with Britain.[9] Asakai Koichiro, the head of the Japanese liaison office in London, also observed that the POW problems and trade frictions caused public resentment against Japan.[10] Yoshida had many good reasons to concentrate on improving better relations with Britain. One was economic. The first priority was given to economic reconstruction by the Yoshida government. The more opportunity to expand her economy Japan could obtain, the better. Improving Anglo-Japanese relations would provide an opportunity for the Japanese to expand their external trade to China, Southeast Asia and the British Commonwealth, where Japan could not only cooperate with but also come into conflict with the British. The Japanese government had already started negotiating admission to the GATT immediately after signing the peace treaty. It was necessary for Japan to enter the free trade system in order to derive benefits from stable international trade. For this purpose, British support was indispensable, but the latter was reluctant to back the Japanese efforts because of existing economic friction. Thus, solving trade friction between Britain and Japan became one of the most significant policy objectives of Anglo-Japanese relations.

From Yoshida's viewpoint, any improvement in Anglo-Japanese relations should also cover strategic aspects, particularly in relation to China. He was well aware of the resentment in Britain caused by the Yoshida letter. Yoshida had proposed separating communist China from the Soviet bloc by inducing a switch in US policy towards China, though he had yielded to Secretary of State Dulles's pressure. In February 1952, Yoshida told British officials in Tokyo that he wanted to promote 'a tripartite Anglo-American-Japanese policy towards communist China' and that Japan would be able to play the role of a bridge between communist China and the western bloc members.[11] To implement Yoshida's plan, the policy differences over China between Britain, the US and Japan should be resolved. The most difficult obstacle for his China policy was the inflexible attitude of the Americans over Chinese trade with the western allies. Yoshida sought to reverse

Anglo-American divergences over China, and expected that the Americans would amend their rigid China policy in the direction of British policy. This meant that Yoshida was in favour of a kind of *de facto* 'two Chinas' policy.

Development of Anglo-Japanese relations

During the Yoshida period, the evolution of Anglo-Japanese relations took the form of both convergence and divergence. For the purpose of improving Anglo-Japanese relations, the Foreign Office and, in particular, Ambassador Dening recognized the significance of exchanging personnel in various sectors and of promoting mutual cultural understanding. The establishment of the British Council in Tokyo in 1953, and a local branch in Kyoto in the following year, implemented this idea.

More spectacularly, the British government invited a member of Japanese royal family to the coronation of Elizabeth II. The Japanese government accepted this invitation with pleasure and sent Crown Prince Akihito in March 1953. The Crown Prince stayed in Britain for about two months and visited various parts of the country. He was welcomed in most places but could not fully escape expressions of hostility from former POWs. Prime Minister Churchill invited the Crown Prince to lunch at 10 Downing Street on 30 April. But on the same day, his visit to Newcastle was cancelled because of strong objections by a group of POWs there. The newspapers devoted far more column inches to the Newcastle decision than to Churchill's invitation. Akihito's visit to Coventry also encountered opposition from the trade union movement there. Thus, it can be seen that the British could not fully support their government's efforts to improve Anglo-Japanese relations. In other words, the POW question could not be solved simply at inter-governmental level.[12]

Apart from the POW problem, economic frictions were intensified during the Yoshida era. The stressful reality of economic relations was highlighted by Anglo-Japanese divergence over the latter's admission to the GATT. But the British government expressed strong reservations, because of unfair commercial practices by the Japanese pottery and textile industries.

In July 1954, the interim committee of the GATT decided to start the process of formally admitting Japan by recommending its member states to convene multilateral tariff negotiations with Japan by February 1955. Peter Thorneycroft, the President of the Board of Trade, who was determined to resist American pressure and protect domestic industries, proposed in the cabinet to open bilateral negotiations with Japan in order to reach mutual agreements favourable to British industries, which should override the GATT provisions. He was, however, faced with strong American pressure to accept Japan's full membership. The US government suggested that the British government should impose some safeguards on her trade with Japan each time any vital problems occurred. Fearing that the American proposal might be harmful to Anglo-Japanese relations, Thorneycroft decided, instead, to threaten the Japanese with invoking Article 35 of the GATT unless the Japanese agreed to hold bilateral negotiations. He thought that both the Japanese and the Americans had false hopes that the British would climb down in the face of their combined efforts and intended to let them know that their hope was ill-founded.[13] On 23 October, an aide mémoire containing the British proposal was handed to the Japanese government. But the Japanese Foreign Ministry replied that it was not able to accept the British proposal. Consequently, the British government became more inclined to invoke Article 35.

In contrast to the GATT problem, Britain and Japan were more cooperative in promoting economic growth in South and Southeast Asia through the Colombo plan. In July 1953, the overseas negotiating committee of the Churchill cabinet prepared a paper, which noted that the British economic policy towards Japan was 'to encourage Japan to hold and use sterling and to look to the sterling area for her supplies of raw materials'.[14] The British government assumed that the Japanese could contribute to economic development in Colombo plan countries by investing in Southeast Asia.[15]

Overcoming strong opposition from Australia, and mobilizing support from the Asian powers such as India, Pakistan and Ceylon, and the US government, Japan was finally admitted to the Colombo plan in October 1954.[16] What the Japanese government sought was not only economic but also strategic advantage. Building a stable economy in the region was necessary for Japanese trade which was urgently seeking new markets, and was essential to prevent the spread of Communism in Southeast Asia. Economic stability and development was also regarded as contributing to Japan's strategic security.[17] Thus, Japan and Britain started their cooperative steps in Southeast Asia which had been one of the flashpoints of their conflict before the war, although the British government would continue to be wary about Japan's excessive trade expansion into that area.[18] Their efforts seem to have played a decisive role in building the postwar economic circumstances in the area. Given the later British retreat and the dominant economic role played there by Japan since the 1960s, it can be argued that 'succeeding John Bull'[19] occurred in Southeast Asia in economic terms.

The Yoshida mission

On 26 September 1954, Yoshida departed for Western Europe and the United States – the so-called 'Yoshida mission'. As part of his lengthy tour, he visited Britain at the beginning of October. The mission had been planned as early as January and Yoshida defined its general purpose as a 'goodwill mission'.[20]

The agenda for negotiations that the Foreign Ministry officials intended to take up during the mission were mainly economic: a commercial and aviation treaty with Britain, existing domestic resentment over so-called 'unfair competition' on the part of some Japanese industries, and Japan's admission to the GATT. It was also intended to talk about the problems related to Japan's compensation for British POWs and clemency to Japanese war criminals.[21]

Although Yoshida understood the significance of these concerns, he attached more significance to political issues, in particular, coordination of Anglo-Japanese policy towards China,[22] and desired a spectacular success in London. He was reported to have said that the two countries should not concentrate myopically on specific economic questions.[23] As mentioned above, Yoshida had his own policy vision of an Anglo-Japanese coalition over China. This vision may have reflected his self-esteem as a statesman who had the will and ability to take initiatives in world politics. As the Foreign Office accurately analysed, the mission was also designed to reconstruct Yoshida's political reputation and power, which seemed to have been irreversibly undermined by an economic scandal involving some top members of his Liberal Party and of his own mishandling.[24]

Moreover, the Japanese public had become increasingly anti-American, as a result of the end of the occupation and also because of the Daigo Fukuryu Maru Jiken (Lucky Dragon incident) on Bikini Atoll.[25] Anti-American nationalist sentiments were easily translated into anti-Yoshida feelings, because the attitude of Yoshida and his government towards the US government had a clear pro-American outlook, which was now alienating public opinion in Japan. This was also spurred on by the diplomatic defeat of the US in Indochina when the Eisenhower government failed to mobilize British support for a joint military intervention so that as a result the international status of China increased. The international profile of Britain, which had rejected the American request for a joint intervention and successfully presided over the Geneva conference, was also rising as a promoter of détente. The diplomatic defeat of the US and the victory of Britain gave Yoshida's efforts over China through cooperation with Britain the appearance of a bid for diplomacy independent of American control. Thus, his mission to Britain must have been designed to neutralize both domestic criticism and anti-American nationalism.

As already mentioned, the Japanese government regarded Britain as one of the most important partners for its policy towards Southeast Asia. It was reported that as early as May 1953 Yoshida had ordered the setting up of a committee to formulate a suitable policy for developing the Southeast Asian economy.[26] The Yoshida mission was originally scheduled to start in July and to be extended beyond Europe to Southeast Asia, but this was postponed because of political confusion caused by scandal, and his visit to Southeast Asia was removed from the schedule. A guideline for a speech, prepared by the Foreign Ministry in April 1954, stated: 'the central point of the speech is to propose to the British to consult over action plans for coordinating and harmonizing our policy for the development of Southeast Asia and the Colombo plan led by the British'. In addition, the Foreign Ministry recognized that cooperation with the British in Southeast Asia would to a great degree contribute to its China policy. According to Kasumigaseki's analysis, 'the British government is reported to emphasize the significance of SEATO (Southeast Asia Treaty Organization) as an organization for economic cooperation' and 'the British understood that the most effective policy to counter the infiltration of Chinese influence in Southeast Asia was to support economic development in the area and at the same time promote the policy of co-existence'.[27] Based on these analyses, Yoshida was to reiterate his desire to establish an Anglo-Japanese front for a 'counter-offensive against communism' in Southeast Asia.

The Foreign Office considered that the mission would provide a good opportunity to help the Japanese establish their postwar identity as a member of the western alliance. One of its minutes clearly defined the Yoshida mission to Britain as an opportunity to 'demonstrate our readiness to accept Japan into the free world'.[28] The Foreign Office was still suspicious about any shift on the part of Japan towards a neutralist position and was concerned by the declining political power of Yoshida.[29] The British government was inclined, therefore, to avoid the outstanding controversial problems, such as Japanese unfair trade practices and the POWs, although Yoshida should be reminded that they had not gone away.[30]

The British were also aware that Yoshida wanted to discuss China. Ambassador Dening suggested that Yoshida would present his Chinese policy and warned that, however 'woolly' it might be, it should not be ignored because the Japanese attached more confidence to British policies towards Asia than American ones. In other words, Dening suggested that the British government should seize the opportunity to strengthen its influence in Japan.[31] But the Foreign Office took the opposite stance to the ambassador and recommended that Eden should dissuade Yoshida from expecting any support for his plan for an Anglo-Japanese coalition over China.[32] The British government was very careful to avoid giving the impression of ganging up with the Japanese against the US.

Prime Minister Yoshida arrived in London on 21 October. During his stay, he was tirelessly active. On 26 October, he was received in audience by the Queen and expressed gratitude for the hospitality that had been offered to the Crown Prince in 1953. On the same day he was invited to make a speech in the House of Commons. There Yoshida emphasized that Japan had no intention of taking a neutralist position and desired to reconstruct Anglo-Japanese political cooperation for stabilization in the Far East and to establish economic cooperation in Southeast Asia. Touching on the alleged unfair trade activities, Yoshida explained that the postwar democratization of the Japanese economy and industrial relations 'render impossible what is called 'social dumping' by Japan'. He added: 'When you study the true conditions of Japanese economy you will find that there is no ground for fear of deadly competition from us' and requested Members of Parliament to take a more sympathetic attitude to Japan's admission to the GATT. Finally, he promised to settle the problem of compensation for British POWs by all means as soon as possible and asked for parole for Japanese war criminals.[33]

27 October must have been the busiest day for Yoshida during his visit. He had meetings with the Foreign Secretary Anthony Eden, the representative of the National Federation of Far Eastern Prisoners of War, and Prime Minister Churchill. Eden and Yoshida discussed all the items on the agenda and followed the lines prepared by their diplomatic officials. Yoshida asked Eden for more favourable consideration for Japan's admission to the GATT and amnesty for Japanese war criminals. Eden requested Yoshida to take the POW question more seriously, and Yoshida promised to consider the question faithfully.

Denis Allen, the head of the Far Eastern Department, recalled after the Yoshida mission that he had been struck by 'the manner in which Yoshida kept on coming back to the subject of China'.[34] In his meetings with Eden and Churchill, Yoshida referred to the necessity for both governments to attempt to detach the Chinese from the Russians. Yoshida said to Eden, 'Because the market in China is extremely significant to the Japanese economy, it is necessary to detach China from Russia in order to secure the market'. Eden responded that the embargo on China was consolidating Sino-Soviet ties and that promoting trade relations between China and the western powers might be effective in undermining her relations with Russia. But he emphasized that cooperation with the Americans was essential over trade with China, and that Japan and Britain should avoid giving any indication of an Anglo-Japanese coalition against the US.[35] Yoshida reiterated his vision during the meeting with Churchill. Churchill went no further than expressing 'sympathy with his general aims'.[36]

Yoshida also had meetings with non-governmental groups. On 25 October, the representatives of the Federation of British Industries (FBI) called on him and exchanged views. They expressed their suspicion that the Japanese government was assisting exporting industries with governmental subsidies or a favourable tax regime. Yoshida retorted that the Japanese government could not afford to do so and had withdrawn its subsidies. In response to the FBI's complaint about the export thrust of Japanese textile industries, Yoshida suggested that the increase in exports from Japan would also beneficial to the British. As for unfair commercial activities by Japanese pottery industries, the FBI representatives admitted that the friction had been gradually eased, but complained about the continuation of dumping of small pottery. Yoshida promised to persuade those industries to join a trade union, which would be able to restrain them from dumping.[37]

Two days later, Yoshida held a meeting with representatives of the National Federation of Far Eastern Prisoners of War. The representatives demanded that the Japanese government should carry out its obligation under Article 16 of the peace treaty, that is, compensate the POWs and fix a specific timetable. They added that the problem was not financial but one of principle. Yoshida rather rudely retorted: 'I thought that this question had already been settled.' But he promised to put the item of the compensation into the next budget plan.[38]

It was natural that the POW question was one of the main foci of attention on the part of the British, because that had been an unforgettable and deep wound generating strong anti-Japanese sentiments.

But the British government was reluctant to go further than reminding the Japanese of the existence of the problem, because it considered that the problem had been on the way to a settlement.[39] In fact, the Japanese government had reached almost the final stage in resolving this question before Yoshida's visit, being ready to pay £6,050,000 in compensation.[40] Although the Ministry of Finance was reluctant to approve this, it finally agreed to the payment. It was stated in a minute by the Foreign Ministry of 29 November that the POW question was deemed to be finally settled when the Japanese government paid £4,500,000 to the International Red Cross in May 1955.[41] From then on, at least for the rest of the 1950s, the POW question was not to be taken up by either government as an intergovernmental issue. But a question of such a traumatic kind could not be erased by an interstate agreement and still exists as an intractable thorn in British public opinion.

The Yoshida mission was the first postwar visit to Britain of a top political leader of Japan. The mission was successful in generating cordiality in Anglo-Japanese relations. It also provided Foreign Ministry officials with the incentive to solve specific Anglo-Japanese issues before the mission arrived. From Yoshida's viewpoint, however, the mission to Britain must have been disappointing, though he seemed to be very satisfied with the cordiality and hospitality extended by the Foreign Office and Churchill. His attempt at a spectacular diplomatic coup over the China question was blocked by the British, though in a subtle manner. He could not gain any diplomatic fruits in the United States either.

Détente and the quest for autonomy: the Hatoyama period[42]

Yoshida returned to Japan in the middle of November without any diplomatic gains and failed to stay in power. Hatoyama Ichiro, the leader of the Democratic Party, took office in December. He effectively appealed to the existing nationalist sentiment in the Japanese public by proposing a new foreign policy the so-called '*jishu gaiko*' (autonomous diplomacy) to improve Japan's relations with the main arch-enemies of the United States: China and the Soviet Union. Although Hatoyama succeeded in mobilizing much popularity, his party could not win a comfortable majority in the Diet even after the general election in March.

British officials had been anxiously observing this development. To them, Yoshida was far more desirable. Hatoyama's past record as an admirer of Hitler and Mussolini alarmed the Foreign Office and was interpreted as an indicator of his strong nationalistic disposition. His inauguration speech proposing to normalize Japan's relations with her communist neighbours was regarded as an indication of his anti-American and neutralist tendency.[43] Hatoyama's political weakness was also a source of British anxiety. He was regarded as an indecisive and sick old man and was supposed to leave office at the time of the conservative merger. Dening believed that the Hatoyama administration would adopt an opportunistic foreign policy such as normalization with China to mobilize nationalistic popular support. Its indifference to Britain and Europe also disappointed the British ambassador.[44]

As Dening suggested, Hatoyama was not very interested in promoting Anglo-Japanese relations, but he and his entourage were inclined to regard Britain's détente diplomacy during the Churchill and Eden administrations as one of the most suitable models for their autonomous diplomacy. Since 1954 the Churchill–Eden détente diplomacy had demonstrated clearly that even an ally protected and controlled by the United States could promote détente with American arch-enemies, and could, by doing so, increase its international status. For the Hatoyama administration, the British success was a good example to convince their domestic hard-line opponents of the relevance of détente diplomacy towards the Russians. In fact, Hatoyama frequently mentioned Churchill's name as the champion of world peace in his Diet speeches.

In the mid-1950s, the Japanese government was to a great degree preoccupied with Soviet-Japanese normalization talks.[45] Anglo-Japanese political relations mainly revolved around this issue and the economic problems connected with Japan's admission to the GATT. The Japanese government could not ignore the influence of Britain, as a co-author of the San Francisco peace treaty, over the territorial problems involved in normalization talks with the Russians. Soviet-Japanese normalization talks started in London in June 1955. The Japanese officials tried their best to keep in touch with the Americans, but they also conveyed certain significant information on the negotiations in order to obtain advice and support from the Foreign Office. Whitehall was, however, very careful not to offer any advice that suggested its involvement in the negotiating process. The Foreign Office recognized that the normalization talks were destined for failure and realized that the British government had to avoid giving the Japanese any excuse for putting the blame on the British and stirring up nationalist sentiment in Japan.[46]

The Soviet-Japanese territorial dispute could also place the British in a very difficult position with regard to her relations not only with the Japanese but also with the Russians. The Foreign Office had consistently opposed the Japanese territorial demands. The Japanese government desired to restore Japan's sovereignty over at least the four islands located in the southern part of the Kurils: Etorofu, Kunashiri, Shikotan and Habomai. But the Foreign Office took the position that Kunashiri and Etorofu were *de facto* or even *de jure* Soviet territories and that Japanese sovereignty over Shikotan was also doubtful.[47] Anticipating potential furious nationalistic reactions from the Japanese, the British could not express their position openly. At the same time, altering its stance in favour of the Japanese would harm British relations with the Russians with whom the Eden government sought détente. The British government was in a dilemma: it could neither state its basic position, nor amend it in order to support the Japanese claims.

During 1955, the Foreign Ministry came to know that the position of the British government was not at all favourable to its territorial demands. Even the US government was not sympathetic to Japan's claims for Kunashiri and Etorofu until September 1956. Without strong Anglo-American support and faced with the refusal of the USSR to return Etorofu and Kunashiri, Hatoyama decided to restore diplomatic relations with Russia by shelving the territorial questions without concluding a peace treaty. He went to Moscow to sign a joint declaration for normalization in October 1956.

It can be argued that, if the Japanese government had obtained Anglo-American support, negotiations with the Russians would not have reached any conclusion. In other words, the cautious and negative British attitude somehow restrained the Japanese from becoming too rigid over the territorial question and, therefore, Russo-Japanese normalization was achieved. The Soviet Union and Japan terminated their state of war by the joint declaration and it to some extent stabilized the Far Eastern situation by establishing at least a formal channel of communication between the two countries. That being so, the British government, in a sense, contributed to Far Eastern stability by not supporting the Japanese territorial demands.

Hatoyama's policy towards communist China caused little concern within the Foreign Office. Although Sino-Japanese rapprochement had been one of the main foreign policy goals of his administration, the government could not go any further than expressing its intention to recognize and cooperate with some non-governmental attempts to promote trade with China. Peking continuously wooed the Japanese, for example, by stating its readiness to invite Hatoyama and Foreign Minister Shigemitsu in May 1956.[48] But the Japanese government was too preoccupied with normalization with Russia and with related domestic political struggles to respond to the Chinese. The British government did not, therefore, have to be too concerned with a possible Sino-Japanese coalition. In any case, Hatoyama did not stay in power long after the ratification of the Russo-Japanese joint declaration in December 1956. Shortly after the ratification, he retired and was succeeded by Ishibashi Tanzan.

Japan's admission to the GATT

Developments over Japan's admission to the GATT were affected by Hatoyama, who was regarded as more nationalistic and neutralist than Yoshida. The Foreign Office was concerned about the possible worsening of Anglo-Japanese relations in the event of the invocation of Article 35 of GATT and feared that Hatoyama might overreact to the unfavourable British attitudes and turn to a rapprochement with China. It attempted, therefore, to put pressure on the Board of Trade. In the middle of December 1954, Foreign Secretary Eden proposed at a cabinet meeting to abandon the option of invoking Article 35. The President of the Board, Peter Thorneycroft, strongly resisted Eden, insisting that the Conservative government could not ignore the intense domestic pressure from cotton industries in Lancashire, and proposed to postpone the decision not to invoke the article.[49] The struggle between the Foreign Office and the Board of Trade can be characterized as a struggle between the logic of the Cold War and that of domestic political economy. In the event it was a victory for the latter and the British government informed the Japanese of its decision to invoke Article 35 in April 1955.

Here again it should be emphasized that the British government did not intend to obstruct Japan's admission itself. Despite its invoking Article 35, Japan gained full membership of GATT in September 1955. The British fully recognized the necessity to include Japan within an international cooperative procedure for resolving economic disputes and meet the Japanese demand for recognition as a legitimate state within the international regime. What they sought was to take gradual steps to adjust British attitudes and those of Japan to the new international economic rules embodied in the GATT. The governments of both countries now moved to the next stage of establishing a firmer basis for cooperative and mutually beneficial economic relations through bilateral negotiations for a commercial and aviation agreement, which was to be concluded in 1963.

The Kishi period: 'A new phase in Anglo-Japanese relations'

Ishibashi Tanzan who succeeded Hatoyama, did not stay in power very long because of ill health. After his premature retirement, Kishi Nobusuke became prime minister in February 1957. Governmental changes also took place in Britain. After the collapse of the Eden administration following the Suez debacle, Harold Macmillan took office in January. Both prime ministers were faced with difficult situations generated by their predecessors.

Mutual image

Prime Minister Kishi was faced with two contradictory tasks: first, repairing relations with the US, which had deteriorated as a result of Hatoyama's blunt attempts at autonomy through his détente diplomacy; and, secondly, promoting Japan's political autonomy and international status. The frequent cases of trade friction with the US forced the Japanese to search for new and wider markets elsewhere, for instance, mainland China and Southeast Asia, in order to reduce Japan's dependence on the US economy. The Girard case also took nationalist sentiments in Japan in a more anti-American direction.[50] Kishi attempted to carry out his foreign policy to meet both tasks.

Harold Macmillan also had to reconstruct Britain's special relationship with the US. As a result of the Suez fiasco, it had deteriorated, as had the international prestige of Britain. The huge costs of war had devastated the British economy. The long process of withdrawal from the British colonial empire was progressing steadily. Even so, the Macmillan government had to do its best to restore its influence over the Americans and play a significant role, in particular, in the field of the Cold War.

Kishi received a very negative assessment within the Foreign Office. His past record as a minister in the Tojo cabinet during the war raised the suspicion that he might be sympathetic to totalitarian communist regimes. It was also feared that he might adopt opportunistic foreign policies, such as a rapprochement with China, in order to feed the growing Japanese population and keep his hold on political power.[51]

As far as Anglo-Japanese relations were concerned, the Foreign Office observed that the new Japanese government was indifferent to Britain. The first diplomatic blue book published by the Foreign Ministry in

September 1957 contained only a brief reference to Britain covering the British Commonwealth and nuclear tests. Kishi also gave the British officials in Tokyo the impression that he was not very interested in a declining power, such as Britain. The Foreign Office expected the new Japanese government would step up its assertiveness towards the British government.[52] In summer 1957, when the US State Department unofficially recommended that the Foreign Office invite Kishi to Britain, the British did 'not altogether share American enthusiasm for Mr. Kishi' and decided to wait and observe his performance in domestic and international politics. In contrast, Fujiyama Aiichiro, appointed Foreign Minister in July, created a more favourable impression. The British estimated that Fujiyama had, and would have, strong domestic political support even if Kishi fell from power. As an influential businessman, the new Foreign Minister did not make the British officials anxious about a political coalition with China and the Soviet Union, which they had feared. He was also supposed to appreciate the significance of British support and advice much better than Kishi.[53]

On the other hand, Kishi and his cabinet regarded Britain as a very important factor for their foreign policy. Kishi recalled in his memoirs that he had regarded as essential the strengthening Japan's ties with Britain, which enjoyed a 'special relationship' with the US. He also considered that the Japanese should not be too preoccupied with relations with the US and should look more to Europe.[54] The GATT questions had to be settled. Japanese public opinion was furious when the British ignored Japan's request to halt their nuclear tests in April and carried them out in the Christmas Islands in May 1957. One of Kishi's pet policies, the Southeast Asia Development Fund, needed British support. Britain was again regarded as an important partner and was assumed to exercise an effective political leverage on the United States over problems regarding economic and political relations with China. In addition, the Foreign Ministry observed that the British government started to look on Japan as a more significant partner because of its decline in power in Asia after the Suez fiasco, because of the rising international status of Japan, and because of the improving attitudes towards Japan in Commonwealth countries.[55] Earlier, Yoshida had been very careful not to give any suggestion of an Anglo-Japanese coalition against the US. Compared to its predecessors, the Kishi government tended to demonstrate more explicitly its intention to establish such a coalition. During the Kishi period, the Foreign Ministry attempted to invite British political leaders more warmly than previously. In July, for instance, Nishi Haruhiko, the Japanese ambassador to Britain, on the instruction of his prime minister, invited Macmillan to Japan in the winter of 1958, though the invitation could not be accepted because of Macmillan's busy schedule.[56]

The British government could not overlook the new Japanese government, even though it was not at all enthusiastic about Kishi. The British embassy at Tokyo started in August 1957 to move towards the idea of inviting Fujiyama to London. Macmillan and Selwyn Lloyd, the Foreign Secretary, were at first reluctant, but finally approved this proposal.[57] The Japanese government accepted the invitation with pleasure.

Fujiyama's visit to Britain

The general purpose from the viewpoint of the Foreign Office was to exert influence on Kishi through Fujiyama, whom it preferred to his Prime Minister as a diplomatic partner. The British expected that Fujiyama was more conciliatory towards the present British position on nuclear deterrence and could mitigate the fury of the Japanese public.[58] From the Japanese viewpoint, Fujiyama's visit was a very good opportunity 'to revive the atmosphere of past friendship at the time of the Anglo-Japanese alliance' and to convince the British public that the Kishi government had no intention of merely following the course set by the Americans.[59] They were also determined to assert more intensely what they had to assert. Fujiyama stated that Japan would establish a 'new phase of Anglo-Japanese relations'.

Fujiyama arrived at London on 27 September. He met many British governmental leaders including Selwyn Lloyd and Macmillan. The British government extended lavish hospitality which was intended to convey to Fujiyama how significant his visit was regarded by the British. The main aim of the Foreign Office was not to discuss specific problems between the two countries in depth, but to establish goodwill and friendship with Fujiyama and the new Japanese government.[60] Fujiyama met the Foreign Secretary in the morning of 28 September. After lunch, Duncan Sandys, the Defence Minister, joined the meeting. During Fujiyama's stay, this was the most significant meeting, where most of the main issues were discussed. Over the China problem, Fujiyama stated that the urgent task of the free world was to detach China from the Russians, but that the Americans took too rigid a policy towards China to attain that purpose. He continued that Britain and Japan should exchange information and coordinate their policies. Then, unlike his predecessors, Fujiyama clearly proposed cooperation to persuade the Americans to adopt a more flexible policy. The Foreign

Office agreed with Fujiyama's proposal for frustrating Sino-Soviet relations. But it observed that a Sino-Soviet split was unlikely to take place in the near future. Lloyd cautiously avoided responding directly, saying that China and Russia had historically been enemies and that China was not really a Russian satellite but was more independent than was generally understood. When Fujiyama asked for the British view on Chinese representation in the United Nations, Lloyd made it clear that his government had no intention of causing any trouble for the United States.[61] Whereas the Japanese were more positive in building a closer Anglo-Japanese coalition against the US, the British did not alter their previous policy of avoiding any suggestion of ganging up with Japan against the US.

As for the issue of British nuclear tests, the British leaders and Fujiyama diverged sharply. Fujiyama adamantly demanded an immediate halt to British nuclear tests by suggesting that, unless the existing very strong anti-nuclear sentiments in Japan were taken fully into account, Japanese public opinion would become anti-British and anti-American. On the other hand, Lloyd and Sandys tried to convince Fujiyama of the necessity of developing nuclear weapons in order to deter the Russians. Sandys asked Fujiyama to make more effort to bring the Japanese public round in favour of the reality of nuclear deterrence.[62] This clearly demonstrates that the British leaders could not understand how deeply traumatic the experience of Hiroshima and Nagasaki was to the Japanese people.

Another issue of serious divergence was the British invocation of Article 35 of the GATT. Fujiyama urged Britain to follow the Australian government, which had finally agreed in July to open negotiations with Japan to examine the possibility of revoking the application of Article 35. But Lloyd refused and stated that the GATT question was not only an Anglo-Japanese matter but was also a crucial domestic political issue in Britain, though he expressed the understanding of Japan's need to expand trade with Britain.

The Asian Development Fund, one of Kishi's pet policies, was also discussed. The fund was designed by Kishi to build up a multilateral system of financial assistance for the developing countries in Southeast Asia with financial contributions from the US and Britain. It was intended to increase purchasing power in Southeast Asia and prevent the spread of communism there. Fujiyama observed that the British government was more susceptible to Asian opinion than the US government. He therefore wanted British support for the scheme. The British also realized the significance of this plan because Southeast Asia was one of the most important markets for them. But this also made the British very sensitive to the possible danger of Japan's economic penetration into their Asian market. The Foreign Office also estimated that Britain could not afford to contribute financially to the fund.[63] The Southeast Asian countries were expected by the Foreign Office not to be attracted by the plan, because of their memories of the Great East Asian Co-prosperity Sphere. Lloyd showed an interest in the plan, but declined to take part in it, saying that it was impossible for Britain to assist Japan financially.[64]

The next day, Fujiyama met other governmental leaders in charge of economic matters and took up the issue of Article 35 of the GATT and Japan's purchase of a British atomic reactor. The British position on GATT problem had not changed. On the purchase of an atomic reactor, Fujiyama stated that the Japanese government were inclined to buy a British one. This statement seemed to please the British. But the Foreign Minister suggested that his government expected the British to import more Japanese goods in return. Vaughan Morgan, the Minister of State at the Board of Trade, did not fully accept this, but expressed his understanding of the Japanese proposal.

Following the visit of Fujiyama, a joint communiqué was issued on 1 October. His visit did not lead to any specific agreements on the issues raised by the Japanese. Nevertheless, both sides regarded the meetings as a considerable success. The Foreign Office was satisfied with the frank exchange of views with Fujiyama. The embassy to Tokyo also reported that the Japanese Foreign Minister was very impressed by Britain's sophisticated attitudes towards Asia by quoting Fujiyama's statement that the Southeast Asian Development Fund 'was not merely a question of getting the money and complying with the political conditions necessary to get it; it was also necessary to know how and where to use it, and this the British knew'.[65] The Japanese must have been satisfied with British hospitality, which assured them that the British government attached more importance to them than hitherto. In this way the Foreign Ministry was given some encouragement to pursue closer relations with Britain and proposed inviting a senior British minister to Japan. Responding to this invitation, Defence Secretary Duncan Sandys was quite willing to visit Japan in order to assuage the furious Japanese anti-nuclear sentiments. But the Foreign Office finally stopped him, fearing the possible adverse effects of such a visit.[66]

The fact that Fujiyama's visit could not solve any specific Anglo-Japanese questions should not be ignored. On 17 November, Britain carried out a nuclear test on Christmas Island, in spite of Japanese protests. The British embassy was so alarmed that it proposed a visit by Macmillan to Japan to present his case to the Japanese public. The Foreign Office considered that such a visit was out of the question and supposed that the Japanese would become more realistic in the face of the on-going Soviet attitudes towards disarmament.[67]

Developments in 1958

1958 saw the following two significant events affecting Anglo-Japanese relations: the inauguration of Japan as a non-permanent member of the UN Security Council in January and the deterioration of Sino-Japanese relations in May. As for the former, Japan had reached the status where she could, and was determined to, play a significant role as a bridge between West and East. The Japanese government was now able to carry out its Asian policies more positively and intensified its efforts to represent what it defined as the interests of Afro-Asian countries. In the middle of January, Fujiyama began to discuss with the British his plan for building a stable structure in Asia. The Foreign Ministry proposed a meeting between Fujiyama and Macmillan in Singapore on the occasion of Fujiyama's visit to Indonesia for the purpose of signing a peace treaty and of Macmillan's visit to India. The main issue Fujiyama planned to take up was recent developments in Anglo-Soviet relations related to Macmillan's proposal for a non-aggression pact with Russia, the Soviet proposal for a summit conference, and political consultations on international problems in East Asia. On the first two items, Fujiyama voiced his distrust of the Soviet Union and doubts about the relevance of Macmillan's and Soviet proposals. Of more importance was the third item. Fujiyama proposed a tripartite political consultation, saying, 'As a measure to cope with such various international problems in East Asia, Indonesia, Goa, Kashmir, etc., I think it is necessary to establish a combined policy, after full consultations, from the overall viewpoint, among foreign ministers of the United Kingdom, United States and Japan'.[68]

It is clear that the Japanese government was expanding the area in which Japan was willing to take the initiative in setting up an Anglo-US-Japanese coalition. Predecessors of Fujiyama had limited the area for tripartite political coalition to China. Now it included not only China but also South and Southeast Asia. The Kishi government had clearly become more assertive and intended to play a leading role in international affairs in Asia. In this sense, as the Foreign Office staffs observed, the Japanese must have regarded Britain as an effective political lever to influence the Americans and Southeast Asian countries, in order to raise the international status of Japan. Although the Foreign Office was satisfied with the fact that the Japanese still desired closer cooperation with Britain, it was not at all enthusiastic about Fujiyama's proposal. It was presumed that the Fujiyama plan could generate complications in its relations within the British Commonwealth.[69] Fortunately for the British, Fujiyama and Macmillan could not spare enough time to discuss the issue because of their tight schedules. When Ono Katsumi, who became ambassador in May, raised this matter again in conversation with Lloyd, the Foreign Secretary was indifferent to the issue and recommended that he discuss the matter with the head of the Far Eastern Department.[70]

Sino-Japanese relations did not deteriorate until May. The fourth non-governmental trade agreement was signed on 5 March. But two months later, the so-called 'Nagasaki national flag incident' devastated relations. On 2 May, a right wing thug pulled down a Chinese national flag located at a department store in Nagasaki, and the Chinese government made strong accusations against the Japanese government. The man was at once arrested for humiliating the national flag of a foreign country, but freed soon after on the ground that the flag was not the national flag because there were no official diplomatic relations with China. The Chinese government decided to sever all economic and cultural relations with Japan.

These developments undermined Kishi's plan to improve Japan's relations with China. He was very cautious not to make his intentions explicit, because of possible American displeasure. In fact, however, one of the main purposes of appointing Fujiyama as his Foreign Minister was to put him in charge of promoting Sino-Japanese economic and, in the long run, political relations.[71] On the other hand, the Nagasaki incident offered a favourable opportunity for Anglo-Japanese relations, at least from the British viewpoint. The failure of Kishi's ambitions calmed the British nightmare of a Sino-Japanese coalition.[72] The deterioration of her relations with China pushed the Foreign Ministry to promote closer relations and consultations with the British, not only over East Asian affairs but also over the prolonged bilateral question of the Commercial and Aviation Treaty. Ambassador Ono entertained a strong hope of obtaining advice from the British on far eastern problems and proposed that Prime Minister Kishi should visit Britain.

Japan's aspiration to act as a leader of the Afro-Asian states would, however, inevitably cause friction with Britain in areas such as the

Middle East. Since May, the US and Britain had been faced with political instability in Lebanon caused by nationalist groups there and finally decided to send in troops to suppress the nationalistic riots in July. The Japanese government, which had shown increased interest in markets and resources in the Middle East, quickly took an attitude hostile to the Anglo-American expedition. Fujiyama argued at a special session of the UN General Assembly in August that Britain and the US should withdraw their forces as soon as possible. But Anglo-Japanese friction over this issue did not last long, because British troops in Jordan started to withdraw in October.

At the end of 1958, the British and US governments held a consultation over their relations with Japan. Faced with the turmoil in the Far East generated by the Chinese attack on the offshore islands and political instability in Japan caused by Kishi's decision to open negotiations for revising the US-Japanese Security Treaty, Anglo-American diplomats were urged to re-examine their policy towards Japan. As a result of the consultation, both governments agreed on the necessity to make more joint efforts to keep Japan in the orbit of the free world. But there were some discrepancies between them. While both realized that the future of Japan depended upon how Japan could expand her external trade, the British were afraid that the US was intending to encourage the Japanese to expand their trade towards Southeast Asia and Europe, which were regarded by the British as their own markets. The British were still sceptical about the Americans judging the Kishi administration to be a democratic regime. Even so, the Foreign Office now started to realize that it was necessary to conclude a commercial treaty with Japan at an early date and to take a more lenient attitude towards Japan's demand for the withdrawal of Article 35 of the GATT.[73]

Prime Minister Kishi's visit to Britain

The Foreign Office was in favour of Ono's proposal in May 1958 that Kishi should visit Britain. In fact, it started to soften its previous critical attitudes towards him. At the end of July, the Foreign Office opined that Kishi was becoming more firmly committed to the free world. It was also observed that Japan had steadily become more influential with Afro-Asian nations and that it was advisable to welcome Kishi through whom the British might exert some indirect influence on Asian states.[74] These estimations by the Foreign Office were firmly established by May of the next year. They now found that the Japanese were taking a 'reasonably consistent line' as a member of the western bloc, that there was no danger of Japan's trying to recognize the communist government of China, and that she regarded Britain as a more important partner to herself. From the British viewpoint, the Sino-Japanese rifts which had developed since the Nagasaki flag incident and the Chinese attack on Quemoy and Matsu had forced the Kishi government to abandon hope of the early restoration of diplomatic relations with China. Moreover, Kishi's efforts to revise the US-Japanese Security Treaty were also regarded as beneficial because the Japanese would be able to reverse their over-dependence on the United States and calm anti-American sentiments among the Japanese public.[75]

Indeed, in 1959 the Japanese government confirmed the British perception. The Secretary General of Kishi's government stated in February that Britain had now become more significant to Japan, because of its increased global influence due to Macmillan's visit to Russia and the illness of John Foster Dulles. In May, Ambassador Ono suggested that his government aimed to establish much closer relations with Britain by devising joint policies towards Asian countries and China. One of Japan's highest officials also made it clear that the Foreign Ministry had come to the view that closer relations with Britain would be more beneficial and useful than before. The Foreign Ministry expected Macmillan's détente policy, such as his visit to Moscow to solve the Berlin crisis, to contribute favourably to Japan's hopes for a breakthrough in her relations with China in the long run.[76]

Kishi arrived in London on 13 July. The main subjects discussed were disarmament and emerging nationalism in the Middle East and Africa, a general assessment of the world political situation, policy towards China and Anglo-Japanese trade relations. On disarmament, Kishi explained that the anti-nuclear sentiments on the part of the Japanese stemmed from their experiences in Hiroshima and Nagasaki and stressed that the Japanese people strongly hoped for the success of the disarmament talks between the US, Britain and Russia in Geneva. In regard to emerging nationalism in the Middle East and Africa, Kishi expressed the hope that his country might be able to help to 'promote a peaceful solution through the United Nations' to the recent unrest there and proposed Anglo-Japanese cooperation on this issue. He referred to his fear of a possible combination of extreme nationalism and communism emerging in those areas. David Ormsby-Gore, the Minister of State, agreed but carefully avoided any clear commitment to his proposal. Kishi also mentioned the necessity of helping economic development in Africa, and emphasized that

Japan could play a significant liaison role between the West and the East. The Minister of State appreciated Japan's assistance through the UN. Thus, the Japanese started to extend their involvement in international political and economic affairs in those areas. But the British tried to restrain them from becoming too influential in the areas where the British had been one of the main actors and possessed major political and economic interests.[77]

Kishi exchanged views with Macmillan on the general situation of world politics and on policy towards China. After a brief exchange of opinions on the former, he stressed that Japan would stay firmly within the western bloc. Then, they moved on to the China issue. Kishi explained that the hostile attitudes of the Chinese government made it impossible to recognize China and to promote trade with her, because the Chinese were making it a precondition that a political relationship should be established. He reiterated that Japan's basic policy was to promote cooperation with the free world and that, though 'there was the idea of a "two Chinas" solution', neither China nor Taiwan would accept it'. Macmillan responded that the present situation was quite different from that prevailing when Britain had recognized the People's Republic in 1950 and added that the present Anglo-Chinese relations were much worse than had been envisaged at the time. Macmillan also tried to dissuade Kishi from attempting to take advantage of Anglo-American policy divergences over China, take that there was no divergence with the US government. Macmillan implied that the 'two Chinas' policy was not at all feasible and made it clear that the British government would support Kishi's present non-recognition policy towards China.[78]

On the trade issue, Kishi informed Macmillan of Japan's decision to buy the British atomic reactor. The Japanese government intended to reverse Britain's negative attitude towards imports from Japan by buying the atomic reactor.[79] Following this line, Kishi expressed his hope that recourse to Article 35 of the GATT would be lifted and made it clear that his government intended to mitigate the British anxiety about 'the possible flooding of the market by Japanese products by introducing some voluntary restriction on exports to Britain'. Though Macmillan expressed his understanding of Japan's position on this matter, he emphasized that the British government had to defend its own economy. Then the two prime ministers closed their conversation by agreeing to promote closer Anglo-Japanese cooperation.[80]

Kishi also met David Eccles, President of the Board of Trade, and, David Heathcoat Amory, the Chancellor of Exchequer, and repeated his hope for an early lifting of Article 35 and resumption of the most favoured nation status by Japan. The British ministers emphasized the difficulties involved in those matters as Macmillan had done. But they finally opened the way to Japan's most favoured nation status by proposing to hold a joint examination of an adequate safeguard arrangement to protect British industry in order to put an end to the Anglo-Japanese stalemate over the GATT. Kishi fully agreed. Apart from the GATT problem, they touched on an issue related to the recently established European Economic Community. Both sides shared anxiety that the EEC might become an exclusive economic bloc. Having lost their traditional market in China, the Japanese were urged to search for other markets in different parts of the world. Europe was one of the major targets for the Japanese. Kishi said, 'if ... [the EEC] resulted in greater discrimination against outside countries the Japanese Government saw serious objections'. In response, Eccles sought Japanese support for the British 'in pressing the American and Canadian Governments to take a similar view in order to prevent the EEC becoming too protectionist'. At the end of the discussion, problems on Anglo-Japanese cooperation in assistance for developing countries were discussed, and Kishi proposed closer joint efforts through international bodies in order to protect those countries from Soviet influence. But the British were not at all enthusiastic. Amory responded, 'before we could help the under-developing countries, we must earn means to help them'.[81]

The Anglo-Japanese discussions mainly followed the agenda prepared by the Japanese. But at the final meeting on 15 July, Macmillan raised more specific matters on the British claim for compensation for British assets lost during the Sino-Japanese war since 1937. Kishi promised to settle this matter at an early date.[82]

At the end of Kishi's visit, a joint communiqué was issued containing a summary of the conversations and expressing the determination of both parties to promote Anglo-Japanese cooperation on various matters. As stated, the main outcome of the conversations was that the leaders of both countries could have frank exchanges of views on the general international political situation and on their relations. In fact, both governments intended not to solve specific problems, but to generate a friendlier atmosphere between the two countries. In this sense, Kishi's visit was successful from the viewpoint of both governments. In addition, however, they managed to take a further step towards the final solution of the GATT problem when the Anglo-Japanese Commercial and Navigation Treaty was signed in 1962.

After Kishi's visit, there was not much development in Anglo-Japanese diplomatic relations, mainly because Kishi's government was almost exclusively preoccupied with the revision of the US–Japan security pact, which was finally completed in 1960. The domestic turmoil in Japan which was caused by the security pact negotiations forced the Japanese Prime Minister to resign in June 1960.

Conclusions

The 1950s were a period during which Britain and Japan struggled to re-establish their state identities within the context of changing world politics. They tried to redefine their roles in the world, their power and their relationship with other countries. For Britain, it was a modification and readjustment of her identity as a former world power. Although she was in the process of a retreat from power, Britain was still one of the most influential countries in the western bloc and the Far East. After the Cold War structure became dominant in the world political scene, the British tried to maintain that influential status in a manner different from the pre-war period. They intended to manage and stabilize the Cold War structure and believed that they were still capable of influence, in spite of their real power being in decline. It was undeniable that they had to accept US hegemony and depend on her power resources. But the British continued to be very sceptical about the relevance of US Cold War policy and recognized the necessity to restrain the Americans from taking the world to the brink of annihilation, even by taking an opposite stance to the US government. At the same time, it was imperative for Britain to establish her national power in order to recover from the devastation of war. For this purpose, the British leaders had no choice but to maintain good relations with the US and their traditional economic interests in various international regions, and to protect their domestic economy. Thus, the new identity the British were trying to establish was one of Britain as the indispensable ally of the US, which was reliable and influential in the general development of world politics. In other words, postwar Britain was to be an autonomous but loyal ally of the superpower.

For the Japanese leaders, the struggle for a new state identity started from scratch. The first priority was given to reconstructing the country's shattered economy. For this purpose, Japan also had to depend on US power resources. At the same time, Japan had to return to an internationally legitimate status by demonstrating that she had become a peaceful nation and that she was observing postwar international rules.

The Japanese leaders tried hard to re-enter the international community by becoming a member of various international organizations, such as the United Nations and the GATT. Their efforts helped in meeting the need for recovery from the shattering of their national pride. In particular after the end of the occupation, the re-emerging mood of nationalism put pressure on the political leaders to seek a way to escape from over-dependence on the US and to achieve autonomy. For that purpose, they sought ways to expand external trade and to exert some political leverage over their patron. Like the British, the Japanese government tried to establish the state identity of a new Japan as a reliable and autonomous ally of the US, though in various different ways in each administration.

Thus, Anglo-Japanese relations in the 1950s evolved around their international quest for a similar new identity. But the positions of the two countries were quite different. Britain was a status quo power, though she had to some degree been compelled to retreat from that status. On the other hand, Japan started from scratch and her bid for a new identity was oriented towards altering the existing international settings, though not revising them as in the pre-war period. The nature of Anglo-Japanese relations was dependent on how well the British accepted the alteration in terms of their national interests and vision of how the Cold War structure should be.

Britain was largely supportive of Japan's efforts to be recognized as a legitimate international power as a member of the western bloc. The Japanese leaders could enjoy full British support for their admission to the United Nations. The Foreign Office and, in particular, the British embassy in Tokyo were eager to improve Anglo-Japanese relations, while they were determined to request the Japanese to meet the conditions provided in the San Francisco peace treaty, such as compensation for British POWs and for British assets lost during the Sino-Japanese war. The Japanese leaders also regarded it as imperative to reconstruct a close relationship with Britain in order to return to the international community. It was reflected in the fact that Japanese leaders very often referred to the return to the days of the Anglo-Japanese alliance. But in fields related to economic interests, the British could not wholeheartedly support the Japanese. Japan's entry into the GATT encountered British suspicions of the illegitimate nature of some of Japan's commercial conduct. Whereas the Foreign Office was more favourable to Japan's admission, the Board of Trade and domestic economic interest groups were adamantly against it. Even so, both countries finally discovered a meeting point at the end of the 1950s.

Britain's eagerness to improve her relations with Japan reflected her scepticism about the political and diplomatic tendencies in postwar Japan. British officials did not easily accept that Japan could suddenly become a trustworthy democratic country immediately after the end of the war. They also regarded the conservatives in Japan as rather weak. These British observations bred an anxiety about the possibility of Japan changing to a neutral stance or even switching to the communist camp. The British with their state identity as a declining world power, placed their relations with Japan within the context of the Cold War power balance. To demonstrate that Britain, one of the most influential western allies, recognized Japan as a legitimate power was regarded as essential to keep Japan firmly in the orbit of the free world. Along the same lines, the British government remained vigilant over the development of US-Japanese relations. The Foreign Office, distrusting America's ability to handle Asian nationalism, was concerned with the possible deterioration of US–Japanese relations, which was to be avoided at all costs in order to keep Japan within the western bloc. But this prospect also provided the British with a good opportunity to exert influence on both Japan and the US as an honest broker, and with more scope for diplomatic autonomy.

The Japanese conservative leaders looked upon Britain as a useful political instrument to influence the US government, when they wanted to take a position that could be regarded as opposing US Cold War policy. Throughout the 1950s, Japanese governments continuously desired to expand Sino-Japanese trade relations. But US restrictions on her allies' trade with communist China constituted a great obstacle to the Japanese. The British were sympathetic to the Japanese partly because the former also desired to expand trade with China; partly because the Foreign Office recognized that it was desirable for the western allies to give the Japanese more opportunity to expand their economy; and partly because Japan's economic penetration into the Southeast Asian market could be slowed by inducing her to re-enter her traditional market in China. Thus, it was beneficial for both the British and the Japanese to work together to make the Americans reconsider their China policy.

As for political relations with communist China, the Japanese governments tended to promote a *de facto* 'two Chinas' policy. During the decade covered in this chapter, each administration in Japan hoped to improve not only her trade relations but also her political relations with China. It was partly because political relations had to be improved in order to improve trade relations. But, for Japanese political leaders and Japanese public opinion, more importantly, promoting better relations with China meant a bid for autonomy and self-reliance. From the viewpoint of Britain, which had already recognized the communist government of China in 1950, the rigid anti-China policy of the US was a source of anxiety and had to be restrained. Here also, there was good reason for an Anglo-Japanese coalition to change American China policy.

From Yoshida to Kishi, Japanese governments continued to send a clear signal to the British government of their desire to create a common front against the US. But the British disliked making any clear commitment to protest jointly against the US, because their relations with the Americans would deteriorate. At the same time, they could accept the promotion of Sino-Japanese trade relations, but they were determined to prevent a Sino-Japanese political coalition, which, they believed, would drastically alter the world power balance. Thus, Anglo-Japanese cooperation to change US policy towards China could never succeed.

Japanese leaders recognized Britain not only as a political instrument for conducting independent diplomacy but also as the suitable model for it. One can see a similar characterization of Britain in the foreign policy of the Hatoyama administration towards Russia. For Hatoyama, détente with the Soviet Union was partly aimed to achieve more autonomy from the United States. This notion was derived from their understanding of Britain's détente policy under the Churchill and the Eden administrations leading to the Geneva Four-Power Summit in July 1955.

Thus, Anglo-Japanese relations in the 1950s presented a complicated scenario of cooperation, successful or failed, and friction, evolving around their bids for a new postwar state identity. But it can confidently be argued that the British and Japanese diplomatic leaders steadily improved their relations through their efforts to adjust themselves to the newly emerging international political structure. Japan was gradually but steadily incorporated into the western bloc as a legitimate international power with the considerable assistance of British cooperation, and Anglo-Japanese relations entered a new phase of non-power political cooperation and an interdependent relationship. But it is also true that Japan failed to achieve political autonomy through improving her relations with China, partly because of the hostile external attitudes of China and partly because of the difficulty in constructing a close Anglo-Japanese coalition to change the rigid US policy towards China. Britain also gradually lost her political influence in Asia.

Cooperation, Friction and the Search for State Identity 231

In the 1960s, Japan retreated from her ambition for political autonomy and concentrated on her bid to become an economic giant. Britain also retreated from being an influential political force in the Far East and was to look more to European integration as the main stage for her international performance.

Notes

1. This chapter is intended to cover Anglo-Japanese relations after the end of occupation period. For a detailed account on the occupation period, see the previous chapter by Peter Lowe.
2. For the 'Yoshida letter', see the previous chapter. For more detailed accounts, see Hosoya Chihiro, *San Furanshisuko kowa eno michi* (Road to the San Francisco Peace Settlement) (Tokyo: Chuokoron-sha, 1984), ch. 11.
3. Dening to Eden, 28 March 1952, FO 371 99411 FJ1051/16, Public Record Office, Kew.
4. *Ibid.*
5. *Ibid.*
6. CAB 129/66/C(54)92; Foreign Office Minutes by Sir Ivone Kirkpatrick, 6 January 1954, FO371 110413 FJ1051/1.
7. Hosoya, *San Furanshisuko*, pp. 289–90; Tilman Remme, *Britain and Regional Cooperation in South-East Asia, 1945–49* (London: Routledge, 1995), p. 206.
8. Hatano Sumio, 'Tonan ajia kaihatsu wo meguru Nichi-Bei-Ei kankei: Nihon no koronbo puran kanyu wo chushin ni' (Japan-US-UK Relations over the Development of Southeast Asia: Japan's Admission to the Colombo Plan in 1954), in Kindai Nihon Kenkyukai (ed.) *Kindai nihon kenkyu* (Modern Japan Studies), No. 16 (1994), pp. 215–42.
9. Dening to FO, 21 February 1952, FO371 99411 FJ 1051/10; Dening to FO, 5 March 1952, FO371 99411 FJ1051/9.
10. Asakai to Okazaki, 29 March 1952, A'-0127 (700), Microfilmed documents issued by the Diplomatic Record Office of the Ministry of Foreign Affairs in Tokyo (hereafter cited as MOFA). 'A'-0127' indicates microfilm number, and the numbers within parenthesis indicate frame numbers.
11. Clutton to Scott, 21 February 1952, FO371 99411 FJ1051/10.
12. *Asahi Shimbun*, 2 May and 18 May 1953.
13. CAB 129/71/CP(54)314.
14. 'Overseas Negotiations Committee: Japan' 16 July 1953, CAB 134/1095 ON(53)136.
15. Chancery to FO, 30 September 1953, FO371 106981 FZ11014/76.
16. Scott to FO, 10 August 1954, FO371 111908 D11011/7; Gleeson-White to CRO, 27 August 1954, FO371 111908 D11011/14.
17. Minutes by Reading, 15 September 1954, FO371 111908 D11011/7.
18. While US–Japanese trade frictions intensified in 1958, the Foreign Office were concerned with a possibility that the Americans tried to redirect Japanese trade drive more to Southeast Asia. For the British anxiety, see the following documents. Morland to Lascelles, 7 January 1959, FO371 133599 FJ1052/1G; De la Mare to Dalton, 6 December1958, FO371 133599 FJ1052/1.

19. I borrow this phrase from the title of a book by D.C. Watt, *Succeeding John Bull: America in Britain's Place, 1900–1975* (Cambridge: Cambridge University Press, 1984).
20. Okazaki to Matsumoto, 6 February 1954, A'-0135 (26); Minutes by Okazaki, undated, A'-0135 (50–53), MOFA.
21. 'Eikoku to no Juyo Anken' (Significant issues in relations with Britain), undated, A'-0136 (563–578), MOFA.
22. Matsui to Oda, 26 May 1954, A'-0135 (460–465), MOFA.
23. Matsui to Oda, 14 May 1954, A'-0135 (249–254), MOFA.
24. FO Minutes by Mayall, 27 September 1954, FO371 110413 FJ1051/8.
25. On 1 March 1954, a Japanese fishing boat the *Daigo Fukuryu Maru* (Lucky Dragon V) was sprayed by a cloud of radioactive fallout caused by a US thermonuclear experiment at the Bikini Atoll. In September, one of the crew members died, allegedly from radioactive damage.
26. For a detailed account about Yoshida's Southeast Asian policy, see John Dower, *Empire and Aftermath: Yoshida Shigeru and the Japanese Experience, 1878–1954* (Cambridge, Mass.: Harvard University Press, 1979), ch. 12.
27. Minute by the director of Public Information and Cultural Affairs Bureau, 26 August 1954, A'-0137 (73); Minute by the second division of Asian Affairs Bureau, 8 August 1954, A'-0137 (349), MOFA.
28. FO minute by Mayall, 27 September 1954.
29. FO minute by Crowe, 3 August 1954, FO371 110409, FJ1022/1.
30. FO minute by Mayall, 27 September 1954.
31. Dening to Allen, 13 October 1954, FO371 110497 FJ1631/79.
32. FO minute by Rumbold, 27 October 1954, FO371 110498 FJ1631/83.
33. Matsumoto to Ogata, 26 October 1954, A'-0136 (298–299), MOFA.
34. Allen to Dening, 29 October 1954, FO371 110498 FJ1631/85.
35. Matsumoto to Okazaki, 28–29 October 1954, A'-0136 (308–311), MOFA.
36. 'Record of Discussion at the PM's Dinner For Mr. Yoshida on October 27', FO371 110498 FJ1631/85.
37. Matsumoto to Ogata, 25 Oct. 1954, A'-0136 (288–292), MOFA.
38. Matsumoto to Okazaki, 26 October 1954, A'-136 (300), MOFA.
39. FO minute by Mayall, 27 September 1954.
40. See n. 21.
41. 'Yo Shori Jiko Shinchoku Jokyo' (Progress in Settling Significant Issues), 29 Nov. 1954, A'-0136 (516–519), MOFA.
42. For a more detailed account of Hatoyama's foreign policy ideas, see Takahiko Tanaka, 'Soviet–Japanese Normalization and the Foreign Policy Ideas of the Hatoyama Group' in P. Lowe and H. Moeshart (eds), *Western Interactions with Japan: Expansion, the Armed Forces and Readjustment, 1859–1956* (Folkestone: Japan Library, 1990), pp. 45–65.
43. CAB 129/72/C(54)367.
44. Dening to FO, 23 March 1995, FO371 115223 FJ1015/9; Dening to FO, 4 May 1955, FO371 115223 FJ1051/16.
45. For a detailed account of the Soviet–Japanese normalization talks and Anglo-Japanese relations, see Tanaka Takahiko, *Nisso kokko kaifuku no shiteki kenkyu: sengo Nisso kankei no kiten, 1945–1956* (A History of Soviet-Japanese Normalization: Start of the Postwar Soviet-Japanese Relations) (Tokyo: Yuhikaku, 1993). See also Tanaka, 'Soviet–Japanese Normalization Talks in

1955–1956: with Special Reference to the Attitude of Britain' (unpublished PhD dissertation, University of London, 1990).
46. Tanaka, *Nisso Kokko Kaifuku no Shiteki Kenkyu*, esp. pp. 106–12, 184–92 and 262–7.
47. Minute by Bullard, 5 June 1956, FO371 121039 FJ10338/24.
48. *Asahi Shimbun*, 16 May 1956.
49. Memorandum by Eden, 12 December 1954; Memorandum by Thorneycroft, 13 December 1954, CAB129/72/C(54)391.
50. In January 1957, an American GI William S. Girard shot dead Japanese female farm worker collecting empty shell cases on an American rifle range in Gumma prefecture. This incident caused great public anti-American resentment in Japan.
51. Tokyo to Lloyd, 3 August 1957, FO371 127529 FJ1022/16.
52. 'The Recent Situation of Japan's Diplomacy', FO371 127532 FJ1022/67.
53. Morland to Coulson, 29 July 1957, FO371 127529 FJ1022/14; Harpham to FO, 13 Sept. 1957, FO371 127530 FJ1022/33.
54. Kishi Nobusuke, Yatsugi Kazuo and Ito Takashi, *Kishi Nobusuke no Kaiso* (Memoirs of Kishi Nobusuke) (Tokyo: Bungeishunjyu, 1981), p. 393.
55. 'Fujiyama Daijin Hoei Taisho Hoshin: Dai Ichiji Hoshin' (Guidelines for Foreign Minister Fujiyama's Visit to Britain: version I), 12 September 1957, A'-0154 (422–423), MOFA.
56. FO Minutes by Morland, 11 July, 1957, FO371 127543 FJ1051/12; FO371 127543 FJ1051/13.
57. 'The Possibility of inviting the Japanese Foreign Minister to visit the United Kingdom', 29 Aug. 1957, FO371 127530 FJ1022/22; FO minute by Dalton, 2 September 1957, FO371 127530 FJ1022/23.
58. Confidential Minute by Dalton, 2 September 1957 FO371 127530 FJ1022/23.
59. 'Fujiyama Daijin Hoei Taisho Hoshin: Dai Niji Hoshin' (Guidelines for Foreign Minister Fujiyama's Visit to Britain: version II), A'-0154 (425–428), MOFA.
60. Briefing by Dalton, 25 September 1957, FO371 127532 FJ1022/54.
61. Nishi to Kishi, 29 September 1957, A'-0154 (506–528), MOFA; FO Minute, 'Visit of the Japanese Foreign Minister: appendix D', 25 September 1957, FO371 127532 FJ1022/54.
62. Nishi to Kishi, 29 September 1957, MOFA.
63. 'Visit of the Japanese Foreign Minister', appendix F, 25 September 1957, FO371 127532 FJ1022/54.
64. FO Minutes, FO371 127529 FJ1022/11; Nishi to Kishi, 29 September 1957.
65. Morland to Lascelles, 3 October 1957, FO371 127532 FJ1022/59; Lascelles to Morland, 22 October 1957, FO371 127532 FJ1022/59(a).
66. Selby to Dalton, 1 October 1957, FO371 127532 FJ1022/61.
67. Lascelles to FO, 27 November 1957, FO371 127567 FJ1241/1.
68. Harpham to FO, 15 January 1958, FO371 133597 FJ1015/5.
69. Lascelles to FO, 27 January 1958, FO371 133597 FJ1051/10.
70. Record of a conversation between Lloyd and Ono, 13 May 1958, FO371 133597 FJ1051/18.
71. Kishi, Yatsugi, and Ito, *Kishi Nobusuke no Kaiso*, p. 185.
72. Tokyo to FO, 12 March 1959, FO371 141415 FJ1011/1.

73. Morland to Lascelles, 7 January 1959; De la Mare to Dalton, 6 December 1958, FO371 133599 FJ1052/1.
74. FO Minutes by Dalton, 25 July 1958, FO371 133598 FJ1051/37.
75. Morland to MacDermot, 14 May 1959, FO371 141435 FJ1051/28; Tokyo to FO, 12 January 1960, FO371 150561 FJ1011/1.
76. Morland to MacDermot, 14 May 1959, FO371 141435 FJ1051/28; Mayall to Dalton, 27 February 1959, FO371 141434 FJ1015/7.
77. 'Record of conversation between the Minister of State and the Japanese Prime Minister on 13 July 1959', 17 July 1959, FO371 141439 FJ1051/91.
78. 'Record of conversation between the Prime Minister and the Prime Minister of Japan', 27 July 1959, FO371 141439 FJ1051/92.
79. See notes 53 and 57.
80. 'Record of conversation between the Minister of State and the Japanese Prime Minister on July 13, 1959'.
81. 'Note of a Discussion held in the Chancellor's Room in the Treasury 3.00 p.m. on Monday, 13th July, 1959', FO371 141439 FJ1051/96.
82. 'Record of conversation between the Prime Minister and the Prime Minister of Japan on July 15 1959'.

10
Anglo-Japanese Relations since the 1960s: Towards Mutual Understanding – Beyond Friction
Kuroiwa Toru

In this chapter I would like to look at the whole spectrum of Anglo-Japanese relations since the 1960s. In discussing the history of this mutual exchange it is difficult to separate political from diplomatic, economic or cultural issues, since these categories have become closer in recent years. It is the case that economic problems directly become political problems, and cultural issues often develop into diplomatic ones. In certain periods of economic friction or (for example) when Japanese investment became a critical issue in discussions with Britain, such matters became the centrepiece of political and diplomatic relations. History after 1960 should not therefore be restricted to a political and diplomatic approach.

The history of Anglo-Japanese interaction after 1960 should be divided into three periods. It is relatively difficult to say where one period starts and another finishes, but the character of the first period emerged mainly in the 1960s. The characteristics of the second period began to appear in the 1970s and those of the third period became more pronounced in the 1980s. But the features of each decade were not restricted exclusively to their periods. The first is the 'period of the new beginning'. In the 1960s Japan was concerned with re-establishing equal relations with Britain and shedding the role of defeated nation. Its most significant moment came with the signing of the Anglo-Japanese Commercial Treaty of 1962.

The second was the 'period of mutual understanding'. At the time the torrent of Japanese goods flooding into Britain became a problem. Japanese self-regulation of trade became the principal concern as trade issues came to the surface. In order to solve the problem an import promotion mission was sent from Japan to Britain whose objective was to 'Buy British'. Efforts such as these were made to solve the trade friction and to promote the establishment of balanced and equal relations. In the 1970s the Japanese Emperor and Empress visited Britain and Queen Elizabeth and Prince Philip visited Japan. These reciprocal visits were to promote good relations, but also to draw a line under the unfortunate events of the Second World War. When Emperor Hirohito visited London a man threw his jacket onto the Emperor's carriage and the tree that the Emperor planted in Kew Gardens was cut down. These facts showed that the atmosphere of the war period continued into the 1970s.

The third period was that of 'mutual development' not only involving Japan looking to Britain, but Britain beginning to look towards Japan. The call was made by Mrs. Thatcher to 'Look East'. Japanese companies expanded into Britain and British companies tried to establish themselves in Japan. Protectionism in the Japanese market became a problem. The most colourful example of Britain 'Looking East' was the 'Japan Festival' of 1981, and largely because of its success we entered a period where Anglo-Japanese relations 'never had it so good'. Of course Anglo-Japanese relations have not always been rosy. The problem of POWs was a thorn in the flesh throughout postwar Anglo-Japanese relations, and the issue of whaling which arose in the 1970s, although not exclusively an Anglo-Japanese problem, dented Japan's image in the eyes of the British. These problems will recede in the future, but remain bones of contention.

First period: the new beginnning: the Anglo-Japanese commercial treaty

We cannot overstate the importance of the Anglo-Japanese Commercial Treaty. The signing of this treaty on 14 November 1962 elevated the Japanese national position from that of a defeated country to that of an equal partner. Japan had therefore exerted every effort from the 1950s onward into bringing this treaty about. It may be an exaggeration to say so, but Japan took the view that without signing the treaty it would be nearly impossible for her to exist in the international community as an independent nation. The negotiations continued for seven years from start to finish. Two years before the conclusion of the treaty Japanese Foreign Minister Ohira Masayoshi visited Britain as part of regular consultations and held discussions with Sir Alec Douglas Home, the Foreign Secretary, during the course of which the mood of the negotiations improved considerably. When Home invited Ohira to his private Scottish residence, the Japanese side thought 'Britain had shown its willingness to think highly of Japan'.[1] Such an improved atmosphere raised the expectation that the treaty would be successfully concluded.

At the time Anglo-Japanese trade agreements were decided each year with lengthy negotiations that continued for about half the year, so both government and business had become exasperated with the situation. Japanese trading companies made known their frustration at not being able to plan for the long term, and the government realized the folly of engaging officials in forging these agreements for up to half the year. The conclusion of the new treaty was expected, although in Britain there were suspicions of Japan and doubts that Japanese goods were of poor quality and mere imitations of British products.

The President of the Board of Trade, Reginald Maudling, and the Japanese ambassador, Ono Katsumi, who were engaged in the negotiations planned the publication of a report intended to break down the prejudice against Japanese goods. Sir Norman Kipping of the Federation of British Industry was sent to Japan in the autumn of 1961. Sir Norman was very impressed with the state of the Japanese economy and wrote a report entitled 'A look at Japan' at Hakone just before returning to Britain. This report was widely read as it was written by a key British business figure and created a strong impression amongst various leading figures in government, Parliament, the mass media and the business world. When articles of an anti-Japanese nature were carried in the mass media Sir Norman often countered them, taking care to explain about the Japanese economy and providing proof of the quality of Japanese goods.[2] This greatly assisted the conclusion of the treaty and its passage through Parliament.

The treaty was signed on 14 November 1962 in the presence of Prime Minister Ikeda Hayato, who was visiting London, and Prime Minister Harold Macmillan. This treaty took the form of a revision of a previous Anglo-Japanese commercial treaty that had been suspended for 21 years since the Second World War; and with no more discrimination Japan was granted favoured nation trading status. Both countries have since treated each other as 'most favoured nations' in trade and navigation matters. Until that time Britain had used Article 35/(3) of the General Agreement on Tariffs and Trade (GATT), which meant that Japan was discriminated against, but in signing the new treaty Britain gave up its use of Article 35. In return the Japanese gave Britain the safeguard of omitting a list of eight sensitive items such as knives, lighters, fishing tackle, microscopes and toys, and promised that 14 items would be subject to self-regulated export controls. This was a great step towards liberalization because Britain had previously had 62 items whose import from Japan was restricted.

In these negotiations the Japanese side appreciated the British government's efforts to conclude the treaty despite opposition from the business community and trade unions. For example, Counsellor Ishimaru of the Japanese embassy in London who was directing officials in the negotiations, wrote:

> When the remarks of British shipowners about purchasing or giving orders for Japanese vessels based on liberalisation in the trade talks were published in the newspapers, the powerful trade unions launched an opposition movement and it became the lead story in *The Times*. For a while we were inclined to fear the cancellation of liberalisation. But in *The Times* the following day, Transport Minister Marples issued the following statement: 'Because there is no unfair competition on the part of Japan, we should like the trade unions to reconsider their position in order to develop the competitive power of British manufacturing industry'. We appreciated his toughness in adhering to what had once been agreed and not yielding to pressure from interest groups. We now had the assurance that the treaty negotiations would succeed.[4]

This treaty was one of the most important factors that defined the two countries' postwar relations, and with it we can say that both countries resumed normal bilateral relations. The newly born expectations in bilateral relations resulting from this treaty were displayed by newspaper headlines at the time. For example, 'Ruling for the Normalisation of Commerce', 'Expectations for the Expansion of Trade' or 'Bridgehead Established for EEC Trade'.[5] After the treaty was signed the volume of trade expanded rapidly, showing that Japanese expectations had been achieved. Japan at the time was eager to establish itself as an export economy and the policy was to push trade expansion. Thus Japanese officials who succeeded in concluding the treaty probably felt the same sense of emancipation as the Japanese leaders who had been successful at revising the unequal treaties with the Western powers in the Meiji period.

After the conclusion of the treaty the interests of the Japanese government lay in reducing the number of sensitive items and items that were subject to self-regulation. The negotiations about lowering the number of items continued and every year Britain brought down the total of goods that were restricted. Eventually within five years the British government decided to set protocol aside and abolished all remaining restrictions on sensitive items.

The next problems for the Japanese government were how Japanese companies could be stopped from imitating British goods, and how Japanese exports could be expanded further. Concerning the first problem, the Japanese Minister for Trade and Industry decided to admonish the Japanese companies who were identified by the British as the major imitators. But copying British goods was usually small and moved quickly from one product to the next, making it difficult to stamp the practice out. The British claimed that prime examples of the goods copied were woollen wear and china. In order to solve 'Anglo-Japanese friction' in 1965 the management of the Japanese woollen company Daido-Keori and Nihon-Keori and the British based 'Woollen Company of Lancashire' met in Bradford for two days under the guidance of the Japanese embassy in order to discuss the eradication of fake merchandise. The reason that the Japanese woollen companies joined in talks was because cheap imitations were also a nuisance for them. When Japan wanted to raise exports they found that they could not easily export imitation goods and, with the development of the export economy, such export merchandise eventually disappeared. Japan adopted the slogan 'We will catch up with the West and overtake the West' and, in using this slogan, hoped to dispel the notion that Japanese goods were shoddy.

Concerning the second problem, this was a period when the Japanese Export and Trade Organisation (JETRO) was focusing on the promotion of Japanese exports. It arranged in advance in 1965 for the ship *Sakura-Maru* to visit five foreign ports to promote exports. On board the ship they displayed Japanese televisions, transistor radios, motor-bikes, china, clocks, watches, sewing machines and cameras that Japan wanted to export. In Britain the ship moored on the Thames 30 miles outside London and was visited by key figures from British industry. The export of Japanese cars, which later became a cause of conflict between the two countries, had already begun in 1965. At the motor show in Earls Court (London) Nissan appeared for the first time and began the process of establishing a dealer network. In 1966 Toyota began to penetrate the British market by exporting about 700 cars. Fifteen years later, when the numbers exported had increased rapidly, they were forced to impose self-regulation controls.

On the other hand, British exports to Japan had begun to gain a foothold. For their part British exporters to Japan suffered from high tariffs in Japan, especially on whisky which became the focus of British grievances. The reduction of high whisky tariffs has since become an ongoing topic of negotiation. At the time Japanese negotiators claimed that 'the reason whisky sells in Japan is because the price is high; if you made it cheap you could not sell it'. This logic was largely to protect the Japanese whisky industry, but British whisky was respected because it was expensive and sold as a highly priced luxury product.

The reason that British exports entered the Japanese market so late was because of the lack of openness of the market. The Japanese market was highly regulated by the Ministry of Finance and Ministry of Commerce and Industry. The expansion activities of British companies in Japan were often frustrated by the numerous regulations. According to Oba Sadao, the British side themselves stated the reasons that they could not penetrate the market as follows:

1. The occupation of Japan by American forces had given an advantage to US firms and anti-Japanese sentiment among the British persisted.
2. In Europe the integration of the market was progressing with EFTA and the EEC and British companies' priority was to pursue European expansion.
3. There were many British industries which could not reform and renew their technology and management and were therefore losing international competitiveness.[6]

By the mid-1960s a degree of mutual understanding had just begun to emerge. The principal example of the start of mutual co-operation was when emergency financing was granted to the Bank of England by the Bank of Japan in November 1964. There had been a change of leadership to a Labour government in Britain resulting in the pound being heavily sold. Britain decided to borrow $3 billion from the central banks of the main industrialized countries and the Bank of International Settlements (BIS). As part of that finance the Bank of Japan lent $50 million. Very late one night the Governor of the Bank of England, Lord Cromer, telephoned the President of the Bank of Japan, Yamagiwa Masamichi, who understood that Britain needed money but not how much or for what purpose. Then Maekawa Haruo, the director of the bank, telephoned the New York Federal Bank and the Bank of England and realised that they needed emergency financing of

$50 million. Even though it was the middle of the night he telephoned senior officials at the Ministry of Finance and took the decision immediately to grant the requested assistance.[7] Judged from the standpoint of the Japanese bureaucratic system which is characterized by inflexibility and a lengthy decision-making process, this on-the-spot decision by the Bank of Japan and the Ministry of Finance taken during late night discussions was most unusual. It was taken because Japan saw it as a way of cooperating with Britain and of acting as a full member of the international community.

The era of mutual understanding had begun. It was an overture to Britain for greater understanding and a way of Japan wooing Britain. Japan wanted to erase the negative images such as the bad treatment of POWs by the Japanese army, and alter the clichéd impressions encapsulated in British notions of geisha girls and Mount Fuji. In order to replace this image Japan wanted to forge good relations and convey the image of a new Japan. To aid British understanding of the Japanese, the Anglo-Japanese Economic Institute was established by the Foreign Ministry in 1961. This set up and published a monthly journal with funding from the Japanese government. It was written by British journalists who wrote articles that defended Japan. In this way the Japanese government sought to achieve a greater capacity to influence the British. A successor magazine continues today, and the British use it to exchange information on Japan and express opinions.

In an effort to develop mutual understanding there were revisions of British textbooks. If there was an inaccuracy or outright prejudice concerning Japan the Japanese embassy requested scholars such as Richard Storry of Oxford University to locate them and rectify the mistakes through contact with the publishers. It was thought that, if British scholars pointed out the mistakes, the general public would take greater heed of what was being said. These efforts to improve mutual sentiment were based on the idea that it was better for British scholars to lead the way in altering attitudes than it was for the Japanese with their more deferential approach. This judgement was based on the assumption that the British people were traditionally inclined to pay scant attention to the voice of Japan because its economic development was relatively recent, and this had the effect of making the Japanese less sure of themselves. It was in the 1970s that Japan changed this approach and that the Japanese themselves began to change British attitudes to Japan for the better and make them more positive.

The establishment of an association of Anglo-Japanese Members of Parliament was another start towards mutual understanding. Until then only a few senior members of the House of Lords who had known pre-war Japan were enthusiastically interested in, and well disposed towards, Japan. Japan recognized the need to create a new group, so, through the efforts of the Japanese, contacts were made with MPs such as Sir Julian Ridsdale, and the Association of Anglo-Japanese Members of Parliament was formed. At the same time a similar organization was established in the Japanese Diet around Ishida Hakuei. The two groups now had the opportunity to launch exchange visits.

Second period: mutual understanding

In the second period of Anglo-Japanese relations both countries entered a phase of mutual understanding. Although both countries wanted to comprehend the other, the will of Japan to understand Britain was stronger. Or it could be said that the Japanese were determined to make an effort to get Britain to understand that modern Japan was entirely different from pre-war Japan. That effort was displayed in Japan's attempts to transform itself from a defeated country into an economic power-house. The Japanese believed that, in order to expand trade with Britain and more generally in terms of foreign trade and investment, it was essential to make Japan better known and understood abroad. In doing so Japan hoped to smooth its economic advance.

But Japanese expansion was so rapid that there were repercussions from the British side. For example, there were complaints that British industry was becoming bankrupted by the rapidly rising floods of cheap Japanese exports. To dampen such criticism self-regulation of export expansion to Britain was imposed by Japan. It was somewhat strange that Japanese trade missions promoting the import of British goods visited Britain so often searching for British commodities that could be sold in Japan. It would perhaps have been more usual for the companies wanting to sell goods to Japan to have visited the country themselves, but in this case the procedure was reversed. This was because Japanese expansion was so explosive that it had aroused much adverse criticism in Britain.

The visit of the Showa Emperor and Empress in October 1971 was only three days long but it was a remarkable event in Anglo-Japanese relations. It publicly displayed for the first time that the two countries were returning to balanced equal relations. In Britain, however, there was still a strong voice calling for Japan to accept responsibility for its war-time conduct and especially for the maltreatment of its prisoners of war. There was thus a lack of welcome in some quarters for the Emperor's visit. By the 1970s both countries were keen to deepen and enhance their mutual understanding but the war still cast its shadow over events. What particularly concerned Japan during the visit was how to deal with the question of war responsibility. The Emperor's visit had been planned over a year earlier as one stop on a tour of several European countries. The Japanese government decided that it would not tackle the sensitive question of the war. They just put it aside in the manner typical of Japanese bureaucrats.

When it came to the official dinner at Buckingham Palace at the invitation of Queen Elizabeth on 5 October there was a clear difference between the speech of the Queen and that of the Emperor. The Queen said in a speech of welcome: 'We can't say that relations between our two countries have always been peaceful and friendly. Because of that experience we are determined that the same thing will never occur again.' Whilst she did refer to the calamitous events between the two countries during the war, the Emperor, on the other hand, chose to point out that he had visited Britain fifty years earlier, that he respected British social institutions and had met George V, the Queen's grandfather, that the two countries had enjoyed reciprocal royal visits, and that Japan had learnt so much from Britain. He went on to say that he expected further friendship in the future but he never mentioned the war at all. Due to the concern that there would be a debate on his personal responsibility if he mentioned the war, his speech was markedly different from the Queen's. Japan was thus inclined to evade the biggest issue between itself and Britain. The gulf in sentiment between the countries was illustrated by various incidents with British citizens. First, when the carriage carrying the Emperor and the Queen was being driven past Buckingham Palace a black jacket was thrown from the crowd at the carriage. It fell just behind it, though, and neither the Emperor nor the Queen noticed, but the next day's *Times* carried the story with a banner headline. The second incident occurred at Kew Gardens when the Emperor planted a Japanese cedar tree. The next day the tree was found to have been cut down, and chloric acid had been scattered around it. A small card was left with the message 'they didn't die in vain' written on it.[8] The British Foreign Office declared: 'We think that this is incomprehensibly sordid and deplorable.' This protest against the treatment of POWs by the Japanese army showed that, even 25 years after the end of the war, anti-Japanese feeling ran high. *The Times* pointed out the following day that, even though the crowd had been larger than normal for heads of state, there had been no shouts of welcome. *The Sun* newspaper wrote of a 'silence like ice'. In the opinion columns of the mass media there were statements that 'the time to demand apologies for the war has gone', and 'although the memory of the war has not been forgotten it is time to forgive the sins'. So it was by no means unanimous to decry the Japanese. When the Emperor visited Westminster Abbey to lay a wreath at the tomb of the Unknown Soldier, there was a shout from the crowd that it was 'an insult to the dead'. But immediately there came a response: 'Don't make the dead the seed of hate'.[9] So there were citizens who resisted the temptation to express hatred. That implied that there was a body of opinion who thought it best to let bygones be bygones.

Good relations between the two Royal Families were strengthened by the Emperor's visit to Britain. The Japanese Emperor had been very much impressed by the subtleties of British hospitality and the British tendency to preserve tradition, and it was pointed out to him that they had used the same cutlery at Buckingham Palace as they had when he was entertained there as the heir to the throne 50 years before in 1921. On the third day of the Emperor's visit he entertained the Queen at the Japanese ambassador's residence at a return banquet. The Queen spent an hour more than had been scheduled, implying that she was deeply interested in Japan.

In response to the Emperor's visit to Britain there was now an exchange of prime ministerial visits at the beginning of the 1970s. Prior to this three Japanese prime ministers had visited Britain, but no British prime minister had ever visited Japan. Therefore during the Emperor's visit a request was made. When Prime Minister Heath arrived in September 1972 the Japanese were relieved that a British prime minister had finally come. But from the British point of view the opinion had been reached that Japan could no longer be ignored because of its rapid trade expansion and its strengthening international status. The chief purpose of Edward Heath's visit was to hold discussions with Prime Minister Tanaka Kakuei. The main topics of the talks were the international currency and trade liberalization of both countries, amongst other related matters. Economic issues were central to the discussion. This illustrated that the foremost concerns of each country were economic, notably the Japanese trade surplus with Britain which had already become a problem. At the summit Prime Minister Heath said that 'Japan should increase its imports of British goods'. Prime Minister Tanaka responded by saying that 'the dream of all Japanese is to wear British suits and to drink Scotch. So you can understand'. Prime Minister Heath was interested in Tanaka's visit to China and in reference to this he declared 'the Chinese are going to buy Concorde, and if relations between Japan and China are normalised then Concorde will fly to Japan'. By referring to the Chinese purchase of Concorde he showed his desire to drum up sales of UK goods to Japan. When Prime Minister Ikeda Hayato had visited France, President de Gaulle had made a cynical reference to Ikeda as a salesman of transistor radios. But the British prime minister also needed to sell UK goods. In this respect the Japanese and British position was a common one.

The visit of Prime Minister Tanaka to Britain in October 1973 was a follow-up to Heath's visit the previous year. At the time of Tanaka's visit economic matters were still very much to the fore. The Japanese Foreign Ministry was concerned that political matters should be set aside. An Anglo-Japanese joint statement issued after the consultations said that both countries had decided to cooperate on energy matters and that they had agreed that Japan would participate in the development of the North Sea oil industry. In return Japan agreed to invest in underdeveloped areas of Britain. With these agreements Japanese investment began and the economic relationship became closer. These decisions buoyed up the mood of both countries, and stimulated the interest in the Queen's visit to Japan in 1975. A by-product of Tanaka's visit to Britain was the establishment of a Japanese Studies promotion fund called the 'Tanaka Fund' whereby Japan contributed 300 million yen for the purpose of research on Japan in order to enhance mutual understanding. The Tanaka Fund, which was administered by the Japan Foundation Endowment Committee, was the most precious source of funding for British researchers on Japan. In the latter half of the 1980s when interest rates fell sharply, management of the fund became more difficult, but today it still operates on the interest of the investment.

Japanese investment in Britain's 'underdeveloped areas', which had been promised in the communiqué at the time of Tanaka's visit, had begun at the beginning of the 1970s when 12 companies set up in Britain. In 1972 YKK and Nittan arrived, in 1973 Takiron and Sony, and in 1976 Matsushita, NSK and Rinnai, followed in 1978 by Sekisui, Toshiba and Daiwa Sports. Then in 1979 Mitsubishi and Hitachi established themselves. Five of the companies settled in Wales which raised the reputation of that country in the Japanese community. The Welsh

Development Agency issued a PR document entitled 'Wales – The Centre of European Expansion by Japanese Industries'. There were a few inevitable murmurs of complaint from other areas that had not attracted so much investment. Japanese investment to Britain was accelerated further by the development of the Japanese economy throughout the 1980s. This was hailed by both countries as 'the fruit of advances in Anglo-Japanese relations'.[10] At first the British were suspicious of new Japanese companies but they gradually turned their attention to Japanese management practices. For example the custom of chief executives wearing the same clothes and eating in the same dining room as the rest of the workers. Also, instead of forming labour unions, the employers and employees would discuss issues regularly and in depth. The existence of foremen or representatives whose business it was to have a thorough knowledge of the personal circumstances of every worker became common. This style of Japanese management, so alien to British companies, was initially given a bad reception, but in time British employees came to accept it. When the realization dawned that this management style was successful, many seminars were held and several British companies decided to adopt the Japanese model of management. The Japanese management mode thus became established and gained respect in Britain.

When Prime Minister Tanaka visited Britain, it had been agreed at the summit that the first ever trip to Japan by a British sovereign would be undertaken by the Queen and the Duke of Edinburgh and, in accordance with that agreement, the Queen went to Japan in May 1975. There was some dissent in Britain against the trip from the former Burmese camp POWs, but majority opinion supported the start of a fresh relationship 30 years after the end of the war. The Duke of Edinburgh visited the Commonwealth War Cemetery at Hodogaya in a gesture to the dissenters. Apart from this event the trip received a welcome that was both colourful and warm. Especially, after visiting the Ise shrine, the royal couple toured for 2 days in Kyoto, where about 320,000 people turned out to wave flags of welcome. The crowds were more numerous than for any foreign visit since the Second World War. When the Queen ate Japanese food, she broke the tradition that royals never remove their footwear in public and sat on a small Japanese mat. Furthermore she broke the convention that no photography was permitted during meals, allowing a photographer to capture a scene in which she ate using chopsticks. She appeared to take the view that she should follow Japanese custom as much as possible while she was in Japan. The mass media worked itself up into a state of great excitement over her visit. When she walked on the sand at a temple in Kyoto, a journalist took pictures of her footprints and found that the length of her stride was longer than that of ordinary people and the photo was carried with the headline 'The Queen's way of walking'. The humour of the Duke of Edinburgh became popular. At a reception for the Queen and Duke, the Duke asked a famous television broadcaster 'How do you make the news?' The broadcaster answered proudly, 'We use computers for everything'. The Duke always sceptical about modern technology exclaimed 'It's the beginning of the end!' The newscaster was speechless. Then at a welcome reception held by Commonwealth citizens the Duke spoke to a nun from New Zealand. When she couldn't utter a word because of nerves the Duke went closer to her and said, 'Don't worry you can confide in me' and everybody laughed, relaxing the situation. These stories were carried in the papers and the Japanese people felt at home with the royal visitors.

We should also mention the Queen's speech at the welcome luncheon that had been organised by five commercial corporations such as the Keidanren group. The Queen began by saying 'I am pleased that Anglo-Japanese relations were initiated by the letter written by my ancestor King James I, addressed to Shogun Tokugawa Ieyasu'. She went on to say that 'trade between Britain and Japan has increased by six and a half times in the last ten years', 'British industry is paying serious attention to the hugely expanding Japanese market. Japanese products are well known and popular with the people of Britain'. She emphasized that trade relations would be further developed, and said lastly that 'scholars, artists and diplomats have contributed to the relations of the two countries but that it was businessmen who had made by far the largest contribution'. Japanese businessmen were surprised when the Queen mentioned trade matters and in the next day's papers a headline read 'The British Queen makes sales gracefully'.[11] For the Japanese it was incredible that the head of the royal family had referred to business and, by implication, promoted British products. However, the British royal family had traditionally taken responsibility in leading the way in trade matters. They regard themselves as having a large contribution to make on behalf of their country, particularly in the development of foreign relations. People consider it natural that the royal family serves its people in this way as they are supported by the contributions of the taxpayers. This recognition of differences from Japan created a feeling of admiration for the British royal family.

This visit increased the pro-British feelings of the Japanese. It is fair to say that the reception granted to the Queen's visit was warmer than that of the Japanese Emperor's visit to Britain. It is hard to calculate just how much this visit affected the relations of the two countries, but it undoubtedly served to create a good atmosphere between them. The unexpected welcome was a surprise to the British side. Let us take a look at the reaction in the British media. 'Queen receives extraordinary welcome in Tokyo', 'It was a great welcome in contrast to the cooler receptions granted to many who had gone before such as US President Ford', wrote *The Times*. 'It was a great contrast to the cool reception of London's citizens to Emperor Hirohito's visit in 1971', wrote the *Daily Telegraph*. 'Many months have passed since Burma, Singapore, Changi prison and the bombing of Hiroshima. The figure that led Japan to war has welcomed the Queen of Britain. In the past the Japanese flag represented the most fearsome of countries to Britain and it was inconceivable the Queen would have bowed for that flag. But in Tokyo a new generation of ideas brought shouts of "Banzai!" and welcomed the Queen' (*Daily Express*). 'The Queen seems determined to utilise this visit as the best chance to promote the image of British products,' commented the *Guardian*. It is likely that admiration of Britain had been stimulated by the Queen's visit, and this admiration came as a surprise even to the British correspondents. When the Queen did not refer to the war and went as far as to promote British goods those involved in relations between the two countries were encouraged and felt that the postwar period was at last receding into the distance.

From the start of the 1970s Japanese exports to Britain had increased rapidly and damaged British industry. This has become a substantial problem for both countries. The main Japanese products being exported at the time were televisions, cars and motorcycles. These flooded into Britain and caused bankruptcies of companies and factory closures. For example, the British electrical manufacturing group BREMA announced their concern over the threat to British industry from the rapid increase in colour television imports. Half of the total increase in imports was from Japan. Japanese colour television companies headed the expansion, and there was great concern for British industry. In January 1976 the British electrical manufacturer, Thorn Industries, announced the closure of its colour TV braun tube factory in Lancashire. With this development the only remaining television tube manufacturer was Murad, a subsidiary of the Dutch company Phillips, and the industry stated that the cause of its decline was the rapid increase in imports of Japanese braun tubes. The British motorbike was also going to disappear as they could not compete with the rise in numbers of imported Japanese bikes. In August 1975 the government decided to stop financial assistance to the sole surviving motor bike producer NVT and the company was obliged to close. The Minister for Trade and Industry said in the House of Commons: 'The Government has put twenty-four million pounds into the motor-bike industry in the last two years but there is no hope that levels can be boosted by the 1980s even if we put in a further fifty million pounds'. The British industry which had made high quality bikes in the 750–1000cc class was beaten by the Japanese big four manufacturers, including Yamaha, Suzuki and Kawasaki, which mass-produced small or middle range bikes such as 250 ccs.

Japan took two measures to deal with the British reaction to the flood of Japanese exports. The first was self-regulation of exports; the second was to send a trade mission to Britain in order to encourage imports into Japan. Apart from British companies such as colour television and motor bike manufacturers, there were other more powerful industries such as the British car industry that wanted to keep out Japanese exports. The British and Japanese car industries began a consultation process on 18 December 1975 and an agreement was reached the next day between Toyota Eiji, chairman of the Japanese Car Industry Association, and the chairman of the British Automobile Manufacturing and Retail Association. These talks were initiated by the British Minister for Trade, Peter Shore.[12] The Japanese side wanted to make this consultation merely an exchange of information to encourage ties. But the British side wanted to obtain a pledge of self-regulation from Japan and hoped to stop the assault on their industry from Japanese exports. Finally, the Japanese side compromised and agreed to self-regulate: for example, 'in the first quarter of next year imports will be at the same level as in the latter half of 1975'. Since then delegates from both sides of the car industry have consulted and the Japanese have continued to agree to keep exports down to a certain level. Self-regulation restricted imports against the spirit of GATT but, when Japanese exports increased so rapidly that they threatened to destroy British industry, the Japanese were obliged to opt for 'orderly exports'. Apart from cars there were also restrictions on cutlery and china. These were in addition to the self-imposed restrictions on colour televisions and their components, which had also been achieved through bilateral consultations.

As a means of avoiding trade conflict apart from self-regulation, we should also look at trade missions for import promotion. Since 1971 the trade imbalance between the countries had emerged as a large problem. The Japanese trade surplus with Britain had reached

$100 million in 1970 and $200 million by 1971. From January to September 1972 Japanese exports increased to $670 million and imports by contrast stood at $360 million, which represented a rise of 17.6 per cent, and the Japanese trade surplus was still increasing. At talks held in Tokyo in September 1972, therefore, Britain asked Japan to send a 'Buy British' import promotion mission and the Japanese team agreed. In March 1973 the import promotion mission, led by Matsuo Taiichiro (chairman of the Japanese Machine Import Association and Vice President of Marubeni) which included about 30 businessmen and managers from trading companies, department stores and the Trade Ministry, visited Britain. They toured various factories, shops and departments to research the type of British goods that they might be able to buy, how they could send them to Japan and what the production capacity was. They made their study right up to the point of actual import. The mission concluded that 'it is difficult to import large amounts of British products and there is no option available except to accumulate small batches of goods. But the British for their part have no strong desire to increase production even if sales are guaranteed'. They went on to say, 'Britain's way of commerce is the same as that of confectionery companies in Kyoto,[13] that is, they do not make any more of their product after they have sold everything that they have made'. The Japanese side were unhappy with the British approach which they called 'the business way of the aristocracy'.

However there was a strong view from the British side that the problem lay in 'the lack of openness of the Japanese market', especially the protectionism and complexity characteristic of the Japanese market which hindered the export of British products. When the mission met Prime Minister Edward Heath, he pointed out that some Japanese retailers were hindering the entry of British investment and asked the Japanese to act to change the situation. Thus Japan was asked to import British goods actively and to open up the Japanese market.

Another objection of the British side in relation to Japanese importing was the tendency they had to scoop up everything at once. For example, a British newspaper commented that a Japanese businessman sent industrial spies to gather information on British fashion.[14] According to the newspaper, the Japanese would appear every time the designer showed in Paris. The designer claimed that the Japanese had a special force of ten people who came repeatedly onto the stand, and on one occasion a gentleman bought five types of coat, pulling from his pocket £20,000 in cash to pay and that this reckless purchasing was in order to imitate the designs. Furthermore the tabloid reported that at a

Christie's auction the Japanese, purchasing only Impressionist paintings, snapped up half the entire day's turnover worth 400 million Yen. This way of buying drew criticism from the British and also heightened concerns about Japan which was well on its way to becoming an economic power in the world. There was a report from the Japanese embassy in London to the government in Tokyo which read: 'It is significant that amongst the British there is candid evaluation of Japan as a major economic power but also that a feeling of envy has appeared. These sentiments are sharpened by the British realization of the present economic crisis in their own country, and an awareness of the downfall of the British Empire.'

But, when compared to Japanese–American relations, these sentiments did not arouse the same conflicts. This was because measures taken to avoid them, such as the trade regulation and trade missions, had had some effect on British sentiment. It is doubtful whether the import promotion mission had any great effect but the British side had been grateful for it as an attempt to appreciate the goods that Britain had to offer. So the sending of an import promotion mission was well received and similar missions were sent to various other countries in Europe, but the British one had been the first and had trodden new ground. Secondly, Britain recognized the existence of Japan as an economic power increasingly with the commencement of Japanese investment in the country. The amount of Japanese investment rose steadily throughout the 1980s encouraged by the Conservative government although it had started in the 1970s and the British supported its growth seeing its advantages in respect of complaints over the trade surplus. Thirdly, British industry was not so eager to export to Japan and showed less desire to penetrate its market, largely as a result of Britain's emphasis on exporting to the EU countries.

Stimulated by the American media, which had an interest in Japan, the British mass media began to show an interest in the 1970s. For example, the *Economist* of 4 January 1975 ran a special edition on Japan titled 'The Century of the Pacific Ocean 1975–2075?' The article pointed out that from 1 January the century of Japan had started and praised Japan even though they felt it necessary to include a question-mark. It complimented Japan, saying that a stable policy for 30 years following World War II and a health administration that increased life expectancy, combined with an appreciation for beauty, formed the basis for economic growth. A further factor supporting economic growth was 'the ability to shrewdly acquire other countries' technology'. The 'transfer of civil servants to private industry' and 'the method of disposing of inefficient companies by squeezing their finances' as well as 'wages adjustable by bonuses' were mentioned, as was the capability that the Japanese had to 'deal with Arabs because of their over-dependence on oil'. The article was thus slightly cynical in parts of its explanation of the reasons for Japan's growth.

It became common when reporting on Japan to mention the particular Japanese phenomenon of rapid economic growth. The issuing of invitations to British journalists by the Japanese government to come to Japan was considered a useful means of broadening the interest. For example the Japanese government invited Mr Green, editor of the *Daily Telegraph*, to Japan to view Japanese factories and arranged interviews with important businessmen. This kind of invitation began to change clichéd reports such as one that revealed how some Japanese employees had gone to hot springs to get drunk and watch striptease shows on a company junket. Or others that reported on the way of life of members of the Japanese mafia, the *yakuza*. Such images of Japan were predominantly negative. The Japan Foundation, created by the government in 1974, was the main force behind efforts at changing these perceptions.

In the light of the growth in the Japanese economy, a body of opinion emerged with a view to the future that youth exchanges were needed and a programme was devised and proposed by the British. Nicolas Wolfers (now Maclean) proposed that university graduates and postgraduates should be sent to Japan for a year to teach English and learn about Japanese culture, customs and ways of thinking. They had to be bright individuals who had the potential to become future leaders of British society. The programme was intended to create pro-Japanese sympathizers for the future of relations. It was also intended to enhance the teaching of spoken English in Japan and thus promote the country's internationalization, so killing two birds with one stone. When Mr Wolfers proposed this idea to Ambassador Kato Tadao in London, the ambassador ordered Counsellor Sakamoto to promote such a programme. However, the Ministry of Education opposed this plan, citing opposition from the teachers' union Nikkyoso, and from teachers whose pronunciation of spoken English was far from perfect. When the proposed programme was reported in the Japanese press, Koizumi Jun-ichiro, a member of the Diet, was impressed and sought to implement the programme. Eventually, through political lobbying, the programme was authorized as educational policy.

In late 1976, the selection process for British students to be sent to Japan began. Initially, 20 students were to be chosen from 600 applicants, but in fact, in 1978, 23 students were finally allocated places to commence studies. This was the beginning of the Japan Exchange & Teaching programme (JET), which was formally launched 10 years later. For the JET programme, the graduates were selected not only from Britain and English-speaking countries of the United States, Australia, Canada and Ireland; but French, German, South Korean and Chinese students were also selected to teach their respective languages. In 1997, approximately 4,500 foreign students came to Japan. Thus, over a period of 20 years, from an initial British idea coupled with Japanese diplomatic efforts, the programme has flourished. Overall, it has been extremely successful as an educational and cultural exchange between countries. The JET programme, however, was unsuccessful in respect of the subsequent employment of the British youth, who found it difficult to return to work in their home country after having been a little spoilt by the pampering that they had received in Japan, and they often preferred to remain and look for work there.

Third period: mutual development

When the Falklands war broke out in April 1982, the British government expressed dissatisfaction at the Japanese stance and demanded several times that they renounce their pro-Argentina stance. The reason that Japan took a sympathetic stance towards Argentina was largely because of the 20,000 Japanese-Argentinians, whose lives the government wanted to avoid making difficult in Argentina. Also Japan's government took into account the feelings of its people who were naturally inclined to empathize with the underdog. The UK was seen as a relatively powerful nation and Argentina as comparatively weak. When Britain asked Japan to add its voice to the resolution denouncing Argentina at the UN, the Japanese government declined. So the Foreign Secretary, Francis Pym, called Mr Hirahara, the Japanese ambassador, and asked him directly to reverse the decision. Britain was irritated when the Japanese then took the decision to support the ceasefire resolution that it was strongly opposing. Mrs Thatcher wrote about the Versailles summit in her autobiography *The Downing Street Years* as follows:

> We had been talking for about fifteen minutes when a message came through from the Foreign Office and Tony Parsons that a vote was about to be taken in the Security Council and that the Japanese were voting against us. As theirs was the ninth vote required for the

resolution to pass this was particularly irritating. So much for the previous undertakings of co-operation. I tried hard to contact Mr Suzuki, the Japanese Prime Minister, to persuade him to reverse the decision and at least abstain. He could not possibly have gone to bed in such a short time. But I was told that he could not be reached.[15]

As its territory had been invaded by a relatively minor power such as Argentina, Britain felt obliged to avenge its hurt pride. But Mrs Thatcher later explained to Ambassador Hirahara that, if Britain had attacked Nazi Germany at the first sign of invasion at the start of the Second World War, only 20,000–30,000 British and French soldiers would have died, and up to 20 million people could have been saved. She went on to say that

> when this historical lesson had been learned it became our policy to show the world that we will never again allow any form of invasion of even the smallest kind, and to show that invasion will never again be profitable. If we close our eyes to the Argentinian invasion of the Falklands, then they or other countries will continue to invade their neighbour's territory. Therefore Britain supports the Japanese government position demanding the return of the Northern islands both inside and outside the UN because the Soviets snatched the islands after Japan had surrendered. Britain will never again allow invasion.[16]

Tension between Japan and Britain over the Falklands was one of the rare occasions when the two countries had disagreed since the 1960s. There was no real political conflict between the two countries, but the differing approaches were revealed. When the Falklands war ended with British victory, Britain took a mature view of the matter and did not pursue Japan over its stance, so the war did not ruin Anglo-Japanese relations.

Three months after the end of the Falklands war Mrs Thatcher visited Japan as scheduled. She had been to Japan before but this was her first visit as prime minister. Thatcher, who admired Japanese economic growth and respected the hard-working Japanese, wanted to examine the workings of the Japanese economy and to learn from this system how to stimulate the British economy. She had previously proclaimed the need to 'Look East' and was keen to study Japanese growth. Her visit signified a respect for Japan which had placed 40 per cent of its total European investment in Britain. In discussions with Japanese leaders, including Prime Minister Suzuki and Foreign Minister Watanabe, the problems of the Falkland islands and the massacre of Palestinian refugees in the Lebanon were discussed, but only as an exchange of information. The main themes for discussion were economic matters such as self-regulation and liberalization of the market in order to correct the trade imbalance. We should mention that Mrs Thatcher spoke to the chairman of the Nissan car company, Mr Kawamata, at this time and attempted to persuade him to build a factory in Britain, which resulted in the establishment of a factory at Washington, Co. Durham. Thatcher used her political power to full effect in order to revitalize the British economy.

Mrs Thatcher's activity in Japan was very energetic according to Ambassador Hirahara, who accompanied her. While they were flying in a helicopter Mrs Thatcher's husband, Denis, was pointing out a golf course that had appeared below them, and the prime minister would not even leave the articles that she was busy reading about Japan in order to peer out of the window.[17]

The 1980s was the period when Japanese investment to Britain rapidly expanded. In February 1984 Nissan signed a commitment with the DTI to construct a British factory. In July the Yamazaki Tekko company established itself in Britain too as an EEC committee agreed to its receiving a subsidy from the UK government. In June 1985 Honda and British Leyland signed an agreement of co-operation to develop new models of car. Japanese companies continued arriving in Britain, and by the start of 1987 the number exceeded 50. By 1988 the number of Japanese companies had reached 82.[18] According to the DTI, Japanese companies employed 20,000 workers and the volume of investment from 1972 to 1988 was around £1 billion. The Japanese establishing themselves in Britain were surprised by increasingly loud voices beckoning them to mainland Europe. As a result, articles welcoming Japanese investment began to appear such as that in the London *Evening Standard* which was titled 'Welcome to the Japanese Invasion'.[19]

Although Japanese investment had risen, the trade imbalance had not been resolved. In order to find a solution the leaders of the Japanese government and business community often visited Britain. In October 1981 a government economic mission headed by Inayama came and in March 1982 the Esaki mission included the chairman of the Special Research Committee on the International Economy set up by the Liberal Democratic Party. In February–March 1983 the Uemura mission visited Britain, followed in November by the Japanese Market Promotional Mission. Their common objective was to create an environment for the export of British products to Japan. In welcoming these missions the British pointed out the closed nature of the Japanese market and asked for greater openness.

However Britain itself began to make efforts to promote exports to Japan and initiated and ran a campaign called 'Opportunity Japan' (1988). The main aims of the campaign were: to double the volume of exports to Japan in three years; to introduce the chance of investment in Japan to British companies; and to promote Anglo-Japanese co-operation in the markets of third countries. This campaign was very successful and achieved the objective of doubling British exports to Japan within three years. In contrast to the US, Britain did not use the word 'imbalance' or continually attack Japan over the issue, preferring to take the more pragmatic approach of trying to increase exports. This attitude was appreciated by the Japanese and aided their objectives. This spirit of co-operation was beneficial to both countries. After three years of successful operation under 'Opportunity Japan', 'Priority Japan' was run for three years and that was followed by 'Action Japan', all of which were designed to promote exports. With the success of these campaigns in Britain, similar campaigns were started in Europe. For example in France 'Le Japon. C'est possible', and in Holland 'Plan Japon' were launched to promote exports to Japan. Of course, criticisms against Japan's closed market persisted, and in 1987 there was a complaint in the British parliament when Cable and Wireless had its application to enter the Japanese communications market turned down. The calls for Japan to open its market grew steadily stronger. This problem soon became a diplomatic one, and as a result of political pressure Cable and Wireless was granted permission to enter the Japanese market. Membership of the Tokyo Stock Exchange had also become an issue. When UK dealers had been refused access, the exchange had given the somewhat strange reason that their building was not physically big enough to accept them. However it was opened to foreign companies in stages in 1986 and 1988, and then finally, when Mrs Thatcher came to Japan in September 1989, she requested membership for the two remaining British companies wanting to join. The British recognized Tokyo's efforts during the negotiations about opening the market but complained that progress was too slow. That it took a long time to resolve such conflicts was a characteristic Japanese shortcoming.

From the point of view of Anglo-Japanese exchange it was helpful that Crown Prince Hironomiya studied in Britain. The British government was very supportive during his period of study. When the Japanese royal family decided to send the Prince to Britain, it was agreed that he should go to Oxford because Prince Chichibu and Prince Hirohito-Mikasa had studied there, but the Japanese did not know which college would be best for him. So Ambassador Hirahara passed a request to Britain to suggest a college. The Foreign Secretary recommended Merton College giving the reason that it was the oldest college and that student numbers were only about 150 and no Japanese students had ever been there before. Francis Pym told Hirahara, however, that he was not entirely happy with the choice. Surprised, the ambassador asked the reason why, to which Pym replied, 'because I went to Cambridge'.[20] The Crown Prince stayed in Oxford from June 1983 for two years and wrote a thesis which was published in book form called 'On the Thames. Two Years in Britain'. He researched the history of British canals, doing part of his investigation on foot.

He was accepted by the British royal family. Yamazaki Toshio, the then Ambassador to Britain, wrote:

> Once a year there is the 'Trooping of the Colour' parade, to which the Prince was invited and he afterwards went to Buckingham Palace. At that time the royal family suggested 'why not come out on the balcony for a few minutes' and he joined the entire royal family outside where they waved at the crowds gathered in front of the palace. Apparently the British who saw the scene on television were wondering who the dark haired gentleman was, when the commentator explained that it was Prince Hironomiya. The public saw that he was being treated as a member of the family.[21]

This revealed the closeness of the two royal families. The Japanese royals had chosen Britain when deciding where to educate the Crown Prince as they had seen the British royal family as a role model. However, as a result of the divorce of the Prince and Princess of Wales, the Japanese royal family has lost some of its openness because of concerns that, if they became accessible in the British style, they would lose respect from the public. They found that the British royal family was not such a good example to follow.

Proximity became an important factor not only in economic terms but also in terms of cultural exchange. For example, the UK–Japan

2000 Group was launched in 1985. This was organized by the Japanese Foreign Ministry and influential politicians. Businessmen and scholars involved in Anglo-Japanese relations got together and decided to submit a proposal to help promote relations from a civil perspective. The committee's proposal aimed to help the two governments promote exchange on an annual basis. In 1981 the Edo Exhibition was held at the Royal Academy of Arts. Various places hosted initiatives to introduce Japan to the public; the 'Japan Introduction Week' in Glasgow and the Welsh 'Japan Week' in March 1984 were followed closely by the Oxford 'Japan Week' in December 1985. It became common for Japanese film and drama to be shown at the Edinburgh Festival. In 1987 *Macbeth*, directed by Ninagawa Yukio, proved very popular at London's National Theatre. This was the period when Japanese culture became known in Britain. Cultural exchanges showed that Britain was not only interested in the Japanese economy but also in its cultural aspects; we could say that it enriched mutual relations. Its high-point was the Japan Festival of 1991–92.

When in the 1990s political matters between both countries came to the fore it was due to the Gulf War. Although Japan donated $13 billion to the Gulf War due to pressure from the US and the UK, it was accused by the West of a lack of international co-operation. This was because its decision to donate was too slow and too late. Britain, however, understood the situation and gave the Japanese their intelligence on the war. 'The British Foreign Office was of the opinion that Gulf War information should be supplied to the Japanese as much as possible. The intelligence released to the Japanese Foreign Ministry through the London Embassy was far more valuable than that from Washington'.[22] During this period Japan and Britain found that they could co-operate well politically.

The idea for the Japan Festival came from the British. As 1991 was the centenary of the establishment of 'The Japan Society' in London, the society proposed that Japanese culture should be introduced on a grand scale to commemorate the event. Japan and Britain decided to work together in staging the festival. On the British side Sir Peter Parker, former chairman of British Rail, headed the organizing committee, and on the Japanese side Saba Shoichi, Vice-Chairman of Keidanren, were chosen. Sir Peter explained the idea behind the festival as follows:

> Nowadays in Britain the towns are full of Japanese electronic goods and one in five cars in Britain are Japanese designs. Nearly two

hundred Japanese manufacturing companies are established in various parts of the country. However British people know little about Japanese culture, a few members of the intelligentsia excepted. We want to redress that imbalance so let us introduce an exhibition of Japanese culture past and present that is full of variety. We shouldn't concentrate solely on London, but want to introduce it to the whole of Britain, so that we can say 'Now we know Japan'. Active, flexible and full of variety, reserved yet friendly and trustworthy, these kinds of Japanese qualities should be conveyed to the British.[23]

Most of the money was to be collected by the Japanese which was in a stronger economic situation at the time, and the Japanese put the target to be collected at 1 billion Yen. The committee were able to attain their goal as it was the time of the 'bubble economy' in Japan. In fact sponsorship collected in Britain during the whole period of the festival was 5 billion Yen.

The content of the Japan Festival was a mixture of traditional Japanese culture and contemporary culture. As scheduled it was staged not only in London but in other parts of Britain. The activity that caused most excitement was the Sumo performance, and the Kabuki and Bunraku puppeteers. The splendid Kabuki performance of Tamasaburo in 'Heron' touched people's hearts and was praised in all the usually cynical newspapers. Sumo was already very popular because of the weekly digest shows from Japan seen on cable and satellite television channels. On the days it was shown touts appeared who were charging 30 times the value of a ticket. Many people commented that they were impressed by the beauty of Japanese tradition and the dignified courtesy and pride of the Sumo wrestlers.

The Japanese who participated were for their part impressed by the sophisticated eye of the audiences. A famous Japanese actress, Arima Ineko, who had heard about the discerning judgement of London audiences, reported that, though she had performed *Hanare Goze Orin* in identical performances over 400 times in Japan, her legs were trembling for the first five minutes of her London performance.[24] A Bunraku puppeteer recounted that 'in Japan audiences are often not silent. This was the first time in my life that the audience displayed such attentiveness'.[25] The Japan Festival of 1991 can be seen as one of the high-points of past Anglo-Japanese relations. To borrow Harold Macmillan's words we had 'never had it so good'. We should not forget to mention that the Japan Festival Educational Trust was incorporated into the festival. This programme organized groups of volunteers (such as Japanese wives resident in Britain) to visit secondary schools with video tapes that introduced Japan. They also told of their own experiences of Japan in the classrooms. This helped British children to develop an interest in Japan and the trust continued in existence after the festival in order to foster their interest in learning about Japan in schools.

Although Anglo-Japanese relations reached their peak at the time of the Japan Festival, two sticking points remained. One was the problem of compensation for British POWs who had been abused by the Japanese army. The other was the whaling problem. Both issues were understood to have been resolved at government level but, in terms of national sentiment, that was not the case. The Japanese government took the view that the POWs' claims had already been settled. This was because the Japanese government agreed with the British government to pay £75 per person to former POWs in the 1951 San Francisco treaty and this amount had already been paid. But the POWs asserted their right to sue for compensation personally aside from the nation-to-nation settlement. At the time of the 50th anniversary celebrations for VE day and VJ day in 1995, they used the opportunity to demand from the Japanese government a formal apology and compensation. Some of the POWs, angered by the Japanese government's inaction, appealed to the courts in Tokyo, demanding an apology from the government and £14,000 per victim. They mistrusted the Japanese government whom they suspected of preferring to bide its time and wait for the natural solution of them all eventually dying.[26] The Japanese government was not invited to the ceremony commemorating the 50th anniversary of the end of the war at Hyde Park, London, in August 1995 because of objections by the POWs, and the tabloids stirred up anti-Japanese feelings by carrying reports that detailed the maltreatment by the Japanese army again.

The whaling problem is not restricted to Anglo-Japanese relations, but British public opinion turned strongly against Japan because the Whaling Commission that sets catch quotas meets every year in Britain. When the Whaling Commission holds talks, thousands of letters of protest would arrive at the Japanese embassy in London. The voice of protesters became quieter as the numbers caught decreased but, when we assess Anglo-Japanese relations at a popular level, we cannot deny that Japanese whaling practices have aggravated anti-Japanese feelings in Britain.

Notes

1. Interview with Fujisaki Banri, Counsellor of the Japanese embassy in London.
2. Hanaoka Sosuke, 'Memories of the Anglo-Japanese Commercial Treaty: A Japanese Perspective', in Ian Nish (ed.), *Britain and Japan. Biographical Portraits*, Vol. II (Folkestone, 1997), p. 322.
3. GATT Article 35 defined the right of trading countries to withhold MFN status according to their own judgement. Britain discriminated against Japan on account of the low wages paid to workers in Japan.
4. Hanaoka, 'Memories of the Anglo-Japanese Commercial Treaty', p. 323.
5. *Mainichi Shimbun*, 15 November 1962.
6. Oba Sadao, 'Nichi-ei keizai-koryu 400-nen shi (53): Sen-go no Nihon ni okeru Ei-kigyo (jo)' (400-year History of Anglo-Japanese Economic Exchange (53): Post-War British Industry in Japan), *Big Ben* Newsletter, Nippon Club, No. 92 (March 1996), 3.
7. Ota Takeshi, *Kokusai Kinyu. Genba Kara no Shogen: Nichigin Kara Mita Gekido no 30 Nen* (International Finance. Testimony from the Spot: Thirty Years of Turbulence Seen from the Bank of Japan) (Chuo Koron Sha, 1991), p. 25.
8. *Mainichi Shimbun*, 8 October 1971.
9. *Asahi Shimbun*, 7 October 1971.
10. The factors that had induced Japanese companies to establish in Britain were as follows: 1. There were some companies that could not make a profit exporting from Japan due to the high transport costs; 2. Companies wanted to create a base for export to the rest of the EEC which Britain had joined in 1973; 3. They became confident of on-the-spot production due to successes in Southeast Asia and the US; 4. The British government would have put pressure on imports if Japanese companies had not started to produce in Britain; 5. Japan's companies had a feeling that they could manage to communicate better in English than in other European languages; 6. Mining areas like Wales and former industrial areas like Scotland had relatively cheap and well trained labour forces; 7. These under-developed areas provided Japanese companies with good conditions to find land for industry and also companies locating there were provided with tax incentives. Furthermore once one company is shown to be successful there is a tendency for Japanese companies to follow suit. For example five colour television companies all made investments in the UK.
11. *Asahi Shimbun*, 9 May 1975.
12. *Mainichi Shimbun*, 20 December 1975.
13. Words of a Mission member from the retail business.
14. *Sunday Times*, 8 April 1973.
15. Margaret Thatcher, *The Downing Street Years* (London, 1993), pp. 231–2.
16. Hirahara Takeshi, *Eikoku Taishi no Gaiko Jinsei* (Diplomatic Life of a Japanese Ambassador to Britain) (Kawadeshobo Shinsha, 1995) pp. 245–6.
17. Interview with Ambassador Hirahara.
18. Announcement from the British Ministry for Trade and Industry, May 1988. There were several reasons for the increase in the level of Japanese investment: 1. The Japanese can understand English making it easier for them to

transfer technology and train the management; 2. The quality of labour was high and labour costs were low, around half that of Germany's; 3. The infrastructure was secure and to obtain funding firms could utilise the City of London; 4. Central and local governments were very active and provided tax relief programmes; 5. When Japanese companies were set up they had no labour unions but they had prior examples of excellent management-labour relations; and 6. When Japanese companies established in Europe it was possible to export to the rest of Europe even if European integration became tighter. The expansion of Japanese companies into Britain stimulated British industry. The effects were as follows: reform of the production of component parts; management reform such as altering internal communications and the introduction of a single employee dining room; and unification of workers and management and the stabilisation of industrial relations. Oba Sadao, 'Nichi-ei keizai-koryu 400-nen shi (57): Zai-ei nihon kigyo no genjo' (400-year History of Anglo-Japanese Economic Exchange (57): The Present Situation of Japanese Industry in Britain), *Big Ben* Newsletter, Nippon Club, No. 96 (November 1996), 3.
19. *Evening Standard*, 10 September 1991.
20. Interview with Ambassador Hirahara.
21. Yamazaki Toshio, in *Koryo* (Old boys' school magazine of the First High School), (October 1986), 18.
22. Interview with senior officials of the Japanese Foreign Ministry.
23. *Nikkei* Newspaper, 3 February 1992.
24. Author's interview.
25. Author's interview.
26. Interview with Arthur Titherington, Chairman of the Japanese Labour Camp Survivors Association.

11
Distant Friends: Britain and Japan since 1958 – the Age of Globalization

Christopher Braddick

>Friends agree best at a distance.
>
>(English proverb)

In recent years the text of Anglo-Japanese relations has been peppered with expressions of mutual affection. It was not always thus. Perhaps it is no more than government propaganda, but if the history of postwar Anglo-Japanese relations can reasonably be characterized as an evolution from enmity to amity, then it is worthwhile considering what accounts for this transformation. Is it the product of some fundamental values held in common, or merely a temporary coincidence of interests? Does it result from the rational calculations of individual policy-makers in London and Tokyo, from the pressures imposed by important domestic interest groups, or does the re-emergence of some intangible, but none the less genuine, emotional bond lie behind the improvement? Have powerful third parties, like the US, helped or hindered the strengthening of Anglo-Japanese ties?

Our interest, moreover, is not confined to the influences on Anglo-Japanese relations, but also extends in the opposite direction. In other words, we should consider how important Anglo-Japanese relations have been for the wider world, as well as for London and Tokyo. In the first half of the twentieth century, one might reasonably argue that from alliance to war this was one of the key bilateral relationships shaping the course of world history. But not even the most Anglophile Japanese (or Japanophile Briton) would make this claim for the post-1945 period. Surely it is not coincidental that, despite the hyperbole of politicians and diplomats, their relationship has been virtually ignored by scholars. What factors explain this decline? Does it reflect revised foreign policy priorities? Or are the bilateral developments of the past four decades less a reflection of the actions of individual states and more the result of the deeper structural changes – postwar decolonization, Cold War polarization, institutional multilateralization, economic globalization and regionalization – that have occurred within the international system? These are some of the key questions that will be addressed in this chapter.

'Le rapprochement Anglo-Japonais' (late 1950s–mid-1960s)[1]

> Kino no teki wa kyo no tomo [Yesterday's enemy is today's friend].
>
> (Japanese proverb)

In 1958, when Britain and Japan should have been preparing to commemorate the centenary of their modern diplomatic ties, bilateral relations were still 'as chilly as they could be'. [2] This assessment from the newly appointed Japanese ambassador to London, Ono Katsumi, might be dismissed as exaggerated and not a little self-serving, were it not for the extraordinary comments of his counterpart, Sir Daniel Lascelles: 'The whole urge of [the] needy, incredibly industrious and politically rather unscrupulous or merely amoral [Japanese] is away from the ideological inhibitions of the so-called free world and towards a renewal of the struggle for hegemony of Asia'.[3] Was Japan once more a threat?

Twelve years of peace had seen very little progress made towards healing the grievous wounds inflicted by four years of war. British attitudes ranged from the cautiously optimistic to the positively hostile. While *The Economist* was reasonably sanguine regarding Japan's prospects for achieving economic and political stability, 1958 also saw the publication of Lord Russell of Liverpool's best-seller: *The Knights of Bushido: The Shocking History of Japanese War Atrocities*.[4] On the Japanese side there reportedly remained 'a great reservoir of friendship and respect for the British people, in spite of the unfortunate breaking of the thread'. [5] This was said by some to be based on a gross overestimate of British power.[6] But *Gaimusho's* first *Diplomatic Blue Book* published the previous autumn had laid down the 'three basic principles' of Japan's foreign policy: cooperation with the free world; support for the UN; and maintenance of close ties with Asia.[7] As a leading member of NATO, a permanent member of the UN Security Council and the head of a Commonwealth that reached into South and Southeast Asia, Britain was a significant factor in every respect.[8] In contrast, London's postwar focus on relations with the United States, the Commonwealth and Western Europe – Churchill's 'three circles' – left Japan on the sidelines.

Anglo-Japanese relations seemed frozen in a state of 'suspended animation', but a thaw, as yet unremarked, had set in. The impetus came mostly from the Japanese side, and Foreign Minister Fujiyama Aiichiro's visit to London in September 1957 represented the first push. No significant progress was made on any of the long-standing obstacles to Anglo-Japanese reconciliation: Britain's nuclear testing at Christmas Island, which had sparked a near-riot at the Tokyo embassy in May; London's invocation of GATT Article 35, allowing it unilaterally to discriminate against Japanese exports; compensation from Japan arising from the pre-1941 'China Incident'; and protection of British copyrights. However, Fujiyama and Foreign Secretary Selwyn Lloyd agreed to increase cooperation to aid Southeast Asian development and to exchange low-level intelligence on China.[9] Japan was certainly keen to present relations in a positive light.[10] Fujiyama's official report concluded that 'this visit lessened the sense of rift (*tairitsu*)', and, he hoped, 'laid the foundation stone for future cooperation'.[11] The British confirmed that it had 'helped to restore political relations'.[12]

Seeking to maintain the momentum, at Tokyo's request Fujiyama met Prime Minister Macmillan in Singapore on 19 January 1958. After disagreeing on the wisdom of supplying aid to Indonesia, Fujiyama proposed holding joint Japan–UK–US political consultations aimed at producing a common Asia policy.[13] London politely declined this offer, however, concerned lest it raise difficulties vis-à-vis the Commonwealth and SEATO.[14]

Japan's new ambassador, Ono Katsumi, was eager to set about rebuilding relations: 'My predecessors, Matsumoto and Nishi, have with your help exerted themselves in the removal of rubble resulting from the war. I see before me a road ready to be paved,' he told the Japan Society. 'Cooperation between our two countries is important not only to ourselves, but to the other nations of the free world, especially those of South-East Asia and the Pacific area,' he declared.[15] Just a week after his arrival in May, Ono had proposed that Prime Minister Kishi visit Britain. Foreign Secretary Lloyd advised caution: 'there ha[s] been a steady improvement in Anglo-Japanese relations but British public opinion needed nursing along step by step and we must not overdo things'.[16]

The first fruit of the Anglo-Japanese détente appeared in mid-June, with the signing of an agreement on the peaceful uses of atomic energy. This allowed British companies eventually to win the contract to build Japan's first commercial nuclear power plant at Tokai Mura.[17] Any afterglow was short-lived, however, as the following month's Anglo-American military intervention in the Middle East attracted strong condemnation in Japan, although the government refrained from publicly denouncing their actions.[18]

Whilst this crisis was ebbing, another was brewing in the Taiwan Straits. Discomfited by Washington's belligerent response, Tokyo began to revive Yoshida Shigeru's idea of closer relations with Britain as a counterweight to its overwhelming dependence on the US.[19] Unbeknown to the Japanese, however, at President Eisenhower's suggestion, secret Anglo-American consultations had recently begun on a joint approach to Japan. The Americans, repeatedly emphasizing their desire for 'the closest cooperation ... on Japanese matters', sought British assistance in their efforts at 'leading Japan into free world paths', and especially at preventing Japanese diplomatic recognition of Beijing. The British government found itself in a rather awkward position. Generally more tolerant of left-wing views and aware of the risk of appearing to be 'ganging up' on the Japanese, London would not 'prejudice our relations with the US or Commonwealth on their account, or pull their Chinese chestnuts out of the fire for them' but, having recognized the PRC in 1949, it was hardly in a position to advise Tokyo against doing so now.[20]

According to Ambassador Lascelles, Anglo-Japanese relations 'remained somewhat tepid', but his replacement, Sir Oscar Morland – a wiser choice – was more optimistic.[21] He was convinced that 'the Japanese Government do in fact attach great importance to closer cooperation with us'. Moreover, he argued that, 'both in the short term and long term, we can gain a lot from closer cooperation with Japan'.[22] Morland was responding to the latest Japanese proposals offering 'to assist us in containing Communism and in promoting healthy nationalism in the Middle East and ... work[ing] out with us a common policy as regards the underdeveloped countries of Asia and Africa'.[23] At the Far Eastern Department, N.C.C. Trench's reaction was similar:

> Although there are matters over which our interests clash, the Japanese have over the past eighteen months or two years shown signs of wanting closer relations with HMG ... It is clearly in our interests to encourage this attitude in the Japanese not only because

it is valuable to have in Asian councils a voice friendly to us (although the Japanese tend to overestimate their influence in Asia) but also because it is essential to keep the Japanese lined up with the West against the increasing power of China, while offering them a policy in this respect rather less rigid than that of the Americans.[24]

Kishi was invited to visit London in mid-July 1959. The Foreign Office briefs recommended that Britain 'should encourage Japanese attempts to draw closer'. Japan was recognized as 'now playing an independent and on the whole responsible role in world affairs'. Britain's main aim was 'to prevent Japan from allying herself with the Sino-Soviet bloc'. Thus it was felt wise to provide the Japanese 'with some sort of safety-valve for their views on the wrong-headedness of America's China policy'. On the trade front it was noted that: 'it will be increasingly awkward for us to maintain our discrimination against Japan ... when the only other countries so discriminated against are in the Soviet bloc'. At the same time, the 'unscrupulous ... clever and adaptable' Kishi was regarded with some suspicion, and 'any Japanese proposals for formal bipartite or tripartite consultative machinery' were still unwelcome.[25]

At the popular level distrust of Japan ran deeper: 'The fact that the former militarists and ultranationalists are totally discredited and the country staunchly anti-militarist ... is either unknown or discounted. And so many [Britons] continue to believe that Japan is nursing an urge to rearm and again indulge in power politics whenever a suitable opportunity occurs'. It is perhaps a sign of the importance Tokyo attached to Kishi's forthcoming trip that the author of these comments, Hessell Tiltman (Tokyo special correspondent for the *Manchester Guardian*), was recruited by Gaimusho to offer suggestions on how to handle British public opinion.[26] His advice was closely followed.[27]

In London the two premiers agreed that 'close cooperation should be the guiding principle of Anglo-Japanese relations'. China was the main focus of their conversation. 'The Japanese Government could not recognise the Peking regime at present,' Kishi declared, adding that 'the basic principle of Japanese policy ... was to cooperate with the free world'. Macmillan responded in like terms: 'Despite our recognition of Peking, our relations with the Chinese remained cool and we stood firmly with the Americans and our other allies on the broad issues'. On economic matters Kishi offered 'voluntary restrictions on exports in exchange for [Britain] dropping Article 35'.[28] The Chancellor of the Exchequer and President of the Board of Trade (BOT) fell back on the hostile public opinion defence, and the latter – the centre of resistance to an agreement – insisted on 'adequate safeguards'. In response to Kishi's offer to support European economic integration as long as it led to an 'expansion of trade', its president, Sir David Eccles, claimed that 'we were fighting Japan's battles'. Finally, a consensus was reached on the need to cooperate in assisting underdeveloped countries, although both sides complained of a lack of funds.[29] *The Economist* complained of a 'widespread impression that the Japanese Prime Minister came to London with nothing to offer and left empty-handed'.[30] Kishi felt otherwise. On his return journey he said that 'he intended ... to conduct Japan's foreign policy on the basis of a trinity formed by Japan, the US and the UK'. Moreover, once back in Tokyo he told a press conference that Macmillan had supported Japan's non-recognition of China as 'wise and realistic'. Questions were raised in the Commons and Kishi was eventually forced to tell the Diet that he had been 'misquoted' in both cases.[31]

In his 'annual review for 1959', Morland offered a realistic assessment of Japan's courtship of Britain: commercially, they wanted London to 'remove and encourage by our example others to remove discrimination against Japanese imports', while, politically, they hoped that Britain would 'exert our influence on America in a way that will assist their objectives in China and South-East Asia'. In sum, 'they would like to have us as useful friends, provided that it does not cost them too much'. Morland recommended that London adopt the same attitude: 'We have now much to gain from promoting closer relations provided that we too can do this without any important sacrifice'.[32]

For the next six months Tokyo's attention was monopolized by the crisis surrounding the revision of the US–Japan Security Treaty, which eventually forced Kishi to resign in July 1960. Anxious to restore a degree of normality to Japan's foreign relations, the new government, led by Yoshida protégé Ikeda Hayato, immediately set about reviving its stalled approach to Britain. Trade Minister Ishii Mitsujiro visited London in August and assured his hosts that Japan remained 'staunchly pro-Western', and 'strongly ... felt the need for closer Anglo-Japanese ties'.[33]

The last months of 1960 were notable for two symbolically important Anglo-Japanese agreements: the settlement of Britain's 'China Incident' claims and the conclusion of a Cultural Convention.[34] Ambassador Ono was now speaking optimistically of Britain beginning to view Japan as 'her equal partner' rather than 'a mere commercial competitor'. He cited three reasons for this: 'the anti-Japanese sentiment of the British people arising from the war has been gradually declining'; 'the UK has recognised the rapid rise of Japan in the international community'; and somewhat contradictorily, its own interests in Asia having shrunk, 'to the UK, Japan today is not as important as she used to be'.³⁵ In private, Ono was putting his theory to the test by repeatedly inviting Prime Minister Macmillan to visit Japan. Not surprisingly, Ambassador Morland was enthusiastic.³⁶ The Foreign Secretary was supportive too, arguing: 'It is very much in our interests to do all we reasonably can to keep her on the right side. Her price now is not high: she wants only our friendship and goodwill in commercial as well as political fields'. Macmillan, however, decided that he could not go before mid-1961.³⁷

In January 1961, the Foreign Office prepared an assessment of the 'Japanese attitude towards the UK'. It described how 'the Japanese feel that the UK adopts a very cold and stand-offish attitude towards them', although they still hold 'a very strong feeling of admiration' for Britain. The author warned that 'the Japanese have only very shallow ideological roots and many of them would not boggle at switching their allegiance to the Communist bloc if they thought that was to their material advantage'. Moreover, he recognized that 'in any difference of opinion between the US and ourselves, the Japanese will always tend to side with the US'. The report concluded that 'we shall need to pay more attention to them, not sporadically, but as a matter of permanent and settled policy'.³⁸

A few days later, the respected Japanese economic daily, *Nihon Keizai Shimbun*, noted how 'British feelings towards Japan have improved remarkably', dating the transformation from 1958. It clearly distinguished, however, between the Establishment's view and that of the 'masses', where 'anti-Japanese feeling, stemming from ignorance and prejudice is still deep-rooted'. Nevertheless, it concluded that 'Anglo-Japanese relations are entering a new era'.³⁹

By March, Ambassador Ono was confidently predicting to the inaugural meeting of the Anglo-Japanese Parliamentary Group: 'There is no doubt that the "long and dreary winter" in Anglo-Japanese relations is about to come to an end'. Concretely, he suggested greater cooperation on the 'China problem' and the 'Africa question'.⁴⁰ Earlier that week, he had told the Foreign Secretary, Sir Alec Douglas Home, that Japan favoured a 'two Chinas' policy, and wanted the British government to help seat both in the UN, but it was his African proposal that was to attract most attention in Whitehall.⁴¹ It was one of the main topics of discussion at a large inter-ministry conference held in June to discuss Anglo-Japanese relations. The Colonial and Commonwealth Relations Offices worried about Japanese technical assistance. The BOT criticized 'so-called Japanese "aid" [which] took the form of long-term credit guarantees', while the Foreign Office's position was that 'the time has come to seek closer relations with Japan'. A consensus was reached in favour of promoting the exchange of business leaders, information and culture, and on the provision of technical training, although Ambassador Morland admitted that 'lax security in Japan made the exchange of confidential information difficult'.[42]

The British desire for a fresh start with Japan was revealed even more strongly in the preparations for a visit by Foreign Minister Kosaka Zentaro in July 1961. The Foreign Office offered a warning: 'beware of sentimental hankering after "the good old days" ... We can not return to the Anglo-Japanese Alliance ... Our relations must be based on the facts and conditions of today'. This repudiation of the past also extended to the negative elements, for it claimed that: 'anti-Japanese feeling has so abated that it need no longer be a serious factor in considerations of our policy towards Japan'. There were now 'no major political irritants in Anglo-Japanese relations', but the Foreign Office felt 'it would be an error to assume that because she is now on our side, we can afford to neglect her. A change in her political orientation is by no means impossible'. The 'main problems' were said to lie 'in the commercial field'. Negotiations for a Treaty of Commerce were continuing, but support for Japan's admission to OECD was 'difficult' because it was a regional organization. Still there was scope for increased trade and 'partnership in joint commercial ventures'.[43]

Prior to Kosaka's arrival, Macmillan reluctantly decided to postpone his planned visit to Japan: 'a journey of comparatively secondary importance'.[44] Although the Prime Minister's letter of apology to Ikeda implied that Japan was one of Britain's 'friends and allies', Ambassador Morland could not help complaining that London was 'unduly preoccupied about Europe and thinking about Japan and the Far East [is] out-of-date'.[45]

Kosaka opened the talks by reporting that, when Ikeda had met President Kennedy a fortnight earlier, the former 'had mentioned his desire to establish as close relations with the UK as we had with the US' – suggesting a major readjustment of Japanese foreign policy – 'and President Kennedy had welcomed this'.[46] According to the American record, however, Ikeda had said something quite different: 'The Prime Minister advanced the request that the US undertake to establish with the Japanese in Asia a relationship similar to that enjoyed by Britain, under which the two governments consult continually on foreign policy problems of common concern'.⁴⁷ This implied a certain jealousy on Tokyo's part at the Anglo-American 'special relationship', rather than a desire for balanced relations with both London and Washington. Nevertheless, Kosaka was probably being sincere when he stated that 'Japan desired the UK to keep her attention focused on Asia and rely upon Japan'. In response, Macmillan observed that facing 'very similar' problems produced 'a natural sympathy between Britain and Japan'.⁴⁸ However, the main topic of discussion was again China. Kosaka stressed the importance of building a common UK–US–Japan policy and, with the UN moratorium procedure being no longer practicable, they agreed that Taipei should be pressured into accepting a diminished status.⁴⁹ With other ministers, Kosaka warned that the Security Treaty with the US alone was 'inadequate' to bind Japan to the free world, when her 'proximity to China and Russia meant she was exposed to strong Communist propaganda'. On Africa, he suggested combining Britain's 'great experience' with Japan's 'feeling of kinship with the people of Africa … as a "coloured race"'!⁵⁰ Kosaka also tried to inject a sense of urgency into the negotiations on the Treaty of Commerce; differences narrowed slightly.⁵¹ The next day, he claimed that there existed 'a spiritual bond between the UK and Japan'. Unmoved, Selwyn Lloyd, now Chancellor of the Exchequer, still wanted relations to 'proceed step by step', and he resisted Japan's admission to the OECD.⁵²

Commenting on Kosaka's visit, the embassy in Tokyo came out strongly in favour of Japan's entry to the OECD. The Far Eastern Department, believing that 'Kosaka's visit was more successful even than our fondest hopes', wanted to be supportive, but recognized that 'there is still a certain amount of residual hostility towards Japan in official circles outside the Foreign Office'. As a *'pis-aller'*, the embassy proposed establishing 'a high level Anglo-Japanese Economic Committee' modelled on the US–Japan one. It was also impatient to conclude the Commerce Treaty, correctly deducing that Britain's application to join the EEC increased pressure on Tokyo to make concessions.⁵³

In a speech to the Diet in January 1962, Ikeda referred portentously to the likely prospect of Britain joining the EEC producing a new European superpower greater than either the US or Soviet Union.⁵⁴ He sought to counter this with his 'three-pillar theory', an early version of trilateralism, which proposed an international economic system built on North American, Western European and Japanese poles. This scenario informed Tokyo's approach to London throughout the coming year. Some Japanese, however, thought that they could turn the new situation to their advantage by quickly concluding the Treaty of Commerce with Britain and persuading it to keep the EEC 'outward-looking', supplanting Britain's close economic ties with Commonwealth countries, and reducing their own 'lopsided' dependence on the US.[55]

In Britain there was some sympathy for Japan's predicament. The previous autumn, Sir Norman Kipping, director-general of the Federation of British Industry, had visited Tokyo and returned urging greater and freer trade with Japan.[56] Seven months later Frederick Erroll, President of the BOT, became the first senior cabinet minister to visit Japan. Erroll sought to reassure his hosts, telling them: 'I'm convinced that whatever our future relations with the EEC may be, there is a wide scope for developing trade between Britain and Japan'.[57] That summer, *The Economist*'s Norman Macrae visited Japan and in a very influential survey first suggested that Britain could learn important lessons from it.[58] Paul Johnson, the well-known political commentator, added his voice to the chorus.[59]

Disregarding all this advice, however, when negotiations on a Treaty of Commerce resumed in July, the British proposed an 'EEC clause', allowing the treaty to lapse on their accession to the Community. This was flatly rejected, as it would have negated the whole purpose of the agreement for the Japanese. Both sides were subject to internal pressures as negotiations entered their end game. On the eve of the new round of talks, Gaimusho had published a booklet conceding most of the outstanding points. The next day, however, MITI and the Finance Ministry reportedly lambasted the paper and refused to accept it. While negotiations were proceeding, an inter-ministry meeting decided that Japan should threaten to exclude Britain from the benefits of Tokyo's liberalization programme unless they revoked Article 35.[60] If resistance from certain sectors of British business had not diminished – especially the Lancashire textile industry – at least the BOT was supportive.[61] The Prime Minister's position, however, is a matter of dispute. According to Erroll, 'Macmillan was against the whole idea .... He saw it as a threat to British industry and commerce'. Yet this assessment was contradicted by Ambassador Ono, who believed that, 'behind the success of the ultimate treaty was no doubt the fact that the prime minister gave it his personal backing'.[62]

Overcoming all of these difficulties – after six years of fitful negotiations – a treaty was finally ready for signing when Ikeda visited the UK in November 1962. The Japanese Premier publicly hailed the agreement as 'epoch-making', and even compared it to the San Francisco Peace Treaty in significance. Ikeda was a little nearer the mark when he told Macmillan: 'It was the beginning of a new era of Anglo-Japanese cooperation and partnership'. As its title implies, the Treaty of Commerce, Establishment and Navigation was a long, complex and wide-ranging agreement, but the extension of most favoured nation treatment was its key provision.[63] Ikeda's 'most amicable' talks with British leaders were not confined to economic issues, however. The Foreign Office's expectation that Japan was 'anxious to cooperate with the UK in political matters, particularly those affecting China and the emergent nations', proved accurate.[64] Ikeda now proposed reviving a scheme – first suggested by Yoshida eight years earlier – for 'driving a wedge between China and the Soviet Union' by improving economic relations with the former. Ikeda also offered to 'act as a bridge between the West and Africa'.[65] Finally, Ikeda told Home: 'Britain's presence was essential' in Southeast Asia.[66] The British response was generally positive, although the Chancellor of the Exchequer was careful to exclude the possibility of a special bilateral relationship developing: 'Although some Japanese have recently talked nostalgically of the Anglo-Japanese Alliance, I believe Ikeda and his government realize that conditions today are not those of the beginning of the century and that our relations must now be conducted on a wider, multilateral basis'.[67]

When France then vetoed Britain's application to join the EEC, it came as a 'rude shock' to the Japanese, some of whom now felt that the Treaty of Commerce had given away too much.[68] Hence, one of the 'principal objectives' of Home's visit to Japan in late March 1963 was 'to convince the Japanese that we are still worthwhile political and commercial partners following the breakdown of the Brussels negotiations'.[69] In the short term at least they need not have worried, for, whereas the Treaty had been given a fairly rough ride in Parliament on the eve of Lord Home's arrival, not a single vote was cast against Diet ratification.[70]

Home's visit was the first ever by a British Foreign Secretary. Frustrated by Washington's Sinophobia, Ikeda told his guest that he 'considered that British policies towards China were very much more sensible and wise than American policies'. Home's response was encouraging: 'It was ... up to Britain and Japan to try and make the US see the error of her ways'. Ikeda was also critical of America's politicized aid programme. However, he still hoped to create some kind of formal trilateral structure to harmonize policies on Asia.[71] The second of Home's 'principal objectives' was to persuade the Japanese that 'we seek more than trade with Japan and that we mean what we have said about developing closer cooperation and consultation between our two countries'.[72] This prompted him – somewhat reluctantly – to offer Japan foreign minister-level consultations, perhaps twice a year. The Japanese readily accepted.[73] Home was careful to emphasize that 'we have no demands to make of Japan. And we, of course, seek no exclusive or even special relationship'.[74] Press speculation about a revival of the Anglo-Japanese Alliance was played down back in Whitehall, where the reaction was less than enthusiastic.[75]

The first round of foreign ministerial consultations took place in September, when Foreign Minister Ohira travelled to Castlemains, Home's estate in Scotland. Ohira now accepted that 'The biggest problem in Asia is Communist China', but nevertheless felt 'neglect of China' was preferable to America's 'containment' strategy. On Southeast Asia a compromise was reached: Japan would 'cooperate with the formation of Malaysia', and Britain would accept its close association with the Philippines and Indonesia as long as Sukarno 'refrained from expansionist ideas'.[76] At the BOT, Ohira expressed Japanese fears that without Britain the EEC would become 'more inward looking'.[77]

Britain had no intention of competing with the Americans for influence over Japan. Indeed, the Foreign Office stressed the need to keep the US government fully informed on the consultations.[78] The same observation applies to the secret exchanges that had been taking place since May on the possibility of Anglo-Japanese defence cooperation. This idea was first broached by Kitamura Takeshi, secretary-general of the National Defence Council, and the first defence official to visit the UK since the war. At the Ministry of Defence he spoke of the need for Japan to increase its international security role and counterbalance its dependence on the US by building a strong political relationship with Britain. Concretely, he suggested broadening the exchange of political information and expressed an interest in the purchase of British military equipment and joint military research and development. The Foreign Office response was basically favourable, although concern was expressed regarding Japan's poor security and the need to 'avoid involvement in purely Japanese defence problems', as well as the likely reaction of the Americans and domestic public opinion.[79] Home was willing to 'discount' the last worry and, after discussions with the Pentagon, the State Department confirmed that the US would in principle raise no objections. Like Ambassador Morland in Tokyo, however, they expressed scepticism as to how far Kitamura was speaking for his government.[80] In July, Vice-Foreign Minister Shima confirmed that Kitamura's statements had not been authorized, although he too welcomed the idea 'in principle'.[81] It seems that Gaimusho was less than enamoured with Boeicho's initiative; hence Japan's inconclusive official reply, which was delivered a month later.[82]

Britain's arms industry was very enthusiastic about breaking into a new market.[83] But in a mirror image of the Japanese situation, while the Foreign Office offered active support, opposition from within the defence establishment frustrated its efforts. Whether it was providing training for Japanese military personnel or supplying the latest weapons, the Admiralty and War Office objected on security grounds.[84] A series of revealing defence discussions took place between British Embassy staff and senior officials at Boeicho and Gaimusho. Yet the former remained pessimistic about the prospects for an agreement, warning that 'at present there is little scope, or enthusiasm on Japan's part for defence cooperation with us'.[85] By June 1964, the Foreign Office was also expressing doubts: 'if they conclude that security considerations are preventing us from giving them information which is released to other countries politically less or at any rate no more important to us than Japan, our relations might suffer'.[86] It was to be another six months, however, before London finally conceded that 'the idea of some general arrangement about Anglo-Japanese defence cooperation is now dead'. The Japanese government had just announced that lack of an Official Secrets Act prevented it from satisfying the requirements of Britain's proposed Memorandum of Understanding. In a rare display of humility, the Foreign Office acknowledged that the British approach had been 'premature and too obviously commercial in intent'. At the Tokyo embassy it was regarded as 'the end of a chapter. Certainly not the end of our cooperation in the field of defence'.[87] In fact, the high tide of Anglo-Japanese cooperation had passed, and it was to be more than 20 years before it surged again.

Rising sun and setting sun: Anglo-Japanese rivalry (mid-1960s–late 1980s)

> More worship the rising than the setting sun.
>
> (Pompey)

There had always been elements of competition as well as cooperation in Anglo-Japanese relations and, as London and Tokyo struggled to adjust to their changing relative status within the international system, so the balance gradually shifted. As its GNP outstripped Britain's, a more self-confident Japan began to reassess its relationship with the 'old empire'. Their rivalry would mostly take the form of commercial competition, but it was not without its politico-strategic dimensions. In the mid-1960s, beneath all the diplomatic pleasantries, one can detect the first stirrings of an Anglo-Japanese tug-of-war over Asia. Not a traditional struggle for power, but a clash between conflicting visions of their respective roles in the region. Japan campaigned to keep Britain – a country grown weary of imperial responsibilities and aching to withdraw – politically and militarily engaged in the East, while Britain tried to encourage a reluctant Japan to shoulder a share of the burden commensurate with its newly acquired economic power.

Their growing sense of rivalry may also have been influenced by the replacement during 1964 of many of the key individuals responsible for the recent improvement in relations. First came the arrival of Sir Francis Rundall as Britain's new ambassador to Japan. In the 'annual review for 1963', relations were described as 'very cordial', but perhaps a hint of jealousy can be detected in his comment: 'The US now enjoys the special position in Japan which used to be ours'. More important, however, was his critique of Japanese foreign policy for its 'preoccup[ation] about being all things to all men', resulting in 'a chronic immobilism'.[88] Three months later, Rundall highlighted two Japanese features: 'the extremely rapid economic growth and the excessive caution of politicians'. Regarding Anglo-Japanese relations, he felt that, over and above their desire to be liked by everyone, 'the Japanese retain considerable respect and some liking for us'. But '[t]he most essential thing, and perhaps the hardest', Rundall concluded, 'is to treat them as equals'.[89]

The second round of foreign minister talks were held in early May in Tokyo. There were no major breakthroughs but the British felt that the Japanese were at least being more forthcoming, and thought it meant a lot to them 'to be accepted back in the big league'. Talks focused on the Malaysia–Indonesia and China–Taiwan disputes. Unlike Washington, London was not enthused by Ikeda's plan to settle 'confrontasi', and blamed Anglo-Japanese differences over Malaysia on the 'jealousy in Japan of the influence we can exert in Asia'. Foreign Secretary R.A. Butler succeeded in convincing his hosts that 'the time is not ripe to launch some sudden new initiative'. Similarly, the Japanese were apparently relieved to hear that Britain wanted Taiwan to 'remain a separate entity apart from the mainland'.[90] On economic matters, Butler reassured his hosts that British credits to the Communist states were based on purely commercial principles, and both sides expressed some dissatisfaction with access to the others' market.[91] *The Economist* described the visit as 'rewarding, if unexciting, perhaps more rewarding because it was unexciting'.[92]

In the second significant appointment of the year, Vice-Minister Shima Shigenobu replaced Ono Katsumi as ambassador in June. A change of tone was soon apparent. In his first major public speech, Shima caused puzzlement at the Foreign Office by choosing to emphasize the persistence of differences of opinion between Japan and Britain.[93] Nor was this an isolated incident. When Funada Naka, the right-wing speaker of the House of Representatives, visited London the previous month, he had declared that 'we are of course competitors in a growing number of markets, notably China, and we do not agree on all international issues, for example, Indonesia and Malaysia, and Singapore'.[94] These early indications of a cooling of Japan's ardour for Britain became more pronounced in the wake of Tokyo's rejection of the defence cooperation treaty, and its cessation of the regular 'board meetings' between officials from the British Embassy and Gaimusho's European Affairs Bureau, both in December 1964.[95]

The return of the Labour Party to power in the autumn of 1964 after 13 years in opposition prompted mixed reactions in Japan. Whereas opposition leaders welcomed the result and immediately dispatched missions to see what lessons could be learnt, it aroused considerable anxiety within Japanese government circles.[96] The Liberal Democratic Party (LDP) and Japanese embassy in London let it be known that they were concerned at Labour MPs' lack of knowledge of Japan and their own incomprehension of Labour policies.[97] After the election, the Foreign Office did its best to scotch rumours of a new policy towards China, but Gaimusho continued to question the generous credits London was using to support its trade with the communist states.[98] Another cause for concern was the way the international money markets responded to Labour's victory with a run on the pound. With approximately 30 per cent of its trade still conducted in sterling, it was clearly in Japan's interests to see a strong pound, and she willingly joined in the international rescue package.[99]

The high level of Japanese popular interest in the British election is noteworthy given that it coincided with the fall of Khrushchev, China's first nuclear test, and the Tokyo Olympics. In contrast, news of Ikeda Hayato's retirement three weeks later, and the backroom manoeuvring that led to the naming of Sato Eisaku as his successor, slipped by almost unnoticed in Britain. As another Yoshida protégé and the younger brother of Kishi Nobusuke, Sato might have been expected to further his predecessors' efforts to strengthen relations with the UK. Ironically, however, having long criticized Ikeda for his 'low posture' foreign policy, he was to oversee perhaps the quietest period in postwar Anglo-Japanese relations.

The foreign ministerial consultations continued, albeit with declining frequency and interest.[100] The impression of business as usual was a strong one, but there was already an underlying sense of the political relationship having reached a plateau. In January 1965, Foreign Minister Shiina Etsusaburo travelled to London. With the predictable exceptions of Indonesia and Labour's imposition of a 15 per cent import surcharge, 'General agreement was reached on all major problems'. Yet as the Foreign Office conceded: 'little new came out of the exchanges'.[101] Foreign Secretary Michael Stewart returned the visit in October. In Tokyo, he lauded the 'close friendship' uniting the two countries. The views expressed were almost identical; the only exception being Sato's insistence that China now represented the main threat to the 'free world' and 'might attempt to drive a wedge between the UK and Japan'.[102] In a rare public comment on Anglo-Japanese relations a few weeks later, Prime Minister Sato emphasized the two countries' 'common interests ... as major trading nations' and their 'deep interest in and responsibility for the political stability of Asia'. He concluded: 'a tremendous advance has been accomplished in mutual recognition and trust'.[103]

Despite the politicians' rhetoric, at the ambassadorial level there remained considerable dissatisfaction with the status quo. In May, when it was suggested to him that 'Anglo-Japanese relations were now very good', Ambassador Shima had replied, 'Ah, but what is their substance?'[104] Consulted on this, Ambassador Rundall was defensive: 'American advice obviously carries most weight,' he conceded, 'but I think we are listened to and consulted as often as anyone else.' Rundall placed the blame for any shortcomings on Tokyo: 'The basic fact is, I think, that Japan has no close bilateral foreign relations with any other country because she has not yet got a foreign policy'.[105] In his 'annual review', he again criticized Japan for being 'as passive as she can get away with.' Rather poetically, Rundall compared the state of Anglo-Japanese relations to 'a suit of clothes which has been worn long enough to become comfortable'. But he did not disguise the existence of 'latent causes of friction'.[106] Bilateral relations were dominated by the 'low politics' of trading quotas, air traffic rights, dumping and copyright protection. Talks were 'often acrimonious', and the British negotiators, finding their Japanese counterparts 'obstinate and tiresome', were left 'bruised and resentful of Japanese tactics'.[107] The Beatles, whose visit in the summer of 1966 suddenly made British diplomats the object of many politicians' attention (seeking tickets for their grandchildren), provided only a brief respite.[108]

In Washington's opinion, Britain still 'clearly ... undervalued Japan'.[109] This was unfair. In December 1966, the Foreign Office produced draft 'guidelines for British policy towards Japan up to 1975', which opened with the statement: 'Whether we like it or not ... Japan is not a country we can ignore'. It listed three key British interests vis-à-vis Japan: that she should never again become a totalitarian power (of the right or left); that she should contribute to peace, stability and economic development in Asia; and that she should buy as many British goods and services as possible. The report's key recommendation was that Japan be persuaded 'to play a more positive role in Asia'. The authors also recognized that economically Britain and Japan were 'basically competitors', and hence warned that 'comparatively minor commercial frictions ... can have disproportionately large effects on our relations overall'.[110] At the fifth round of consultations two months earlier, Foreign Minister Shiina had stated quite openly that Japan did 'not wish to see British influence greatly reduced in South East Asia'. In other words, he wished to see British forces help to maintain security in the region, thereby allowing 'the Japanese role in Asia [to remain] economic and not military'. In return, Shiina announced Japan's intention to increase its foreign aid to one per cent of GNP.[111]

The sixth round of Anglo-Japanese consultations were delayed until January 1968, by which time the situation in East Asia had been transformed. The two sides agreed to 'seize every opportunity' to bring peace to Indochina, expressed satisfaction at the normalization of relations between Indonesia, Malaysia and Singapore, and hoped 'in the long run' to end Beijing's isolation. But most significant for Anglo-Japanese relations was Britain's recent decision to withdraw its forces from bases 'east of Suez'. Foreign Secretary George Brown had to assure Foreign Minister Miki Takeo of Britain's continuing interest in the political and economic stability of the region. He also pressed Miki to increase Japan's foreign aid and expressed concern about Japan's strong economic relationship with Rhodesia, where Ian Smith's white government had unilaterally declared independence on 11 November 1965. Miki promised action. Brown was grateful for their 'frank and deep exchange of views'. Contemplating the whole series of foreign ministerial talks, the *Japan Times* commented: 'These consultations have wrought much good if they have achieved nothing spectacular'.[112]

Thereafter political relations were apparently allowed to drift once again as the two governments became preoccupied with more pressing matters: the negotiations on the reversion of Okinawa in Japan's case, the second application to join the EEC in Britain's. In early May 1969, the seventh round of consultations revealed little new thinking from either party. It is clear, however, that Foreign Minister Aichi was pressed on trade with Rhodesia, foreign aid and import tariffs, particularly those affecting whisky. Finally, he was called upon to answer widespread accusations of Japanese mistreatment of dogs imported from Britain.[113] The so-called 'Anglo-Japanese dog wars' had been grabbing headlines for several months, and did nothing to improve Japan's popular image in Britain. Increasingly concerned by foreigners' perceptions of Japan, Gaimusho had commissioned Gallup to begin conducting annual public opinion surveys in the UK on the subject in 1967. The latest poll found that distrust of Japan was indeed on the rise, albeit primarily because of fears that Japanese goods were undercutting Britain's export drive.[114] Similarly, Britain's popularity amongst Japanese was declining slightly.

After a long slumber, Anglo-Japanese relations at last began to awake that autumn, following London's decision to revise its policy towards Tokyo. The key strategic objective was unaltered: to further Japan's integration into the western camp, thus preventing a possible Sino-Japanese alliance. But commercially Britain now sought to learn from Japan's remarkable economic success.[115] In what was to date the UK's largest ever export promotion, a successful 'British Week' was held throughout Japan in October, although the simultaneous visit by Anthony Crosland, President of the BOT, proved rather less so. In a radical departure from established policy, Britain had recently proposed the complete abolition of restrictions on bilateral trade. The first reaction from MITI was positive, but the reply Crosland received in Tokyo was dismissed as 'totally unsatisfactory'.[116] When Foreign Secretary Stewart visited Tokyo in April 1970, Gaimusho suggested that major concessions would be forthcoming on the crucial whisky issue, but a month later, the Japanese government succumbed to pressure from the domestic distillery lobby, leaving whisky to poison relations for the next two decades.[117] According to Reginald Cudlipp, Britain and Japan were 'now firmer friends than ever they were'.[118] In June, however, the Tories, led by Edward Heath, returned to power, ushering in an era of escalating economic conflict only partly relieved by a new found interest in multilateralism.[119]

It is surely not coincidental that Anglo-Japanese trade rivalry became a more serious irritant to relations after 1971, the first year that Japan enjoyed a substantial visible trade surplus with Britain. Nor was it accidental that British support for trilateral economic cooperation should gain ground as its admission to the EC finally neared realization and as US–Japan relations were at their lowest ebb, following the so-called 'Nixon shocks' and Washington-imposed settlement of the long-running US–Japan textile wrangle. Fearing the consequences of such a bilateral 'solution', in March the CBI had called for a Euro-American united front to press for Japanese liberalisation but to no avail.[120] Japan redirected exports to Europe on a huge scale to compensate for its lost American markets. Britons responded with dire warnings of 'the Japanese threat'. Denis Healey, a future Labour Chancellor of the Exchequer, cautioned Europeans not to follow the US example: 'it's difficult to imagine that a Japan thus twice rebuffed by the Western world wouldn't turn inwards and rely once more on her military power for both political and commercial influence'.[121] Dismissing any such military threat as inconceivable, Sir John Figgess, British commissioner general at 'Expo 70' in Osaka, nevertheless warned of the danger that 'uncontrolled overseas marketing by the Japanese could set off a trade war'.[122]

The ninth round of Anglo-Japanese consultations in June merely served to highlight differences over policy on China (where Britain opposed a 'two Chinas' policy), and trade (especially whisky and 'special preferences' for Hong Kong).[123] Nor did the Emperor's historic but controversial visit to the UK that autumn do much to relieve the tension.[124] Domestic pressure on the British government continued to mount in line with the spiralling trade deficit, inflation and unemployment figures. Following the failure of EC–Japan negotiations, Trade and Industry Secretary John Davies flew to Tokyo in June 1972, and, in return for 'voluntary self-restraint' (VSR) agreements on ball bearings, polyester fibres and colour televisions, promised to become Japan's future friend inside the EC.[125]

Against this background, in September Edward Heath became the first incumbent British premier to visit Japan. Economic issues dominated the generally cordial talks. After meeting with Japan's new Prime Minister, Tanaka Kakuei, Heath declared: 'we think alike'. Heath resurrected Ikeda's 'three pillars' of a decade earlier, emphasizing the need for 'concerted action by the three great political and economic groupings of the free world', but he also warned that, unless Japan adjusted its export strategy and opened its markets wider, the rise of protectionism was inevitable. Moreover, Heath was critical of Japan's foreign aid contribution, and tried to interest the Japanese in buying Concorde.

Welcoming Britain's forthcoming accession, Tanaka wanted Heath to persuade the EC to adopt 'outward-looking policies'. Similarly, while keeping Japan and China apart had long been a British priority, Heath openly supported Tanaka's forthcoming trip to Beijing to normalize diplomatic relations.[126] The Japanese press united in welcoming Heath, frequently referring to 'the long history of friendship between the two nations'.[127] The media in London was rather less appreciative, and a subsequent Gallup poll revealed only a slightly more 'friendly' (and no more knowledgeable) British public than before.[128]

As a direct result of Heath's visit, Britain stepped up its efforts to crack the Japanese market, with the establishment of an 'Exports to Japan Unit' at the DTI and the opening of a British Marketing Centre in Tokyo.[129] However, Tanaka's visit to Britain in autumn 1973 produced an even more innovative strategy to compensate for Japan's snowballing visible trade surplus. As part of his 'resource diplomacy' Tanaka proposed joint exploitation of North Sea oil reserves, offering productive investment in depressed UK regions in return. He was apparently disappointed by the lukewarm British response. Yet, according to one contemporary British commentator, 'This is a visit and relationship to which the Government attaches an importance that goes far beyond the interests of trade and belongs to the high political strategy of the Western world'. Tanaka and Heath did agree on the need to develop closer contacts between the three power centres of the non-communist world, although the Japanese side reportedly had some reservations lest this damage fragile relations with its Asian neighbours or lead to joint Euro-American action against Japan's trade surpluses. Finally, Heath advised Tanaka, who was returning home via Moscow, to resist Soviet advances in Asia.[130]

In January 1974, in the wake of the first 'oil crisis', Trade Minister Nakasone Yasuhiro repeated Tanaka's 'investment for oil' offer. London replied that Japan's chances of securing a stake in the North Sea would depend on its contribution to Britain's onshore development.[131] However, wary of catching the 'English disease' *(igirisubyo)*, to date only four Japanese manufacturers had established facilities in Britain. The strikes that helped to force the Tories from office in March did little to persuade others to join them.

The new Labour government immediately came under intense pressure from business and union leaders to impose import controls. According to one official: 'There was a strong feeling in British government and industry that the Japanese were not trading fairly', but initially the former preferred to leave the latter to negotiate VSRs.[132] For the next few years, the headlines were dominated by a raft of trade disputes, from cars, televisions and audio equipment, to steel, ships, and air routes.[133] It was not all bad news, however. In May 1975, Queen Elizabeth received a very warm welcome in Japan, setting off a consumer craze for anything British, and for a while thereafter the embassy in Tokyo and the DTI attempted to declare a truce in the trade war with Japan.[134] In November, Anglo-Japanese relations took on another dimension with the inaugural meeting of the G-7 in Rambouillet. The seven leading capitalist economies foreswore protectionism, but the British government could not long ignore a balance of trade in cars that was 63:1 in Japan's favour.[135] A reluctant MITI eventually agreed to keep Japan's share of the British car market below 11 per cent: a 'temporary arrangement' that was to survive for 17 years! Japan's television makers responded to their own VSR by building factories in Wales, although not without encountering strong opposition from existing competitors, which the British government was not always able to overcome.[136]

Relations reached their nadir during the years 1976–79. The Japanese, who had successfully reversed their own economic slowdown, seemed incapable of comprehending the strength of British concerns. The Japanese believed that they were being made a scapegoat for Britain's stagflation and mass unemployment. When *Keidanren* chairman Doko Toshio led a mission to Europe in October 1976, the British government accused Japan of pursuing an export strategy that went to 'the brink of dumping', and threatened import controls in retaliation. Doko countered that Britain still enjoyed a massive surplus on trade in services.[137] Ambassador Kato Tadao spoke of 'the remarkable closeness of Anglo-Japanese relations today, compared with my two previous tours'. According to him, 'Britain retain[ed] her unique position in Europe in our foreign policy considerations'.[138] Japan continued to view relations with the EC as a 'series of bilateral relationships'.[139] In contrast, Prime Minister James Callaghan decided, against the advice of his officials, to raise Britain's complaints at the EC summit in November 1976. EC anti-dumping duties were imposed on Japanese ball bearings two months later. In April 1977, Trade Secretary Edmund Dell flew to Tokyo and in what *The Times* described as 'the toughest language ever employed by a visiting European politician', demanded that Japan double its British imports within two years.[140] Japanese ministers further inflamed the situation with ill-considered statements blaming Britain's economic woes on its 'inclination towards Communist policies', workers' lack of discipline and the large number of immigrants.[141]

Charges of racism were meanwhile levelled against the British people and press.[142] Admittedly, in autumn 1977, a Gallup poll found that Britons topped the list of Europeans who associated words like 'selfish', 'sly', 'imitators' and 'cruel' with the Japanese, but such persons were greatly outnumbered by those who saw the Japanese as 'hard working', 'polite' and 'efficient'. In addition, many more Britons regarded Japan as a 'reliable friend' than did not, although compared to other Western Europeans they were easily the most suspicious of Japan.[143] As one Australian observer commented: 'British–Japanese relations could stand a lot of improvement, which essentially means modernization on both sides'.[144]

Economically, there were signs of such a 'modernization' during this period with a new interest in industrial cooperation. Reports by a Parliamentary Committee on Science and Technology and the National Economic Development Council recommended encouraging inward investment and purchasing technology licences. Several firms, most notably British Leyland and Honda, were soon putting such ideas into practice.[145] Politically, however, things seemed to be going backwards. In January 1979, on the pretext that they were only to discuss political and strategic problems, Callaghan and three other G-7 leaders met in Guadeloupe without Japan. Tokyo's pride was obviously hurt, but this was as nothing compared to the storm provoked two months later by an EC working paper which referred to the Japanese as: 'a country of workaholics who live in what Westerners would regard as little more than rabbit hutches'. The British author, Sir Roy Denman, a senior commission bureaucrat, claimed such 'funnies' were merely included to make it more readable, but it led to accusations in Tokyo that there was a 'British mafia within the EC bureaucracy' controlling policy towards Japan.[146]

Much changed when the Tories won the May 1979 election and Margaret Thatcher became Britain's first woman prime minister, but Anglo-Japanese relations showed little immediate sign of improvement. As Thatcher's first ambassador to Japan later observed: 'There was, of course, nothing sentimental in her approach. She was determined to force concessions out of a reluctant Japanese government'.[147]

Foreign Minister Sonoda made an unscheduled trip to London two weeks later, and stressed the importance of Anglo-Japanese relations in promoting tripolar diplomacy. Foreign Secretary Lord Carrington replied that the British government and people generally had a favourable view of Japan, and any hostility was the result of envy at its economic success. Sonoda undertook to continue orderly exports and increase investment if desired.[148] The British government did not officially respond to Sonoda's offer until January 1980, when Trade Secretary John Nott visited Tokyo. Like his predecessors, he called for Japanese export restraint and complained about barriers to British exports (especially for whisky, confectionery and services), but he also supported productive investment in the UK as a means of redressing the ballooning trade imbalance.[149] Voluntary restraint agreements (VRAs) now covered nearly half of all Japanese exports to Britain, but the bilateral trade gap still doubled between 1979 and 1981, while Japan's annual direct investment in the UK nearly tripled during the same period.

Britain was now pursuing a clear five-prong economic strategy towards Japan – promoting Japanese investment; joint ventures; removing obstacles to British exports; technological collaboration, and Japanese export restraint – but examples of contradictions between policy and practice were numerous. Ambassador Sir Hugh Cortazzi recognized that his 'first priority had to be economic relations', yet the British Marketing Centre in Tokyo was now closed.[150] The Tories advocated 'free trade', but that summer when the European Commission was working to end all quota restrictions on Japanese exports, Britain leaned towards the hard-line positions of the French and Italians and insisted on keeping the limit on cars.[151] Moreover, in April 1981, when Lord Carrington visited Tokyo, he warned that protectionism remained an option.[152] At the time, it was said that 'the British [government] remains suspicious of Japanese intentions', but in a series of private meetings between the DTI and MITI that began in September, the latter agreed to act as a 'marriage broker' to promote hi-tech commercial projects between British and Japanese firms.[153]

Meanwhile minor progress was discernible on Anglo-Japanese political cooperation. On the two key issues of the day – sanctions against the Soviet Union (for invading Afghanistan) and against Iran (for taking US hostages) – they agreed on a common line. Tokyo also provided aid to the newly independent Zimbabwe in support of the Carrington peace agreement. Then in September 1980, joint naval exercises were conducted for the first time since the war.[154]

In June 1982, Suzuki Zenko undertook the first official visit to Western Europe by a Japanese premier for nearly eight years. According to Foreign Minister Sonoda, Japan now felt it needed to have close relations with Britain and France in order to gain a big voice vis-à-vis the US and Soviet Union, but in London Suzuki's call to strengthen Euro-Japanese ties met with little enthusiasm. Suzuki suggested that Tokyo was ready to play a more active role in international affairs, but for the British government the easing of trade friction represented an essential precondition. Warning of rising domestic protectionist pressures, Thatcher again insisted that Japan open its market further. Suzuki firmly denied that it was closed, however, and described protectionism as 'a suicidal act' that would lead to 'the stagnation of the free economic systems of the West'. Carrington was on more fertile ground when he expressed Britain's hope that Japan would contribute to free world security by increasing its aid to developing countries. A fortnight later, Suzuki announced the doubling of Japan's ODA within five years.[155]

Suzuki's visit to Britain may have been 'singularly unspectacular', but it led to fresh calls to improve relations with Japan. In a well-argued analysis, Professor Joseph Frankel suggested that the rapidly growing trade imbalance prevented 'the basic community of our major international interests' from being 'transformed into political cooperation'.[156] Sir Michael Wilford, a former Tokyo ambassador, agreed. He believed that Britain had much to learn from Japanese management, technology, industrial organization and state planning. But Wilford felt that the British view of Japan was prejudiced by three factors: the POW issue; memories of pre-war Japanese industrial practices; and an unwillingness to recognize why Japan had been so successful industrially. In consequence, he concluded, 'the bulk of Britons do not understand the Japanese ... [and] all too often ... despise them'.[157] Yet a Gallup poll conducted for Gaimusho presented a rather different picture. The vast majority of Britons believed that feelings towards the Japanese people had become friendlier or more respectful, largely because of their admirable economic achievements or conduct when visiting Britain. Most people thought that future relations could best be promoted through expanded trade and investment, especially increased British exports to Japan and cooperation in developing high technology. Moreover, surprisingly few respondents blamed rising imports of Japanese goods for worsening British unemployment or supported strengthened import controls.[158]

Efforts at building a new political relationship received a major setback during the Falklands war in spring 1982. The full story has yet to be revealed, but it is clear that the fundamental disagreement over how to respond to the Argentinian invasion of the British South Atlantic dependency constituted a serious crisis in Anglo-Japanese diplomatic relations. London expected Tokyo's wholehearted support and found its ambivalent attitude 'very disappointing'. Prime Minister

Suzuki twice spurned personal requests from Thatcher to impose economic sanctions on Buenos Aires, but even worse in her view was Japan's support for a UN resolution calling for an immediate ceasefire, mutual withdrawal of troops and a negotiated settlement. The Japanese government was reportedly concerned about the fate of some 30,000 Japanese residents in Argentina and perhaps $1.2 billion in bilateral trade, but Washington's hesitant support for Britain may have been the most decisive factor.[159] By the time of the G-7 summit in June, British forces had retaken the islands. Thatcher still made a point of complaining to Suzuki over Japan's behaviour, but she was mollified by the unanimous support expressed for Britain, albeit *post bellum*.[160]

By the autumn relations seemed to be back on track. Perhaps the shock of the Falklands rift had helped to make both sides realize the value of a stronger political relationship. Thatcher made her first official visit to Japan in late September. Arriving in her most combative mood, the 'iron lady' criticised the weak yen and demanded that Japan open its market, restrain exports, promote technological cooperation and increase investment in Britain, where only 24 Japanese manufacturers had as yet established themselves. Nissan Motors (which had postponed a decision on building a plant in the UK) and Fanuc (the robot maker) were subjected to the full force of Thatcher's 'feminine charm'. She also played the saleswoman, touting British planes and oil rigs, and declared that the trade imbalance could not continue 'without threatening the breakdown of the free trading system'. She countered the old argument that British firms were not trying hard enough by pointing to their great success in other markets and warned that Japan's policy response would be 'judged by results'.[161] On the political front, agreement was reached on the institution of multi-level official consultations on a wide range of politico-strategic issues including East–West relations, Asia, the Middle East, and defence.[162] More controversially, both sides declared their opposition to Washington's strengthened sanctions against Moscow and their support for Soviet energy projects. Thatcher also took the opportunity to extol the virtues of small government and told the Japanese that 'economic strength generates not only political responsibilities but defence obligations too ... Japan should be capable of defending herself, her sea-lanes and other vital approaches'.[163] A positive response on these two points, however, would have to await the accession of Nakasone Yasuhiro to the premiership two months later.

Media reaction to Thatcher's visit was mixed. While the western press reported that she made an 'excellent impression', responses amongst the Japanese ranged from 'appalled' and 'disappointed' to 'overwhelmed' and 'captivated'. On the right, she was lauded for taking on the trade unions and held up as a model for Japan's leaders, while on the left she was pilloried for tripling unemployment.[164]

The first half of 1983 saw further progress in the Anglo-Japanese defence relationship. In January, Foreign Minister Abe Shintaro travelled to Europe, in part to discuss the establishment of formal Japanese representation at NATO. Unlike France, Britain was said to have a 'quite pragmatic' attitude. In March, a British defence minister held long discussions with senior Self-Defence Force (SDF) officers in Tokyo and agreed to expand the existing staff talks. He was succeeded a few weeks later by two senior Foreign Office officials responsible for defence issues. They shared Japan's concern that the ongoing Intermediate Nuclear Force (INF) reduction negotiations in Geneva should not allow the Soviets simply to transfer their missiles from Europe to Asia.[165] This was followed in May by the inclusion, at Nakasone's request, of a controversial phrase in the Williamsburg G-7 summit statement: 'The security of our countries is indivisible and must be approached on a global basis'.[166] In April 1984, Foreign Secretary Geoffrey Howe went so far as to declare that there was 'no major problem on which Britain and Japan do not share broadly the same outlook'.[167] At the G-7 summit held in London two months later, Thatcher publicly held up Japan (and the US) as economic examples for Britain to follow. Nakasone spoke of his belief that the world was entering 'a new era ... in which Japan and the countries of Western Europe will work together for world peace'.[168] Similarly, Japan's *Diplomatic Bluebook* stated that 'Japan and the Western European countries share basic values of freedom, democracy and market economies ... and we also share a great responsibility for world peace and prosperity in today's harsh international climate'.[169] At home, however, Nakasone adopted a rather different tone: 'West European countries are in a dejected mood because the center of the world economy is shifting from the Atlantic to the Pacific', he claimed, 'they are jealous because Japan and the US are stepping up their ties with the advent of the Pacific age'.[170]

The mid-1980s were to prove another relatively quiet period in Anglo-Japanese relations. The highlight was undoubtedly Japan's acceptance of Britain's proposal to establish a 'track two' forum of scholars, businessmen, journalists, politicians and bureaucrats to promote better long-term relations. The 'UK–Japan 2000 Group' (soon to be renamed the UK–Japan Twenty-First Century Group) held its first meeting in February 1985, and in subsequent annual get-togethers served as a catalyst, helping to set the agenda – both current and future – across the entire range of bilateral interactions.[171]

Meanwhile Japan's visible trade surplus with Britain renewed its inexorable climb, doubling again between 1985 and 1988 to stand at an unprecedented $8 billion. Enraged by the 'unfair' victory of a Japanese-led consortium in the competition to build Turkey's second Bosphorus bridge, Thatcher warned that 'a very real trade war, with its attendant political and diplomatic consequences, could break out between East [meaning Japan] and West'.[172] Things came to a head during 1987. In the previous November, Trade Secretary Paul Channon had visited Tokyo and unsuccessfully requested an end to discrimination against European alcohol, skis, telecommunications and financial corporations. A personal letter from Thatcher was no more effective.[173] The British government was running out of patience with Japan: 'The mood has changed in Britain in the past few years. The issue used to be whether to retaliate against Japan. The issue now is how to retaliate'. On 2 April, the cabinet agreed to threaten Japanese banking and insurance companies operating in the City of London, unless the Japanese government fulfilled its 1985 promise to allow foreign companies (including Britain's Cable and Wireless) one-third of Japan's telecommunications market.[174] This was a high-risk strategy, but the brinkmanship eventually paid off. Soon after Takeshita Noboru's selection as premier in November 1987, the Cable and Wireless issue was resolved, and the Ministry of Finance finally agreed to admit four British firms to the Tokyo Stock Exchange.[175] Then a GATT panel ruled that Japan's liquor tax regime was discriminatory, forcing the government to revise it.[176] In another significant innovation, Gaimusho responded to criticism of Japan's ineffective aid record by inviting the British Crown Agents to help implement part of its assistance programme for Africa.[177] The Japanese economy was buoyant, direct investment in the UK was booming, and for the first time in two decades the bilateral visible trade gap was narrowing. Suddenly, the economic disputes that had plagued relations for years were evaporating and a bright new future seemed to beckon.

'A new partnership'? (late 1980s–late 1990s)

> A friendship broken may be soldered but never made whole.
> (English proverb)

In January 1988, Geoffrey Howe journeyed to Tokyo for what he later judged to be 'by far' his 'most important' visit.[178] He spoke of how, 'In the interdependent world of 1988, linked by economic, political and shared security interests, Britain and Japan are both individually key players. But even more important, there are new things we can do together'. Calling for a partnership 'with no hectoring on the one side and no soft-soaping on the other', he listed ten areas for cooperation that would promote democratic values and support the free trade system.[179] In talks with his opposite number, it was agreed that henceforth ministerial and senior official level meetings would be held annually, and non-governmental exchanges between parliamentarians, businessmen and youths encouraged. They spoke of having laid the foundations for a 'new, dynamic and plain-speaking partnership'. Howe did not neglect to mention the remaining economic problems, but the attempt to draw Japan into an overtly political relationship at a time of serious US–Japan friction was unmistakable.[180] According to *The Economist* both sides now desired 'a special relationship' that went 'beyond trade and investment'. For historical reasons Britain still occupied 'a special, sentimental corner in the hearts of the Japanese', but more importantly, it argued, they were 'intrigued at the way Britain's diplomatic influence around the world persists, even though its economic power does not'. In short, the Japanese felt that they again had something to learn from Britain, a view soon confirmed by the new ambassador to Britain, Chiba Kazuo.[181]

This paradigm shift was broadened two months later by Trade Secretary Lord Young. In Tokyo to launch the 'Opportunity Japan' campaign, which aimed to help British business double its exports to Japan within three years, he declared: 'We must shift our perception of Japan as a problem, and see it as an opportunity'. Having taken the medicine prescribed by American and Japanese corporations, Young pronounced the 'English disease' cured. He was optimistic about the future: 'While Anglo-Japanese relations may have been confrontational for the past twenty years, I hope the next twenty will be an era of harmony'.[182]

The next move in this carefully orchestrated campaign was to have been provided by Prime Minister Takeshita when he visited London in May, but his 'international cooperation initiative' proved rather anticlimatic: 'a plop not a splash'. Takeshita described how Japan aimed to contribute to the maintenance of peace through non-military means, expand its aid budget, and especially promote international cultural exchanges. Aware of the EC's plan for further integration in 1992, Takeshita called for an upgraded European–Japanese relationship within the trilateral framework. Apparently immune to the new spirit of cooperation, or perhaps deliberately adopting the role of 'hard man', Thatcher picked away at the old economic scabs and the British press largely ignored the visit.[183]

According to David Howell, chairman of the House of Commons' Foreign Affairs Committee and a confirmed Japanophile: 'The British do not really want to see Japan as a great military power again', but, he asked, 'Is it right that others should do Japan's peacekeeping for it?' Answering his own question Howell declared: 'European policy-makers should seek, indeed demand, the much closer involvement of Japan in all the "hot" world issues'. Ambassador John Whitehead was optimistic: 'There is growing recognition in Britain and Japan of our interdependence and common interests in world political as well as economic affairs'.[184] Yet in August, when an LDP Northern Territories Map Mission visited London to solicit support for this key Tokyo foreign policy objective, the response was equivocal.[185]

In retrospect, the European Commission's former director of relations with East Asia, Simon Nuttall, recognized that 'The British had historically been among the most anti-Japanese .... In 1988, however, the British changed tack, reckoning that the Japanese were of greater benefit to the UK as large-scale investors'. Moreover, this had altered the balance of opinion within the EC as a whole, so that 'the Community followed suit'.[186]

While relations were being transformed at the governmental and business levels, the resurrection of a long-dormant issue – POW compensation – prompted a sudden outpouring of anti-Japanese feelings amongst the British public. This may in part have been a reaction to 'the official rhetoric of Anglo-Japanese cordiality', but it also coincided with media attacks on the terminally ill Emperor Hirohito for his 'war crimes'.[187] Awareness of the conspicuous consumption in Japan and the sense that time was running out for the ageing British survivors, may also have played a part. The Japanese government's position had always been that all claims for compensation had been settled by the San Francisco Peace Treaty of 1951, as a result of which former British POWs had each received £76. However, a new, hard-line group, the Japanese Labour Camp Survivors Association (JLCSA), was now demanding £10,000 per veteran.[188] Conscious of the popular mood, Thatcher sent Howe and Prince Philip to the Commonwealth War Cemetery in Yokohama the day after they had attended the funeral of the Emperor in February 1989, but this did nothing to resolve this issue.[189]

Visits to the UK by Foreign Minister Uno Sosuke and Trade Minister Mitsuzuka Hiroshi restored momentum to the improving Anglo-Japanese relationship. The former agreed with Howe on the need for burden sharing in defence and preventing the EC from developing into 'fortress Europe'. The latter invited Britain to join a Japanese supersonic jet project, and was assured by Young that Japanese cars built in Britain would be treated as British by the EC. Thatcher sounded the only sour note when she expressed concern regarding the Recruit scandal.[190]

Young returned the visit in May and declared, in what was to become a cliché of the 1990s, that Anglo-Japanese relations had never been better. Yet such an assessment was to a degree belied by his pressing the government to lower airfares and improve access to the Japanese market, especially the distribution system and Tokyo Stock Exchange.[191] The Prime Minister took up many of the same points during her fifth visit to Japan in September. Prior to departure, Thatcher had complained that Japan constructed 'deliberate barriers' to foreign imports. Upon arrival she expressed the hope that the 1990s would be a decade of 'unprecedented partnership between Britain and Japan' but maintained the pressure on Japanese protectionism. On the political front, Japanese moves to normalize relations with Beijing so soon after the Tiananmen massacre met with Thatcher's disapproval. On the other hand, she declared her support for Gorbachev's reforms and urged Prime Minister Kaifu Toshiki to increase aid to the post-communist government of Poland.[192] By January 1990, when Kaifu visited Britain, the fall of the Berlin Wall had symbolized the ending of the Cold War in Europe, and they apparently reached a compromise. Thatcher basically endorsed Kaifu's view that China should not be isolated internationally, and in return he conceded that Britain and Japan should work together to support the democratic reforms in Eastern Europe with financial and technical assistance. In addition, they agreed to coordinate their aid policies towards Africa. More generally, Thatcher described Britain and Japan as sharing the same values of freedom, democracy and the market economy, and concurred with Kaifu on the need to create an 'unprecedented partnership and friendship' for the next century.[193]

A remarkable transformation took place within the Labour Party during 1990, resulting in a bipartisan Japan policy. It began with a visit to Japan that autumn by Gordon Brown, Shadow Trade Minister. On his return, he made it clear that 'the Labour Party warmly welcomes Japanese investment in the United Kingdom'. Shadow Chancellor John Smith followed in spring 1991, and in a bold attempt to appropriate 'Japan' from the Tories thereafter held it up as a model of state involvement. Trade Minister Nakao Eiichi held talks with Labour leaders during his stay in London in May 1991.[194] Labour's change of heart was all the more surprising when one considers that it came against the background of a media backlash against Japanese 'Trojan horses' and 'screwdriver' plants. Nor were critical assessments of Japan confined to the tabloids. A survey of how Japan was reported in the British press during the first half of 1991 revealed that, with the exception of the *Financial Times*, the broadsheets, both conservative and liberal, tended to adopt a 'negative' attitude.[195] Moreover, another poll conducted for Gaimusho in autumn 1990 found that, compared to other EU citizens, many fewer Britons considered Japan 'reliable', and many more felt that it was 'not fulfilling a suitable international role'. On the other hand, two-thirds of them thought it important to co-operate with Japan, albeit that the EU and North America had first priority.[196]

The following summer, with election rumours circulating, members of the pro-Japan lobby (mostly Tories) were reportedly concerned at the weak links between the Labour Party and Japanese business community. Labour supporters countered by pointing to the latter's 'excellent relations with top union leaders', but that autumn saw the Trades Union Congress pass a resolution attacking the 'feudal and alien' Japanese attitude towards industrial relations. An extremely acrimonious debate had revealed the depth of resentment in some quarters against so-called 'beauty pageants', after which 'single-union' and 'no-strike' deals were signed. TUC General Secretary Norman Willis did his best to repair the damage, but a fact-finding mission to Japan in February 1992 found business leaders still smarting from the resolution's 'crude anti-Japanese sentiments'. The fall in the amount of Japanese investment in the UK, which began in 1991, most probably reflected the bursting of Japan's 'bubble economy', but union attitudes may have been a factor in Britain's declining share of the total, alongside the Tories' growing Euroscepticism. Japanese companies in the UK were reportedly relieved at the Tory election victory the following April, one official going so far as to assert that investment would have been frozen otherwise.[197] Labour learnt its lesson in time for the next election; the Tories did not.

By this time much had changed in official Anglo-Japanese relations. The end of the Thatcher era in November 1990 had come as a shock to most Japanese, and Tokyo was anxious that her successor, John Major, continue their 'global partnership'.[198] The Gulf War, which had begun with Iraq's invasion of Kuwait in August, did not precipitate the kind of crisis in Anglo-Japanese relations that it provoked in US–Japan ties. Japan was reportedly pleased with the high quality intelligence it received from Britain during the war, which reportedly surpassed that supplied by the US. In September, on a visit to Tokyo, Foreign Secretary

Douglas Hurd hinted that Britain expected Japan to do more to help the Allies, but mantra-like he repeated that bilateral relations had 'never been better'. Then in February 1991, with the fighting over, London politely requested its share of Tokyo's promised $9 billion contribution.[199]

In March, David Howell, now chairman of the UK–Japan 2000 Group, proposed the signature of a new 'UK–Japan Friendship Agreement'. His aim was not to create an exclusive special relationship, but for Britain to 'guide and encourage Japan's expanding links with ... Europe', and for Japan to return the favour in the Asia-Pacific region.[200] That same month, the DTI declared its 'Opportunity Japan' campaign a success, having nearly doubled British exports to Japan.[201] It immediately followed this up with the announcement of a successor – 'Priority Japan' – with the same export-doubling target but also incorporating the ideas of learning from Japanese technology and business techniques, promoting investment in Japan, and selling to Japanese firms worldwide.[202] Trade policy was now primarily decided at EU level.[203] According to Sir Geoffrey Howe, the former Foreign Secretary, in a tripolar world order it was 'important for Britain and Japan to sustain and develop the strongest possible relationship' to prevent US–Japan 'collusion'. Hence London's strong support for the EU–Japan Joint Declaration of July 1991, which recognized their 'common attachment' to certain political and economic values, and placed relations on a firm foundation for the first time.[204] Yet Britain risked EU unity to ensure that Japanese cars produced in the UK were excluded from the EU–Japan import limit agreed at that time.[205]

That autumn politics took a back seat, however, as Britain experienced the largest arts festival ever staged in Europe – 350 events at 250 locations spread over three months at a cost of some £20 million – all in the name of 'demystifying and challenging misconceptions' about Japan. One commentator was moved to speak of 'an informal Anglo-Japanese Alliance', although the Japan Festival was not without its critics. Some thought it simply too big and too ambitious, but a number of conspiracy theorists suggested something more sinister: that the Japanese corporations funding the event were really aiming to increase their political influence in Britain by winning 'the hearts and minds' of the public. If so, then the results were decidedly mixed.[206] At the popular level, 'bad news' continued to dominate Anglo-Japanese relations during 1992. Press stories ranged from Japanese mistreatment of whales and dolphins and shipments of Japanese plutonium from Britain and France, to the Sagawa Kyubin corruption scandal, Japanese companies in the UK 'evading' taxes, Shirayama's controversial purchase of County Hall in London, and the prices charged by Japanese computer game companies.[207]

It took a former ambassador to sound a warning note: 'Anglo-Japanese relations today are probably as good as they have ever been ... But it would be a mistake to think that the relationship will necessarily continue to grow closer', Sir Hugh Cortazzi cautioned.[208] The elites pressed on regardless. In November 1991, a minister confirmed that the British government had 'made a strategic decision to press for an open relationship with Japan and for the closer integration of Japan into the world community, instead of concentrating on specific issues like market opening and the various taxation and securities squabbles of the past'. Ambassador Kitamura Hiroshi responded by listing four significant areas of current cooperation: aid for the Soviet Union; UN arms control; Cambodia, and Hong Kong.[209] The following month, Gaimusho's *Diplomatic Bluebook* acknowledged that during the last few years 'bilateral relations have developed into a new stage of mutual consultation and cooperation in coping with a wide range of international issues'.[210] In February 1992, Ambassador John Whitehead offered the most detailed exposition of British policy towards Japan to date. He first discussed their 'common interests', which were global in character, and included free trade, stability and security, human rights and good government. He pointed out that bilateral ties had increasingly to be seen in a Euro–Japanese context, where Britain's role was to show that relations were not a zero-sum game.[211] The following month, the 'buddhas' of the UK–Japan 2000 Group 'envisaged a growing "global partnership" between Britain and Japan in the political, security, and economic fields'. According to David Howell, they believed that there was 'some very special chemistry in the relationship and that its significance is growing'.[212]

On the Japanese side, Britain was assuming ever-greater importance. That summer, Miyazawa Kiichi became the eighth postwar Japanese Prime Minister to visit Britain. Prior to his arrival, Ambassador Kitamura published an article asserting that: 'For Japan, Britain is the standard-bearer of an outward looking Europe'. Moreover, he thought that 'Japan should emulate the positive features of British diplomacy'. Kitamura preferred to avoid comparisons with the Anglo-Japanese Alliance, but none the less was convinced that 'the currently thriving Anglo-Japanese relationship is a major asset for Japanese diplomacy and a catalyst that can help promote Japan's future foreign policy goals'.[213] Miyazawa himself thanked

Britain for the way it had led Europe to adopt a more positive attitude towards Japan. The Foreign Office must have been gratified to hear a Japanese leader publicly declare for the first time that 'the UK is the linchpin of Japan's relationship with Europe'.[214] A few months later, 'a senior Japanese minister' seemed to ascribe an almost talismanic quality to Anglo-Japanese relations, telling newly appointed Ambassador John Boyd that, 'whenever Britain and Japan were friends, all was well with the world, but when we fell out, things went wrong more widely'.[215]

In 1993 doubts about the relationship started to resurface at the highest levels. In January, Michael Heseltine, president of the BOT, confidently wrote that Britain had 'gone a long way towards the achievement of key economic aims and creating a plain-speaking but constructive relationship with Japan'.[216] Yet, while he claimed some credit for improving the situation, the author of the concept, Sir Geoffrey Howe, still felt that 'for Europe, Japan matters far less than it does for the US and features low down our agenda of foreign policy issues'.[217] That same month, Ambassador Kitamura repeated that: 'Anglo-Japanese relations are at present in excellent shape in every arena'. But he also expressed concern that, with the bursting of Japan's bubble economy, British firms were losing interest in the Japanese market and mutual trade and investment were actually declining.[218] In Tokyo, his counterpart noted that Britain's bilateral trade deficit with Japan was proportionately greater than that suffered by the US, and dusted off the whisky bottles and aero engines as items that Japan should buy more of.[219] Foreign Secretary Douglas Hurd visited Tokyo in April and discussed efforts to prevent North Korea's nuclear weapons programme and aid to Russia. On his return home, however, he confessed to feeling 'a twinge of unease' whenever he read his brief for a trip to Japan. Always it 'starts off with the same sentence "UK–Japan relations are excellent" .... If there is no friction', Hurd wondered, 'is it because there is not enough contact?'[220] A new Gallup poll conducted the following month revealed that a majority of Britons did not share the Foreign Secretary's opinions.[221]

In September 1993, Prime Minister John Major visited Tokyo and declared Britain's support for Japan's claim to a permanent seat on the UN Security Council, and, despite the views of accompanying businessmen, its opposition to Washington's approach to 'managed trade'. Hosokawa Morihiro, Japan's new reformist premier, repeated that Britain was the key pillar in Japan's relations with Europe. Major even spoke of Britain and Japan enjoying a 'strategic partnership'. Bilateral politico-military talks were now a biannual event and defence staff talks had recently been added. They agreed to an exchange of diplomats. The number of visits by senior military officers and civilian defence officials had increased greatly, Japanese SDF personnel regularly attended British staff colleges, and in the past year Britain had supplied 16 per cent of Japan's defence imports.[222] In short, the 'defence pact' envisaged in the mid-1960s was now a reality. Yet a mere 12 per cent of the British public saw the politico-security field as an appropriate area for Anglo-Japanese cooperation, and Major's visit was to be overshadowed by a much more vocal group of critics, namely, the former POWs.

In June 1991, MPs had called on the Japanese government to provide generous compensation for these men: to no avail.[223] Thus things stayed until the LDP fell from power in the summer of 1993. Hosokawa then caused a sensation by becoming the first Prime Minister to admit that Japan had waged a 'war of aggression'. Despite complaints from Japanese officials that he would raise hopes for compensation, Hosokawa went on to express 'deep remorse and apologies for Japan's past actions, which caused unbearable suffering and sorrow for so many people'. The 12,000-strong JLCSA asked Major to press their case for compensation and threatened legal action against the Japanese government and companies that used forced labour, should he fail. Despite the Japan Federation of Bar Associations issuing a report supporting the case for compensation, Major accepted Hosokawa's assertion that the issue was legally settled at San Francisco. However, Hosokawa did agree to examine Major's proposal for 'non-governmental measures' to resolve the issue. The JLCSA expressed its disappointment.[224] This turned to anger when it emerged that the two governments had agreed to establish a special foundation to collect donations from Japanese who felt the former POWs deserved compensation. No one seems to have consulted the POWs themselves, who denounced the project as tantamount to charity. Nor indeed the former *zaibatsu*, for they all refused to contribute to the fund or even meet with its head. In August 1994, Japan's new Socialist Prime Minister, Murayama Tomiichi, announced a 10-year, ¥100 billion fund to atone for Japan's wartime atrocities and was considering including some measures for former Allied POWs. In December, the Major plan collapsed amidst much acrimony and the following month the JLCSA, together with groups from Australia, New Zealand and the US, launched a lawsuit in the Tokyo District Court demanding $22,000 in individual compensation and an explicit apology.[225]

In spring 1995, with the fiftieth anniversary of the end of the Second World War approaching, a MORI poll conducted for the Japanese embassy revealed that British impressions of Japan and Germany were generally similar – slightly favourable – albeit both were based on a self-confessed lack of knowledge.[226] But the ceremonies marking the end of war in the European and Pacific theatres exposed a sharp division in attitudes. Whereas German leaders were invited to attend the VE-Day events in May, Japanese leaders were excluded from most of the VJ-Day ceremonies in August.[227] *The Economist* was highly critical: 'The British have taken the fiftieth anniversary of Japan's surrender as an occasion for raking up old enmities, not being glad of new friends'.[228] British ministers and Prince Philip reportedly attended a 'bitter service of "thanksgiving for victory over Japan"', but Japanese ministers similarly marked the occasion with visits to Yasukuni shrine. Murayama had wanted the Diet to pass a resolution turning Hosokawa's apology into an official government statement, but in the face of determined right-wing opposition, he could only force through a watered-down version. Murayama sent a private letter to Major conveying his 'deep regret and apologies that Japan's past acts have left deep scars on many people, including POWs'. But this backfired when he subsequently denied that it was a letter of apology, prompting a flood of protests in Britain: the JLCSA threatened to boycott Japanese goods. This was withdrawn when Murayama finally got it right with an 'historic' apology on 15 August, and the JLCSA proposed a settlement fund be established with government and perhaps corporate contributions. Had the process of reconciliation finally begun?[229]

Concluding thoughts

> A state worthy of the name has no friends – only interests.[230]
> (President Charles de Gaulle)

Having examined the past four decades of Anglo-Japanese exchanges one can safely conclude that bilateral relations have broadened, deepened and intensified. The frequency of contact, levels of interaction and range of issues involved have increased exponentially. Yet it has not been a simple geometric progression. We have identified three distinct phases, divided by two quiet transitional periods. The first phase began in the late 1950s with a Japanese initiative to heal the postwar rift, to which Britain's response was cautious, but positive. Tokyo's motives were clear: economically, to prise open European and Commonwealth markets; and politically, to balance to some extent its overwhelming dependence on Washington. Japan looked to Britain as an alternative role model. London's prime concern was to help keep Japan in the 'free world' by playing long stop to America's wicket keeper. This first phase came to an end in the mid-1960s, when Japan's GNP overtook Britain's, and the collapse of defence talks and the replacement of leaders on both sides revealed the limitations of their political relationship.

The hiatus that followed was disturbed in the early 1970s by the onset of serious trade friction that was to chafe for nearly two decades. Similar trade structures made Britain and Japan natural competitors: a competition that Japan was winning. While the 'English disease' became an object for industrial Japan to avoid, many Britons began to see Japanese industrial methods as 'best practice' and even envied Japan's 'one-party democracy'. Nor was there a substantial strategic relationship – as with the US – to compensate for the trade imbalance. Japan sought to persuade Britain to remain militarily engaged in Asia, while London pressured Tokyo to accept greater international political responsibilities. Neither was very successful.

A second lull developed in the mid-1980s, at the end of which the apparent resolution of a number of long-running trade disputes provided London with the opportunity to redefine the Anglo-Japanese relationship. With Britain abandoning the battering ram for something more sophisticated, the last decade has seen relations go from strength to strength. Britain has regained its status as a role model: diplomatically; politically; and perhaps even economically. Meanwhile the Japanese development model has been badly tarnished in the wake of numerous financial scandals, the lingering ill effects of the collapsed 'bubble economy', and the devastating Asian economic crisis.

A variety of factors determined the course of Anglo-Japanese relations during this 40-year odyssey. Not surprisingly, certain key individuals – prime ministers, foreign ministers and ambassadors – exerted a disproportionate influence, for good or ill, but government institutions were more important in the long run. The differing perspectives of the two foreign ministries on the one hand, and the more wary economic, defence and various 'domestic' ministries on the other, slowed progress and sometimes threatened to scuttle the entire process. Moreover, both the British and Japanese governments have on occasion succumbed to pressure from powerful domestic interest groups. The enthusiasm of big business usually outweighed the concerns of the media, trades union movement, environmental or veteran lobbies. The people of Japan and Britain suffer from a profound mutual ignorance, but especially threatening is the divergence between elite and mass perceptions in Britain. If there is an emotional bond between Britain and Japan then it is 'a one-sided love affair'. Japanese of virtually all persuasions readily subscribe to the idea of amicable ties stretching back into the distant past, and Britain has ranked consistently high in their polls of 'most liked' countries. The British, in contrast, still harbour suspicions of Japan. In Whitehall, policy-makers feel uncomfortable with both the sentimental and historical dimensions to bilateral relations, preferring to base ties on contemporary conditions and clearly defined common interests. Shared core values may form the bedrock of their relationship, but the practice of 'democracy' and 'human rights', 'capitalism' and 'free trade' vary between Japan and Britain. The 'great island nations' idea does have geopolitical significance, but is frequently overdrawn. Moreover, when it comes to day-to-day foreign policy decisions, perceived national interests are inevitably more important. Certainly, as status quo powers their views on international problems often coincide, but policy differences remain, for example, on nuclear deterrence, Burma, whale hunting and Third World debt relief.

Concerning influential external actors, the US has usually worked to promote better relations between its two allies. On one level Britain and Japan compete to maintain American interest in their region. Conversely, when Washington has been subjected to joint Anglo-Japanese pressure, for example over the Soviet pipeline projects in the early 1980s, it has reacted negatively. The EU meanwhile has generally followed Britain's lead on Japan policy, although these days trade strategy is basically set in Brussels.

Finally, the connection is of considerable value to both parties. The last decade has seen Japan become Britain's third largest direct foreign investor and 'number two' trade partner outside the EU. Similarly, from Tokyo's perspective, Britain is second only to the US as a host for Japan's direct foreign investment, and is its 'number two' trade partner inside the EU. At heart, the relationship remains an economic one, although the 'Action Agenda' and more recently the 'Common Vision' have highlighted the strength of the political and strategic arteries. Still, the nature of international relations has changed too much to make comparisons with the Anglo-Japanese Alliance meaningful. Relations will not regain the wider significance they enjoyed during the early decades of this century. Indeed in an era of globalization few bilateral relationships retain their former status. But that is not to say they are unimportant: bilateral ties still form the basic building-blocks of all diplomatic activity. 'Unspectacular' is the adjective most frequently applied to Anglo-Japanese diplomatic contacts – which helps to explain the lack of scholarly attention – but in many respects theirs has become the key relationship linking western Europe and east Asia, and a force for stability worldwide. There was, of course, nothing inevitable about relations taking this positive turn, nor is the process irreversible, but with continuing efforts on both sides Britain and Japan will probably remain distant friends.

Notes

1. *Le Monde*, 16 April 1963, cited in Albrecht Rothacher, *Economic Diplomacy between the European Community and Japan, 1959–1981* (Aldershot: Gower, 1983), p. 103.
2. Ono Katsumi, 'The Changed Climate of Anglo-Japanese Relations', *Japan*, 10 (April 1964), 6.
3. Lascelles to Foreign Office [hereafter FO], 'Annual Review for 1957', 11 March 1958, FO371/133577 (FJ1011/1), Public Records Office, Kew.
4. *Economist*, 8 March 1958.
5. 'Ambassador Ono speech to the Japan Society Dinner', 2 July 1958, FO371/133598 (FJ1051/31).
6. *Economist*, 20 October 1956, 247.
7. Gaimusho, *Waga gaiko no kinkyo* (Tokyo, 1957), 7.
8. With Britain's active support, Japan had gained entry to the UN in December 1956 and a non-permanent seat on the Security Council a year later.
9. Record of Conversation [hereafter RC], Lloyd & Fujiyama, 28 September 1957, PREM 11/1910. Two days later Fujiyama actually stormed out of a TV studio when interviewer Robin Day presented him with concrete evidence of illegal Japanese copying of British ball bearings. *Hong Kong Standard*, 1 October 1957.
10. Gaimusho had proposed inserting in the joint communiqué a reference to the 'most amicable atmosphere reviving memories of the Anglo-Japanese Alliance days'. The final version merely stated that: 'satisfactory progress was being made in the restoration of close and friendly relations between the two countries'. O-A kyoku to Nishi, 18 September 1957, A-0154, 560, Gaimusho Shiryokan [GSK]; 'Joint Communique', *Japan Society of London Bulletin [JSLB]*, 24, February1958, 5.
11. Fujiyama Aiichiro, 'Rengo Okoku homon ni kan suru hokoku', October 1957, A-0154, 730, GSK.
12. Lascelles, 'Annual Review for 1957'.
13. Singapore to FO, 19 January 1958, FO371/133597 (FJ1051/7). Disregarding Macmillan's warnings, Fujiyama signed a reparations agreement with Jakarta the next day. Nishihara Masashi, *The Japanese and Sukarno's Indonesia* (Honolulu: East-West Center, 1976), p. 53. See also Lord Hood (Wash.) to FO, 5 February 1958, FO371/133597 (FJ1051/13), and BrEmbTok to FO, 15 Jan. 1958, FO371/133597 (FJ1051/5).

14. Dalton (CRO) to Wellington, 23 January 1958, FO371/133597 (FJ1051/6).
15. 'Ambassador Ohno speech to Japan Society Dinner', 2 July 1958, FO371/133598 (FJ1051/31).
16. Lloyd to Lascelles, 13 May 1958, FO371/133597 (FJ1051/18).
17. *Keesing's Contemporary Archive* [KCA], 16266 & 16522; *Economist*, 21 June 1958, 1111–12. The plant began operation in 1966, and was finally decommissioned on 31 March 1998.
18. *Economist*, 23 August 1958, 611, and Lascelles to Morland, 22 August 1958, FO371/133598 (FJ1051/39).
19. RC, Ono & Morland (FED), 28 August 1958, FO371/133598 (FJ1051/40).
20. Although no records of the talks were supposed to be kept, some details can be found in FO371/133599 (FJ1052/3), FO371/141435 (FJ1051/34, 41), & FO371/141443 (FJ1071/1, 2). At one point the French were also involved. de la Mare to Dalton, 18 February 1959, *ibid.*, Hood to MacDermot, 16 May 1959, Morland to MacDermot 14 May 1959, FO371/141435 (FJ1051/25, 28).
21. Lascelles to FO, 'Annual Review for 1958', 12 March 1959, FO371/141415 (FJ1011/1).
22. Morland to MacDermot, 14 May 1959, FO371/141435 (FJ1051/28).
23. Lansdowne to Hoyer Millar, Enc. in Trench to MacDermot, 16 June 1959, FO371/141436 (FJ1051/40). Morland interpreted the last to mean that the Japanese hope 'we can help them in economic penetration and trade in those countries', although there was also talk of 'agreeing spheres of influence over economic assistance to underdeveloped countries'. Trench to Heppel, 21 May 1959, FO371/141436 (FJ1051/41).
24. *Ibid.*
25. Briefs for talks Kishi, 2 July 1959, FO371/141437 (FJ1051/53).
26. Tiltman advised that three points be stressed: 1) 'Japan's desire for the closest and most cordial relations possible between the two nations'; 2) 'postwar Japan's significant role as the most advanced democracy in Asia, and the nation's contribution to stability in Asia and the free world', and 3) 'the basic problems with which today's Japan is confronted … and Japan's own efforts to overcome them'. Memo from Hessell Tiltman, 'PR Approach to Prime Minister Kishi's visit to UK', 5 May 1959, A-0148, 673-4, GSK.
27. Ono to Fujiyama, 23 June 1959, A 0148, 683–4, GSK.
28. RC, Kishi & Macmillan, 13 July 1959, PREM 11/2738.
29. Note of Discussion, Amory, Eccles & Kishi, 13 July 1959, FO371/141439 (FJ1051/96).
30. *Economist*, 25 July 1959, 210.
31. Morland to Lloyd, 8 September 1959, FO371/141440 (FJ1051/112), Morland to FO, 12 August 1959, FO371/141439 (FJ1051/98), BrEmbTok to FED, 18 August 1959, FO371/141439 (FJ1051/101), Minutes by [illegible], 31 August 1959, FO371/141440 (FJ1051/106).
32. 'Annual Review for 1959', Morland to FO, 12 January 1960, FO371/150561 (FJ1011/1).
33. He also appealed for British investment in Japan. Lloyd to Morland, 24 August 1960, FO371/150580 (FJ1051/23).
34. *KCA*, 17690 & 17837.
35. Ono Katsumi, 'The Japanese Ambassador at Cambridge', *JSLB*, 33 (February 1961), 7–10.

36. 'Annual Review for 1960', Morland to Home, 3 January 1961, FO371/158477 (F1011/1).
37. For. Sec. to Macmillan (draft), Enc. in de la Mare to Hurd, 1 December 1960, FO371/150581 (FJ1051/34).
38. Minute by de la Mare for For. Sec., 26 January 1961, FO371/158491 (FJ1051/6).
39. *Nihon Keizai Shimbun*, 29 January 1961.
40. Ono Katsumi, *JSLB*, 34 (June 1961), 16–19.
41. For. Sec. to Morland, 23 March 1961, FO371/158491 (FJ1051/18), Mayall (Tokyo) to de la Mare, 27 April 1961, FO371/158484 (FJ103110/7).
42. 'Meeting to discuss Anglo-Japanese relations', 2 June 1961, Enc. in de la Mare to Phillips (BOT), 8 June 1961, FO371/158493 (FJ1051/46). See also: Hitch to de la Mare, 3 January 1962, FO371/164971 (FJ1051/4), Memorandum of Conversation, Dillon & Lee, US–UK Bilateral Talks, Washington, 16 February 1961, *FRUS* 1961–63, IX, Foreign Economic Policy, 113, 'Briefs for visit of Foreign Minister Kosaka', 14 June 1961, FO371/158493 (FJ1051/58).
43. 'Briefs for visit of Foreign Minister Kosaka', 14 June 1961, FO371/158493 (FJ1051/58).
44. Prime Minister's Personal Minute to Secretary of State, 15 June 1961, FO371/158493 (FJ1051/59/G).
45. de la Mare to Peck, 21 June 1961, FO371/158494 (FJ1051/6/G), Macmillan, FO to Tokyo, 28 June 1961 (FJ1051/62/G), Morland to Hoyer Millar, 28 July 1961, FO371/150580 (FJ1051/25).
46. RC, Macmillan & Kosaka, 5 July 1961, FO371/158494 (FJ1051/80).
47. Memorandum of Conversation, Ikeda & Kennedy, 21 June 1961, *FRUS* 1961–63, XXII, North-East Asia, 692–9.
48. RC, Macmillan & Kosaka, 5 July 1961, FO371/158494 (FJ1051/80).
49. In the event all such efforts failed and, when Kosaka and Lord Home met at the UN General Assembly in September, they were left with no alternative but to support the US 'important question' resolution, which successfully delayed Beijing's admission to the world body for another ten years. RC, Home & Kosaka, New York, 22 September 1961, FO371/158497 (FJ1051/114).
50. RC, Kosaka & Home, 7 July 1961, FO371/158494 (FJ1051/80).
51. Note of Meeting, Kosaka & Maudling, 5 July 1961, FO371/158495 (FJ1051/83).
52. Note of Meeting, Kosaka & Lloyd, 6 July 1961, FO371/158495 (FJ1051/83).
53. Warner (Tokyo) to Peck, 17 August 1961, and Peck to Warner, 2 October 1961, FO371371/158497 (FJ1051/110), de la Mare to Morland, 29 January 1962, FO371/164971 (FJ1051/7).
54. Gaimusho, *Waga gaiko no kinkyo* (June 1962), 6.
55. Rothacher, *Economic Diplomacy*, pp. 94–5; Saito Shiro, *Japan at the Summit* (London: Routledge, 1990), pp. 28–9; *Far Eastern Economic Review*[FEER], 8 February 1962, 319; 'Japanese Ambassador Visits Birmingham', *JSLB*, 39 (February 1963), 25.
56. Julian Ridsdale, *JSLB*, 36 (February 1962), 12–14; Hanaoka Sosuke, 'Memories of the Anglo-Japanese Commercial Treaty', in Ian Nish (ed.), *Britain & Japan: Biographical Portraits II* (Richmond, Surrey: Japan Library, 1997), p. 322;

Economist, 30 Sept. 1961, 1284; Reginald Cudlipp, 'One Man's Thoughts on Anglo-Japanese Relations', *Pacific Community*, 1 (July 1970), 657; Rothacher, *Economic Diplomacy*, p. 95.
57. *FEER*, 24 May 1962, 389.
58. 'Consider Japan', *Economist*, 1 & 8 September 1962, 792–819, 913–32.
59. Paul Johnson, 'The Tortoise and the Hare: Asia's Next Decade', *New Statesman*, 1 June 1962, 792.
60. Rothacher, *Economic Diplomacy*, pp. 96–8; *FEER*, 30 August 1962, 380–3.
61. *Economist*, 10 November 1962, 593.
62. Carol Kennedy, 'The Treaty that Started it All', *Anglo-Japanese Journal*, 5(2) (September–December 1991), 2–3. Ono's view was apparently based on Macmillan having told him that Japan bought many books from the family publisher. Hanaoka, 'Memories', p. 326.
63. In return for revoking Article 35 of GATT (and supporting Japan's full membership of OECD), the treaty offered Britain a 'quite exceptional' triple-layer of protection: continued import restrictions on 'sensitive items'; 'voluntary' Japanese export restraint on certain goods; and the right to impose emergency quota restrictions where imports caused or threatened 'serious injury' to domestic producers. Most contentious had been the last safeguard, which ironically was never to be used. It specifically forbade an appeal to GATT, although if Britain did not offer compensation, Japan had the right to retaliate. For the full text, see: *Contemporary Japan* (1963), 769–86. See also: Robin Gray, 'The Anglo-Japanese Commercial Treaty of 1962: A British Perspective, in Nish, *Britain & Japan*, pp. 314–15; Sir Hugh Cortazzi, 'Britain and Japan: A Personal View of Post-war Economic Relations', in T.G. Fraser and Peter Lowe (eds), *Conflict and Amity in East Asia* (Basingstoke: Macmillan, 1992), p. 166.
64. 'Brief for Japanese Prime Minister's Visit', 6 November 1962, FO371/164975 (FJ1052/11).
65. Five rounds of talks were held in London between April and December 1962. Thereafter it was decided that meetings 'on the ground in Africa' would be more useful. For details see: FO371/164972 (FJ1051/23), FO371/164973 (FJ1051/41,48,51), and FO371/170755 (FJ1051/3,20).
66. RC, Ikeda & Macmillan, 12 November 1962, and Ikeda & Home, 14 November 1962, FO371/164976 (FJ1052/21).
67. RC, Lloyd, Maudling & Ikeda, 13 November 1962, FO371/164976 (FJ1052/23).
68. *FEER*, 14 February1963, 291–2; Rothacher, *Economic Diplomacy*, p. 102.
69. 'Briefs for Secretary of State's talks in Japan', 22 March 1963, FO371/170759 (FJ1052/22).
70. *FEER*, 29 November 1962, 446; Mori Haruki, 'Aspects of the Development of Anglo-Japanese Commercial Relations', *JSLB*, 73 (June 1974), 10–11; *KCA*, 19171, 19397.
71. RC, Home & Ikeda, 2 April 1963, FO371/170759 (FJ1052/27), 3 April1963, (FJ1052/29).
72. 'Briefs for Secretary of State's talks in Japan', 22 March 1963, FO371/170759 (FJ1052/22). See also Morland to FO, 21 December 1962, FO371/164974 (FJ1051/67).
73. *FEER*, 25 April 1963, 205.
74. FO INTEL No. 48, 'Anglo-Japanese Relations', 15 May 1963, FO371/170755 (FJ1051/1).

75. At the Foreign Office, E.H. Peck was privately 'appalled by the scale and frequency now proposed for this consultation', and hoped to avoid the need for 'a crescendo of Anglo-Japanese relations improving ad infinitum'. The economic ministries meanwhile preferred to use their 'own channels'. Peck to MacLehose, 17 April 1963, and MacLehose to Peck, 22 Apr. 1963, FO371/170755 (FJ1051/6, 11,12).
76. Home also sympathized with Ohira's complaint about Singapore's demand for reparations from Tokyo. Record of Meeting, Home & Ohira, 3 September 1963, FO371/170757 (FJ1051/46), Ohira & Home, 3 September 1963, A-0365, 1162–93, GSK.
77. Minute President BOT's Meeting with Ohira, 5 September 1963, FO371/170757 (FJ1051/53), Cortazzi to Bentley, 23 October 1963, FO371/170757 (FJ1051/61).
78. McKenzie Johnston to Bentley, 'Report on Visit of Ohira', 12 September 1963, FO371/170757 (FJ1051/55). As MacLehose explained later: 'Our main purpose in suggesting regular consultations to the Japanese ... was to bring them closer into Western counsels. Since the war they have been and indeed remain largely dependent on the US both for their security and for their economic prosperity .... Although relations between Japan and the US are good, both we and the Americans saw dangers in such narrow external relations. If Japan fell out with the US and there was no other Western country for her to turn to, she might go to the Chinese. With American encouragement we therefore decided to try and help the Japanese feel more a part of the free world as a whole'. 'Briefs for Anglo-Japanese Consultations', 27 April 1964, FO371/176015 (FJ1051/43).
79. Scott (MOD) to Peck, 27 May 1963, Burrows to FED, 'Meeting with Kitamura', 22 May 1963, and MacLehose, Enc. in Cabinet Office (MOD), 29 May 1963, FO371/170778 (FJ1192/3, 4, 6).
80. BrEmbWash to FO, 26 June 1963, Enc. in Minute by Waterfield, 8 July 1963, MacLehose to BrEmbTok, 6 June 1963, Morland to MacLehose, 14 June 1963, and Ormsby Gore (Wash.) to FO, 11 July 1963, FO371/170778 (FJ1192/7, 9, 11).
81. Morland to FO, 23 July 1963, FO371/170778 (FJ1192/11).
82. Morland to FO, 30 Aug. 1963, FO371/170778 (FJ1192/14).
83. Riddoch (MOD) to Bentley, 19 September 1963, FO371/170778 (FJ1192/17), MacLehose Minute, 10 Dec. 1963, FO371/170779 (FJ1192/27), BrEmbTok to Cheke, 20 December 1963, FO371/170779 (FJ1192/28).
84. For example, an invitation to attend the Jungle Warfare School in Malaya prompted such fierce criticism it had to be withdrawn. Similarly, supply of the Tigercat/Seacat missile was blocked for more than a year, even though it had already been sold to a number of Latin American countries. Perkins (War Office) to MacLehose, 21 November 1963, FO371/170779 (FJ1192/25, 21), MacLehose to Williams (MOD), 20 March 1964, FO371/176030 (FJ1192/16).
85. Another factor was Japan's limited defence budget and dependence on the US: 'The Japanese are unlikely to decide on a firm policy so long as there's any chance of screwing aid out of the Americans'. Cortazzi to Bentley, 16 November 1963, FO371/170779 (FJ1192/24), Cheke to FO, 11 October 1963, FO371/170778 (FJ1192/20), FO to BrEmbTok, 12 Dec. 1963, BrEmbTok to Cheke, 17 December 1963, MacLehose to Phillips (BOT), 1 January 1964, FO371/170779 (FJ1192/28).

86. It was still hoped to review the process 'after a year or so'. Bentley to Cortazzi, 22 June 1964, FO371/176030 (FJ1192/25).
87. Memorandum of Discussion, Cheke & Hogen, 17 December 1964, Cheke to MacLehose, 17 December 1964, 14 January 1965, Bentley memo 21 January 1965, FO371/181094 (FJ1192/1).
88. Rundall to FO, 'Annual Review for 1963', 13 January 1964, FO371/175999 (FJ1011/1).
89. Rundall to Butler, 9 April 1964, FO371/176017 (FJ1052/2).
90. RC, Butler & Ohira, 2 May 1964, and Rundall to FO, 3 May 1964, FO371/176016 (FJ1051/50, 51).
91. Record of Meeting, Butler & Ohira, 4 May 1964, Cortazzi to MacLehose, 8 May 1964, Rundall to Butler, 13 May 1964, FO371/176016 (FJ1051/51, 57, 55), Rundall to Caccia, 7 May 1964, FO371/176017 (FJ1052/7).
92. *Economist*, 9 May 1964, 581; *FEER*, 21 May 1964, 365; *KCA*, 20284.
93. MacLehose to Peck, 7 October 1964, FO371/176049 (FJ1103/30).
94. Bentley to Cortazzi, 14 September 1964, FO371/176018 (FJ1052/21). Cortazzi tried to put a positive gloss on Funada's speech by suggesting that it had been written by Gaimusho and 'intended primarily to demonstrate that Anglo-Japanese relations had advanced to such a degree that we can now speak freely and frankly about the problems on which we are not agreed'. Cortazzi to Bentley, 25 September 1964, FO371/176018 (FJ1052/28).
95. Cheke (Tokyo) to MacLehose, 31 December 1964, FO371/181106 (FJ1691/1).
96. Cortazzi to Bentley, 15 October 1964, 23 October 1964, FO371/176018 (FJ1052/23,27,35).
97. Cortazzi to Bentley, 30 October 1964, 6 November 1964, FO371/176018 (FJ1052/38,39).
98. Record of Discussions, MacLehose & Hogen, MacLehose & Nakayama, 9 November 1964, FO371/176018 (FJ1052/42, 43). A joke reportedly doing the rounds in Gaimusho claimed that Britain's trade fair in Beijing was a greater threat to Japan than ten Chinese nuclear tests! *Economist*, 28 November 1964, 1017.
99. Record of Meeting, Walker & Shiina, 15 January 1965, FO371/181081 (FJ1051/15).
100. Hugh Cortazzi, 'The Relationship between Japan and the UK: Retrospect and Prospect', Gyosei International College, 30 January 1992, 6.
101. 'Prime Minister–Japanese Foreign Minister Meeting'; Record of Meeting, Walker & Shiina; Jay & Shiina, 15 January 1965, FO371/181081 (FJ1051/9,15) /181082 (FJ1052/21).
102. Record of Meeting, Stewart & Shiina, 19 October 1965; Stewart & Sato, 20 October 1965; and Stewart speech to Asian Affairs Research Council Tokyo, 19 October 1965, FO371/181084 (FJ1051/63,66,67,70).
103. Sato Eisaku, *Japan*, 17 (January 1966); Rundall to Peck, 8 December 1965, FO371/181084 (FJ1051/73).
104. Gore-Booth to Rundall, 31 May 1965, FO371/181085 (FJ1052/10).
105. Rundall to Gore-Booth, 30 June 1965, FO371/181085 (FJ1052/15).
106. Rundall to Stewart, 'Annual Review for 1965', 6 January 1966, FO371/187076 (FJ1011/1).

107. Cortazzi, 'Economic Relations', 167–9, and, 'Britain and Japan: A Personal View', *Japan Society Proceedings* [JSP], 118 (autumn 1991), 49.
108. 'The Beatles visit Japan', July 1966, FO371/187127.
109. Thompson (Wash.) to de la Mare, 20 July 1966, FO371/187115 (FJ1192/18).
110. Permanent Undersecretary's Steering Committee, 'Policy Towards Japan', 8 December 1966, FO371/187096 (FJ1051/30). See also Ronald Dore, 'Japan's Place in the World', *World Today*, 22(7) (July 1966), 296.
111. RC, Brown & Shiina, 1 November 1966, F371/187099 (FJ1052/36).
112. In 1965 Tokyo had enthusiastically backed London's non-recognition policy, and over the next couple of years had progressively strengthened trade controls in line with UN sanctions. Nevertheless Japanese companies were engaged in illegally purchasing huge quantities of chrome ore from Rhodesia and Japan remained Salisbury's biggest source of imports. *Japan Times* [JT], 9–11 January 1968; Rothacher, *Economic Diplomacy*, p. 116; KCA, 21132, 21420, 21631, 21836, 22163, 22524, 22924.
113. Rothacher, *Economic Diplomacy*, p. 116; *JT*, 3–4 May 1969.
114. *FEER*, 21 September 1969, 803.
115. Rothacher, *Economic Diplomacy*, p. 147.
116. *Japan*, 32 (October 1969), 6–9; *FEER*, 21 September 1969, 803, 87(2), 10 January 1975, 50; *Economist*, 11 October 1969, 78; Rothacher, *Economic Diplomacy*, pp. 116, 145–7; Cortazzi, 'Economic Relations', *op. cit.*, 172.
117. Rothacher, *Economic Diplomacy*, pp. 150, 154; *JT*, 20–21 April 1970.
118. Reginald Cudlipp, 'One Man's Thoughts on Anglo-Japanese Relations', *Pacific Community*, 1 (July 1970), 660. Cudlipp was director of the Anglo-Japanese Economic Institute, a body established by the Japanese Embassy in 1961.
119. Watanabe Taizo, 'New Tasks for Japan', *JSLB*, 63 (February 1971), 3.
120. Rothacher, *Economic Diplomacy*, p. 155.
121. *Sunday Times*, 3 October 1971.
122. Sir John Figgess, 'The Outlook for Japan', *World Today*, 27(11) (November 1971), 485.
123. *JT*, 12–13 June 1971.
124. There were protests, albeit muted when the Queen restored him to the Order of the Garter. *Economist*, 2 October 1971, 14–15, 16 October 1971, 33; *KCA*, 24932; Stephen Large, *Emperor Hirohito and Showa Japan* (London: Routledge, 1992), pp. 182–5.
125. *Economist*, 10 June 1972; Rothacher, *Economic Diplomacy*, pp. 161, 163–5.
126. *KCA*, 25515; *JT*, 15–21 September 1972; *Economist*, 23 September 1972, 78–80; Rothacher, *Economic Diplomacy*, pp. 164–5.
127. *Mainichi Shimbun*, 17 September 1972; *Nihon Keizai Shimbun*, 17 September 1972; *Asahi Shimbun*, 16 September 1972.
128. *Asahi Shimbun*, 4 June 1973.
129. Cortazzi, 'Economic Relations', 174; *FEER*, 10 January 1975; Rothacher, *Economic Diplomacy*, p. 168.
130. *Observer*, 30 September 1973; *JT*, 1–3 October 1973; *KCA*, 26253, 26632; *Economist*, 29 September 1973, 15; Saito, *Japan at the Summit*, pp. 40–1; Rothacher, *Economic Diplomacy*, p. 171.

131. *Economist*, 19 January 1974; *JT*, 12–3, 17 January 1974; Rothacher, *Economic Diplomacy*, p. 173.
132. Cortazzi, 'Economic Relations', 174; Rothacher, *Economic Diplomacy*, p. 175.
133. J.W.M. Chapman, 'Britain, Japan and the China Aviation Tangle, 1974–76', *Proceedings of BAJS*, 1, Part 1 (1976), 169–94.
134. I.H. Nish, 'Queen Elizabeth and Japan', *Contemporary Review*, 227 (1317) (October 1975), 184; Rothacher, *Economic Diplomacy*, p. 177.
135. *JT*, 10 May 1976.
136. *Economist*, 7 May 1977, 107; Rothacher, *Economic Diplomacy*, p. 240.
137. Hakoshima Shinichi, *Japan Quarterly*, 26 (1979), 482; Rothacher, *Economic Diplomacy*, pp. 220–2. The methods used by the two sides to measure trade in services are very different; hence there is wide disagreement on the size of Britain's invisible surplus. *FEER*, 31 December 1976, 43.
138. This was not saying much since his earlier stays in London had been from 1939–42 and 1953–54. Kato Tadao, *JSLB*, 80 (November 1976), 10.
139. Kosaka Tokusaburo, director general of the Economic Planning Agency, cited in Endymion Wilkinson, *Misunderstanding: Europe Versus Japan* (Tokyo: Chuo Koronsha, 1981), p. 234.
140. Rothacher, *Economic Diplomacy*, p. 234. In marked contrast, Margaret Thatcher, the leader of the opposition, who was in Tokyo at the same time, praised Japanese 'efficiency' for its economic success. Yet when pressed even she had to concede that some British industries required 'limited protection' from Japanese competition. *JT*, 15, 17 April 1977.
141. Rothacher, *Economic Diplomacy*, pp. 226–9, 241–2; Amaya Naohiro, cited in Wilkinson, *Misunderstanding*, p. 228.
142. Masaru Yoshinori, 'Psychological Aspects of Euro-Japanese Trade Frictions', in Gordon Daniels and Reinhard Drifte (eds), *Europe and Japan: Changing Relationships since 1945* (Ashford, Kent: Paul Norbury, 1986), p. 54; Murray Sayle, 'Anglo-Japanese Relations', *New Statesman*, 96 (2489) (1 December 1978), 738.
143. Gaimusho, Joho Bunka Kyoku, *EC 5 kakoku tai Nichi yoron chosa* (Tokyo: Hakuhodo, May 1978).
144. Sayle, 'Anglo-Japanese Relations', p. 738.
145. Wilkinson, *Misunderstanding*, p. 77; Rothacher, *Economic Diplomacy*, pp. 262–3; Hanabusa Masamichi, *Trade Problems between Japan and Western Europe* (New York: Praeger/RIIA, 1979), p. 103.
146. Hakoshima Shinichi, *Japan Quarterly*, 26 (1979), 485; Rothacher, *Economic Diplomacy*, pp. 259–61.
147. Cortazzi, 'A Personal View', 50.
148. *JT*, 19, 23–4 May 1979; *Daily Yomiuri*, 3 June, 8 July 1979.
149. *JT*, 22–3 January, 21 May 1980.
150. Cortazzi, 'Economic Relations', 175–9.
151. Rothacher, *Economic Diplomacy*, pp. 270, 272; Wilkinson, *Misunderstanding*, p. 211.
152. *JT*, 7, 9 April 1981.
153. Jill Hills, 'Foreign Policy and Technology: The Japan–US, Japan–Britain and Japan–EEC Technology Agreements', *Political Studies*, 31(2) (June 1983), 207, 221; Wolf Mendl, *Western Europe and Japan between the Superpowers* (London: Croom Helm, 1984), p. 136; *Economist*, 3 April 1982, 31.

154. Reinhard Drifte, 'Japanese Security Policy and European Security', in Daniels and Drifte, *Europe and Japan*, p. 65; Rothacher, *Economic Diplomacy*, pp. 268–9.
155. Gaimusho, *Waga gaiko no kinkyo* (Tokyo, 1982), 403; *JT*, 18–9 June 1981; Saito, *Japan at the Summit*, p. 72; *Daily Yomiuri*, 12 July 1981.
156. Joseph Frankel, 'British–Japanese Relations', *World Today*, 37(7–8) (July–August 1981), 243–6.
157. Sir Michael Wilford, *JSLB*, 96 (March 1982), 2–4.
158. Gaimusho Joho Bunka Kyoku, *EC 6 kakoku tai Nichi yoron chosa*, unpublished report, May 1982, Tokyo.
159. Japan's was in fact the casting vote that ensured that the resolution passed. Margaret Thatcher, *The Downing Street Years* (London: Weidenfeld & Nicolson, 1993), pp. 231–2; Cortazzi, 'Personal View', 47; *Daily Yomiuri*, 11 April, 16 May 1982.
150. Saito, *Japan at the Summit*, pp. 74–5; *Daily Yomiuri*, 20 June 1982.
161. *JT*, 20, 21, 22 September 1982; *Daily Yomiuri*, 26 September 1982.
162. Tanaka Toshiro, 'European–Japanese Political Cooperation', *Keio Journal of Politics*, 5 (1984), 88–9.
163. *FEER*, 8 October 1982, 40–1, 16 June 1983, 71.
164. *Sankei Shimbun*, 23 September 1982; *Daily Yomiuri*, 26 September 1982; *FEER*, 8 October 1982, 40.
165. *FEER*, 16 June 1983, 71; *JT*, 14, 29 April 1983.
166. Saito, *Japan at the Summit*, p. 78; *Daily Yomiuri*, 5 June 1983.
167. *JT*, 26, 27 April, 9 June 1984.
168. *JT*, 12, 13 June 1984; Saito, *Japan at the Summit*, p. 81.
169. Japanese Foreign Ministry, *Diplomatic Bluebook* (Tokyo, 1984), 57.
170. *Daily Yomiuri*, 22 July 1984.
171. Patrick Jenkin, *Japan Society Review*, 106 (summer 1987), 9; Robert Taylor, *China, Japan and the EC* (London: Athlone Press, 1990), pp. 106–7; *JT*, 7 December 1998.
172. *Daily Yomiuri*, 12 May, 2 June 1985; Saito, *Japan at the Summit*, p. 84.
173. *KCA*, 35385.
174. *FEER*, 16 April 1987, 62–3.
175. Negotiations on the latter issue had started in 1983. For a participant's account, see Sir Geoffrey Littler, *JSP*, 123 (spring 1994), 5–16.
176. Saito, *Japan at the Summit*, p. 89.
177. By 1994 they had administered grants worth more than $1 billion. Peter Berry, 'The Crown Agents and Japan', in, *Anglo-Japanese Collaboration: On to a Global Partnership*, Anglo-Japanese Economic Institute, London (1995), 54–6; Chris Somes-Charlton and Ivan Alexander, 'Japanese Aid: Cooperation with Crown Agents, *Anglo-Japanese Journal*, 3(4) (Jan.–Mar. 1990), 9–11.
178. *JT*, 11 June 1988.
179. The ten areas were: East–West relations; the Iran–Iraq War; terrorism; global economic stability; the free trade system; investment strategies; capital markets and stock exchanges; agriculture; aid; and communications. *Britain and Japan: Partners for Prosperity*, Anglo-Japanese Economic Institute, London (1988), 31, 35.
180. *KCA*, 35646; *JT*, 12, 13 January 1988; Brian Bridges, *1992: Process and Euro-Japanese Relations*, JATI International, Reading (1990).

181. *Economist*, 16 January 1988, 52; *JT*, 13 March 1988.
182. Yamazaki Toshio and Nirasawa Yoshio, 'Satcharizumu no shori to Nichi-Ei kankei no shintenkai', *Sekai Keizai Hyoron*, 32(6) (June 1988), 41; *JT*, 2, 15–17 March 1988.
183. Japanese Foreign Ministry, *Diplomatic Bluebook* (Tokyo, 1988), 222–3; *JT*, 4, 5, 7 May, 6 June 1988.
184. *JT*, 13 March, 25 April, 11 June 1988.
185. First reports stated that the FO had reversed established policy. Takeshita happily informed the Diet of Britain's public backing. But a few days later the ambassador explained that opposition to Soviet occupation of the islands was not equivalent to recognition of Japan's assertion of sovereignty. *Asahi Shimbun*, 2, 5 August 1988.
186. Simon Nuttall, 'Japan and the EU: Reluctant Partners', *Survival*, 38(2) (summer 1996), 108.
187. Roger Buckley, 'The Emperor Question Again: Anglo-Japanese Relations, 1945 and 1989', *Journal of Social Science* (ICU), 29(3) (1991), 153. The Japanese government lodged an official protest at criticism of the Emperor appearing in the tabloid press. Watanabe Michio, an influential right-wing politician, even called on the government to take legal action. *JT*, 23 September 1988.
188. *JT*, 14 May 1988.
189. *JT*, 26 February 1989.
190. *JT*, 15 Jan., 3 February 1989.
191. *JT*, 24–5 May 1989.
192. Lynda Chalker, 'Anglo-Japanese Collaboration on Aid', *Anglo-Japanese Journal*, 4(1) (Apr.–June 1990), 17–18; *KCA*, 36892; William Nester, *Japan and the Third World* (Basingstoke: Macmillan, 1992), pp. 164–5; *JT*, 16, 19–22 September 1989.
193. *JT*, 13 January 1990.
194. *JT*, 19 December 1990, 1 May 1991.
195. D.W. Anthony, 'How Japan is Reported in the British Press', in *Research Papers in Japanese Studies*, 1 (February 1996), Cardiff Business School, 69–92; *JT*, 7 September 1990.
196. Gaimusho Daijin Kanbo Kaigai Hokoka, *EC 7 kakoku tai Nichi yoron chosa*, unpublished report, November 1990.
197. *JT*, 10 June, 12, 17 September, 22 November 1991, 11 February, 11 April 1992. The late Professor Keith Thurley criticized Japanese investment in the UK from a rather different perspective: 'Japanese business is being used as a deliberate political device to meet the needs of retooling British industry, revitalizing industries and creating changes in the organization of labour ... there is a degree of exploitation of the Japanese by the British and that bothers me'. G. Murray, *Synergy: Japanese Companies in Britain* (Tokyo: PHP Institute, 1991), p. 212.
198. *JT*, 24, 29 November 1990.
199. *JT*, 11 September 1990, 3 February 1991.
200. *JT*, 7 March 1991.
201. Exports increased from £1.5 to £2.7 billion, although it should be noted that its share of the Japanese market actually fell slightly.
202. The over-ambitious 'Priority Japan' campaign failed to reach its export target and was replaced by 'Action Japan' (with a goal of £3.5 billion) in

April 1994. Ishikawa Kaoru, 'Kengamine no Nichi-O kankei', *Gaiko Forum* (July 1991), 42–9; *JT*, 25 April 1991, 29 February 1992, 19 September 1993.
203. Sir Geoffrey Howe, 'Japan and the US: A European Perspective', *World Today*, 48(7) (July 1992), 127.
204. *JT*, 22 June 1991; Roger Buckley, 'Forgetting the Past, Considering the Future: Anglo-Japanese Relations and the 1990s', *Journal of Social Science (ICU)*, 30(2) (1991), 1–12; Leon Brittain, 'Towards Further Cooperation and Interdependence', *Euro-Japanese Journal*, 1(2) (Aug.–Nov. 1994), 11–13.
205. This led to the abandonment of Britain's long-standing Japanese car import quota the following year. *JT*, 26 May, 22 June 1991, 7–8 February, 11 April 1992.
206. *JT*, 15 June, 13, 18 September, 31 December 1991.
207. *JT*, 24, 27 February, 25, 30 March, 24 June, 12 August, 17 October, 26 December 1992, 13 November 1993
208. Cortazzi, 'The Relationship', 10.
209. *JT*, 21 November 1991. The subsequent passage of the UN conventional arms sales register resolution, an Anglo-Japanese initiative, was particularly satisfying.
210. Japanese Foreign Ministry, *Diplomatic Bluebook* (Tokyo, 1991), 296.
211. *JT*, 23 February 1992.
212. *JSP*, 119 (spring 1992), 71; *JT*, 18 March 1992.
213. Kitamura Hiroshi, 'Genjitsushugi gaiko no kikubari to shitatakasa', *Chuo Koron*, 107(6) (June 1992), 86–97.
214. *JSP*, 120 (autumn 1992), 66. According to a former Foreign Secretary, in June 1991 Prime Minister Kaifu had acknowledged in private that Britain was 'the keystone in the arch of Japan's relations with the European Community'. Sir Geoffrey Howe, *Conflict of Loyalty* (London: Pan, 1995), p. 688.
215. *JT*, 19 November 1992.
216. Michael Heseltine, 'Anglo-Japanese Relations: Britain's Positive Approach', *Anglo-Japanese Journal*, 6(3) (Jan.–Apr. 1993).
217. Howe, *Conflict of Loyalty*, 126–7.
218. Kitamura Hiroshi, 'Anglo-Japanese Relations: A Global Perspective', *JSP*, 121 (spring 1993), 63–71.
219. *JT*, 28 January 1993.
220. Douglas Hurd, 'Britain's Relations with Japan: Excellent – Could be Better', *Anglo-Japanese Journal*, 7(1) (May–August 1993), 2; *JT*, 7 April 1993.
221. Gaimusho Daijin Kanbo Kaigai Hokoka, *EC 7 kakoku tai Nichi yoron chosa*, unpublished report, June 1993.
222. Admiral Sir James Eberle and Yamamoto Tadashi (eds), *Britain and Japan: The New Era* (London: UK–Japan 2000 Group, 1994), 9, 11; *JT*, 21 September 1993.
223. *JT*, 8 June 1991.
224. *JT*, 9, 11, 15, 18–19, 21 September, 11 December 1993; *KCA*, 39637; Numata Sadaaki, *Britain and Japan: A Diplomat's Eye* (London: Anglo-Japanese Economic Institute, 1997), 9.
225. *JT*, 27–8 May, 17, 26 December 1994, 31 January 1995; *KCA*, 40319, 40360.
226. MORI, *GB Public Attitudes towards Japan*, unpublished report, April–May 1995.
227. *JT*, 13 June 1995.

228. *Economist*, 26 August 1995, 14–15.
229. *JT*, 13, 15, 18, 19 August 1995.
230. R.T. Tripp, *The International Thesaurus of Quotations* (Harmondsworth, Middlesex: Penguin, 1976), p. 923.

Index

Abe Shintaro, 286
Acheson, Dean, 186–7
Aichi Kiichi, 280
Ainscough, Thomas, 84
Akihito, Crown Prince (Heisei Emperor), 98, 178, 196, 206, 210
Allen, Denis, 211
Allen, Louis, 151
Amau Eiji, 6, 30, 34, 37
Amery, Leopold, 5, 28
Anami, General, 131
Anglo-Japanese Commercial Treaty (1962), 226, 235–9, 272–3
Anglo-Japanese Economic Institute, 241
Anglo-Japanese Parliamentary Group, 269
Anti-British sentiment in Japan (1939–41), 18
Anti-Comintern Pact (1936), 32, 34
Anti-Japanese feeling in UK (1939–41), 19
ANZUS Pact (1951), 183
Arita Hachiro, 18, 41–2
Ariyoshi Akira, 34
Asakai Koichiro, 205
Ashton-Gwatkin, Frank T., 14–15, 53, 78, 81
Ashton-Rose, Major T.S., 161
Asian Development Fund, 219
Astor family, 40
Atomic bombs, 131, 138, 143
Attlee, Clement, 142–3, 174
Australia, 114–15, 123, 140, 182–5, 188, 191, 207, 219; Trade diversion policy, 71
Automedon incident, 44

Ba Maw, 119, 123
Badoglio, Marshal, 122
Bagge, Widar, 129
Baldwin, Stanley, 72
Banff Conference, 1933 (IPR), 93–4

Barlow, (Sir) Thomas D., 66
Barnby (Lord), 9
Beatles in Japan, 279
Best, Antony, 19
Bevin, Ernest, 174, 183
Bhore, (Sir) Joseph, 57
Blamey, General Thomas A., 139
Boon, Major Cecil, 161
Bose, Rash Behari, 117, 120
Bose, Subhas Chandra, 120–1, 123–4, 126–7, 137
British Council, 206
British nuclear tests, 217–21, 224, 265
British Pacific Fleet, 140
British POW issue, 160–2, 196, 202, 206–8, 210–12, 260, ch. 7 passim
Brown, George, 279
Brown, Gordon, 292
Bullwinkel, Vivian, 151
Burma, 136–7, 149, ch. 7 passim
Butler, R.A., 39, 43–4, 276–7
Byas, Hugh, 97

Cable and Wireless, 256, 289
Cadogan, (Sir) Alexander, 33
Callaghan, General C.A., 154
Callaghan, James, 283–4
Carrington, Lord, 284–6
Casablanca Conference (1943), 141
Chamberlain, Neville, 7–12, 20–1, 31, 34–6, 39–42, 74, 79, 103
Channon, Paul, 289
Chatfield, (Admiral Sir) Ernle, 33
Chiang Kai-shek, 15, 20–1, 38–9, 119–20, 125, 187
Chiba Kazuo, 290
Churchill, Winston S., 28, 32, 40, 125, 136–8, 142–3, 183, 189, 196, 206, 210–13
Clague, J.D., 160
Clare-Lees, (Sir) William, 86
Clive, (Sir) Robert, 7
Close, Captain J.C., 151

Clutton, George, 178–9
Colombo Plan, 207–9
Cooper, Lt Cmdr. G.T., 167
Coral Sea, battle of, 117
Cortazzi, (Sir) Hugh, 285, 295
Craigie, (Sir) Robert, 16–18, 38–9, 40–4
Cripps, (Sir) Stafford, 120
Cromer, Lord, 240
Crosland, Anthony, 280
Cudlipp, Reginald, 280
Cunliffe-Lister, (Sir) Philip, 62–3, 74, 82–4

Davies, John, 281
Dell, Edmund, 283
Dening, (Sir) Esler, 144–5, 187–8, 202–3, 206, 210, 213
Denman, Roy, 284
Doko Toshio, 283
Dorman-Smith, (Sir) Reginald, 136
Dulles, John F., 181–7, 192, 196, 205
Dutch East Indies, 70–1

Eccles, (Sir) David, 268
Eden, Anthony, 35–6, 37–8, 40, 98, 138, 142, 152, 187, 210, 213, 215
Edo Exhibition, London (1981), 258
Edwardes, Arthur, 31, 36–7, 40
Edwards, J.O., 167
Elizabeth II, Queen, 246–8, 283
Erroll, (Sir) Frederick, 272
EXPO, Osaka (1970), 281

Falklands War (1982), 253–4, 286–7
Federation of British Industries, 9, 32, 70–1
Figgess, (Sir) John, 281
Fisher, (Sir) Warren, 7, 10, 20–1, 31, 36, 79
Frankel, Joseph, 286
Fujihara Iwaichi, 120
Fujiwara Ginjiro, 53
Fujiyama Aiichiro, 217–22, 265
Fukui Shinpei, General, 154
Funada Naka, 277

Gaitskell, Hugh, 185
Gascoigne, (Sir) Alvary, 175–6, 180–1

GATT, 188–90, 194, 201, 205–10, 215–17, 225, 228, 237–8
George V (King), 9
German-Italian-Japanese Military Agreement (1942), 118
Greater East Asian Conference (1943), 123–4
Greater East Asia Co-prosperity Sphere, 113, 115, 117, 124, 195
Grew, Joseph, 140–1
Gulf War, 258
Gullett, (Sir) Henry, 72
Gwynne, H.A., 31, 36

Hachizuka Kunifusa, Captain, 158
Halifax (Lord), 37–9, 42, 140
Hammersley, S.S., 73
Hashimoto Ryutaro, 196
Hatoyama Ichiro, 190–1, 212–15
Hayashi Senjuro, General, 13–14
Heath, Edward, 244–5, 250, 280–2
Hirahara Takeshi, 253–4
Hirohito (Showa Emperor), 5, 15–16, 113, 143, 176–7, 236, 242–3, 291
Hironomiya, Crown Prince, 257
Hirota Koki, 6–8, 10, 14, 36, 99, 128
Hoare, (Sir) Samuel, 31, 56, 87, 98
Holmes, Colonel C.R., 157
Holmes, Colonel E.B., 154–5
Home, (Sir) Alec Douglas, 237, 269, 273
Hongkong, fall of, 116, 150–1
Horinouchi Kensuke, 16
Hosokawa Morihiro, 196, 296
Hosoya Chihiro, 1, 8, 74, 111
Howe, Geoffrey, 288–9, 291
Howell, David, 291, 295
Hurd, Douglas, 293–4, 296

Ikeda Hayato, 237, 268, 271, 273, 277
Ikeda Shigeaki, 16–17
Imai Itaru, Colonel, 163
India, 54–68
Indian National Army, 117, 120, 137
Indo-Japanese Trade Convention (1937), 90
Inoue Toshikazu, 9, 10
International Military Tribunal for the Far East, 149

Ishibashi Tanzan, 11, 15, 191, 215
Ishida Hakuei, 242
Ishii Mitsujiro, 268
Ismay, General (Sir) Hastings, 142
Itagaki Seishiro, General, 144
Ito Takeo, General, 150–1
Iwakuro Hideo, 120

Japan Cotton Spinners Association (Osaka), 60–5, 67, 94
Japan Festival, UK (1990–1), 258

Kadono mission (1937), 91
Kaifu Toshiki, 292
Kanin (Prince), 15
Katayama Tetsu, 176
Kato Tadao, 252, 283
Kawabe General, 126
Keidanren, 247, 283
Kennedy, President J.F., 270
Kipping, (Sir) Norman, 237, 272
Kisaka Junichiro, 2
Kishi Nobusuke, 191–5, 216–27, 265–7
Kitamura Hiroshi, 295–6
Kitamura Takeshi, 274–5
Kiyozawa Kiyoshi, 17
Koiso Kuniaki, General, 121, 127–9
Koizumi Junichiro, 252
Konoe, (Prince) Fumimaro, 16, 19, 112, 115, 130
Kosaka Zentaro, 270–1
Kurusu Saburo, 64

Ladybird Incident (1937), 38
Lancashire Cotton Corporation, 60–1
Lascelles, (Sir) Daniel, 264
Laurel, Jose P., 123–4
League of Nations, chs 1 and 2 passim
Lees-Mody Pact (1933), 56, 64
Leith-Ross, (Sir) Frederick, 7, 10–1, 15, 20–1, 34–5, 39, 89–90
Lindley, (Sir) Francis, 4, 63, 66–9, 83
Lloyd, Selwyn, 218–22, 265, 271
Lowe, Peter, 20
Lyons, Joseph, 72

MacArthur, General Douglas, 125, 127–8, 139, 144, ch. 8 passim

MacDonald, J. Ramsay, 56
Macmillan, Harold, 196, 216–25, 237, 265–9, 272
Macrae, Norman, 272
Maekawa Haruo, 240–1
Major, John, 293, 296, 297
Makino Nobuaki, 9, 12, 36, 55
Manchester Chamber of Commerce, 32, 62–3, 66–8, 82–3
Manchukuo Petroleum Co., 95–6
Marco Polo Bridge incident (1937), 112
Marples, Ernest, 238
Masuda Hiroshi, 11
Matsudaira Tsuneo, 9, 69
Matsui Keishiro, 30
Matsuoka Yosuke, 6, 19–20, 43, 57
Matsuura Masataka, 16–17
Maudling, Reginald, 237
Miao Bin, 128
Midway, battle of, 112, 117
Miki Takeo, 279
Mitsuzuka Hiroshi, 291–2
Miyazawa Kiichi, 295–6
Modin, Air Commodore C.O.F., 151, 159
Mohan Singh, 120
Morgan, Vaughan, 220
Morland, (Sir) Oscar, 266–70, 274
Morrison, Herbert, 178–9, 183–6
Mounsey, (Sir) George, 98
Mountbatten, Admiral Lord Louis, 139, 143–4, 146
Murayama Tomiichi, 196, 297–8
Mutaguchi, General, 126
Muto Teiichi, 18

Nagai Kazu, 18
Nagano Osami, Admiral, 115
Nakajima Kumakichi, 57, 64, 94
Nakamura Aketo, General, 169
Nakamura Shigeo, Colonel, 158
Nakao Eiichi, 292
Nakasone Yasuhiro, 287–8
Nehru, Jawaharlal, 117, 186, 195
New Zealand, 140, 182–3, 185, 188
Nimitz, Admiral Chester, 125, 127
Nippon Kogyo, 167–8
Nish, Ian, 2, 4, 5, 35

Nishi Haruhiko, 218
Nomonhan, battle of (1939), 116
Northern Territories issue, 254
Nott, John, 284
Nuttall, Simon, 291

Oba Sadao, 240
Ohira Masayoshi, 236–7, 274
Oil, 91–8, 101
Okada Gentaro, 65
Ono Katsumi, 222–4, 237, 264–5, 268–9
Ormsby-Gore, David, 224
Ottawa Conference (1932), 51, 81
Ozaki Hotsumi, 14

Pacific Defence Council, 191
Parsons, Sir Antony, 253
Percival, General A.E., 136, 154–5, 159
Piggott, (Major-General) F.S.G., 39
Potsdam Declaration (1945), 130–1, 142–3
Pym, Francis, 253, 257

Quebec Conference (1943), 139

Reading (Lord), 4–5
Ride, (Colonel) L.T., 160
Ridsdale, (Sir) Julian, 242
Roosevelt, President F.D., 119, 125, 138
Runciman, Walter, 56, 62–6, 68–9, 74, 82–4, 87
Rundall, (Sir) Francis, 276, 278
Russell of Liverpool, Lord, 264

Saionji, (Prince) Kimmochi, 5
Sakai Tetsuya, 8, 35
Sakonji, Admiral Naomasa, 168
Sandakan 'Death Marches', 150, 169
Sandys, Duncan, 218–19
San Francisco Conference (1951), 186
Sansom, (Sir) George B., 54–7, 69, 79, 89, 103, 140–2
Sato Eisaku, 277
Sato Naotake, 13–15
Sawada Setsuzo, 4–5, 55–7
SEAC, 126, 139–40, 145

SEATO, 209, 265
Shanghai Incident (1927), 27–8; (1932), 4
Shawcross, (Sir) Hartley, 185, 188
Shidehara Kijuro, 175–6
Shigemitsu Mamoru, 8, 10, 14, 30, 36, 39–40, 42–4, 112, 122–5, 127–8, 215
Shiina Etsusaburo, 277, 279
Shima Shigenobu, 275, 277–8
Shimada Shigetaro, 121
Shore, Peter, 249
Simla Conference, 55
Simon, (Sir) John, 3, 6, 31, 63, 74, 83
Singapore, fall of, 116, 132, 135–6, 145, 153–6
Sitwell, General H.D.W., 155–6
Smith, John, 292
Smithsonian Exhibition, 196
Sonoda Sunao, 284, 285
Soviet-Japanese normalization talks (1955), 213–14
Stalin, Joseph, 125, 138, 142–3
Staton, Air Commodore W.E., 152
Stewart, (Sir) Kenneth, 61
Stewart, Michael, 277, 280
Stilwell, General Joseph W., 126, 136–7, 139
Stimson, Henry L., 6
Storry, Professor G.R., 241
Streat, (Sir) Raymond, 88
Sugita Ichiji, Colonel, 154
Sugiyama Hajime, 15
Suzuki Keishi, Colonel, 119
Suzuki Teiichi, 3
Suzuki Zenko, 254, 286–7

Taji Yasushi, 95, 97
Takahashi Korekiyo, 11, 52–3, 62, 71
Takamatsu (Prince), 14
Takeshita Noboru, 289–90
Tanaka Kakuei, 244–6, 281–2
'Tanaka Fund' (1973), 245
Taylor, A.J.P., 59
Terauchi Hisaichi, Marshal, 144
Thailand–Burma Railway, 162–4, Ch. 7 passim
Thatcher, (Lady) Margaret, 253–6, 284–8, 291–3

Thomas, (Sir) Shenton, 159
Thompson, (Sir) Ernest, 72
Thorn Industries, 248
Thorne, Christopher, 131, 135, 140–1
Thorneycroft, Peter, 188–9, 206–7, 215
Tientsin Crisis (1939), 17–18, 40–1
Tiltman, Hessell, 267
Togo Shigenori, 12, 116, 129–31
Tojo Hideki, General, 112, 116–17, 119, 121, 124–7, 153
Tokunaga Isao, Colonel, 161
Tokyo Stock Exchange membership, 256
Torrance, Brig. K.S., 155, 159
Toyoda Teijiro, Admiral, 131
Toyota Eiji, 249
Trautmann, Oskar, 16
Treasury Group, 78–9, 86–7
Trench, N.C.C., 266
Tripartite Pact (1940), 19
Trotter, Ann, 15
Truman, President Harry S., 141–3, 174, 181–2, 196
Tsuda Shingo, 57, 73, 94
Tsunoda Jun, 20
Tsurumi Shunsuke, 2

Uchida Yasuya, 54
Uemura Mikio, General, 153
Ugaki Kazushige, 17, 39, 40

Uno Sosuke, 291

Vischer, Dr Carl Matthaus, 162

Wavell, General Archibald, 137
Whaling disputes, 260
Whitehead, (Sir) John, 295
Wilford, (Sir) Michael, 286
Willingdon (Lord), 56
Willis, Norman, 293
Wilson, (Sir) Horace, 31, 39, 66, 68, 86–7
Wingate, General Orde, 126, 137
Wolfers, Nicolas (MacLean), 252
World Economic Conference, 1933 (London), 51

Yalta Conference (1945), 45
Yamagiwa Masamichi, 240
Yamamoto Isoroku, Admiral, 118
Yamashita Tomoyuki, General, 154
Yamazaki Toshio, 257
Yonai, Admiral Mitsumasa, 129, 131
Yoshida Shigeru, 11–15, 20–1, 36, 39, 176–9, 190, 205–6, 209–12, 217, 266; visit to London (1954), 189, 208; 'Yoshida letter', 205
Young, Lord, 290, 292
Younger, Kenneth, 183, 186

Zentsuji POW camp, 162